Communication and Human Behavior

Fifth Edition

Communication and Human Behavior

Brent D. Ruben

Rutgers University

Lea P. Stewart

Rutgers University

Boston • New York • San Francisco
Mexico City • Montreal • Toronto • London • Madrid • Munich • Paris
Hong Kong • Singapore • Tokyo • Cape Town • Sydney

Executive Editor: Karon Bowers
Series Editor: Brian Wheel
Series Editorial Assistant: Heather Hawkins
Senior Marketing Manager: Mandee Eckersley
Editorial Production Service: Omegatype Typography, Inc.
Manufacturing Buyer: JoAnne Sweeney
Composition and Prepress Buyer: Linda Cox
Cover Administrator: Kristina Mose-Libon
Electronic Composition: Omegatype Typography, Inc.

Between the time Website information is gathered and published, some sites may have closed. Also, the transcription of URLs can result in typographical errors. The publisher would appreciate notification where these errors occur so that they may be corrected in subsequent editions.

Library of Congress Cataloging-in-Publication Data

Ruben, Brent D.
    Communication and human behavior / Brent D. Ruben, Lea P.
Stewart.—5th ed.
      p.   cm.
    Includes bibliographical references and index.
    ISBN 0-205-41790-6
    1. Communication.   2. Human behavior.   I. Stewart, Lea.
II. Title.
P90.R78   2006
302.2—dc22

                                        2004063375

Printed in the United States of America

10 9 8 7 6 5 4 3 2 1   10 09 08 07 06 05

Contents

9   *Media   186*

13 *Organizations* **294**

14   *Cultures and Societies   324*

Preface

Each generation faces its own unique problems and prospects. For us there are the challenges of fast-paced technological change, race relations, health care, evolving concepts of marriage and family, changing gender roles, drug and substance abuse, and international conflict.

We also face a host of smaller, but no less significant, challenges on a daily basis: a relationship that doesn't work out, a low grade we receive, a job that doesn't come through, a friend who no longer seems to care, the prejudice or discrimination that inflicts pain, a parent who doesn't understand, a marital conflict that can't be reconciled, or a child who disappoints loved ones.

Whether approached from the perspective of psychology or communication, political science or art, literature or sociology, a knowledge of human behavior can be of great value in our efforts to comprehend and deal with the circumstances we encounter. It can also help us understand ourselves, our actions, our motives, our feelings, and our aspirations.

Perhaps the greatest value comes from approaches which draw on a number of disciplinary perspectives. This fifth edition of *Communication and Human Behavior* aims to provide this kind of framework.

About the Fifth Edition

Previous editions of *Communication and Human Behavior* have been well received by students and instructors at the many colleges and universities where they have been adopted. This response has been very gratifying. It has also meant that a number of helpful comments and suggestions on the book have been provided, and as a result this fifth edition improves on its predecessors in a number of respects.

The basic approach—viewing communication as a fundamental life process that is necessary to our lives as individuals, and to our relationships, groups, organizations, cultures, and societies—remains the same. However, in this fifth edition, new and expanded chapters, and refinements in content and organization further clarify the meaning, importance, and implications of this perspective.

The result is a book that is appropriate for an even broader range of audiences than previous editions.

Communication is a topic that, in a certain case, is extremely basic, involving daily activities that we all take for granted—speaking, writing, and listening. At the same time, it is a complex phenomenon that plays a pivotal and far-reaching role in all human affairs.

The challenge for the authors of an introductory text is to capture, explain, and illustrate these more familiar facets of communication, and then to relate and integrate them into a broader framework for understanding the complexity and pervasiveness of human communication processes.

Communication and Human Behavior addresses these challenges by providing a book which is expansive and yet integrated, rigorous yet readable, and which links theory and practice.

It does this by:

- Providing a broad introduction to the process and field (Chapters 1 and 2).
- Presenting an historical context in which to better understand communication today (Chapter 3).
- Focusing on communication as a basic life process (Chapter 4).
- Analyzing human communication in terms of "invisible" as well as "visible" aspects of the process (Chapter 5).
- Explaining how we receive messages (Chapter 6), and also how we create and send messages using verbal codes (Chapter 7) and nonverbal codes (Chapter 8), and the role media play in these processes (Chapter 9).
- Examining the role of communication in multiple contexts of human life, including individual (Chapter 10), relationships (Chapter 11), groups (Chapter 12), organizations (Chapter 13), cultural/intercultural (Chapter 14), and public and mass communication (Chapter 15).

Research Profiles

This edition of *Communication and Human Behavior* features research profiles from some of the most eminent scholars in the field of communication today. These individuals truly represent the state-of-the-art in current communication research in a variety of areas ranging from health care to electronic communication to intercultural issues. We would like to thank these individuals for their contributions to this volume. We know that our students' experiences will be enriched because of their willingness to share their expertise with us.

Communication and Human Behavior Distinguished Panel of Experts

Mark Aakhus, Associate Professor, Department of Communication, Rutgers University

Ulla Bunz, Assistant Professor, Department of Communication, Rutgers University

Stacey L. Connaughton, Assistant Professor, Department of Communication, Purdue University

Stan Deetz, Professor, Department of Communication, University of Colorado at Boulder

Mark Frank, Associate Professor, Department of Communication, Rutgers University

Kathryn Greene, Associate Professor, Department of Communication, Rutgers University

Eric E. Harlan, Instructor, Business and Communication, Mississippi University for Women

James Katz, Professor, Department of Communication, Rutgers University

Young Yun Kim, Professor, Department of Communication, University of Oklahoma

Igor E. Klyukanov, Associate Professor, Department of Communication Studies, Eastern Washington University

Gary L. Kreps, Professor and Mandell Endowed Chair in Health Communication, George Mason University

Robert Kubey, Associate Professor, Department of Journalism and Media Studies, Rutgers University

Linda C. Lederman, Professor, Department of Communication, Rutgers University

Jenny Mandelbaum, Associate Professor, Department of Communication, Rutgers University

Mary Beth Oliver, Associate Professor, College of Communications, Pennsylvania State University

Ronald E. Rice, Arthur N. Rupe Professor in the Social Effects of Mass Communication, Department of Communication, University of California–Santa Barbara

Nancy Signorielli, Professor, Department of Mass Communication, University of Delaware

Amy R. Slagell, Associate Professor, Department of English, Iowa State University

Joseph Turow, Robert Lewis Shayon Professor of Communication, Annenberg School for Communication, University of Pennsylvania

Patti M. Valkenburg, Professor, Amsterdam School of Communications Research, University of Amsterdam

Itzhak Yanovitzky, Assistant Professor, Department of Communication, Rutgers University

Acknowledgments

A great many people have contributed to the formation of the ideas presented in this book and in earlier editions. In some cases the contributions have been in written form. In other instances, valued assistance has come also through personal contact over the years. We want to express our sincere thanks to the many colleagues at Rutgers, friends, and students who have contributed to this book and to our thinking about communication and human behavior over the years.

Many people have assisted particularly in the development of this edition. First, we want to express appreciation for the helpful reviews provided by Julie Apker, Western Michigan University, and Loril Gossett, University of Nevada.

We also want to express our appreciation to Jenny Mandelbaum, Mark Frank, Alan Stewart, Marc Ruben, Sara García Gil-Perotin, and Jann Ruben who reviewed and provided comments and suggestions on portions of the manuscript. Ann Volpe provided support at various stages in the processing of the manuscript for which we are also very grateful. Shakira Johnson did an outstanding job providing pictures for this edition.

Thanks to Patrick Carter for the original work, "Images We Hold in Common," which appears in Chapter 5. We remain grateful to Chris Kilyk, Nat Clymer, Hong Ha, John Jacobson, Bill Gilhooly, Robert Convoy, Rich Budd, and Bill Gudykunst, who provided photos and/or processed photos taken by Brent Ruben.

We also want to acknowledge Lloyd Chilton, former Communication Editor at Macmillan, whose early encouragement was essential to the launching of the *Communication and Human Behavior* project, and Steve Dalpin, Prentice Hall Speech Communication Editor, for his guidance in the preparation of the third edition of the book.

We would like to thank the following students for their helpful input during the process of preparing this revision: Arite Bouhlas, Carey Curry, Kiku Dasgupta, and Nancy Tetreaux. We are especially grateful to Catherine Leichtnam for her very careful reading of the text and helpful suggestions, and Travis Russ for his help with the instructor's manual and website.

Finally, we are very appreciative of the support and helpfulness of Allyn and Bacon. Special thanks to Karon Bowers, Brian Wheel, Jennifer Trebby, and Heather Hawkins.

B.D.R.
L.P.S.

Communication and
Human Behavior

1 Introduction— Definitions and Theories

In this chapter

Why . . .

- Communication affects all facets of our lives.

- Success in one's career may well depend on communication.

- Well-educated people are not necessarily competent communicators.

- Personal theories can be as important as scholarly theories.

- Defining communication can be difficult.

Why Study Communication

Communication Is Fundamental to Our Lives

- A recent graduate interviews for a job.
- Friends hundreds of miles apart exchange e-mail messages.
- A doctor talks with a patient about a health problem and suggests lifestyle changes.

- Individuals from very different backgrounds struggle to overcome cultural differences that are barriers to working together on a group project.
- Family members converse using sign language.
- Candidates present political speeches and debate their positions before a live audience.
- The leader of a club guides the group through a discussion of the agenda.
- Viewers watch their favorite film on a DVD.
- Representatives from the management team and a union meet to negotiate a contract.
- A passenger on a train converses with a friend a thousand miles away via cell phone.
- Spouses use their cell phones to call home from the video store to discuss dinner plans.

In each of these situations, and in the dozens of other circumstances that confront us every day, the process of communication is absolutely fundamental. No activity is more basic to our lives—personally, socially, or occupationally. Indeed, communication is so essential that we often take it for granted, much as we do breathing.

If communication is as natural as breathing, why is it necessary to study and learn more about the process? Good question. The short answer is that there are a number of decisions to be made as we engage in communication, and the way we think about the process can make a substantial difference to those decisions and to the consequences which result. The way we understand communication influences the way we think about and react to situations and people. The way we act and relate to others, in turn, can make a major difference in how they respond to us. And, over the short- and long-term, the consequences of these actions and reactions will have significant implications for the kinds of relationships we form, whom we become as people, and the way we contribute as members of families, groups, communities, organizations, and the societies in which we live.

A more detailed answer to the question, "Why should one study communication?" includes a consideration of the following points.

Communication Is Complex

The realization that communication is a *basic* process does not, in any way, imply that it is easily understood or controlled. To the contrary, communication is exceedingly complex and multifaceted. Examples abound in personal, family, community, professional, technological, national, or international settings. Whether one thinks of the goal of improving intercultural and international understanding, overcoming the high divorce rate, or reducing teenage smoking and substance abuse, the communication challenges are daunting.

The communication understanding and skills necessary to be more successful in the many complex situations we face as humans are not simply a matter of common sense. If they were, would these problems emerge in the first place? In point of fact, competence in communication requires what might be called *uncommon* sense. Common sense, for instance, suggests that other people are very much like we are, and that their likes and dislikes, perspectives, concerns, and information needs are generally like our own. While this may sometimes be a workable assumption, more often it is not. "Uncommon sense" leads one to continually question one's own assumptions and to become more attentive to others' needs and perspectives. It is also "uncommon sense" that guides us to attend more carefully to the communication situation and to become more analytical in our dealings with others and to recognize the need to develop an ever-broadening array of communication understanding and skills.

We all face challenges in our personal, family, and workplace relationships. Even when we look carefully at the situations that we assume are going well, we almost always find that there are opportunities for improvement. Whether we think of relationships with roommates, romantic partners, parents, colleagues at work, or acquaintances from another culture, face-to-face, on the telephone, or online, an understanding of communication is essential to the outcomes we desire.

Communication Is Vital to Occupational Effectiveness

Careers in all fields call on one's ability to analyze communication situations, develop effective communication strategies, collaborate effectively with others, and receive and present ideas effectively through various communication channels. At least half of the work force in industrialized countries such as the United States, Japan, Sweden, and England engage in communication or information-related work, and this number has increased dramatically over the past 100 years.[1]

In many jobs, such as those listed in Table 1.1, communication is primary. In many other occupations, technical and disciplinary expertise go hand-in-hand with communication knowledge and ability. This is the case in fields like teaching, management, health care, international business, personnel, counseling, politics, sales, computer applications, library and information science, and speech pathology. To perform competently, a teacher, a counselor, or a politician needs *technical* ability plus *communication* ability.

Studies of the needs of various occupations consistently reaffirm the importance of specific communication competencies in the workplace as among the most critical to success. One extensive study of employers found that fourteen skills and traits, ranked in the following order, were regarded as most important:[2]

1. *Integrity and honesty.* Choosing ethical courses of action
2. *Listening.* Attending to and interpreting verbal messages from others
3. *Reading.* Locating, understanding, and interpreting written information in documents such as manuals, graphs, and schedules
4. *Oral communication.* Communicating ideas and information through verbal presentations
5. *Written communication.* Communicating ideas and information through documents such as letters, manuals, reports, and graphs
6. *Responsibility and self-management.* Exerting high levels of effort, striving to achieve goals, monitoring progress, and exhibiting self-control
7. *Problem solving.* Recognizing problems and devising and implementing plans to solve them
8. *Knowing how to learn.* Acquiring and applying new knowledge and skills
9. *Self-esteem.* Maintaining a positive view of one's self and job
10. *Sociability.* Working and interacting well with others
11. *Diversity.* Functioning effectively in a multicultural and diverse work environment

TABLE 1.1 *Selected Communication Careers*

Managing Communication
(Integrating communication operations, programs,
and services with the mission of an organization)

Corporate Communication	Internal Communication
Publishing	Information Management
Media Management	Communication Centers
Employee Communication	Advertising Management
Public Affairs	Technical Information
Communication and Information Policy	International Communication
Telecommunication Management	Information Services

Preparing Communication Products and Services
(Preparing, packaging, or repackaging communication
products or services for use by others)

Editing	Advertising Production
Science and Technical Writing	Community Outreach
Speech Writing	Reporting
Marketing Communication	Abstracting
Audio, Video, and Website Production	Consumer Advocacy
Computer Information Services	Broadcast Journalism
Public Relations	Documentary Film Writing
Conference and Special Events Coordination	Public Information
Customer Relations	Information Retrieval

Analyzing Communication
(Studying the foundations and theories related to communication
systems, processes, programs, and services, and/or assessing their functioning)

Communication Research	Individual Interviewing
Market Research	Focus Group Interviewing
Public Opinion Research	Academic Research
Audience Analysis	Customer Satisfaction Analysis

Communication Education and Training
(Providing instruction or training in communication)

Professional Development	Leadership and Staff Development
Communication Training	Human Resource Development
Organizational Development	

12. *Decision making.* Prioritizing goals, generating alternatives and considering risks, choosing the best alternatives
13. *Math.* Performing basic computations and approaching problems by using appropriate math techniques
14. *Creative thinking.* Generating new ideas

Interestingly, the managers surveyed were generally dissatisfied with college graduates' levels of preparation in each of these skill areas—particularly with communication competencies in writing, speaking, and listening.

Although the many studies of desired workplace competencies vary somewhat in their specifics, there is a general agreement that the following communication competencies are essential:[3]

- Writing
- Listening
- Public speaking
- Interpersonal and group communication
- Leadership
- Networking
- Teamwork and collaboration
- Meeting skills
- Communication/information technology skills
- Intercultural sensitivity and skills

Communication knowledge and skill are also basic to leadership, as is apparent in the following array of capabilities identified as necessary for effective leaders.[4]

Managing Interpersonal Relationships
- Energizing and empowering others
- Building and managing teams
- Interpersonal flexibility

Gaining Influence and Managing Information Flow within Organizations
- Influencing others
- Building information networks

Achieving Results for the Organization
- Planning and implementing
- Decision making
- Strategic thinking
- Technical knowledge
- Results orientation

A Good Education Does Not Ensure Good Communication Competence

A good education does not ensure that we will become competent in communication. One reason is that many aspects of communication are rarely addressed in most K–12 academic programs and often insufficiently in colleges and universities. For example, schools place little formal emphasis on listening concepts and practices, perhaps because educators feel that it's just common sense or everyone knows how to do it. Both assumptions are obviously unjustified.

Another important aspect of communication that receives little attention in school is nonverbal communication, though research demonstrates that some of the most significant messages in human communication are created and conveyed through nonverbal behaviors. Interpersonal and group communication skills that are necessary to effective collaboration with members of a workgroup, family, club, or community group are also often lacking in formal education. Supporting this conclusion is a study of Harvard graduates who identified collaboration skills as the single most important competence for their careers.[5] Graduates surveyed said they had received little or no instruction in this area, even in their formal university educations.

Ironically, in some instances, advanced education and training can actually be an impediment to competent communication. This is sometimes the case with physicians, scientists, engineers, and others with technical training who become very effective in communicating with individuals with an educational background similar to their own, but much less successful when interacting with people who lack their expertise and training.

Communication Is a Popular and Vibrant Field of Study

As we discuss in Chapter 2, the field of communication is relatively new as a discipline but, at the same time, is one of the oldest fields. Historians generally trace the beginnings of the study of communication and human behavior to the early Greeks. Ancient Greece was an oral culture, and affairs of business and government were conducted through spoken communication. It was, therefore, not surprising that an interest in understanding the theory and practice of communication would emerge during this era. Interest in communication study grew primarily out of philosophy at a time when that discipline was concerned with all aspects of the pursuit of knowledge.

The scientific revolution and the growing trend toward specialization in the pursuit of knowledge led to the development of separate disciplines for the study of behavior, and communication was among these. August Comte (1798–1857) gave the name *sociology* to the study of society and social existence, whose founders include Emile Durkheim, Max Weber, and Karl Marx. A decade later the psychological laboratories of Wilhelm Wundt and William James were established. The origins of anthropology also date to the middle of the nineteenth century and the work of British scholars Maine, Tylor, and Frazer. In the twentieth century, political science and communication, two other fields with an ancient heritage, took on contemporary identities as disciplines in their own right. Communication emerged as a behavioral discipline in the 1950s to join the growing list of social sciences, each of which approaches the study of human behavior from a particular vantage point.

The modern field of communication focuses on the *study of information-related behavior*. As a discipline, communication has also maintained intellectual ties with the humanities—especially philosophy, literature, religion, cultural studies, and art. There are also significant connections between communication and professional fields such as law, medicine, business, information science, cognitive science, social work, education, computer science, and library science. In medicine, for instance, there is a long-standing interest in communication between caregivers and patients, and a significant number of communication researchers see health as a very fruitful area in which to examine and apply a wide array of communication concepts. Information scientists concerned with the storage, retrieval, and dissemination of knowledge regard communication as essential, and information storage and retrieval are increasingly important topics to many who study communication.

High Tech/Low Touch Technology • Eric E. Harlan

Communication is an exciting field of study that has many important applications in today's increasingly complex society. Technological innovations are occurring every day. Professor Harlan's research reminds us of the importance of using communication theory to adapt technology to the needs of people.

• • •

With high technology affecting more areas of society than ever, my research deals with the human interface with high technology. I found the inspiration for this research in my grandmother's attic. One day while looking for some items stored there, I came across the automatic coffeemakers my sister and I had given our grandmother for Christmas over the years. When I asked my grandmother why she had never used the coffeemakers, she replied that they were too complicated for her to use and she was afraid she would do something wrong and burn her house down. That conversation launched my research.

The best technology in the world does nobody any good if it is too sophisticated for people to use, or if they are too intimidated by the technology to even try. I take this thought and use it to find ways technology can benefit such people invisibly by finding ways to "hide" the technology behind familiar interfaces.

I also study ways to adapt new and existing technology for use by the elderly and differently abled. I design systems to enable people without use of limbs or senses to interact with and work in the abled world. In addition, I design systems to monitor elderly persons living alone (like my grandmother) to make sure that they take their medications on time and that they are safe and secure.

I also work with the high-technology industry to find ways that technology can assist people to live safely, comfortably, and more productively. Someday your household, workplace, and personal devices will all communicate with each other to better serve your needs as long as you are comfortable interfacing with these devices. Thus, my research works toward the final integration of "wet ware" (the human brain) with hardware and software.

Today, communication is both a behavioral or social science and an applied liberal art. The discipline shares with psychology, sociology, anthropology, and political science the pursuit of knowledge about human individuals and social activity. The communication field also draws on the traditions of the humanities and the professions. Thus, another of the attractions of the field is the opportunity to study a single discipline that combines the social science, humanities, and professional traditions.

So, the question, "Why study communication?" comes down to this: whether you are interested in the social sciences, the arts, or the professions; whether your interests are primarily occupational or mainly academic; whether your interests reside in better understanding yourself, relationships, groups, organizations, cultures, or international relations; whether your focus is more applied or more theoretical, communication is an extremely important and useful area of study.

Theories: Guides for Analysis and Action

Communication and Human Behavior is a book about thinking—thinking about communication. That makes it a book which emphasizes *theory*, not skills. This is not to say that communication skills are insignificant. We believe they are very important. We also believe that to be successful in the practice of communication over time, there is a critical need for a broad understanding of how the process works to guide our thinking and action. Providing this kind of theoretical framework is the goal of this book.

Personal Theories

Essentially, theories are guides to understanding. It has often been said that there's nothing as practical as a good theory, and that certainly applies to theories of communication.[6] Theories help us to describe, explain, predict, and sometimes control phenomena and circumstances we encounter.

We all have *personal theories* about a range of things—about relationships, doors, friends, and weather, for instance. Our personal theories, which are sometimes called native theories by some social scientists, allow us to navigate in our physical and social environment. For example, our personal theories help us describe particular places and things, explain how to develop close relationships, predict the weather, or control the volume of a television set using a remote control. If we didn't have these theories, we would have to approach each situation we encounter as completely new and unique. We would be unable to think about new situations in more general terms and would be unable to draw on previous experiences in our efforts to describe, explain, predict, or control them. We usually give little conscious thought to the nature of our native theories, how they were developed, or how we are using them. They are based on everyday experience, tend to be taken for granted, are private, and are fairly stable over time.

Based on Everyday Experience.   Personal theories are developed over time in response to the situations and people we encounter. For example, our theories about relationships are based on personal experiences with acquaintances, friends, colleagues, and family members over the course of our lifetime.

Taken for Granted.   Most of us do not think very much about our personal theories, the manner in which they are formed, or the way we use them. Once developed, we generally accept them on faith. For instance, we each have our own theories about doors, and we take these theories for granted. We don't think about how we formed these theories and give little conscious attention to our theories when we turn a door knob. We push or pull a door with full confidence that it will open.

Private.   Personal theories are based on experiences which are to some extent unique for each of us. We often do not discuss our theories or the experiences on which they were based. Our theories about friends are based on our personal experiences, for example, and we generally discuss them only in a limited range of circumstances.

Stable.   Once formed, personal theories are generally quite resistant to change. Our personal theories tend to guide us to see and interpret what we observe in particular ways. Often we ignore or unintentionally distort observations that don't fit in with our personal theories. We are likely to cling to our theories about friends even after we have encountered evidence which seems to contradict our theories. For instance, if a friend has told us something that we know to be untrue, we are likely to tell ourselves he or she probably believed it was true or else altered the facts for a very good reason. Most likely, this kind of event could occur any number of times before we would conclude that the person is purposely lying and no longer worthy of being thought of as a friend.

Scholarly Theories

Theories of a scholarly or scientific nature are similar to personal theories in terms of their basic functions: they, too, are used to describe, explain, predict, and sometimes control objects, people, and events. However, in contrast to personal theories, they are based on systematic observation and testing. They are also questioned, public, and subject to modification.

Based on Systematic Observation and Testing.   Scholarly theories are developed through research involving systematic observation, information gathering, and analysis. Studies may be conducted in experimental laboratories or in natural settings. Data is gathered purposefully by means of interviews, questionnaires, or careful observations; and the results are systematically analyzed. For example, a theory about relationships may be based on the analysis of information derived from direct observations or videotapes. Or a theory could result from interviews or surveys of a cross-section of individuals in varying types of relationships.

Questioned.   Unlike personal theories, which tend to be accepted on faith once they are formed, scholarly theories are continually questioned. Scientific theories are regarded as tentative, and are reexamined through follow-up studies and analyses. Consider the example of doors and door knobs: We have personal theories that allow us to predict that when we turn the door knob, and push or pull, a door will open. Rather than be content with a personal theory that door knobs open doors, a scientific theory would be continually and methodically tested to ensure predictability. Thus, engineers in a corporation that manufactures door entry and lock systems would test and retest their products to determine precisely how likely it is that the door knob mechanism will operate as intended. They might want to determine the average number of uses a sample of door entry mechanisms can tolerate before they fail to function. Then they would want to further study how and why breakdowns occur, and then develop and test theories about how to correct the problem.

Public.   The methods and results of scholarly and scientific theories are disseminated to other scholars and scientists. The goal is to allow others to further evaluate particular theories in terms of at least three standards:

- Validity—accuracy
- Reliability—consistency and dependability
- Utility—usefulness and applicability

A scholarly theory will be reported at conferences and in journals, book chapters, and books so that other scholars and students can test and apply the ideas. (Exceptions to the public nature of research occur in the case of studies that are done within a proprietary context and findings are purposely not shared for reasons of security or confidentiality.)

Subject to Modification.   Because scholarly and scientific theories are public—and generally published—they are available, accessible, and subject to refutation or modification based on new information. Thus, scientific theories can be modified as findings from new research emerge.

Combining Personal and Scholarly Theories

We all have personal theories of communication and human behavior. Like other such theories, our views of communication are based on a lifetime of experience. They are personal. We take them for granted, and they tend to be fairly stable. There are also many scholarly and scientific theories regarding communication and human behavior.

In this book, we will be examining a number of these scholarly and scientific theories. A familiarity with these theories has great value in its own right in helping us to become more aware of the nature and dynamics of communication. Exploring these theories can have the additional value of encouraging and providing tools for a more critical evaluation of our personal theories. That is, we can begin to subject our own theories to some of the more rigorous academic standards associated with scholarly theory development and testing. Do our personal theories hold up in light of more systematic observation and testing? Do we continually question their validity, reliability, and utility? Can we benefit from discussing our personal theories with other people to see where they converge and where they differ? Are we able to modify our personal theories when evidence warrants? By comparing our personal theories with scholarly theories, we can better understand each and narrow the gap between the two and, in the process, also enrich our understanding of human behavior.

Defining Communication

Few words are used in as many different ways, by as many different people, as the word *communication.* To some, communication brings to mind an image of a speaker addressing an audience from behind a podium, the lively discussion among colleagues at a meeting, or an exchange of glances between lovers. Others associate the term primarily with media—newspapers, television, books, radio, film, or the Internet. For still others, communication has to do with computers, PDAs, telephones, satellites, or military command and control.

Communication can be a debate, a sermon, a memorable night at the theater, the efforts of a child striving to conquer stuttering, Morse code, e-mail, a roadside sign, or a thoughtful walk on the beach. Communication is what we think of when we see two friends conversing over coffee, a tear, an outstretched arm, a knowing smile, people using sign language, a kiss, an obscenity scrawled on a rest room wall, even a monk absorbed in silent meditation.

The multiple uses of the term *communication* can be confusing. People who are unfamiliar with the field may wonder whether the term has any limits. Is everything communication? How does being interested in communication differ from being interested in life?

To address the issue, it is important to understand that

- *Communication* is the name of a discipline, as well as the label for a phenomenon. That is, the term refers both to an academic field and a focus of study.
- *Communication* has popular, professional, and technical meanings. The term is commonly used in a very general way by the general public, in a more focused occupational framework in professional circumstances, and in a still more specialized manner in technical and academic settings.

Quite obviously, there are a number of different meanings of the word *communication.* In fact, in one classic study, communication scholars Frank Dance and Carl Larson identified 126 published definitions.[7] The *Oxford English Dictionary* alone lists a dozen definitions. Let's look briefly at a sampling of definitions:

"Communication means that information is passed from one place to another."[8]

"Communication . . . include(s) all the procedures by which one mind may affect another."[9]

"The transmission of information, ideas, emotions, skills, etc., by the use of symbols—words, pictures, figures, graphs, etc."[10]

"In the main, communication has as its central interest those behavioral situations in which a source transmits a message to a receiver(s) with conscious intent to affect the latter's behavior."[11]

"The process of taking something into account."[12]

"The imparting, conveying, or exchange of ideas, knowledge, or information whether by speech, writing, or signs."[13]

"Communication occurs when one person or more sends and receives messages that are distorted by noise, occur within a context, have some effect, and provide some opportunity for feedback."[14]

Not surprisingly, these definitions of communication, and others, have elements in common; they also have a number of differences in terms of the level of observation, the question of intent, the point of view, and the issue of outcome.[15]

Level of Observation

One can study communication on the level of cells, ants, or bees, the level of individuals, relationships, organizations, a particular culture or society, or the international level. Definitions may focus on any one, several, or all of these levels.

The Question of Intent

Scholars often disagree about whether messages have to be intentionally created to be considered communication. Virtually all communication theorists agree that intentional acts that are noted and reacted to should be considered communication.[16] Thus, if an individual asks another person a question and the person answers, it seems clear that communication has occurred because we can presume that the speaker intended to convey a message. Some scholars would limit their definition of communication only to these acts.[17] They believe that communication refers only to those events in which there are purposely created messages. Such scholars might well exclude from the definition of communication those situations in which it is unclear that an individual meant to create or convey a message to others—even if the behavior had meaning to others.

Other scholars argue that communication occurs any time behavior is attended to and interpreted, whether it was intentional or not.[18] Unintentional behavior that has meaning to a receiver might include a yawn in class being perceived by others as boredom. The yawner may not have been intending to communicate to others, but the other students (and perhaps the teacher!) attached a specific meaning to the behavior.

Point of View

Communication can be defined in a way that emphasizes the perspective of a message source (e.g., a public speaker or writer). Definitions can also emphasize the perspective of the receiver (e.g., a listener or reader).

For instance, from a speaker's perspective, the word *communication* is generally used to refer to those circumstances where a listener got the message the sender had in mind. An example might be one in which a message sent was successful in persuading another person as to the correctness of a particular point of view on a given topic. Considered from a receiver's perspective, however, an event where he or she became more convinced that they had no desire to listen further to the speaker would certainly constitute communication, even though it might not be viewed in this way from the source's perspective.

The Issue of Outcomes

Some definitions of communication include only situations in which a particular outcome occurs, for example, situations in which understanding, acceptance, and agreement result from an interaction. However, such a definition might not see communication as having occurred if misunderstanding, disagreement, or some other negative outcome resulted from a situation.

Fundamentals of Communication

To make sense of these many distinctions, to explain the field to others, and to organize our study of the field, we need a comprehensive and unifying definition of communication. A definition that meets these goals should include and integrate the following fundamentals of communication.

Communication Is a Process

Communication is a *process*—an activity that has many separate but interrelated steps that occur over time.

When we prepare for and deliver a public presentation, for instance, we are not engaged in a single, static act. We move, instead, through a sequence of interrelated activities as we plan, gather materials, rehearse, present the speech, and perhaps adjust the presentation as we're giving it, based on the audience's reaction.

The communication that occurs in a conversation is, similarly, an activity composed of a number of interrelated steps occurring over time. Consider the following:

"Hi, how are you?"
"Fine, and you?"

Even in such a simple exchange, a number of steps are involved as messages are created, sent, received, interpreted, and responded to.

Communication Is Essential for Individuals, Relationships, Groups, Organizations, and Societies

For us as individuals, communication is our link to the world, our means of making impressions, expressing ourselves, influencing others, and giving of ourselves. It is also our means of learning about the world and other people, becoming who we are, being entertained, persuaded, humored, deceived, or informed.

It is through communication that we form relationships of all kinds—from the casual exchanges that take place between a customer and a hot dog vendor or between strangers waiting in line at a movie theater, to the intimate conversations between lovers or members of a family. For friends, acquaintances, family, or colleagues at school or work, communication is the means of pursuing joint activities, relating to each other, and sharing ideas.

In groups, organizations, and societies, communication is the means through which we coordinate our own needs and goals with those of others. Within larger organizations, societies, and the world community, communication provides the web of connections that allows for collective action, the establishment of a common identity, and the development of leadership.

Communication Involves Responding to and Creating Messages and Transforming Them into Information That Can Be Used

It is through the process of creating and interpreting messages that we interact with our surroundings and one another. A *message* is any symbol or collection of symbols that has meaning or utility. Messages may involve verbal codes—such as spoken or written language—or nonverbal codes, involving appearance, gestures, touch, or other means. Examples include a speech, letter, wink, flag, poem, advertisement, or painting.

RESEARCH PROFILE

Important Issues in Health Communication • *Gary L. Kreps*

We all need accurate, timely, and relevant information to maintain healthy lifestyles. Professor Kreps's work demonstrates how the effective use of health communication messages is important at a variety of levels, including individuals, groups, organizations, and society.

• • •

Communicating relevant information is critically important for directing health care and promoting public health. Ideally, the best information should be used to guide decisions about health promotion. Yet, those who need relevant health information often do not have it, and this breakdown in communication leads to unnecessary suffering and death. I study the role of communication in health care and health promotion to develop effective strategies for communicating accurate, timely, and relevant health information.

Health communication operates on many levels. Interpersonally, consumers seek information and support from friends, family members, and health care providers to evaluate health risks and make good choices about health-promoting activities. Health care providers also communicate interpersonally to seek information from their clients and colleagues to diagnose and treat health problems. Group communica-

tion is used to help make complex health decisions and provide social support within health teams, ethics committees, and support groups. Health care systems depend on communication of accurate and timely information between interdependent departments and groups to enable adaptation and coordination of care. Even at the societal level of communication, many communication technologies (including radio, television, film, and the Internet) are used to disseminate relevant health information to different segments of society.

I study the ways different levels and channels of communication are used to inform and persuade people about pursuing healthy behaviors (such as nutritional and exercise patterns) and avoiding unhealthy behaviors (such as smoking and substance abuse) to prevent health problems. I study communication strategies to promote screening and early detection of health threats. I examine ways communication informs diagnosis of health problems and promotes collaborative health care treatments. I study ways communication promotes social support. I even study the ways communication helps people die peacefully and with dignity. These are all critically important applications of communication knowledge!

Responding to messages, and transforming them into information we can use, involves an activity often termed *information reception* or *interpretation*. This has to do with the way we attend to, attach significance to, and use information—as individuals and in relationships, groups, organizations, or societies. Information-processing is a complex activity. Our interpretations are not a tangible commodity that can simply be transported from one individual, organization, or society to another. Rather, they are transformed and changed in various ways as messages are shared between one person or location and the next, through a process we will examine in some detail later.

We engage in message creation through verbal and nonverbal behavior. For example, we create messages when we introduce ourselves to someone, since we are in the process of constructing a meaningful message—at least, it is meaningful to us. And, of course, the person who we are meeting is engaged in message interpretation when he or she notices, attaches meaning to, and makes use of our introductory comments.

In face-to-face settings, messages are conveyed from person to person or place to place verbally and nonverbally. In other situations, communication technology—or *media*—play an important role by extending our "natural" capabilities for communication. In these instances, communication between the individuals, groups, organizations, or societies is *mediated.*

Communication Involves Adapting to People and the Environment

We create and interpret messages—as individuals, and in relationships, groups, organizations, and societies—to relate to the environment and to the people around us. In some cases, the process consists primarily of adjusting to the circumstances in which we find ourselves. More often, communication involves actively creating situations and coordinating our actions with others. As we shall see, the same basic dynamics occur in groups, organizations, and societies, but on a progressively larger scale.

Communication: A Definition

We can combine these fundamentals to derive the following definition of communication:

> Human communication is the process through which individuals in relationships, groups, organizations, and societies create and use information to relate to the environment and one another.

This definition is helpful for thinking about the nature of communication and for explaining it in fairly straightforward terms to others. It also provides a useful framework for organizing the ideas presented in this book.

Goals of Communication and Human Behavior

This fifth edition of *Communication and Human Behavior* is a book aimed at helping you think cogently and systematically about communication and its relationship to human behavior. It is based on the assumption that the way we think about communication makes an important difference in the way we understand what is going on around us and in the way we conduct our lives.

The book has three goals:

1. To introduce communication as an area of study. *Communication and Human Behavior* provides an overview and explanation of communication theories, basic concepts, key scholars, issues, and applications.
2. To provide a framework that helps make connections between communication theory and communication processes in action. The objective is to help you develop a communication-oriented perspective on events taking place around you—personally, socially, in work situations, nationally, and internationally.
3. To provide tools to help you use this communication-oriented perspective to analyze, better understand, and be more competent in your own communication behavior.

Implications and Applications

- Communication is a pervasive part of contemporary life with relevance to our lives as individuals, family members, professionals, and members of communities and society.

- Theories are guides to action, and therefore an understanding of the nature of communication is not only valuable in its own right, it also contributes to one's success in practical matters.

- As individuals, we each develop personal (native) theories of communication based on our life experiences. These theories can be enhanced by reconciling them to scholarly and scientific theories developed following more systematic standards.

- The study of communication theory can help one better understand human behavior, more fully appreciate the skills and techniques that are important to achieving communication goals, and improve one's ability to reflect upon and make sense of one's own behavior.

Summary

In a broad range of settings and contexts, communication plays a basic and fundamental role. So essential is the role of communication that it is easily taken for granted and thought to be common sense. When one considers the many problems that result from poor communication, however, the complexity and challenges associated with the process make it clear that this is not the case.

Popular and scholarly writings speak to the importance of communication in our personal and occupational lives. The process is fundamental in many jobs and more generally contributes to professional effectiveness in nearly every field. Communication theory and skills are not assured by one's education, as many of the critical aspects of the phenomenon are underemphasized in formal education. Because of its relevance, its importance, and its many challenges as a topic and field, communication is an extremely popular field.

Theories are the building blocks of understanding. Theories of behavior provide guides to understanding and action. They help to describe, explain, predict, and sometimes control human affairs. Over the course of our lifetimes we each develop personal theories based on our experiences that are quite stable once developed. We typically spend little time analyzing or discussing these theories. In contrast, scholarly and scientific theories are systematically developed, publicly shared, and carefully tested with the goal of achieving validity, reliability, and utility. The two types of theories can be quite complementary and mutually informative.

Communication theories and definitions are numerous and sometimes contradictory. They vary depending on their level of observation, assumptions relative to intention, point of view implied, and perspective on the issue of outcomes. The definition that serves as the foundation for this book is: Human communication is the process through which individuals in relationships, groups, organizations, and societies create and use information to relate to the environment and one another.

Notes

1. Jorge R. Schement, "Porat, Bell, and the Information Society Reconsidered: The Growth of Information Work in the Early Twentieth Century," *Information Processing and Management,* Vol. 26, No. 4, 1990, pp. 449–465; Raul Katz, *The Information Society* (New York: Praeger, 1988); Marc U. Porat, *The Information Economy: Definition and Measurement (OT Special Publication 77–12), Volumes 1–9* (Washington, DC: Department of Commerce/Office of Telecommunication, Government Printing Office, 1977), pp. 1–3. Also see discussion by Anthony Debons, *The Information Professional: Survey of an Emerging Field* (New York: Marcel Dekker, 1981).

2. Carl E. Van Horn, *Enhancing the Connection between Higher Education and the Workplace: A Survey of Employers* (Denver: State Higher Education Executive Officers and Education Commission of the States, Oct., 1995).

3. Brent D. Ruben, *Pursuing Excellence in Higher Education: Eight Fundamental Challenges* (San Francisco: Jossey-Bass, 2004), pp. 65–69.

4. Based on Deborah Stahl, "Managing in the 1990s: Versatility, Flexibility and a Wide Range of Skills. A New Study Outlines the Requirements for Managerial Success in a Complex and Fast-Changing Business World," *AT&T Journal,* March, 1989, pp. 8–10.

5. Richard Light, "How Assessment Has Changed Teaching and Learning at Harvard," University of Texas-Ford Motor Company Consortium on Higher Education Quality, Dearborn, MI, 1996.

6. Kurt Lewin, *Field Theory in Social Science: Selected Theoretical Papers by Kurt Lewin,* edited by D. Cartwright (Westport, CT: Greenwood Press, 1975, c. 1951), p. 169.

7. Frank E. X. Dance and Carl Larson, *The Functions of Human Communication: A Theoretical Approach* (New York: Holt, Rinehart, Winston, 1976).

8. George A. Miller, *Language and Communication* (New York: McGraw-Hill, 1951), p. 6.

9. Gerald R. Miller, "On Defining Communication: Another Stab," *Journal of Communication,* Vol. 16, No. 2, June, 1966, p. 92.

10. Claude Shannon and Warren Weaver, *The Mathematical Theory of Communication* (Champaign, IL: University of Illinois Press, 1963), p. 96.

11. Bernard Berelson and Gary Steiner, *Human Behavior* (New York: Harcourt Brace Jovanovich, 1964), p. 527.

12. Lee Thayer, *Communication and Communication Systems* (Homewood, IL: Richard Irwin, 1968).

13. J. A. Simpson and E. S. C. Weiner, Eds., *The Oxford English Dictionary,* 2nd Ed., Vol. III (Oxford: Clarendon Press, 1989), p. 578.

14. Joseph A. DeVito, *Human Communication* (Boston: Allyn and Bacon, 2003), p. 2.

15. The discussion of levels of analysis, the question of intent, and normative judgment is based on Dance and Larson, 1976, pp. 27–28. See more recent and extensive discussion of these issues in John D. Peters, *Speaking into Air: A History of the Idea of Communication* (Chicago: University of Chicago Press, 1999), chap. 1.

16. Stephen W. Littlejohn, *Theories of Human Communication,* 5th ed. (Belmont, CA: Wadsworth, 1996), p. 9.

17. Michael T. Motley, "On Whether One Can(not) Communicate: An Examination via Traditional Communication Postulates," *Western Journal of Speech Communication,* Vol. 54, 1990, pp. 1–20.

18. Peter A. Andersen, "When One Cannot Not Communicate: A Challenge to Motley's Traditional Communication Postulates," *Communication Studies,* Vol. 42, 1991, pp. 309–325.

2 The Field of Communication

In this chapter

Why . . .

- Communication is one of the oldest yet newest disciplines.

- Early Greeks saw communication theory and practice as critical.

- The popularity of communication is a mixed blessing.

- Communication is an activity, a social science, a liberal art, and a profession.

Early Communication Study

It is difficult to determine precisely when and how communication first came to be regarded as a significant factor in human life. According to historians, considerable concern about communication and its role in human affairs was expressed prior to the fifth century B.C., in classical Babylonian and Egyptian writings and in Homer's *Iliad*.[1] An essay written about 3000 B.C. offers advice on how to speak effectively, while *The Precepts,* composed in Egypt about 2675 B.C., provides guidance on effective communication.

One of the most familiar historic statements on the importance of communication appears in the Bible. In the opening passage of the Old Testament the spoken word is described as the incredibly powerful force through which God created the world—God said, "Let there be light; and there was light." This statement carries considerable rhetorical power for people who belong to various religious communities.

As with other disciplines that have sought to explain human behavior, the beginning of systematic theory development in communication can be traced to the Greeks. Their initial interest sprang from the practical concerns of day-to-day life. Greece had a democratic form of government, and virtually all facets of business, government, law, and education were carried on orally. Greek citizens also had to be their own lawyers. Accused and accuser alike presented their cases before a jury of several hundred persons who would have had to be convinced of the rightness of a position. Lawsuits were common in Athens, and, as a result, public speaking in legal contexts became a preoccupation.

Rhetoric and Speech

What might be considered as the first theory of communication was developed in Greece by Corax and later refined by his student Tisias. The theory dealt with courtroom speaking, which was considered the craft of persuasion. Tisias became convinced that persuasion could be taught as an art and provided encouragement for instructors of what was called *rhetoric*. Corax and Tisias developed the concept of message organization, suggesting that a message should have three parts corresponding to today's concepts of introduction, body, and conclusion.

The sophists were a group of itinerant teachers in Athens in the fifth century B.C. who set up small schools and charged their pupils for tutoring. Protagoras of Abdara taught concepts that are embodied in the modern idea of debate. He taught that a good speaker should be able to argue both sides of a proposition. In addition, he encouraged students to write short messages that did not refer to a particular occasion to be used whenever they were called upon to speak in public.

Gorgias of Leontini was a contemporary of Protagoras and was one of the first to advocate the use of emotional appeals in persuasive speeches. Gorgias was especially concerned about style and the use of appropriate figures of speech.

Isocrates, another famous Greek Sophist, wrote speeches for others to deliver and was very influential in his time. He is known for his belief that an orator should be trained in the liberal arts and should be a good person.

The writings of two other scholars—Cicero (106–43 B.C.) and Quintilian (A.D. 35–95)—also contributed to the broadening theory of communication. Like Plato and Aristotle, Cicero developed rhetorical theories and saw communication as both an academic and practical matter. His view of communication was so comprehensive that it included all of what is now considered the domain of the social sciences. He believed a successful speaker was a knowledgable person. Quintilian is remembered primarily as an educator and synthesizer, bringing together in his writing the previous five hundred years' thinking about communication.[2] His practical guidelines demonstrate how a good communicator should be educated.

The view that communication was critical to virtually all aspects of human life was widely held during the Classical period.[3] However, the comprehensive perspective that characterized communication during this era was largely reversed in the Medieval and Renaissance periods. With the decline of the oral tradition and democracy, much of the interest in communication also waned, and the study of rhetoric was dispersed among several different fields. By the end of the fourteenth century, most of the communication theory that had originally been developed in rhetoric was now being studied in religion.

RESEARCH PROFILE

Research in Rhetoric • Amy R. Slagell

The field of communication has a long, rich tradition rooted in classical rhetorical scholarship. Professor Slagell points out the relevance of studying rhetoric in our contemporary world.

• • •

In the field of communication, to study rhetoric is to study the art of effective discourse. The term *rhetoric* is complex, since it refers to analyzing how and why certain combinations of ideas, language, and delivery have been effective in discourse used in past situations, creating successful discourse in response to current contexts, and to articulating theories about how language and symbols both shape and are shaped by reality. People working in the area of rhetoric might study how speakers, such as U.S. women fighting for the right to vote, created arguments in speeches, writings, and public demonstrations aiming to show that women could be citizens as well as mothers. Some rhetorical scholars also do research to advise today's public speakers how to produce discourse that will be effective in their workplaces or at city council meetings, for example, while others theorize about how the language

we use constructs certain worldviews about gender or race.

One common element that runs through my scholarship is critical engagement of rhetors' choices. Why, I might ask, did the speaker choose this place to share these ideas, put the ideas in this strategic order, use a particular argument or piece of evidence, or use a certain metaphor? We may even ask why a speaker used a particular delivery strategy; for example, why did Colin Powell hold up a small vial of powder to underscore his claim that Saddam Hussein was a threat, when he delivered his address to the United Nations urging their support for armed intervention in Iraq? As a teacher and researcher I aim to heighten awareness about speakers' choices by asking questions such as these and by examining the effectiveness and ethical implications of these choices. We can examine the world of discourse with a critical eye as a way to encounter the choices, the strategies, the ideologies, and sometimes the minds responsible for the discourse. Such investigations also help us think strategically about our own choices, our own efforts to have an impact on those around us through the gift of language.

Eventually, the work of Augustine led to a rediscovery of classical Greek theory. His writings applied communication to the interpretation of the Bible and other religious writings, and to the art of preaching. In so doing, Augustine united the practical and theoretical aspects of communication study.

Early in the seventeenth century, Sir Francis Bacon included both speechmaking and writing that was designed for more practical purposes in his theories. He proposed an ethical basis for communication and argued that the function of true rhetoric was the furtherance of good. His ideas had a major influence on later writers.

During the eighteenth and nineteenth centuries, emphasis in communication study was placed on written argument and literature. There was also great interest in speaking style, articulation, and gesture, leading to the formation of the National Association of Elocutionists in 1892. The elocutionists were a powerful force at this time who produced a very stylized mode of delivery that included vocal manipulation and physical gestures.

George Campbell, a contemporary of the elocutionists, wrote on the philosophical aspects of rhetoric. He maintained that rhetoric had four purposes: to enlighten, to please the imagination, to move the passions, or to influence the will.

Another eighteenth-century writer, Hugh Blair, proposed theories that could be applied either to writing or to speaking. His book, *Lectures on Rhetoric and Belles Lettres,* was very influential at the time.

By the end of the nineteenth century, most colleges and universities were organized into departments, and rhetoric and speech were often taught within departments of English.

Journalism

The other field that contributed significantly to the heritage of communication study is *journalism.* Like rhetoric and speech, journalism also dates back several thousand years. The practice of journalism began some 3,700 years ago in Egypt, when a record of the events of the time was transcribed on the tomb of an Egyptian king. Years later, Julius Caesar had an official record of the news of the day posted in a public place, and copies of it were made and sold.[4]

Early newspapers were a mixture of newsletters, ballads, proclamations, political tracts, and pamphlets describing various events. Like speech and rhetoric, they were forms of public communication. The mid-1600s saw the emergence of the newspaper in its modern form; and the first paper published in the United States, *Publick Occurrences Both Forreign and Domestick,* appeared in 1690 in Boston.

The 1900s–1930s: Development of Speech and Journalism

In the early twentieth century, speech emerged as a discipline in its own right. In 1909, the Eastern States Speech Association—now the Eastern Communication Association—was formed, and in 1910, held its first annual conference. The National Association of Academic Teachers of Public Speaking, which became the Speech Association of America and the Speech Communication Association—now, the National Communication Association—was formed in 1914.[5] In 1915, the *Quarterly Journal of Public Speaking* was first published, followed soon after by the *Quarterly Journal of Speech. Communication Monographs* began publication in 1934. Unlike previous publications which emphasized speech practices, the new journal stressed research. Most of the studies published in the early volumes dealt with speech phonetics and phonology, physiology and pathology.[6] By 1935, the speech association had 1700 members, and speech was well established as a field.

Although the practice of journalism dates back many years, formalized study in the area did not progress rapidly until the early 1900s. In 1905, the University of Wisconsin offered what were perhaps the first courses in journalism, at a time when there were few, if any, books on the topic. By 1910, there were half a dozen volumes available, and between 1910 and 1920, some twenty-five works on journalism and newspaper work were compiled, signaling a pattern of continued growth.[7]

The advent of radio in the 1920s and television in the early 1940s resulted in the wider application of journalistic concepts. These new media gave impetus to the development of a broadened view of the nature of journalism.

Interest in communication was not limited to speech and journalism. In philosophy, scholars wrote about the nature of communication and its role in human life. Anthropologists, psychologists, and sociologists focused on communication and its role in individual and social process; and writers in the area of language also contributed to the advancement of communication study.

The 1940s and 1950s: Interdisciplinary Growth

In the 1940s and early 1950s, the scope of the field of communication broadened substantially. A number of scholars from the various behavioral and social science disciplines began to develop theories of communication which extended beyond the boundaries of their own fields. In anthropology, for example, research concerned with body positioning and gestures in particular cultures laid the groundwork for more general studies of nonverbal communication. In psychology, interest focused on persuasion, social influence, and, specifically, attitudes—how they form, how they change, their impact on behavior, and the role of communication in these dynamics. Researchers were especially concerned with issues of persuasion, including how propaganda persuaded individuals, how public opinion was created, and how the developing media contributed to persuasive efforts.[8] Kurt Lewin and his colleagues conducted a major research program on group dynamics. Carl Hovland and Paul Lazarsfeld conducted early research on mass communication.

Sociologists and political scientists studied the nature of mass media in various political and social activities, such as voting behavior, and other facets of life. In zoology, communication among animals began to receive considerable attention among researchers. During these same years, scholars in linguistics, general semantics, and semiotics, fields that focused on the nature of language and its role in human activity, also contributed to the advancement of communication study.

Studies in rhetoric and speech in the late 1940s and 1950s broadened to include oral interpretation, voice and diction, debate, theater, physiology of speech, and speech pathology. In journalism and mass media studies, growth and development were even more dramatic, spurred on in no small way by the popularity of television and efforts to understand its impact. In a number of classic works in the 1950s, the focus on specific media—newspapers, magazines, radio, and television—began to be replaced by a more general concern with the nature and effects of *mass media* and *mass communication.*

By the end of the 1950s a number of writings had appeared that paved the way for the development of more integrated views of communication. It was during these years that the National Society for the Study of Communication (now the International Communication Association) was established with the stated goal of bringing greater unity to the study of communication by exploring the relationships among speech, language, and media.[9] These developments set the stage for the rapid growth of communication as an independent discipline.

The 1960s: Integration

In the 1960s, scholars synthesized thinking from rhetoric and speech, journalism and mass media, and the other social science disciplines. Among the noteworthy contributions to this integration were landmark books such as *The Process of Communication* (1960), *The Effects of Mass Communication* (1960), *On Human Communication* (1961), *Diffusion of Innovations* (1962), *The Science of Human Communication* (1963), *Understanding Media* (1964), and *Theories of Mass Communication* (1966).

The generalized views of communication reflected in these volumes were applied beginning in the middle of the decade. The term *communication* was linked to *speech* and *rhetoric* in basic books on the field during these years. In 1966, *Speech Communication: A Behavioral Approach* appeared, and two years later, *An Introduction to Rhetorical Communication* was published. In the mid-1960s, major volumes also linked *communication* with *culture* and *persuasion.* Additionally, the first books with *interpersonal communication* in their titles were published during this decade.

Communication was of interest in many disciplines during the 1960s. Sociologists focused on group dynamics, social relations, and the social origins of knowledge. Political scientists wrote about the role of communication in governments, governance, public opinion, propaganda, and political image building, providing the foundation for the development of the area of political communication that was to blossom a decade later.[10]

In administrative studies, writings on organizations, management, leadership, and information networks provided the basis for the growth of *organizational communication,* an area of study that also emerged in the 1970s. Writings in anthropology and linguistics, together with those in communication, set the stage for the emergence of intercultural communication as an area of study. Advances by zoologists during the 1960s encouraged the study of animal communication.

The 1970s and Early 1980s: Growth and Specialization

The expansion and specialization that began in the late 1960s reached new heights in the 1970s. *Interpersonal communication* became an increasingly popular area, as did the study of nonverbal interaction. Information science, information theory, and information and communication systems were other topics of increasing interest. During these same years, *group, organizational, political, international,* and *intercultural communication* emerged as distinct areas of study.

Rhetoric, public speaking, debate, theater, speech pathology, journalism, mass media, photography, advertising, and public relations continued to grow and prosper alongside communication, speech communication, and mass communication. New areas such as instructional, therapeutic, and developmental communication also became attractive to researchers and practitioners. Feminist scholars in communication also began to contribute to many of these areas.

Increased interest in communication study during the 1970s was also evident in periodicals and scholarly journals. Increased research activity led to a remarkable increase in the publication of books and periodicals. The first publications with the term *communication* in their titles were published in the mid-1930s, and during the 1950s four more appeared. Eight new periodicals appeared during the 1960s, and the 1970s brought the arrival of seventeen new publications bearing *communication* in their titles. A number of new academic journals were introduced, and several other journals of speech and journalism added the word *communication* to their titles to reflect a broadened focus. By the end of the decade, *Ulrich's International Periodical Dictionary* listed one hundred and thirty-seven publications on communication.

The expansion and diversification of communication study was reflected in college and university curricula. A number of new departments of communication were formed throughout the 1970s, and some programs in speech changed their names to speech communication or communication. The same was true in some journalism departments, where the shift was from journalism to mass communication, communication, or communications.

The Popularity of Communication

Interest in communication was apparent in the popular, as well as the academic, realm. In 1975, the *Harper Dictionary of Contemporary Usage* listed communication as a "vogue word—a word . . . that suddenly or inexplicably crops up . . . in speeches of bureaucrats, comments of columnists . . . and in radio and television broadcasts." This notoriety focused attention on the importance and relevance of communication and brought individuals with various perspectives and backgrounds to the field. However, it also resulted in such widespread use that the meaning of communication became somewhat less precise.

Discipline, Activity, and Profession.   One factor that contributed to the ambiguity of the term during this period of increasing popularity was the use of a single term to refer to a field of study, a set of activities, and a profession. People study communication, people communicate (or more accurately, engage in communication), and people earn their livelihood creating communication products and services. This potential source of confusion does not occur in most other disciplines. For example, scholars study psychology and English, but they do not "psychologize" or "Englishicate." They study English literature and write. Or they study psychology and engage in therapy or counseling. In these fields, as in most others, different terms are used to differentiate the discipline from the phenomenon itself and from its professional practice. With communication, one word refers to the discipline, the activity, and the profession.

In an attempt to clarify the distinction, some writers suggested the terms *communication science* or *communication studies* to refer to the discipline, and *communicologist* and *communication scientist* or *communication researcher* to refer to those within it. The phrase *communication professional* was sometimes used to refer to individuals who earned their livelihoods engaged in communication activities. These terms were not widely adopted, leaving a source of confusion that continues to the present day.

Communication and Communications.   Another factor adding to the confusion was the use of *communication* and *communications*. Traditionally, *communications* had been used to refer to media or to specific messages being transmitted through these media. *Communication* has historically been used to refer to the activity of sending and receiving messages (through media or face-to-face) and to the discipline as a whole. With the increasing interest in communication technology, the term communications began to be used interchangeably with communication in popular—and sometimes academic—contexts, blurring what had originally been a useful technical distinction.

The Late 1980s and 1990s: The Information Age

The *Information Age* is a popular term used to refer to the period beginning in the late 1990s, and in many senses continuing to the present time. This has been a period in which communication and information technology came to play an increasingly important role in our society. So pervasive are the impacts of these new media and the communication and information services they have created, that it is difficult to find an aspect of our personal and professional lives that has not in some way been affected.

Information As a Commodity

During the 1980s and 1990s, there was an increasing interest in information communicated via messages as an economic good or commodity—something that can be bought and sold— and in the technologies by which this commodity is created, distributed, stored, retrieved, and used. In the United States communication and information companies have emerged as some of our largest businesses. Communication and information became central in the telecommunication, publishing, Internet, and computer industries, as well as in banking, insurance, leisure and travel, and research. People in these fields spent an increasing amount of their time packaging information into products and services that could be sold in domestic and foreign markets. In the United States, Japan, Sweden, England, and a number of other countries at least half of the society's labor force was engaged in communication and information-related work.

Converging Media

New and converging media were a fundamental feature of the landscape of the period. Certainly the most obvious change during this period was the growth of the Internet, and other information storage, transmission, and retrieval systems using computers.

During these years, media were brought together to form hybrid technologies that permitted communication sources and receivers to carry out functions that were once difficult, time-consuming, or even impossible. In earlier periods, specific technologies had more or less specific uses. Television was a medium for viewing mass-produced and -distributed programs which reached the set via the airwaves. During the Information Age, television became not only a medium for the mass distribution of standardized programs but also a device for use with the Internet, DVDs, personal photos, interactive video games, cable systems, and a display for print as well as visual computer output. The telephone underwent a similar transformation. Designed for one-to-one conversation, telephones and telephone lines were used not only in this way but also in conjunction with computers and facsimile machines for the transmission of text and graphics as well as voice. Typewriters, once used exclusively for print correspondence and report preparation, were combined with the telephone and television screen to form new, hybrid telecommunication systems.

Thus, the infamous "Information Age" brought new labels, new and hybrid media, extended concepts of communication and information, changing economic realities, and new jobs for an increasing number of communication and information workers. During these years our perspective broadened to include newer media and the nature and function of communication technology in general. The Information Age greatly heightened attention to the pervasive role of technology in our lives and its impact on human behavior.

The Twenty-First Century: Communication Study Today

This chapter has traced the development of the discipline from its early beginnings, through periods marked by interdisciplinary development, through its emergence and growth as a discipline in its own right through the end of the twentieth century. From this overview, one can draw a number of conclusions about the present period that are helpful in understanding communication study as it exists today.

Ancient and Newly Emergent

The core of modern communication study has its origins in the work of the early Greek philosophers. The 1900s, however, brought a number of changes to the discipline, including a new name. Within the last fifty years, the scope of the field has broadened, its structure has changed, and every facet of it has grown substantially. In this respect, communication can be viewed as a newly emergent field, the newest of the disciplines concerned with the study of human behavior.

Discipline and Interdisciplinary Link

As has been the case for at least the past half century, communication in the present period is a strong discipline in its own right. At the same time, interest in communication extends well beyond the boundaries of the communication field.

This duality attests to the central role of communication in human affairs. And, at a time when the boundaries between these and other fields are becoming less rigid, communication serves as an important intellectual link among scholars of various persuasions and points of view.

In communication studies, we approach issues such as these from the perspective of the creation, transmission, interpretation, and use of information by individuals in relationships, groups, organizations, cultures, and societies. The value of integrating our efforts with the works of scholars in other disciplines has become increasingly apparent. Potential connections exist with a number of areas, including

- *Cognitive psychology and neuroscience.* Focus on perception, thinking, interpretation, memory, and use of information
- *Cultural and critical studies.* Focus on the historical, social, political, and cultural influences on message creation, transmission, interpretation, impact, and use
- *Economics.* Focus on the production and consumption of information as an economic resource
- *Computer science and electrical engineering.* Focus on the storage, retrieval, manipulation, and transmission of information
- *Information science.* Focus on information classification, management, and storage

- *Journalism.* Focus on information sources, content, public communication, and mass media
- *Literature.* Focus on the creation and reader interpretations of textual material
- *Marketing.* Focus on user needs and preferences in relation to adoption and use of messages, products, and services
- *Philosophy.* Focus on ethical dimensions of the communication process involving both individuals and the mass media

Personal and Professional Applicability

The importance attached to communication in contemporary life can also be seen in the extent to which the phenomenon is regarded as essential to our personal as well as our occupational roles. The shelves of libraries and book stores are filled with writings emphasizing the importance of communication to the establishment and maintenance of meaningful interpersonal and family relationships. And, but a few rows away, are an equal number of writings describing the importance of communication to successful professional and organizational functioning. Such writings talk about the importance of communication for individual leaders, team collaboration, organizational effectiveness, and marketplace competitiveness, among other topics.

Old and New Technology

Speaking and listening are as basic to communication and human behavior at the dawn of a new millennium as they were at the time of the ancient Greeks. And yet, in the present period, we benefit from any number of technologically enhanced forms of communication, which give permanence and portability to the messages of face-to-face communication. Beyond taken-for-granted media such as newspapers, radio, television, and magazines are a broad array of new technologies that find their way to the market every year. Whether one thinks of customized news and information Web applications, Internet innovations, cell phones, MP3 software and players, wireless local networks, global positioning systems, high definition LCD television screens/monitors, sophisticated video games, or the many other emerging tools, toys, and technologies, the possibilities for new forms of communication are quite remarkable. And yet as we shall discuss in greater detail later, for all the new forms of communication, many if not most of the basic communication challenges and functions remain. Inquiring minds might legitimately ask if all the new communication forms that fill our pockets, briefcases, homes, and offices have improved the quality of our lives. Are we better informed than we were fifty years ago? Are we better entertained? Is world understanding improving? Are our personal and family relationships better, more meaningful? These are good questions, we think, and are precisely the kind of questions that should increasingly be addressed by those interested in communication study in the 2000s and beyond.

Problem and Solution

Few topics are as pervasive in the popular culture as communication. We have become so accustomed to hearing and reading commentaries on the challenges we face in crossing social, demographic, political, gender, cultural, lifestyle, religious, or occupational boundaries that it

RESEARCH PROFILE

Children and the Internet • *Patti M. Valkenburg*

Is the Internet a global medium that enables people to access information and communicate with others in a new and beneficial way, or is it going to destroy family life and interfere with our interpersonal relationships? Professor Valkenburg's research examines the world of electronic communication and provides some answers to these important questions.

• • •

The Internet is currently the fastest growing medium used among children and teenagers. According to on-line industry research, over 20 million North American children and teenagers were online in 2003. This number is projected to increase to 36.9 million by 2005.

The rapid emergence of the Internet has been accompanied by diametrically opposed views about its social consequences. There are those who see the Internet as a powerful, positive force that will promote family cohesion and make the world a better place. Others, however, hold more pessimistic views about the implications of the Internet for family life, friendships, and identity development.

A major concern about the Internet is that it encourages children to spend more time alone in front of the screen, talking to strangers and forming online friendships instead of friendships with their real-life peers. Because these online relationships are seen as more superficial than real-life relationships, it is believed that the Internet increases loneliness, social isolation, and fragmentation of families and social groups.

Another concern stems from the Internet's anonymous nature and reduced auditory and visual cues. These characteristics of the Internet provide children with many opportunities to experiment with their identities. Some authors argue that children benefit from the possibilities to carve out different identities on the Internet, just as they profit from imaginative play in early childhood. Many others, however, fear that anonymous Internet communication engenders irresponsibility, interpersonal deception, and disinhibited behavior.

Although these concerns are recurrently raised in the literature, most of them are highly premature, because empirical research on the social consequences of the Internet for children is still very scarce. Only by longitudinal research is it possible to develop a true understanding of the positive and negative consequences of the Internet. This is the focus of my research at the Amsterdam School of Communications Research in the Netherlands.

is easy to overlook the central role communication is perceived to play in these matters. In such conversations, communication—or, more precisely, the lack thereof—is seen as the fundamental *problem.* And yet, as John Peters has pointed out, communication is also seen as the essential *solution.*[11] Paradoxically, communication is seen as both a chasm and a bridge.[12] The significance afforded to the phenomenon in our time is quite remarkable, and a factor that contributes to the vitality and importance of communication study and communication practice.

Practical Skill and Fundamental Life Process

Another interesting contrast regarding communication study today is its breadth. In many communication courses, the primary emphasis on communication continues to be as a skill, and more specifically on the set of techniques associated with creating and disseminating messages, orally or in written form, in face-to-face or technologically mediated settings. There are other courses, however—more often the type that would make use of a book such as this—that approach communication theoretically, viewing it as a fundamental life process, one that is basic to our physical, personal, social, political, and cultural existence. The fact the communication study encompasses such a broad range of interests is a source of some confusion, and frequently requires definitional clarification in discussions. At the same time, as in previous periods, this breadth also creates what is a useful tension for the field—a tension between the search for practical technique and the quest for theoretical understanding. Each makes a useful and complementary contribution to the field in its effort to advance human knowledge and capability.

Implications and Applications

- Communication has long been regarded as important to the practice and understanding of human affairs.
- In the past several decades, communication study has become an increasingly popular academic subject.
- Communication study offers students the richness and diversity of the liberal arts tradition, blended with the applied focus of a professional field.
- Communication study today continues to be the center of a very strong discipline in its own right, and also the basis for linkages between scholars and practitioners from many other fields in which communication is important.
- Paradoxically, communication is both the basis for many of the problems of human affairs and also the potential solution.

Summary

Communication has a rich and lengthy history, which can be traced back to Babylonian and Egyptian writings prior to the fifth century B.C. The initial contributions to communication study came from scholars in what was termed *rhetoric*. They viewed communication as the practical art of persuasion. Aristotle and Plato, who were particularly significant to early communication study, saw rhetoric and the practice of public speaking not only as an art but also as a legitimate area of study.

Along with rhetoric and speech, journalism also contributed to the heritage of communication study. As with rhetoric, journalism initially was concerned primarily with practical rather than theoretical matters. By the beginning of the twentieth century, rhetoric and speech were clearly established as disciplines in their own right; and journalism began to take shape as a field as well.

During the early twentieth century, interest in communication continued in rhetoric and speech, and the advent of radio and later television led to the wider application of journalistic concepts and the development of more theories of the overall process. The 1940s and 1950s were years of interdisciplinary growth, as scholars from various disciplines advanced theories of communication that extended beyond the boundaries of their own fields.

The 1960s were a period of integration. A good deal was done to synthesize the writings of rhetoric and speech, journalism and mass media, as well as other disciplines. A number of landmark books appeared within the field.

During this most recent period of history, additional models of the communication process were advanced, extending the work of earlier scholars.

The 1970s and early 1980s were a time of unprecedented growth within the field. It was also a period in which much specialization occurred, giving rise to progress in our understanding of interpersonal, group, organizational, political, international, and intercultural communication.

Continuing growth and interdisciplinary advancement have distinguished the communication field in the late 1980s and 1990s, and developments of the Information Age have been important influences. Converging media, along with economic and marketplace developments, have underscored the pervasive impact of communication and communication media on our lives.

At the opening of the twenty-first century, the discipline of communication and the phenomena it studies are center stage in human affairs. The subject is at once ancient and newly emergent, a discipline in its own right and an interdisciplinary crossroad for scholars from a wide variety of fields. Communication is as relevant to personal as it is professional affairs, and the role of new and old technology continues to be a focus of the times and the discipline. As John Peters has noted, communication study is concerned with both the major problem and most hopeful solution of contemporary life, and the focus of the field of communication is at once on some of the most practical of skills and on the most fundamental of life processes.

The overview of the history of communication reveals a number of changes during the 2,500-year heritage of the field—changes both in the theory of the communication process and in the discipline in which it is studied.

We have seen that the communication field is both ancient as well as a product of the twentieth century, interdisciplinary in heritage, the home of scholars and professionals, a discipline which benefits from the approaches of both the humanities and behavioral sciences, and an area in which media are of continuing concern.

Notes

1. For a detailed summary of the early history of speech and rhetorical communication study overviewed here, see Nancy L. Harper, *Human Communication Theory: History of a Paradigm* (Rochelle Park, NJ: Hayden, 1979), pp. 16–68, and James C. McCroskey, *An Introduction to Rhetorical Communication* (Englewood Cliffs, NJ: Prentice-Hall, 1986), pp. 261–272.

2. Harper, 1979, pp. 27–30.

3. For a comprehensive and thoughtful discussion of the history of communication study, see John D. Peters, *Speaking Into Air: A History of the Idea of Communication* (Chicago: University of Chicago Press, 1999).

4. J. F. Frank, *The Beginnings of the English Newspaper 1620–1660* (Cambridge, MA: Harvard University Press, 1961), p. 2.

5. See H. Cohen, *The History of Speech Communication: The Emergence of a Discipline, 1914–1945* (Annandale, VA: National Communication Association, 1994).

6. E. G. Bormann, *Theory and Research in the Communicative Arts* (New York: Holt, 1965), pp. 16–17. See

also Penny Demo, "Celebrating Our 75th Anniversary and Our Early Publications," in *Spectra,* May, 1989, p. 4.

7. Grant M. Hyde, "Foreword," in *Survey of Journalism.* Ed. by G. F. Mott (New York: Barnes & Noble, 1937), p. viii.

8. Jesse G. Delia, "Communication Research: A History," in *Handbook of Communication Science.* Ed. by C. R. Berger and S. H. Chaffee (Newbury Park, CA: Sage, 1987), pp. 25–30.

9. Carl H. Weaver, "A History of the International Communication Association," in *Communication Yearbook 1.* Ed. by Brent D. Ruben (New Brunswick, NJ: Transaction-International Communication Association, 1977), pp. 607–609.

10. Wilbur Schramm, *The Beginnings of Communication Study in America: A Personal Memoir* (Thousand Oaks, CA: Sage, 1997).

11. Peters, 1999, p. 5.

12. Peters, 1999, p. 5.

3

The Evolution of Communication Theory

In this chapter

Why . . .

- Theories are resistant to change even in the face of contradictory findings.

- Communication is an activity, a social science, a liberal art, and a profession.

The Evolution of an Idea

Scholars and practitioners have been thinking about the nature of communication for more than 2,500 years. The terms they have used, and the examples on which they have focused, have varied with the times, but the fundamental goal—the pursuit of an understanding of the role communication plays in human affairs—has remained unchanged.

With so much being written about communication throughout the history of interest in the phenomenon, in so many varied fields, and focused on so many different areas of application, how is it possible to identify the core concepts of communication theory? One of the best ways to do this is by examining models of communication. Models can take various forms, but regardless of their specific characteristics, all share a common purpose, which is to miniaturize, simplify, highlight, and emphasize fundamental features of the object, process, or phenomenon they are created to represent. Thus, whether the model is of a toy airplane, a building, or a DNA molecule, the goal is to present a coherent view of what the creator believes to be particularly important about the focus of his or her study.

So it is that the models to be presented and discussed in this chapter offer an excellent way to examine the nature and better understand the fundamentals of the communication process. Moreover, examining and analyzing models chronologically, as we have chosen to do, has the additional advantage of highlighting the ways in which the core concepts of communication theory have evolved over the years.

Not surprisingly, given the history of the field, most of the earliest perspectives on communication focused on public settings in which an orator spoke to a listener or group of listeners with the goal of persuading them of the correctness of a particular point of view.[1] Gradually, thinking broadened to focus on private as well as public speaking; nonverbal and technologically mediated as well as verbal communication; multiple speakers and listeners as well as individual sources or receivers; and outcomes that include such things as entertainment, parent–child socialization, relationship building, culture building, and many others along with persuasion. Imbedded in these changes are a number of more subtle but critical shifts in thinking about some of the invisible dynamics that occur as people engage in communication. We think you'll agree that the journey is an interesting one, with rather profound implications for understanding the nature of communication and its role in human life.

Origins of Communication Theory: Early Greece

Aristotle (385–322 B.C.) and his teacher Plato (427–347 B.C.) were the most central figures in early communication study. Both regarded communication as an art or craft to be practiced, and as an area of study. As Aristotle noted in the opening paragraph of his classic work on rhetoric:

> To a certain extent all men [and women] attempt to discuss statements and to maintain them, at random or through practice and from acquired habit. Both ways being possible, the subject can plainly be handled systematically, for it is possible to inquire the reason why some speakers succeed through practice and others spontaneously; and everyone will at once agree that such inquiry is the function of science.[2]

Aristotle saw communication as the means through which citizens participated in democracy. He described communication in terms of an *orator* or *speaker* constructing an *argument* to be presented in a *speech* to *hearers*—an *audience* as depicted in Figure 3.1. The speaker's goal was to inspire a positive image of himself or herself and to encourage the members of the audience to be receptive to the message. As Aristotle wrote

> [R]hetoric exists to affect the giving of decisions . . . the *orator* must not only try to make the argument of his [or her] *speech* demonstrative and worthy of belief; he [or she] must also make his own character look right and put his *hearers,* who are to decide, in the right frame of mind.[3] (Emphasis added)

For Aristotle, communication was primarily a verbal activity through which speakers tried to persuade—to achieve their own purposes with a listener through skillful construction of an argument and delivery of a speech.

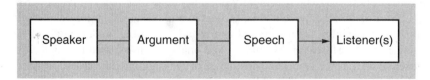

FIGURE 3.1   *Aristotelian View*

RESEARCH PROFILE

Helping People in Conflict • *Mark Aakhus*

Communication is a multifaceted field that encompasses studies of individuals, groups, organizations, and societies. Professor Aakhus's research demonstrates how communication theory can be applied in a variety of contexts.

• • •

My work focuses on the emergence and management of conflicts that arise as people attempt to make decisions, solve problems, and learn. This research brings together ideas about argumentation and social interaction to explain decision making, conflict resolution, and the organization of work.

Among the real-world phenomena that I investigate are couples trying to negotiate divorce settlements, organizations trying to develop workable information systems, groups trying to formulate collective action, decision makers trying to sort out disagreement among experts, communities grappling with development issues, households trying to coordinate the rush of life, and individuals searching for the meaning of good work in their professional practice.

In these studies, I look at the practices and technologies people use to regulate and shape their communication and the consequences of how people handle complex situations. This means that I conduct basic research that explains how communication works in settings of decision making, conflict resolution, and learning and also applied research that models, designs, and tests practices and technologies intended to augment communication in practical, real-world settings.

One set of studies I have done examines third-party interventions by communication specialists to help resolve complex situations. These studies are among the first to articulate the expert-service provided by meeting facilitators, who implement group decision support systems, and dispute mediators. I have identified implicit models and practices these people use to shape a disputant's expression of conflict and the use of reason. These studies offer insight into improving intervention and understanding neutrality in third-party intervention.

Another set of studies examines the design and use of information and communication technology (ICT) to augment human interaction and reasoning by facilitating argumentation. These studies demonstrate otherwise inconspicuous but important influences on discourse quality and reasoning among the technology users. This has led me to create and test applications that facilitate reflective learning in work and professional practice.

Many scholars consider Aristotle to be the greatest theorist of rhetorical communication. His classic work, *The Rhetoric,* was written about 330 B.C. and contains three books emphasizing the speaker, the audience, and the speech.

Book I focuses on the means of persuasion, which Aristotle argues are *ethos* (the nature of the source), *pathos* (the emotion of the audience), and *logos* (the nature of the message presented by the source to the audience). He claims that proof is the essential element for a successful persuasive speech. He differentiates three contexts for speaking: deliberative speaking before the government, forensic speaking in a court of law, and epideictic speaking on ceremonial occasions.

Book II examines the nature of the audience and how the speaker can evoke an audience's emotions. Aristotle argues that demographic factors of an audience (such as age and social class) will influence how they perceive a message.

The final book deals with style and stresses clarity as an important component of an effective message. Aristotle emphasizes how a message is constructed and gives little attention to delivery.

McCroskey identifies three essential elements in Aristotle's theory of rhetoric: all arguments must be based on probabilities (what an audience believes to be true) since absolute verifiable truth is not possible in most cases; audience adaptation (understanding what is likely to persuade someone) is the key to an effective message; and amorality (his theory can be used for both worthy or unworthy ends).[4]

Plato, in his writings, outlined what he thought would be necessary for the study of rhetoric to contribute to a broader explanation of human behavior. He believed that the field would need to include the study of the nature of words, the study of the nature of human beings and their ways of approaching life, the study of the nature of order, and the study of the instruments by which human beings are affected.[5] Thus, although much of the earliest interest in what we now call communication focused on public speaking, it was recognized that in order to understand fully how persuasion operated it would be necessary to develop a broader and more comprehensive theory.

The Twentieth Century

As the field of communication emerged as a discipline in its own right in the 1940s, 1950s, and 1960s, the influence of ideas advanced by early Greek scholars and extended in subsequent writings was still very much in evidence. The ways of thinking about the nature of communication began to change as the field developed, and this evolution was evident in the models of the process that were published and popularized. Among the most influential of these models were those of Harold Lasswell, Claude Shannon and Warren Weaver, Wilbur Schramm, Elihu Katz and Paul Lazarsfeld, and Bruce Westley and Malcolm MacLean. Each of these scholars offered perspectives on the nature of communication that built on the earliest concepts of the phenomenon.

Lasswell's View of Communication

One of the most often cited characterizations of communication was advanced by political scientist Harold Lasswell in 1948 as an outgrowth of his work in the area of political propaganda. Lasswell provided a general view of communication that extended well beyond the boundaries of political science. He said that the communication process could best be explained by the simple statement:

"Who says what to whom in what channel with what effect."[6]

Lasswell's view of communication, as had Aristotle's some two thousand years earlier, emphasized the elements of *speaker, message,* and *audience,* but used different terminology (see Figure 3.2). Both scholars viewed communication as a one-way process in which one individual influenced others through messages.

Lasswell offered a broadened definition of *channel* that included mass media along with speech as part of the communication process. His approach also provided a more generalized view of the *goal* or *effect* of communication than did the Aristotelian perspective. Lasswell's work suggested that there could be a variety of outcomes or effects of communication, such as to inform, to entertain, to aggravate, as well as to persuade.

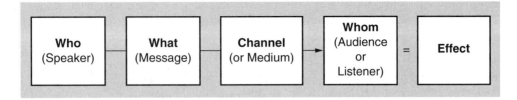

FIGURE 3.2 *Lasswell's Model*

Shannon and Weaver's Model

About a year after the introduction of the Lasswell perspective, Claude Shannon published the results of research he had undertaken for Bell Telephone to study the engineering problems of signal transmission. The results of his study provided the basis for what came to be known as the Shannon and Weaver model of communication (see Figure 3.3).

Shannon and Weaver described the communication process in this way:

> Communication include(s) all the procedures by which one mind may affect another. This, of course, involves not only written and oral speech, but also music, the pictorial arts, the theatre, the ballet, and in fact all human behavior.[7]

The Shannon and Weaver concept represented an important expansion of the idea of communication from the act of speaking or writing in a public setting or through mass media, to activities such as music, art, ballet and the theater—in fact, all human behavior.

Like Lasswell, Shannon and Weaver saw communication in terms of a one-way process by which a message was sent from a source through a channel to a receiver. Their model was somewhat more detailed, however, because Shannon and Weaver made several distinctions that the other models had not. Specifically, they differentiated between a *signal*

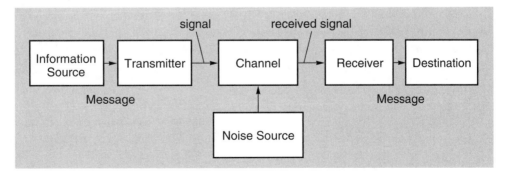

FIGURE 3.3 *Shannon and Weaver's Model*

From *The Mathematical Theory of Communication* by Claude E. Shannon and Warren Weaver. Copyright 1949, 1998 by Board of Trustees of the University of Illinois. Used with permission of the University of Illinois Press.

and a *message,* an *information source* and a *transmitter,* and a *receiver* and *destination.* They described the workings of the model as follows:

> The *information source* selects a desired message out of a set of possible messages. . . . The selected message may consist of written or spoken words, or of pictures, music, etc. . . . The *transmitter* changes the *message* into the signal which is actually sent over the *communication channel* from the transmitter to the *receiver.*[8]

If one considers the example of a dramatic series carried by cable television, the *channel* is the cable; the *signal* is the varying electrical current carried by the cable; the *information source* is the performers, their backdrop, and so on; the *transmitter* is the set of devices (camera, audio and video amplification system, and so on) that converts the visual and vocal images of the performers into electrical current.

In this example, the *receiver* is the television set and cable converter equipment. The receiver's purpose is to change the signal back into a *message* that can be received and interpreted at the *destination* (a cable viewer, in this case).

Shannon and Weaver introduced the term *noise* as the label for any distortion that interferes with the transmission of a signal from the source to the destination. In our example, an illustration of noise would be electrical interference, leading to audio or video distortion, in the cable line. They also advanced the concept of *correction channel,* which they regarded as a means of overcoming problems created by noise. The correction channel was operated by an observer who compared the initial signal that was sent with that received; when the two didn't match, additional signals would be transmitted to correct the error.[9]

Schramm's Models

In an article published in 1954 entitled, "How Communication Works," Wilbur Schramm provided several additional models of communication, including the one shown in Figure 3.4.

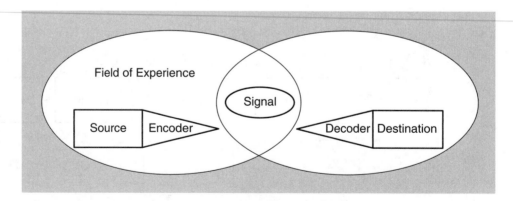

FIGURE 3.4   *Schramm's Model*

From *The Process and Effects of Mass Communication* by Wilbur Schramm. Copyright 1954 by Board of Trustees of the University of Illinois. Used with permission of the University of Illinois Press.

Describing this model, Schramm said

> A *source* may be an individual (speaking, writing, drawing, gesturing) or a communication organization (like a newspaper, publishing house, television station or motion picture studio). The *message* may be in the form of ink on paper, sound waves in the air, impulses in electric current, a wave of the hand, a flag in the air, or any other signal capable of being interpreted meaningfully. The *destination* may be an *individual* listening, watching, or reading; a member of a *group,* such as a discussion group, a lecture audience, a football crowd, or a mob; or an individual member of a particular group we call the mass audience, such as the reader of a newspaper or a viewer of television.[10]

Schramm saw communication as a purposeful effort to establish a *commonness* between a source and receiver, noting that the word *communication* comes from the Latin *communis,* which means common:

> What happens when the source tries to build up this commonness with [the] intended receiver? First, the source encodes [a] message. That is, he [or she] takes the information or feeling he [or she] wants to share and puts it into a form that can be transmitted. The pictures in our heads can't be transmitted until they are coded. . . . Once coded and sent, a message is quite free of its sender. . . . And there is good reason . . . for the sender to wonder whether [the] receiver will really be in tune with him [or her], whether the message will be interpreted without distortion, whether the picture in the head of the receiver will bear any resemblance to that in the head of the sender.[11]

Schramm also introduced the concept of *field of experience,* which he thought to be essential to determining whether a message would be received at the destination in the manner intended by the source. He contended that without common fields of experience—a common language, common backgrounds, a common culture, and so forth—there was little chance for a message to be understood. In this respect his work significantly expanded the thinking of Shannon and Weaver.

Schramm suggested the importance of *feedback* as a means of overcoming the problem of noise. He said that feedback "tells us how our messages are being interpreted. . . . An experienced communicator is attentive to feedback and constantly modifying [the] messages in light of what he [or she] observes in or hears from [the] audience."[12]

The Schramm view of communication was more elaborate than many others developed during this period and added new elements in describing the process. In addition to reemphasizing the elements of source, message, and destination, it suggested the importance of interpretation and the role of field of experience. Whereas other models had acknowledged that the receiver might be either a single person or a large audience, this model suggested that a source could also be one individual or many.

Katz and Lazarsfeld's Model

In 1955, political scientists Elihu Katz and Paul Lazarsfeld presented a *two-step flow* concept of communication in their book *Personal Influence.* The model was based on earlier research in which they found that information presented in the mass media did not reach and have an impact on individuals as previous views of communication seemed to suggest it would. Specifically, their research found that political radio and print messages had a negligible effect on individuals' voting decisions.

In searching for an explanation for this lack of effect, they developed a view that linked interpersonal dynamics to mass communication. They determined that undecided voters were influenced more by people around them than by information provided by the mass media; husbands and wives were influenced by their spouses, club members by other club members, workers by their colleagues, children by their parents, and so on. Their research also indicated that some people were consistently more influential than others, leading them to conclude that "ideas often seem to *flow* from radio and print *to* opinion leaders and *from them* to the less active sections of the population"—in a two-step flow (see Figure 3.5).[13]

Although research has since suggested that the two-step concept is only applicable in some situations, this formulation has been very influential over the years. It served to link face-to-face and mass communication, and also introduced the idea of opinion leaders. It also has served as the basis for the development of *diffusion theory,* which describes the process by which new ideas and technological innovations are introduced and adopted within a group, organization, or community.

Westley and MacLean's Model

A somewhat different approach to communication was developed by Bruce Westley and Malcolm S. MacLean, Jr. They suggested that the communication process begins with *receiving* messages, rather than *sending* them. To be more precise, Westley and MacLean's view indicates that the process actually begins with a series of *signals* or potential messages. As depicted in Figure 3.6, there are a large number of signals—potential messages—in a communicator's environment, which are referred to as "Xs" in their model.

Signals may involve a single sense modality such as sight or sound (X), or they may involve a combination of several modalities, for instance, sight, sound, and touch. The designation for such a signal would be X_{3m}—the "*3m*" indicating that three modalities are involved.

The model indicates that in a given situation only some of the many signals (Xs) in one's environment at any point in time are attended to by an individual (A). When individual A processes these signals and interprets them, what is, in effect, a new message (X^I) results. It is this new message—A's personal representation of the sum of all the Xs—that is passed along when individual A describes what he or she saw or heard to a second individual (C).

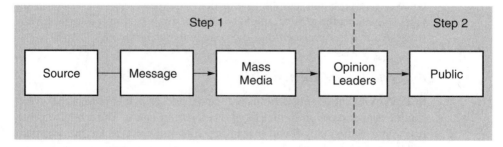

FIGURE 3.5 *Katz and Lazarsfeld's Model*

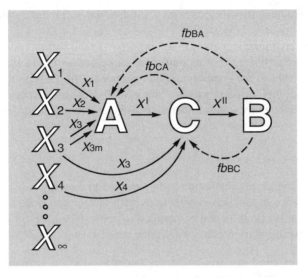

FIGURE 3.6 *Westley and MacLean's Model*

Source: Bruce Westley and Malcolm S. MacLean, Jr., "A Conceptual Model for Communication Research," *Audio-Visual Communication Review* (Winter, 1955). Reprinted by permission of the Association for Educational Communications and Technology. Copyright © 1955 by AECT.

As an illustration, consider that A is a reporter who goes to a crime scene to gather facts and write a story for an editor, who in turn may modify the story before including it in the script of the evening newscast. In this example, the reporter is A. The "facts" he or she gathers are Xs. The story that is written based on the facts is X^{I}. The editor to whom the story is submitted is C. The final version of the story included in the script for the newscast is X^{II}, and members of the viewing audience are Bs.

Two other parts of the model require explanation: first, note the arrow in the model from X_3 to C. This would describe a situation in which individual C had direct exposure to the same signal—X—as did individual A. In our illustration, suppose, for instance, that the editor drives by the scene of the crime and sees the same three bodies that reporter A notices.

Next, note the dotted arrows from B to C, B to A, and C to A. These represent feedback—response signals sent from B to C, B to A, and C to A, respectively. Let's refer, once again, to the illustration. A letter from an audience member to the editor is an example of fb_{BC}. A phone call from the audience member to the reporter would be designated fb_{BA}. Questions posed by the editor to the reporter or a letter of commendation for a fine story would be classified as fb_{CA}.

Obviously, the Westley-MacLean model is considerably more complicated than others; and the additional elements, lines, and arrows result in a view of communication that is broadened in four important ways.

- Accounts for the relationship between interpersonal communication and communication involving mass media

- Suggests that communication begins with an individual receiving messages rather than sending them
- Describes how many of the signals that are important to the communication process may not be intentionally sent (For example, the three bodies in the example above came to be significant to the communication experiences of the reporter and editor despite the fact that this message was not intentionally sent by anyone.)
- Emphasizes the changes messages undergo as they are passed along from one person to another

Dance's Model

In 1967, Frank Dance developed what came to be referred to as a helical-spiral view of communication. The Dance model was substantially different in appearance from others before it. The choice of this visual form was intended to convey the idea that communication is a complex and evolutionary process. As Dance noted

> If communication is viewed as a process, we are forced to adapt our examination and our examining instruments to the challenge of something in motion, something that is changing while we are in the very act of examining it.[14]

The helix, shown in Figure 3.7, was a way of combining the desirable features of the straight-line models with those of the circle, while avoiding the weaknesses of each.[15] To the circular feedback models, the Dance perspective added a concern with the dimension

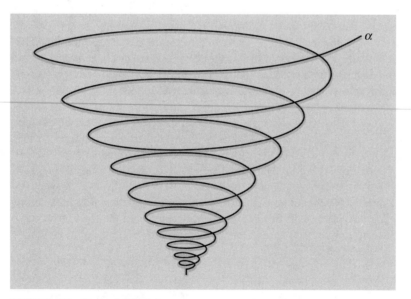

FIGURE 3.7   Dance's Model

Source: "Toward a Theory of Human Communication," in *Human Communication Theory: Original Essays* ed. by Frank E.X. Dance. Copyright © 1967. Reprinted by permission of the author.

of *time,* suggesting that each communicative act builds on the previous communication experiences of all parties involved. For instance, an exchange between two friends could be represented as a particular point on the helix. The history of the relationship is represented by previous points on the line, and the future by subsequent points.

Watzlawick, Beavin, and Jackson's Model

In 1967, Paul Watzlawick, Janet Beavin, and Don Jackson wrote *Pragmatics of Human Communication,* which provided a general view of communication based on psychiatric study and therapy. Their approach and many of the concepts and propositions they advanced have been extremely influential in communication thinking.

The Watzlawick-Beavin-Jackson view, presented in a general form in Figure 3.8, portrayed communication as a process involving a give-and-take of messages between individuals.[16] The perspective stressed the view that communication is not something that occurs only when a source intentionally chooses to send messages. Rather, they asserted that because we are always behaving, "one cannot not communicate."[17]

Communication was characterized as an ongoing, cumulative activity between individuals who function alternatively as sources and receivers, as shown in Figure 3.8. Their writings suggested that in order to understand how communication worked, one needed to look beyond the messages and channels to the meanings that the individuals involved attach to the words and actions they create.

Thayer's Model

In 1968, Lee Thayer's book, *Communication and Communication Systems,* provided an interdisciplinary view of the subject.[18] Like other approaches of the period, Thayer placed

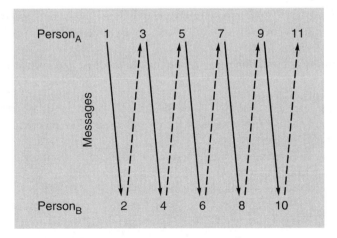

FIGURE 3.8   *Watzlawick, Beavin, and Jackson's Model*

Source: Adapted from *Pragmatics of Human Communication,* Paul Watzlawick, Janet H. Beavin, and Don D. Jackson. Copyright © 1967 by W. W. Norton & Company, Inc. Reprinted with permission of the publishers.

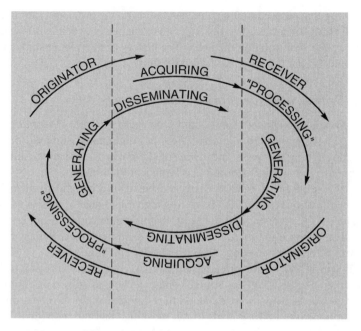

FIGURE 3.9   *Thayer's Model*

Source: Communication and Communication Systems by Lee Thayer, page
269. Copyright © 1968. Reprinted with the permission of Richard D. Irwin, Inc.

increasing emphasis on communication as a dynamic process through which individuals
create and interpret information—which he saw as complex, dynamic, and highly personalized. To emphasize this way of thinking, Thayer proposed the concepts of individual's "take-
into-account-abilities" and "take-into-account-susceptibilities." He contended that our
abilities and susceptibilities guide the way we acquire, process, generate, and disseminate information, as shown in Figure 3.9.

The model portrays communication as a dynamic process, and emphasizes several
other key ideas:

- The message a receiver acquires is never identical to the one a source transmits.
- Receivers acquire those messages which they are capable of processing (compre-
  hending) in some manner.
- People serve as both originators and receivers, and the shift from one to another is
  not always clear cut.
- Information received can serve as feedback.

Communication Theory in the Twenty-First Century

In general, the themes and concepts that were central to communication theory-building
during the middle decades of the twentieth century were carried forth in the 1980s and
1990s with some shifts in terminology and emphasis.

Reflecting the increasing disciplinary and popular attention being devoted to "the Information Age," discussions of the communication process during these years increasingly used the terms "information" and "technology" to refer to what earlier were generally termed "messages" and "media." Theories of communication that included a focus on media (or technology) tended to minimize the distinction made between *mass* and other forms of communication in which technology is involved. This change was prompted, in part, by the realization that newer media and technology made it possible for receivers to be actively in control of the time and place in which communication occurs, and in the uses of messages and information.[19] This change was also quite consistent with the increasing emphasis on the role receivers play in the models of communication discussed previously.

Also notable during the late 1980s and 1990s was the influence of cultural studies in communication theory development.[20] While such authors tended not to depict the process in visual forms, as were a number of the previous theories, these approaches emphasized the important role political, social class, or cultural influences play in framing the context in which specific communication events occur. They highlighted the notion that the participants in communication events are seldom equal in the power and influence they bring to the situation, and inequities of various kinds can play a dramatic role in communication dynamics and outcomes. These and other interdisciplinary influences, thus, continued to contribute significantly to the models and theories of the field.

In the first decade of the twenty-first century, popular models of communication carry forth the traditions of the decades that preceded them. In most of the widely used introductory textbooks in the field, for instance, communication is described as a process of interaction, or a transaction, between individuals involving messages, media, and feedback. Typically, authors also acknowledge the role of noise, context, setting, or other factors which may shape, interfere with, or in other ways influence communication effects or outcomes.[22]

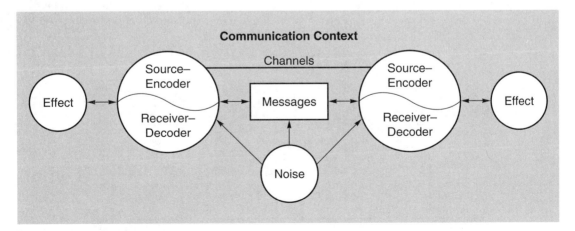

FIGURE 3.10 *DeVito's Model*

From Joseph A. DeVito, *Human Communication: The Basic Course, 9/e.* Published by Allyn and Bacon, Boston, MA. Copyright © 2003 by Pearson Education. Reprinted by permission of the publisher.

One popular textbook author, Joseph DeVito, for instance, illustrates the communication process in the manner shown in Figure 3.10, and defines communication this way:

> . . . communication occurs when one person (or more) sends and receives messages that are distorted by noise, occur within a context, have some effect, and provide some opportunity for feedback.[23]

Reflections on the Evolution of Communication Theory

Paradigms and Anomalies

The earliest perspectives on communication were concerned with public speaking with the goal of persuasion. Orientations broadened to include communication in private as well as public settings, nonverbal and technologically mediated as well as verbal messages, multiple as well as single sources and receivers, and a broad array of purposes, functions, and outcomes.

Amidst many of the obvious changes in form, certain underlying themes remained relatively constant for most of the 2,500-year history of the field. Perhaps the most fundamental of these traditional themes is the view that communication consists of a source constructing and transmitting a message to one or more receivers in order to bring about a particular effect. In this way of thinking, as depicted in Figure 3.11, communication is a one-way event consisting of a one-way transfer of information from source to receiver(s). This $S \rightarrow M \rightarrow R = E$ characterization of communication has been so pervasive in the thinking of the field that it represents what philosopher Thomas Kuhn and others refer to as a *paradigm*. Paradigms are broad theoretical orientations that guide the work of scholars in a field over a substantial period of time. They are pervasive and highly influential, and shape and are reflected in scholars' theories, research, and practice.[24]

Eventually, the paradigms of a field change. Although there is no simple explanation as to how and why this happens, it is often the case that change is stimulated by new ob-

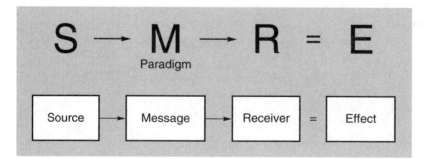

FIGURE 3.11   *One-Way Transfer of Information*

servations and evidence that cannot be accommodated by the prevailing paradigm. Research findings, observations, or events that cannot be explained by, or are inconstant with, existing paradigms are termed *anomalies.* Often, then, anomalies are the stimulant for discarding one paradigm and searching for an alternative.[25]

From our review of the recent history of communication models, it is evident that this kind of change has been occurring in communication. Further examination reveals that the anomaly that has given impetus to this transition is relatively simple: *message sent is not equal to message received—MS ≠ MR.*

Even as Aristotle advanced his orator-to-listener view of communication, he and his contemporaries acknowledged that the persuasive efforts of the speaker were not always successful. It was presumed that the match between the message sent and that received could be made more predictable if sources learned more about how to construct and deliver messages effectively.

The models and writings of Shannon and Weaver, and most especially Schramm, provide evidence of a recognition of the MS ≠ MR anomaly and the beginning of a changing view of communication. Shannon and Weaver's concept of *noise* represented the first formal acknowledgement in a basic communication model that the *message sent by a source* and the *message received by a receiver* often do not correspond. At the same time the concept of *noise,* as they explained it, offered an explanation as to why the two often may not coincide. The notion of a *correction channel* or *feedback,* suggested by Shannon and Weaver and elaborated on by Schramm and others, went one step beyond acknowledging that the message sent and the message received often do not match by providing a mechanism for remedying the problem.

The *field of experience* concept, introduced by Schramm, represented yet another means of explaining why the "picture in the head" of the source might not be duplicated in the head of the receiver following the transmission of a message. The idea of *opinion leaders* and *the two-step flow,* first suggested in the work of Katz and Lazarsfeld, again reflected an awareness of the fundamental anomaly. The two-step concept provided an explanation for the lack of predictive value of the classical paradigm.

The work of Westley and MacLean dealt with the MS ≠ MR anomaly by creating a model that did not begin with the sending of messages, but rather with an individual surrounded by *Xs*—information sources—some of which were intentionally provided by other people and some not. This way of thinking provided a logical and broadened explanation as to why the message as interpreted by a receiver often had little in common with the message as intended by a particular source.

Other changes in the ways scholars described the communication process occurred as a consequence of the recognition that the message as received often did not correspond well to the message that was sent. The Katz and Lazarsfeld model, for instance, presented the view that sender-to-receiver effects are more often *mediated* than *direct.* Dance emphasized that communication should not be viewed as a static event. Like Watzlawick, Beavin, and Jackson, Thayer emphasized that communication was a complex and dynamic process involving generating, disseminating, acquiring, and processing information. His work also placed greater emphasis on the receiver as a force in controlling communication outcomes.

The DeVito model (Figure 3.10) incorporates the components that were utilized in previous portrayals of the communication process. While bearing a striking visual resemblance to models of the mid-twentieth century, subtleties such as bidirectional arrows and references to context update the older perspectives to take recent advances into account.

Communication Theory Today

Our review of communication models suggests that whereas the S $\rightarrow$ M $\rightarrow$ R = E paradigm predominated during much of the history of the field, the past forty years have brought a number of changes to this perspective. The evolution of the concept has been:

- From source- and message-centered to receiver- and meaning-centered
- From one-way to interactive and transactional
- From event- to process-oriented
- From an exclusive emphasis on information transmission to an emphasis on interpretation and relationships, as well as information transmission
- From public speaking to a framework that takes account of communication in a variety of contexts including the individual, relationships, families, groups, organizations, societies, and media

The more recent models and theories have substantially broadened our understanding of the nature of communication. They have also provided a foundation for the development of more comprehensive explanations of the role of communication and human behavior.

Implications and Applications

- Theories of communication have continued to evolve from the earliest Greek scholars to contemporary times.
- Evolving communication theories have moved from a focus on the persuasive intent of speakers to a more interactional process involving the participation of both a sender and receiver.
- Communication theories continue to evolve to reflect a cultural perspective that acknowledges that participants in an interaction may not have equal power in that interaction.
- Newer theories of communication include the role of the mass media and changing technologies available to participants in a face-to-face interaction or mediated communication situations.

Summary

Scholars and practitioners have been thinking about the nature of communication for more than 2,500 years. From its early beginnings, communication was seen as a process in which a speaker constructed messages to bring about desired responses in his or her receivers—the classical S $\rightarrow$ M $\rightarrow$ R = E perspective. The earliest models of communication focused

TABLE 3.1 *Models of Communication: An Overview*

Model	How Communication Works	Major Factors Stressed in Explaining Communication Outcomes	Directional Flow
Aristotle	Speaker constructs messages that bring about persuasive effects among listeners.	source and message	one-way
Lasswell	Speaker constructs messages, selects a channel, and thereby brings about a range of effects among listeners.	source, message and channel	one-way
Shannon-Weaver	Source encodes message and transmits through channel to receiver.	source, message, noise	one-way with feedback
Schramm	Source encodes message and transmits information through channel to receiver, if they have a shared field of experience.	source, message, receiver	one-way
Katz-Lazarsfeld	Source encodes messages and transmits information through mass media to opinion leaders who relay it to public.	channel, message, receiver, opinion leader	one-way (mediated)
Westley-MacLean	Source selectively encodes messages and transmits information in modified form to receiver who decodes, encodes, and transmits information in modified form to other individual(s) with feedback at every step.	receiver, meaning, feedback	circular (through feedback)
Dance	Individuals encode and decode messages based on previous communication experiences	process, time	helical-spiral
Watzlawick-Beavin-Jackson	Individuals exchange messages through behavior, the meaning of which varies with each person depending largely upon the communicative relationship between them	receiver, meaning, process, metacommunication	two-way
Thayer	Individuals generate and disseminate, acquire and process information in an on-going, dynamic process	receiver, originator, information processing and disseminating	circular
DeVito	Individuals send and receive messages that are distorted within a context, have some effect and provide opportunities for feedback	sender, receiver, distortion, feedback	bidirectional, interactive

on one-way, linear processes in which a speaker attempted to formulate a message in order to influence an audience in a particular way. This model assumed that the message sent was (or at least should be) the message received.

Building on this framework, descriptions of communication were developed by scholars including Lasswell, Shannon and Weaver, Schramm, Katz and Lazarsfeld, and Westley and MacLean.

Real-life experience indicated to many scholars that a one-to-one correspondence between intended message and received message did not exist and, thus, more interactional (or transactional) models in which the speaker and the receiver were both seen as important participants in the communication process were created. Additional models of the communication process were advanced by Watzlawick, Beavin, and Jackson, as well as Thayer. Therefore, a broader view of communication has emerged that emphasizes meanings, interpretation, and complex, gradual processes.

Theories and models developed in the last several decades reflected the influences of the Information Age, and often incorporated terms "information" and "technology." Table 3.1 summarizes the theories and models discussed in this chapter. Theories of communication that took account of media (or technology) tended to minimize the distinction made between *mass* and other forms of communication in which technology is involved. Many theories of the period also emphasized the important role of political, social class, or cultural influences in framing the context in which specific communication events occur. Current theories and models carry forth the traditions of the decades that preceded them, and communication is generally described as a process of interaction, or a transaction, between individuals involving messages, media, and feedback—a process in which such factors as noise, context, setting, or other factors which may share, interfere with, or in other ways influence effects and outcomes.

Notes

1. For a detailed summary of the early theories of speech and rhetorical communication see John D. Peters, *Speaking into Air: A History of the Idea of Communication* (Chicago: University of Chicago Press, 1999).

2. Aristotle, *Rhetoric and Poetics,* translated by W. Rhys Roberts (New York: Random House, Modern Library, 1954), in Harper, 1979, p. 20.

3. W. Rhys Roberts, *Works of Aristotle* (Oxford: Clarendon Press, 1924), p. 1377b.

4. McCroskey, 1986, p. 266.

5. Harper, 1979, p. 22.

6. Harold D. Lasswell, "The Structure and Function of Communication in Society," in *Mass Communications.* Ed. by Wilbur Schramm (Urbana, IL: University of Illinois Press, 1960), p. 117.

7. Claude E. Shannon and Warren Weaver, *The Mathematical Theory of Communication* (Urbana, IL: University of Illinois Press, 1949), p. 3.

8. Shannon and Weaver, 1949, p. 7.

9. Shannon and Weaver, 1949, p. 68.

10. Wilbur Schramm, "How Communication Works," in *The Process and Effects of Mass Communication.* Ed. by Wilbur Schramm (Urbana, IL: University of Illinois Press, 1954), pp. 3–4.

11. Schramm, 1954, p. 4.

12. Schramm, 1954, p. 9; see also, Norbert Wiener, *The Human Use of Human Beings: Cybernetics and Society* (New York: Avon Books, 1967), pp. 47–81, for a similar view of feedback.

13. Elihu Katz and Paul F. Lazarsfeld, *Personal Influence: The Part Played by People in the Flow of Mass Communications* (New York: Free Press, 1956), p. 32.

14. Frank E. X. Dance, "Toward a Theory of Human Communication," in *Human Communication Theory: Original Essays.* Ed. by Frank E. X. Dance (New York: Holt, 1967), pp. 293–294.

15. Dance, 1967, pp. 294–295.

16. Paul Watzlawick, Janet H. Beavin, and Don D. Jackson, *Pragmatics of Human Communication: A Study of Interactional Patterns, Pathologies, and Paradoxes* (New York: Norton, 1967), pp. 48–51.

17. Watzlawick, Beavin, and Jackson, 1967, pp. 51–54.

18. Lee Thayer, *Communication and Communication Systems* (Homewood, IL: Richard D. Irwin, Inc., 1968).

19. Joseph Turow, *Media Today: An Introduction to Mass Communication* (Boston: Houghton Mifflin, 2002); Carolyn Marvin, *When Old Technologies Were New: Thinking About Electric Communication in the Late Nineteenth Century* (New York: Oxford University Press, 1990).

20. James W. Carey, *Communication as Culture: Essays on Media and Society* (Boston: Unwin Hyman, 1989); Simon During, *The Cultural Studies Reader* (New York: Routledge, 1999); John Fiske, *Introduction to Communication Studies* (New York: Routledge, 1990); David Morley and Kuan-Hsing Chen, Editors, *Stuart Hall: Critical Dialogues in Cultural Studies* (New York: Routledge, 1996).

21. See also, Richard W. Budd and Brent D. Ruben, *Interdisciplinary Approaches to Human Communication,* 2nd ed. (New Brunswick, NJ: Transaction, 2003).

22. See, for example, Richard Campbell, Christopher R. Martin, and Bettina Fabos, *Media and Culture: An Introduction to Mass Communication,* 4th ed. (New York: Bedford Books, 2003); Joseph A. DeVito, *Human Communication: The Basic Course 2003,* 9th ed. (Boston: Allyn and Bacon, 2003), pp. 2–9; Denis McQuail, *McQuail's Mass Communication Theory,* 4th ed. (Newbury Park, CA: Sage, 2000); William J. Seiler and Melissa L. Beall, *Communication—Making Connections,* 5th ed. (Boston: Allyn and Bacon, 2003), pp. 17–18.

23. DeVito, 2003, p. 2.

24. Thomas S. Kuhn, *The Structure of Scientific Revolutions,* 2nd ed. (Chicago: University of Chicago Press, 1970), pp. 1–42.

25. Kuhn, 1970, pp. 52–65.

4 Communication—A Basic Life Process

In this chapter

Why . . .

- Communication is one of life's most fundamental processes.

- Many similarities exist between animal and human communication.

- Towels on the beach or newspapers on a seat of a train can be forms of communication.

- Adaptation is the most basic function of communication.

Contributions to the study of communication and behavior come from scholars in a number of fields. As we have said, communication is an activity that is fundamental to the lives of individuals, relationships, groups, cultures, and societies. Even more basically, as we will see in this chapter, it is a process that is essential to the lives of animals as well as humans. While animal communication is clearly not the focus of this book, an appreciation of the role communication plays in activities of all living systems is very helpful as a foundation for better understanding the role this process plays in human affairs.

Communication Processes in Animals and Humans

All animals and humans are *open systems,* which is to say they participate in continual give-and-take exchanges with their environment. These exchanges, or *interactions* as they are often called, are essential to life. The basic process is one in which a living system takes in, uses, and in the process transforms, materials that are necessary to its life functioning.

With plants, the process is termed *photosynthesis,* and involves the input, use, and transformation of chemicals and other substances necessary to growth. A number of environmental inputs are essential to the photosynthesis process, including sunlight, heat, water, and carbon dioxide. The creation of oxygen is one of the by-products of this transformation. Oxygen—an output of plant systems—becomes an input for animal systems, which require an intake and use of oxygen, and which, in turn, use and then ultimately transform into carbon dioxide. Animal metabolism also requires the intake of food substances. The food is a necessary ingredient for animal tissue growth, and the organic wastes, which are by-products of the transformation, are returned to the environment.

As one moves from plants to animals, the nature of the system–environment interaction becomes increasingly complex. Animals not only depend for their survival on chemical and physical exchanges but also on communication. Through communication animals and humans create, gather, and use information to interact with and adapt to their environment and its inhabitants.

Just as animal and human systems take in oxygen and foodstuffs and transform them into materials necessary to their functioning, they also take in, transform, and use information. In this most basic sense, *communication is the essential life process through which animals and humans create, acquire, transform, and use information to carry out the activities of their lives.*

Communication Modes

The information used to guide behavior is derived by processing messages in the environment. The world in which animals and humans exist is filled with a vast array of such messages. Some of these, such as the words exchanged between friends, or the mating call of a bird, are purposefully created by living things. Other cues, such as the flash of lightning or the sound of a falling tree are not. Both purposeful and nonpurposeful cues are vital as potential sources of the information that shapes behavior.

Visual Messages

For humans, visual messages are particularly important; a wave and a smile from a friend, a blush of embarrassment, a tear, new clothes or a new car, and the headlines of a newspaper, or the subject line on an incoming e-mail, are all potential sources of information that can hold great significance for us when they are noticed and attended to, as illustrated in Figure 4.1.

Some animals also make substantial use of visual cues. The color and calls of birds, the alluring colored wings of a butterfly, the rhythmic light of the firefly, and the movement of head, ears, or tail by primates all serve as valuable information sources.[1]

As significant as sight is for humans and some animals, it is generally not as crucial as other communication modes in most species. Many animals lack the visual capacities necessary for processing light and depend instead on touch, sound, smell, or taste as primary modalities for relating to their environment or to one another. See Table 4.1.

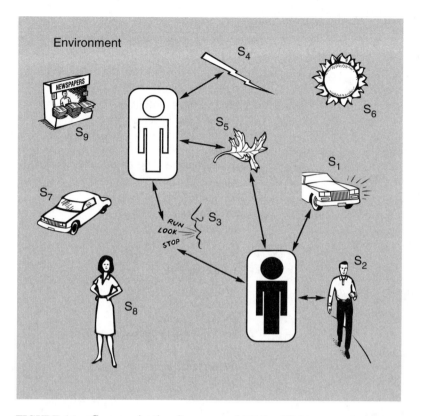

FIGURE 4.1 *Communication Sources and Modes* Within an environment there are a number of potential message sources to which a living thing may attend and react, represented by S_1 through S_9 in the illustration above. Some of these messages may be produced by inanimate sources, such as the visible flash of lightning or the touch of a leaf blowing past in the wind—S_4 and S_5. Other messages, S_1, S_2, and S_3, taking the form of a smell, taste, sound, or sight, are produced by other living things. These messages may be unintended, like the sound created by a person walking down the street (S_2), or they may be more purposeful, such as honking a car horn (S_1) or spoken words S_3. At any instant, many potential messages are not taken account of at all—S_6, S_7, S_8, and S_9—and thus have no information value at that moment in time for the people involved.

Tactile Messages

For animals and human beings, touch, bumping, vibration, and other types of tactile messages are important. From before birth through the first months and years of life, physical contact plays a critical role in the biological and social development of human infants, as well as the young of other species. Tactile messages remain crucial throughout the lives of many animals, in parent–young relations, courtship and intimate relations, social greetings,

TABLE 4.1   *Communication Modes*

Modality	Form of Message
Visual	*Sight* Facial Displays Movement of Body Parts Distance and Spacing Position Dress Other Symbols, Adornment, and Emblems
Tactile	*Touch* Vibration Stroking Rubbing Pressure Pain Temperature
Olfactory and Gustatory	*Smell and Taste (Pheromones)* Body Odors Special Chemicals Food Sources, Fragrances, and Taste
Auditory	*Sound* Incidental Sounds Vibrations Whistling Drumming Rubbing Vocalization

play, and aggression and combat. These cues also play a vital role in self-defense and self-preservation. Receptors in the skin and other locations throughout the body are sensitive to heat, cold, pressure, and pain and, when detected, these cues serve as signals that safety is threatened. For humans, tactile signals are the major source of the symptoms, such as fatigue, nausea, dizziness, muscular strain, or apprehension, that we use to determine if we are ill and to diagnose the problem and its location.

Olfactory and Gustatory Messages

Many animals also use olfactory and gustatory information to relate to their environment and to one another. *Pheromones* is the technical term used to refer to these chemical messages. Pheromones are carried through water or air. Vertebrates receive these messages through a nose, fish through a nose or odor-sensitive cells on the body, and insects by means of sensors located in their antennae. Some of the chemically based messages, such as the smell of rain, have inanimate sources. These messages are so powerful that pheromones released by Australian orchids can fool male wasps into believing that the flowers are female wasps.[2]

As with other modes, the brain and nervous system filter out irrelevant cues and guide the system to respond only to those signals to which the animal is attuned or to which it has learned to attend. Although humans have the set of organs thought necessary for chemical message production and reception, olfactory information plays a less substantial role in the activities of humans than in the lives of many other animals.

Auditory Messages

For humans and many animals, auditory messages provide critical links to the environment and to one another. Some sounds—thunder, an earthquake, or the surf splashing against the shore—have inanimate sources. Other auditory messages are produced by living things through speaking, whistling, honking a horn, drumming, or striking a part of the body against an object, the ground, or another part of the body. For example, see Figure 4.2. Additional messages are created as an extension of human activity, such as those which result from the firing of a rifle or operating an engine. In the case of all auditory messages, the produced vibrations are transported through air or water.

In order for auditory signals to be useful, the vibrations must be detected, received, and processed by means of a special organ which converts the data into electrical impulses that can be interpreted by the brain. Lower-order animals generally respond to sound either by approaching or moving away from the source; most higher-order animals and humans are able to act on auditory messages in a number of ways due to prior learning. Auditory messages are important in the lives of a wide range of species, including birds,[3] insects, and primates, in addition to humans, all of which depend on these cues in caring for their young, learning, courtship and mating, and "language" acquisition and use.

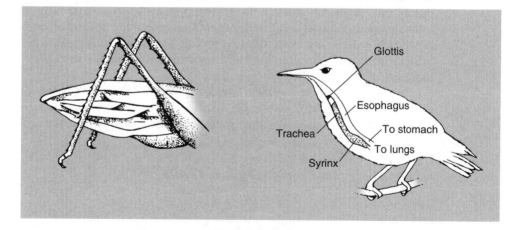

FIGURE 4.2   *Insect and Bird Sound Production*   Many insects produce a sound called *stridulation* by rubbing their hind legs against their bodies. The inner thigh of the hind legs contains a saw-like ridge of teeth (a *file*) that produces a range of sounds when pulled across a wing vein (or *scraper*). Birds, which lack the larynx associated with sounds of most mammals, produce sounds by means of a *syrinx*.

Basic Life Functions of Communication

The significance of communication and the various information-processing modes is clearest when one considers some of the basic life functions they serve. See Table 4.2.

Courtship and Mating

Although differences exist in the specific courtship and mating practices of various species, all involve communication. Humans and other animals must be able to identify other individuals of their own species. Also, individuals must attract and sometimes persuade one another, and the mating activity must be synchronized.

As with other species, human courtship involves the identification and attraction of mates. These processes occur primarily through visual, auditory, and tactile modes, although some studies suggest that chemical cues may also play a role. Human courtship and mating involve persuasion and negotiation. Humans arrange the terms, timing, and implications of their intimate relations, and in these interactions communication plays an indispensable role.

Members of all animal species identify, locate, and attract one another by emitting and responding to cues of one kind or another. The songs of grasshoppers and crickets serve this purpose, as does the odor of moths and the light flashing of fireflies. See Figure 4.3. With birds, mating involves the creation and reception of auditory messages ranging from a simple, repetitive, and not necessarily musical call to complex song-and-dance presentations, acrobatics, and rituals. In some species male birds build and decorate nests, which they use to advertise their availability to prospective mates.

For many animals, mating involves not only identifying and attracting an individual but also synchronizing the timing of sexual activities in order for fertilization to occur. The oyster and certain other marine animals apparently acquire the information needed for the proper timing of fertilization from the ocean tides. Reproduction begins in the spring, following a migration toward a breeding ground. The increased daylight in this season triggers the change in hormonal functions through which reproductive cycles are coordinated.[4]

For some insects, recognition, attraction, synchronization, and coordination occur as a result of messages provided by chemicals. With moths, for example, the female sex pheromone triggers a sequence of activities in the male, starting with the activation of the

TABLE 4.2 *Basic Life Functions of Communication*

Courtship and Mating
Reproduction
Parent–Offspring Relations and Socialization
Navigation
Self-Defense
Territoriality

FIGURE 4.3 *Visual Signal Patterns of Firefly Messages* Male lightning bugs begin their flight during early evening hours of the spring or summer, flashing the luminescent light on the abdomen to attract a mate. In many species, the female does not fly, but rather signals the male from the grass, guiding him to her location. Because there are often a number of different varieties of fireflies in any one area, different codes are necessary in order for individuals to identify and attract members of their own species. These codes consist of distinctive flash and flight patterns—dots, swoops, curves, lines, zigzags, and the timing of flashes.

Source: Margaret Cosgrove, *Messages and Voices.* Copyright © 1974 by Margaret Cosgrove. Reprinted with the permission of Dodd, Mead and Company, Inc.

animal, followed by its movement toward the chemical source, and culminating in courtship and copulation. Pheromones are so vital an information source in the mating process that if a small quantity of the chemical is placed on some nonliving object, nearby male moths exhibit the entire sequence of mating and copulation actions toward that object that are normally associated with the presence of the female moth.[5]

Reproduction

Of course, offspring of any species, as they reach adulthood, bear a strong physical resemblance to their parents. A bear cub grows up to look and act like a bear, not a cat or a dog. Physiologically, structurally, in general appearance, and in a number of behavioral patterns, the young of any species replicate or reproduce their parents. This reproduction comes about through a biological communication process in which the sperm cell of the male parent and female egg cell merge to provide a blueprint for the growth and development of the offspring.

DNA, located within cells, is the molecular basis of heredity. The general pattern of growth of living things is through division of cells. A single cell divides to produce two, each of which divides to produce two more, and so on. In some organisms, this continues until thousands, millions, or billions of cells are produced. Division, growth, and development proceed according to the blueprint, as the cells form into layers and masses that fold together and intermesh to form tissues, organs, and more complex structures.

Reproduction of human offspring by their parents begins at the moment of conception as the sperm and egg join. The egg cell, most of which is filled with food, is about one two-hundredth of an inch across. In this space are all the instructions that represent the mother's contribution to the inherited characteristics of the child. The sperm cell, which is only about 1/80,000 the size of the egg, carries only the messages necessary to the father's contribution to the developmental blueprint. Through the union of these two cells, all the information needed for the continuity of the species is transmitted in what is undoubtedly life's most fundamental communication process.

The genetic blueprint specifies an arrangement of highly organized cell networks, designed to facilitate intercellular information exchange. Intercellular communication within the nervous system of animals and humans involves the transfer of information, encoded electrically and chemically, between two or more cells. The cellular connections are continuously responsive to internal and external stimuli, and resulting changes in patterns of connectivity underlie many of life's complex adaptive behaviors, including development, learning, and memory.

Parent–Offspring Relations and Socialization

Children's survival depends on relations with adults. The human infant, in fact, is dependent on others of his or her species longer than are other creatures. In lower-order animals, the survival of a species and the communication capabilities necessary to this end are largely assured through inheritance. For this reason, among amphibians, reptiles, and fish, little or no contact between adults and their offspring is necessary after birth. However, with social insects, birds, and mammals, early parent–offspring relations are essential to survival. Even before baby ducklings are born, sounds in the egg may help the parents prepare for the tasks ahead. Visual, auditory, tactile, gustatory, and olfactory signals are also necessary to the feeding process—often in ways that we might not expect. Adult birds, for instance, seem to react to auditory cues from their babies, rather than to visual messages, in determining how many offspring are present and, therefore, how much food to bring.[6]

With many social animals, extended contact between parent and young is required. When this contact does not occur, the important role of communication in the survival of a species is underscored. Some birds that are raised without interaction with others of their kind become totally confused about their identity. Konrad Lorenz was the first to study the processes by which birds and other animals learn or imprint their identity in early social interaction. He observed

> One of the most striking as well as pathetically comical instances . . . concerned an albino peacock in an Australian zoo, the lone survivor of a brood that had succumbed to a spell of bad weather. The peafowl chick was placed in the only warm room available, . . . the one in which the giant tortoises were housed. Although the young peacock flourished in these sur-

roundings, the peculiar effect of its reptilian roommates on the bird became apparent not long after it had attained sexual maturity and grown its first train: Beginning then and forever after, the peacock displayed his magnificent plumes in the famous "wheel" position *only* to giant tortoises, eagerly if vainly courting these reptiles while ignoring even the most handsome peahens with which the zoo supplied him.[7]

Navigation

The term *navigation* refers to the purposeful movement of an animal through space, from one location to another. Goal-directed movement of this kind is necessary for nearly all of life's activities, including mating, food location, and self-defense.

Anyone who, as a child, experimented with ants or other insects by placing sticks or rocks in their path probably remembers how skilled they were at determining the presence of an obstacle and adjusting their course accordingly. An ant will leave an odor trail between its nest and a food source that other ants can follow. Even in a simple example of this kind the role of communication is apparent. In order to move systematically from one position to another, a substantial amount of information must be processed. Cues—sound, sight, odor, temperature, or other sources—must be used to determine the present location. Information must also be processed relative to the direction to proceed and progress toward a desired endpoint. Adjusting for impediments, cracks in a sidewalk, or rocks and sticks requires the acquisition and processing of still more information.

Many animals have highly developed navigation capabilities and can travel great distances with precision. The skills of cats, horses, and homing pigeons are well known in this regard, as are those of ducks and geese, who may maintain two seasonal homes several thousand miles apart. Apparently, some animals orient themselves by processing data about landmarks, the sun, or stars. Other animals use a sonarlike system of sounds and echoes for navigation. The echolocation skills of bats are so well developed that in total darkness they can pass between two black silk threads placed less than a foot apart without touching. And, the dolphin's echo system has such sensitivity that the animal can distinguish two different fish at a distance of fifteen to eighteen feet.[8] See Figure 4.4.

One of the most elaborate navigation processes is that used by social bees in locating and securing food. Karl von Frisch found that when a worker bee locates a desirable source of food, it announces the find to other bees in the hive by a dance, as shown in Figure 4.5.[9] The closer the food, the more the tail wags back and forth. The direction of the bee's flight while carrying out the dance indicates the direction in which the food is located.

Navigation processes are also essential for humans, although the communication forms and modalities involved differ. Walking across a room to pick up a magazine, for instance, requires the processing of information relative to one's present location, destination, and incremental progress toward the destination as one moves. When the task is completed, the return trip requires another series of information-processing steps. In a basic sense, a person scurrying along a busy sidewalk at rush hour or driving on a crowded multilane highway has a great deal in common with the navigation activities of the ant, bat, dolphin, or songbird. Each must analyze an immense quantity of information in order to arrive safely at the intended destination.

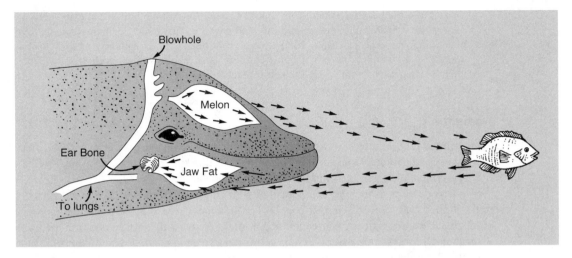

FIGURE 4.4 *Echolocation Technique of Dolphins*   Dolphins send out clicking echolocation signals through the forehead and receive returning messages through the jaw and throat. Whistles are apparently created by forcing air back and forth between the lungs and air sacks connecting to the channel leading to the blowhole. The clicks are transmitted through the water, triking any object in the area. The time it takes the echo to return to the dolphin indicates the distance of the object.

Self-Defense

Communication plays an important role in the processes through which living systems identify and respond to potential threats to their safety and well-being. If an animal senses the presence of a danger—a predator, a falling tree, the headlights of an auto, and so on—it prepares instinctively to defend itself or to flee. As a part of what has been called the *stress response,* hormonal and muscular systems are activated, readying the animal for maximum physical output.[10]

The outlet for this stress energy—the act of fighting or retreating—is often the basis for information used by other animals. This is so, for instance, when the alarm response of one bird evokes a reaction in others who in turn produce their own distress calls. Similarly, as a part of the fight-or-flight response, injured or disturbed fish give off chemical signals that serve to alert other fish of impending danger. And, to the predator, these same cues may be useful in anticipating, countering, and overpowering the actions of its prey. Thus, for living systems, communication is necessary for identifying and reacting to environmental stressors and for signaling others of the need to mobilize for action or dispersal.

Among humans, the natural fight-or-flight response is often constrained or channeled into other culturally sanctioned actions. When this occurs, communication also plays a central role in ways that will become clear in later discussion.

Territoriality

The establishment and maintenance of a home or territory is another activity in which communication is essential. Humans and most other animals become attached to particular

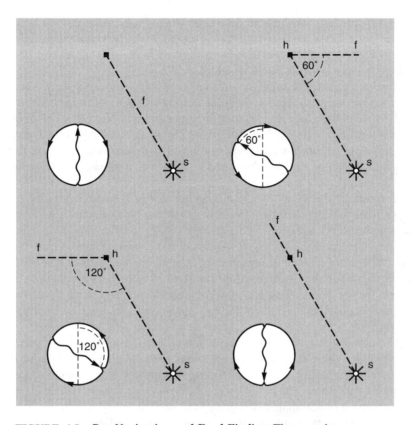

FIGURE 4.5 *Bee Navigation and Food Finding* The scout bee conveys the *distance* of the food by rhythmic tail wagging. The closer the food, the more the tail wags back and forth. The *direction* of the food is indicated by the path traveled by the bee. The direction of movement of the bee while it dances indicates the relationship of the hive (h), the food source (f), and the sun (s). If the tail-wagging dance points upward, the food lies in the direction of the sun. If the dance runs 60° left of straight up, the food is 60° to the left of the sun; if the dance is straight down, the food is in the opposite direction (180° away from the sun), and so on.

Source: Karl von Frisch, *Bees: Their Vision, Chemical Senses, and Language,* revised edition. Copyright 1950, © 1971 by Cornell University. Reprinted with the permission of Cornell University Press.

places, often to those locations where they were born, spent their youth, or mated; and many living creatures mark and even defend these territories.

One of the best examples of animal territoriality is provided by birds. In the spring, some male birds may take possession of an area, hedge, or portion of a meadow. Thereafter, they make an effort to keep out other males by singing. Some birds create songs with two distinct forms, one by which they maintain contact with their partners, and another by which they define and display their territory. Because each bird has a unique song pattern, it is not difficult for other birds to determine when a song belongs to a "neighbor" and a "familiar face," and when it is that of a "stranger."[11] The neighbor whose home is already established represents no threat to the territory; the foreigner may, and his or her presence therefore evokes a much different reaction.

Territories also play an important role in the lives of social insects. Many species go to great lengths to construct their dwellings and to compete for prime housing sites. Often insects can determine the presence of a foreigner and will often attack if an individual violates the territory. Animals also establish and maintain what might be thought of as *mobile* or *transitory territories,* and these, too, involve communication. Some fish and birds, for example, travel or rest in groups, and a stranger that violates the boundary may well meet with considerable resistance.

Territoriality is as important to human life as it is to the lives of many other animals, although often less obviously so. In many situations, humans maintain *personal space*—portable or transitory territories—in a manner similar to other animals. Face-to-face interaction provides another example. In such contexts, interactants become uncomfortable unless a customary amount of personal space is maintained between the individuals. The specifics depend on the situation, culture, and relationship between them. A coat or briefcase on an empty seat in a bus, or a towel or umbrella on the beach may also serve to mark transitory territories, in much the same way as the bird's song claims a section of a grove. See Figure 4.6.

Humans also use communication to mark their territories in more permanent ways. Over the years a great deal of human effort has been directed toward acquiring, dividing, and maintaining space of one kind or another—countries, states, counties, municipalities, and personal properties. The use of fences as territorial boundary markers is an interesting human invention to accomplish this goal, as illustrated in Figure 4.7.

People also spend a considerable amount of time selecting, allocating, and decorating homes, offices, and apartments. The human tendency to create and construct elaborate dwellings would seem to be unsurpassed in the animal world. Whether a garden apartment, condo, brownstone, or home in the suburbs, the acquisition, maintenance, and decoration of home territories becomes an important life activity of many of us. In addition to providing shelter from the elements, territories serve other communicative functions, including the establishment and display of personal, social, economic, and occupational identity and status.

Beyond $S \rightarrow M \rightarrow R = E$: The Adaptation Perspective

In this chapter our focus has been on the role communication plays in the most fundamental activities of life. We have presented a perspective in which communication is viewed as the process through which living beings create, transform, and use information in order to relate to their environment and one another.

The traditional $S \rightarrow M \rightarrow R = E$ approach viewed communication primarily from the perspective of information transmission, where the goal is presumed to be sending messages to establish a commonness between source and receiver. The framework presented in this chapter and throughout the book envisions communication more broadly as the process

FIGURE 4.6 Through various forms of communication, individuals of various species define and maintain personal space.

whereby humans and animals process information in order to adapt—to cope with and shape the demands and challenges of life.

Implications and Applications

- Communication involves far more than speaking and listening, reading and writing. It is a basic life process.
- We tend to assume that *human* communication is much more complex than communication among other animals, and in some respects it is. However, the dance of bees and the echolocation systems of bats and dolphins are examples of the very elaborate communication systems which operate in the animal world.

FIGURE 4.7   Territorial boundary markers play a role in human life.

- In terms of the life functions served by communication, humans have a good deal in common with other animals. As an illustration, we can point to numerous similarities between the courtship and territorial practices of some birds and the courtship rituals and territorial practices of humans that take place on college campuses and in other communities.
- Like other animals, we engage in communication in order to adapt to and coordinate our actions with the environment and one another.

Summary

As special as human communication seems to us, it is important to understand that our ability and need to engage in communication is not wholly unique. We share much in common with many other animals. In this chapter we have considered the role of communication in the basic life processes of living systems, as a foundation for better, more comprehensive understanding of the nature of human communication.

Communication is the process through which animals and humans create, transform, and use messages to carry out the activities of their lives. It is the process through which living things interact with the environment and one another.

Five communication modes are used by animals and humans: visual, tactile, olfactory, gustatory, and auditory. Communication serves a number of basic functions in life activities, including courtship and mating, reproduction, parent–offspring relations, socialization, navigation, self-defense, and the establishment and maintenance of territories.

Notes

1. See Eugene Linden, *The Octopus and the Orangutan* (New York: Dutton, 2002).

2. Erica Goldman, "Orchids Deceive Amorous Male Wasps," *Science Now,* July 9, 2002, p. 2.

3. See P. J. B. Slater, "Fifty Years of Bird Song Research: A Case Study in Animal Behavior," *Animal Behavior,* Vol. 65, 2003, pp. 633–640; M. C. Baker, "Bird Song Research: The Past 100 Years," *Bird Behavior,* Vol. 14, 2001, pp. 3–50; M. P. H. Stumpf, "Language's Place in Nature," *Trends in Ecology & Evolution,* Vol. 16, 2001, pp. 475–476.

4. Niko Tinbergen, *Social Behaviour in Animals with Special Reference to Vertebrates* (London: Methuen, 1965), p. 25.

5. H. H. Shorey, *Animal Communications by Pheromones* (New York: Academic Press, 1976), p. 99.

6. Gerhard A. Thielcke, *Bird Sounds* (Ann Arbor, MI: University of Michigan Press, 1970), pp. 65–66.

7. Hilda Simon, *The Courtship of Birds* (New York: Dodd, Mead, 1977), p. 23.

8. Fernand Méry, *Animal Languages.* Translated by Michael Ross (Westmead, England: Saxon House, 1975), p. 3; for further discussion of echolocation, see Prince, 1975, p. 23; and Forrest G. Wood, *Marine Mammals and Man: The Navy's Porpoises and Sea Lions* (Washington, D.C.: Robert Luce, 1973), pp. 70–83.

9. Martin Lindauer, *Communication among Social Bees* (Cambridge, MA: Harvard University Press, 1961), p. 33. A more detailed discussion of dance and communication among social bees of which this is a summary is provided on pp. 32–58. See also *The Insect Societies,* by Edward O. Wilson (Cambridge, MA: Belknap Press, 1971).

10. See Hans Selye, *The Stress of Life* (New York: McGraw-Hill, 1956). The notion of stress and its relationship to communication will be discussed in more detail in subsequent chapters. See also R. J. Schusterman, C. J. Reichmuth, and D. Kastak, "How Animals Classify Friends and Foes," *Current Directions in Psychological Science,* Vol. 9, 2000, pp. 1–6.

11. Thielcke, 1970, pp. 43–47.

5 Fundamentals of Human Communication

Humans have a good deal in common with other animals in terms of the basics of communication, and yet human communication is also unique in many respects. In this chapter we examine the unique and differentiating aspects of human communication.

The Communication Iceberg

The Visibility and Invisibility of Human Communication

When a person without a background in communication theory listens to two people engaged in conversation, watches a group standing to salute a flag, observes a small group decision-making session, or orders products through the Internet, the communication process appears to be rather simple and straightforward. Messages are sent, messages are received, people behave accordingly, and that's that.

Or so it seems. Actually, in the case of human communication, the aspects of the process that can be easily observed are really only the tip of the communication iceberg, as suggested by Figure 5.1.

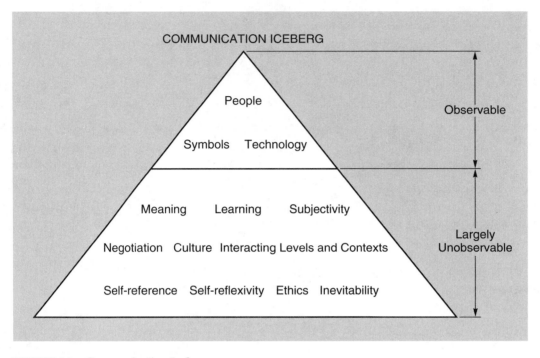

FIGURE 5.1   *Communication Iceberg*

Most of the operations and functions that are necessary to make the communication process "work" are invisible to the untrained eye. Consider the following situation. Bill says: "Jane, please pass the salt." Jane picks up a salt shaker and passes it to Bill. In this circumstance as in others, it seems that meaning has been transferred from Bill to Jane through his verbalized message. However, even in an elementary situation like passing salt, the communication process is far more complex than it appears. And most of that complexity is invisible.

In this simple example, a number of elements are involved in the communication process, and each affects the outcome. First, Bill must decide to engage in communication. Then, he must formulate a message that he believes will convey his desire for the salt. Next, the message must be sent. At this point, Jane has to "decide" to attend to the message, must interpret it appropriately, and must choose to act on it in accordance with Bill's intent.

In order for either party to be able to use language in this transaction, substantial learning is required; "pass" and "salt" are useful symbols only because their meanings have come to be standardized through a complex process of social communication. Given all this, a simple communication event that begins with a verbal request for salt and ends up with the salt being passed is no small accomplishment.

To appreciate fully the complexities of communication, it is necessary to have an understanding of both the "visible" and "invisible" characteristics of human communication.

Visible Aspects of Communication

When we observe communication taking place, three important components of the process are readily observable: people, symbols, and media.

People

In this context, when we refer to *people* we are thinking in terms of individuals functioning as message senders and/or receivers. We include in this category public speakers, as well as individuals speaking to one other person, a group, or an organization. Individuals engaged in writing or other forms of message creation and transmission are also included. We also include individuals who are the recipients of messages in a communication situation, either as listeners, readers, or observers.

Symbols

What do we mean by the term *symbols*? *Symbols* are characters, letters, numbers, words, objects, people, or actions that stand for or represent something beside themselves. There have been many attempts to identify precisely what it is that makes us different from other living things. A number of writers have pointed to our social nature. However, many animals depend for their survival on other members of their species. Other scholars have suggested that our capacity for communication might be the distinguishing characteristic. As we know, however, the production, transmission, and reception of messages is essential to the social lives of many species; and communication in one form or another is necessary to the adaptation and survival of all animals. As humans, we *do* have a unique communication capability; however, we can create and use symbols and symbolic language, and it is this skill and the many consequences of it that perhaps best highlight the special nature of the human animal.[1]

What exactly does it mean to say that humans create and use symbolic language? A *language,* in the most general sense, is a set of characters, or elements, and rules for their use in relation to one another. There are many types of languages. Most familiar are spoken and written languages, such as English, Spanish, or Swahili. The Morse code, Braille, genetic code, and various computer "languages" are less obvious examples. See Figure 5.2.

With language, we code and transmit messages from one point to another using one or more communication modes. Oral, spoken, and other acoustically coded languages make use of the auditory mode. Written or light-utilizing languages utilize the visual channel.

Most languages are based on arbitrary symbolization. While letters and words are the most obvious elements in our symbolic language, there are many others that are important to human life. An illuminated red light located on a pole near an intersection is a symbol, as is George Washington, the Eiffel Tower, or a rectangular piece of cloth with thirteen red and white stripes and fifty white stars on a blue field in the upper corner. Figure 5.3 provides an impressionistic collage of such symbols in a work by Boston artist, Patrick Carter.[2]

Symbols represent things or ideas about things. Words are symbols because they represent objects, ideas, relationships, people, places, and feelings—to name just a few of the concepts or objects that are referenced by words.

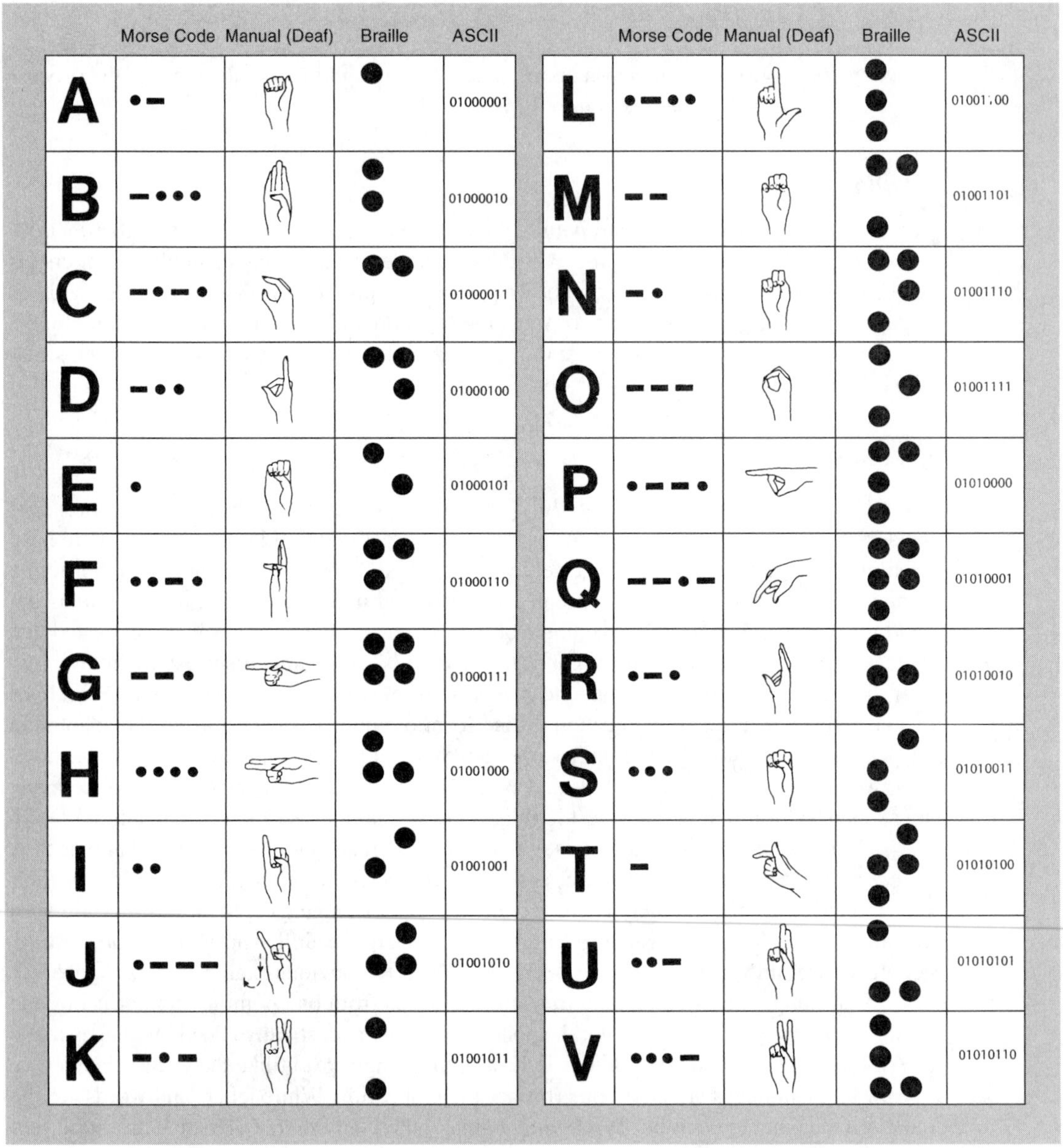

Letter	Morse Code	Manual (Deaf)	Braille	ASCII
A	·-			01000001
B	-···			01000010
C	-·-·			01000011
D	-··			01000100
E	·			01000101
F	··-·			01000110
G	--·			01000111
H	····			01001000
I	··			01001001
J	·---			01001010
K	-·-			01001011
L	·-··			01001,00
M	--			01001101
N	-·			01001110
O	---			01001111
P	·--·			01010000
Q	--·-			01010001
R	·-·			01010010
S	···			01010011
T	-			01010100
U	··-			01010101
V	···-			01010110

FIGURE 5.2 The English alphabet, Morse Code, sign language, braille, and the ASCII (American Standard Code for Information Interchange) computer code are among our most used languages. Each has evolved to meet a specialized set of human needs. The languages differ from one another in their form, yet in terms of the more basic functions served, they have much in common.

	Morse Code	Manual (Deaf)	Braille	ASCII		Morse Code	Manual (Deaf)	Braille	ASCII
W	·－－	(hand)	(braille)	01010111	8	－－－··		(braille)	00111000
X	－··－	(hand)	(braille)	01011000	9	－－－－·		(braille)	00111001
Y	－·－－	(hand)	(braille)	01011001	0	－－－－－		(braille)	00110000
Z	－－··	(hand)	(braille)	01010110					
1	·－－－－		(braille)	00110001					
2	··－－－		(braille)	00110010					
3	···－－		(braille)	00110011					
4	····－		(braille)	00110100					
5	·····		(braille)	00110101					
6	－····		(braille)	00110110					
7	－－···		(braille)	00110111					

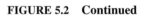

FIGURE 5.2 **Continued**

FIGURE 5.3   *"Symbols We Hold in Common" by Patrick Carter*

The symbols (words) in a language that represent concepts and objects are arbitrary. In most cases, there is no direct or obvious connection between the symbol and the referent (the thing the symbol stands for). Individuals in a society have to learn which words represent which things. For example, we learn that "window" is the appropriate word for the pane of glass that is in the middle of a wall. This symbol may refer to other objects, too. All windows are not the same size and shape, but we continue to use the word "window" to label them. In fact, some windows may even be opaque. Problems in communication often result when we forget that the symbol is not the referent and that many symbols have more than one referent.

Another fundamental, but easily overlooked, illustration of symbolic language is our monetary system. We think little about the communication process that occurs when we go into a store, pick out an item priced at $15, go to the cashier, hand over a ten- and a five-dollar bill, and leave the store with a "thank you" and the item in a bag. This exchange is very much a communication event, one in which symbolic language plays a crucial role. When we give the clerk a ten- and a five-dollar bill, in effect, we are only handing over two pieces of high-quality paper. They have no inherent value, other than the expense of the paper and ink. They are symbols and as such their value to us comes about as a consequence of the meanings we have learned to attach to them—but more about that later. We live, quite literally, in an environment filled with symbols of various kinds, the diversity of which is illustrated in Figures 5.4 and 5.5.

Technology

For most animals, visual, tactile, olfactory, gustatory, and auditory signals are transitory in nature. A sound, a gesture, a touch, a sensation, or an odor may effectively link animals to

FIGURE 5.4 As humans we are literally enveloped in a sea of symbols, an understanding of which is essential to even simple activities like traveling from one place to another, shopping for consumer goods, or enjoying a favorite hobby.

FIGURE 5.5 Familiar symbols may be adapted to fit the needs of the people in a particular neighborhood.

one another and their environment; each is short-lived, and once the message has served its original informational function, no traces of it remain. In most cases, animals must be within sight or hearing range in order to respond to messages from another individual; even olfactory cues used to mark a territory or provide a trail are generally fleeting.

Permanence and Portability.   Through the use of technology, symbols can have permanence and significance apart from the situation in which they were originally used. Information provided in a letter sent to a friend, a book, a poem, a scientific formula, the blueprint for a building, or signs along a highway is not transitory in nature. Such messages may have a virtually unending existence and use. In fact, their life is limited only by our human capacity for preserving the physical materials on which they are recorded.

Technology makes it possible for us to accumulate and transmit information from one generation to the next. This enables us to "bridge" or "bind" time—to use records of the past, as well as the present, and to create messages today that will be a part of the environment of future generations.

Because of technology human communication also has the capacity for "portability"—for bridging space. The objects or persons to which particular symbols refer need not be present in order for the symbol to be useful in communication. Information coded and packaged at one geographic location can be transmitted to persons on another continent. Communication technologies extend and provide an alternative to face-to-face communication, as a means of sending and receiving messages.

When one considers the total spectrum of today's uses of technology—including cell phones, e-mail, and wireless networking, for instance—we realize that few aspects of our personal, social, and occupational lives are exclusively conducted through face-to-face communication. Media play an increasingly pervasive and visible role in our activities.

Invisible Aspects of Communication

Ten other aspects of communication are critical but invisible to the untrained eye. These include: meaning, learning, subjectivity, negotiation, culture, interacting contexts and levels, self-reference, self-reflexivity, ethics, and inevitability.

Meaning

We invent symbols. In order to use them in communication, we also have to invent their meanings and the responses we make to them. To illustrate the point, consider the word *bird. Bird* has no inherent, intrinsic meaning or significance. It is simply a particular pattern of auditory vibrations that comes about by the manipulation of the vocal cords, lips, tongue, and mouth, or a configuration of ink on paper in the case of written language. The characteristics of the word and sounds of its spoken pronunciation comprise a symbolic code that is useful only to those who are able to decipher it. The word is arbitrary in the sense that it has no relation to the animal to which it refers, other than that which we have invented and accepted. Any word could have been chosen in its place.

As another illustration, let's return to the example of a red light at the intersection. In casual conversation, we may say that the light "means" stop. Actually, however, the light means nothing in and of itself. It is a symbol. Its meaning was invented. Through custom and habitual use—and, in this case, legislation—people have come to interpret the symbol as a guide to behavior: to stop. Similarly, the red, white, and blue cloth that we know as the American flag has no intrinsic meaning other than that which we have created and accepted.

Even in the simplest of activities, such as a race, this important characteristic of human communication is apparent.[3] When an athlete hears a starting gun, his or her initial response to the auditory cue is identical to the response of a gazelle. The heartbeat speeds up, and at top running speed the heart pumps five times more blood than normally. Most of the blood is needed for the muscles. There is also a need for twenty gallons of air per minute to supply oxygen to the blood. For the runner and gazelle alike, most of the energy needed by the muscles is lost as heat. Since chemical burn-up by the muscles is too fast to be complete, waste products remain in the blood, leading to fatigue that can be eliminated only when fresh oxygen is introduced into the blood supply.

In all these respects, the behavior of the runner and that of the gazelle are alike. Both creatures function in a manner that is normal for an animal in flight. But, the key point is that the man or woman in the example is not in flight. Where the gazelle's behavior is directed solely by reflex, the runner's actions are not. The behavior of the gazelle is automatic. It could only occur in response to uncontrolled and uncontrollable fears; the runner's response, on the other hand, is a consequence of meaning he or she attaches to the situation and the symbols that comprise it. The runner's behavior is self-initiated, deliberate, and directed by desire—by the meanings attached to the symbols involved.

As humans, we are not only capable of creating events, but also the significance and meaning those events will have for us. We can invent and organize contests, plan and train to participate in them, voluntarily direct our actions during the activity, experience pride and satisfaction upon receiving a ribbon or trophy, and later reflect upon ourselves and our experience. We do all this because of our capacity for inventing and bestowing meaning on the people, objects, and circumstances that surround us—and on ourselves.

Even matters as basic as determining what and how to eat are not solely matters of biology and genetic programming. While many North Americans, for example, look forward with enthusiasm to a juicy barbecued steak, a member of the Hindu faith might well choose the prospect of death by starvation rather than eating the meat of the sacred cow, the holiest of creatures. In a similar sense, decisions as to whether to eat with fingers, fork and knife, or chopsticks, and whether to use one's left hand to eat—as would be acceptable in most countries—or only one's right hand, as is customary in Arab cultures, depend on the meanings we have invented and attached to life's circumstances. See Figure 5.6 and Box 5.1.

Learning

A bird is born knowing how to build the nest necessary for mating and survival; the instructions are inscribed on the chromosomes of the fertilized egg cell from which it developed. Lightning bugs inherit the knowledge needed to emit and respond to luminescent

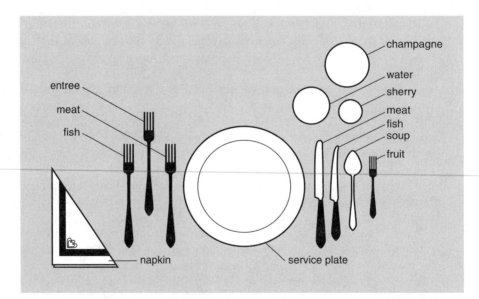

FIGURE 5.6   What to eat, what utensils to use, what order to eat this and that, where to place one's hands when they are not in use, and how to signal one's satisfaction with a meal, exemplify the sorts of concerns that distinguish human symbolic communication from that of other animals. Humans go to great lengths to invent and standardize symbolic practices even with regard to basic biological activities such as eating. Being familiar and fluent with these symbolic realities is often crucial to assuring one's acceptance by those who have themselves learned and accepted a particular symbolic pattern.

BOX 5.1 • *Smiles of a Sumatra Night*

In the longest-running debate on human behavior, nature and nurture have been duking it out for over a century, with nature getting an awful lot of decisions in the past decade or two. Now comes evidence delineating just how much nature shapes our emotional reactions.

When Americans create the expressions associated with anger and fear, the autonomic nervous system swings into gear and puts the body on alert, raising heart rate and altering skin temperature. To determine whether these changes are specific to Americans, and thus learned, or are part of common inheritance, Drs. Robert Levenson, of the University of California—Berkeley, and Paul Ekman, of San Francisco State University, headed off to West Sumatra. There they looked at people as different from us as you can get: the Minangkabau, a matrilineal, agrarian culture that discourages displays of negative emotion.

Yet, when the Minangkabau were taught facial muscle contraction in order to mimic angry or fearful expressions, they registered the same physiologic changes—though they didn't feel the same way. No matter how different we seem, deep down we're all alike, observes the team in the *Journal of Personality and Social Psychology* (Vol. 62, No. 6).

But if biological events turn out to be the same, subjective emotional experience is altogether different. "In our culture, we focus on the physiological sensations that happen when we feel emotions. This is in fact one of the most important aspects of emotion for us," reports Levenson. Ask an American what anger is and he'll tell you what he physically experiences when he is angry. But the Minangkabau didn't feel any emotions when they made the negative facial expressions.

"In their culture, the people are more entwined. Emotions define their relationships, not bodily sensations," explains Levenson. To them, anger is when a friend is mad at you, not how your body responds.

"Physiological responses to emotions are hard-wired into us; they're common for all people," says Levenson. "But what we do with that information is culturally variable."

messages of a potential mate, and bees are apparently born programmed with the information needed to create and interpret the waggle dance. Human beings have to acquire much of the physical and communication skill that is "natural" for many other animals. Unlike lightning bugs, we have to learn the communication patterns associated with courtship. Unlike bees, we have to learn the verbal and nonverbal language necessary to give directions to a friend.

We are born with certain message-responding tendencies—reflexes. The touch of a nipple to the mouth of a newborn infant, for example, is a tactile cue which triggers the sucking response necessary for eating. Likewise, if we accidentally place a finger on a hot stove, a signal is sent to the brain, and in an instant we pull our hand away. Responses such as these are automatic. They are *nonsymbolic* and do not involve symbolic learning. These are what we can term *first-order, information-processing events.*

This kind of automatic, unlearned, nonsymbolic response accounts for a very small percentage of our activities. Most of our experiences require us to process messages based on meanings we have learned. This is evident even in the most fundamental situations. In the case of placing a finger on the hot stove, for example, as soon as we begin to think about the experience of being burned, try to comprehend the reasons for the pain, consider various medical remedies, relate the pain to other sensations in our previous experience, or talk about the event with others, we are involved in a *second-order, information-processing event*—we are using symbols and meanings. For the most part then, our behavior depends not on genetic programs but on the meanings and information value we have learned to attach to particular symbols. Some of the necessary learning—how to read, write, and calculate, for instance—comes from formal schooling. Most of this learning comes from experience. As Geoffrey Vickers has noted:[4]

> Insofar as I can be regarded as human, it is because I was claimed at birth as a member of a communication network, which programmed me for participation in itself.

A moment of reflection will remind us of the underlying complexity of human communication. Whether we consider interactions between scientists using mathematical equations, the "value" of the money we carry around in our pockets, the significance we attach to our flag, a spoken exchange between acquaintances, or facial expressions and gestures between colleagues at work, the symbols and their meanings have to be created, agreed upon, and learned to be useful for communication. Their significance is created by us, and they are useful for communication only to the extent that we learn and are able to use them appropriately.

Subjectivity

The symbols we use in human communication will not necessarily mean the same things to all of us, as aptly captured by the plaque reproduced in Figure 5.7. We relate to messages in a particular way as a product of our experiences. No two of us have precisely the same experiences, and therefore, no two of us attach precisely the same meaning to the messages around us. To put it differently, we do not all encode and decode messages in the same way. Furthermore, even one individual may not attach exactly the same meaning to a particular message at different points in time or in different circumstances.

The subjective aspect of human communication extends to all types of symbols—words, art, money, flags, and so on. When two people look at a work of art, for instance, the meanings it will have for them are in part personal, reflecting their own experience. Consider, again, the illustration in Figure 5.3. Some may see the arch located near the center as the McDonald's "Golden Arch." Some of these individuals will associate the symbol with convenience, speed, and a predictable menu. For others, the arch may symbolize poor nutrition or restricted food choices. Still for others the symbol may be thought of in terms of a famous landmark in St. Louis. Likewise, the man and woman pictured in the upper left-hand corner are likely to evoke a range of interpretations. Some may have no associations at all; others will recognize it as an image often used in advertisements; and some will recognize it as an adaptation of Grant Wood's work, *American Gothic*. The meanings one attaches to this work as a whole will no doubt provide a further illustration of the subjectivity of communication.

FIGURE 5.7   This famous quotation has been attributed to former president Richard Nixon, psychiatrist R. D. Laing, linguist S. I. Hayakawa, and Federal Reserve Chairman Alan Greenspan, among others.

Monetary symbols also illustrate the personal nature of human communication. The value of money is subjective. While a child walking in a crowd may bend down to pick up a penny, many adults will not. To some people, a birthday gift of twenty dollars is regarded as generous; for others it may be seen as insignificant.

A recognition that much of communication is subjective and personal has led to the observation that the amazing thing about human communication is not that it sometimes seems to *fail* but, rather, that it ever seems to *succeed.* Is it any wonder that two lovers, colleagues, or countries come away with very different interpretations of who is to blame in a conflict?

Negotiation

As unique as we and our meanings may be, communication between people generally seems to work pretty well. How can this be? For symbols to work in our efforts to relate effectively to others, our meanings must mesh with the meanings of others. As we engage in communication, we take part in a process of negotiation, through which we reconcile our meanings with those of others.

Unlike efforts by management and representatives of a labor union to arrive at terms for a contract, this negotiation process is essentially invisible. It involves individuals adjusting and readjusting the messages they send and the interpretations they attach to the messages of others, in an effort to make sense of, cope with, and adapt to the demands and opportunities that present themselves.

Culture

The fact that our meanings often seem to mesh reasonably well with other's meanings is no accident, nor it is simply the result of the negotiation that takes place with a given interaction. We learn from and with other people. We are influenced through our participation in groups, organizations, and as members of society. Through this participation, we establish a commonness of cultural experience with other people through social communication. Our symbols and their meanings become shared and standardized—*intersubjectified*—and take on an objective quality that is to say, our symbols come to seem real. Thus, we seldom question whether our money has value or if our words have meaning. With continued use, symbols and their meanings become part of the cultural environment we take for granted.

Through human communication, we create a common culture and a shared view of reality and come to be able to understand one another—to coordinate the meanings for the symbols we use. The more we develop common meanings for symbols with another person, the better the communication process will "work." Store owners who trade pieces of high-quality green paper for goods or services do so because they have learned to attach a similar meaning to the pieces of paper as customers do. Merchants also operate in the belief that the bank and creditors will attach a similar significance to them. When those pieces of paper are "checks," the effectiveness of the communication may dissolve, as the problems of subjective meaning loom large.

Artist Ben Shahn makes this point very eloquently:

> It is the images we hold in common, the characteristics of novels and plays, the great buildings, the complex pictorial images and their meanings, and the symbolized concepts, principles, and great ideas of philosophy and religion, that have created the human community. The incidental items of reality remain without value or common recognition until they have been symbolized, recreated, and imbued with value.[5]

RESEARCH PROFILE

Culture Means Care • *Igor E. Klyukanov*

The discipline of semiotics has much to contribute to the study of communication. Professor Klyukanov's work illustrates the connection between culture and care.

● ● ●

In my research I use the discipline of semiotics to reveal the dynamics of intercultural communication. Semiotics, as the study of signs, was once considered an art of diagnosing a disease; in this light, I am interested in what makes up a healthy cultural identity. I try to determine whether a cultural identity, e.g., ethic or national, is healthy or not based on the ways people use various signs (verbal and nonverbal). For example, some borrowings of another culture's language signs are seen as a misplaced response and can be equated with semiotic fetishism; I try to highlight its ramifications for the recipient culture's identity. Overall, I view a culture's dynamic response to its interaction with another culture as semiotic freedom. As cultures interact with each other, they must come to terms with their Secondness, to use Ch. S. Peirce's term; in this process, they display various degrees of semiotic freedom.

More specifically, in my analysis of the concept of semiotic freedom I use the framework of Semiotic Square (A. Greimás & J. Courtés) made up of four positions—freedom, independence, obedience, and powerlessness. Based on this framework, intercultural discourse can be shown as an interplay of such codes as sovereignty (combination of freedom and independence), pride (combination of freedom and obedience), submission (combination of obedience and powerlessness), and humility (combination of independence and powerlessness). I try to show how these codes are activated through various signs and how different cultures can balance these codes. The ideal degree of semiotic freedom is equated with intercultural tolerance and is seen as a perfect balance between all activated codes.

All cultures strive for this ideal as they are concerned with maintaining their identities. This concern with self-production as a discursive practice is a mode of "care of the self." The word "culture" comes from Latin "cultus" and means, among other things, "care"; in essence, by trying to balance all codes as they are activated in intercultural discourse, each culture tries to take care of itself, i.e., of its Self. Thus, it is crucial that we study how people can use signs freely in their interactions with each other, i.e., how people maintain their (healthy) collective identities.

Culture is a system of knowledge shared by a large group of people.[6] Cultures may be characterized as individualistic or collectivistic.[7] In individualistic cultures (like the United States), individual initiative, achievement, and competition are valued and self-realization is a major goal.[8] Collectivistic cultures (such as that of Kenya) emphasize group goals, shared responsibility, harmony, and group cooperation.[9] Thus, the values cherished by each of these types of cultures can vary greatly. These cultural orientations help explain why advertising messages that are successful in the United States may not work in a collectivistic culture that attaches different meanings to various symbols.

Interacting Contexts and Levels

Human communication operates in various contexts and at various levels. It is the lifeblood of individuals, relationships, groups, organizations, and societies. Intrapersonal, interpersonal, group, organizational, public, mass, and societal communication do not operate in isolation. There is interplay among all levels. The relationships in which we are involved, the groups of which we are members, the organizations we work for, and the society and world community in which we live, all have an impact on our individual communication activities. In turn, intrapersonal communication and the way we feel and think about ourselves influence our interactions in relationships, groups, organizations, and society, as well as public and mass communication. Human communication is the web that unites and gives mutuality to the various forms and levels of human activity.

Self-Reference

The meanings we learn to attach to the symbols we use—and the symbols others use—always reflect our own experiences. As a result, the things we say and do and the way we interpret others' words and actions are a reflection of—and a statement about—our meanings, experiences, needs, and expectations. When a person says, "It certainly is cold out today," "Mexican food is hot," "That movie is excellent," or "That course is very difficult," he or she is talking as much about his or her own feelings, meanings, and experiences as about the temperature, Mexican food, the movie, or course.

It is in this sense that human communication is self-referencing and autobiographical: What we see in and say about other people, messages, and events in the environment always says as much about us as it does about them.

Self-Reflexivity

Another related characteristic of human communication is our capacity for self-reflexiveness or self-consciousness. This human capacity which allows individuals to view themselves as "self," as a part of and apart from their environment, is the core of the communication process.[10] Because of *self-reflexiveness,* we are able to think about our encounters and our existence, about communication and human behavior. This capability enables us to set goals and measure our progress toward them, to have expectations of ourselves, and to recognize when we have met them. On the other hand, it is also through self-reflexiveness that we recognize our failures, expectations we do not meet, and qualities we admire but do not possess.

It is our capacity for self-reflexiveness that allows us to theorize about ourselves and our experiences—to "get outside ourselves" in order to look at ourselves. In effect, we enter into a relationship with ourselves that is similar in many ways to the relationships we have with others. We talk to ourselves, think about ourselves in particular ways, and "act" in particular ways toward ourselves. Our patterns of self-reflexive communication have great implications for how we talk to, think about, and act toward others. These behaviors, in turn, have consequences for how we relate to ourselves.

Ethics

Up to this point, we have discussed various approaches to the communication process without acknowledging that there are some very individual choices embedded within this process. Models of communication deal with an idealized process. In real life, however, individuals often have to make some very difficult choices when communicating with others. For example, most societies value honesty as a fundamental principle. But if a friend who has been seriously ill asks "How do I look?" what is an appropriate response? Truthfully, the friend may look very weak, but if we care about our friend's well-being, is it right to be totally honest and say "You look terrible"? In this instance, many well-meaning individuals might try to cheer up the friend by telling the person he or she looks fine even though this response is a lie.

Deciding when or if it is acceptable to deceive others and what type of deception is acceptable is only one instance of the ethical choices we make every day as communicators. Ethical issues arise in all types of communication situations including interpersonal communication, organizational communication, political communication, advertising, and the news media.[11] It is important to analyze critically our communication behavior in all of these instances. While the choices we make are often personal, consequences often are not, as the meanings others attach to our choices come into play:

To begin thinking about your own ethical responses to communication, consider the following goals:

- *Fostering dialogue.* Richard Johannesen contends that the starting point is dialogue. "And a basic element in dialogue is 'seeing the other' or 'experiencing the other side'."[12] Dialogue is characterized by authenticity, inclusion, confirmation, presentness, a spirit of mutual equality, and a supportive climate. Individuals may engage in dialogue as a first step toward caring for and valuing each other.
- *Valuing diversity.* The United States is a rich mix of individuals from various cultural backgrounds. Although we share many aspirations in common, our communication behavior may differ depending on the situation. For example, some cultural groups demonstrate respect by looking downward instead of making direct eye contact. If we come from a cultural group that regards eye contact as a sign of paying attention and respect, we may misinterpret the other person's behavior. It is important to understand cultural differences while considering the communication process.
- *Tolerating disagreement.* Sometimes we can learn a great deal from individuals who do not agree with us. It is important to learn to defend our beliefs, but this should not come at the expense of learning to listen to others. Individuals can respect each other as people, yet not agree on specific beliefs. While disagreement can be productive, "hate speech" is not. It is important to learn to challenge other people's ideas without name-calling and/or other tactics that foster racism, sexism, or homophobia.
- *Encouraging individuals to understand themselves.* William Gudykunst notes that we are members of many social groups, based on gender, race, ethnicity, sexual orientation, and so on. These group memberships influence our communication. Gudykunst argues that "our personal and social identities influence all of our communication behavior, even though one may predominate in a particular situation."[13] Because of this multiple group membership, we need to understand the groups to which we belong before we can communicate effectively with members of other

groups. As Fern Johnson notes, "Placing value on diversity and respecting the integrity of different cultures requires increasing knowledge about that diversity; and knowledge is always interpreted through a person's own cultural perspective."[14]

- *Valuing integrity.* Finally, consistency between word and deed, between what one says and what one does, is a very fundamental component of ethics.

Inevitability

"We cannot not communicate." This is a phrase coined by Watzlawick, Beavin, and Jackson to emphasize the point that we are inevitably engaged in the process of creating and processing messages during every waking hour of our lives.[15] Our verbal and nonverbal behaviors are ongoing sources of information for others, and, in turn, we are continually and unavoidably processing information about the people, circumstances, and objects in our environment, and about ourselves.

From this perspective, we can see the technical inaccuracy of concepts such as "communication breakdown" or "failure to communicate." Communication is always taking place. Messages are inevitably being created and processed. Most often, what are termed "breakdowns" and "failures" result not from the lack of message sending and receiving but, instead, from differing interpretations of messages, expectations, intentions, or outcomes.

Implications and Applications

- Very few human activities take place without the use of symbols and symbolic language. Even instinctive behaviors, such as pulling away from a source of pain, involve the use of symbols when we wish to talk or think about them.
- The most common symbolic languages are spoken and written languages; but music, computer, art, and sign languages are also forms of human communication.
- The meanings we attach to the people and events around us grow out of our experiences. Thus, whenever we talk or write about someone or something, we are always saying something about ourselves—about what we noticed or thought was worth mentioning, or about our attitudes, opinions, beliefs, values, or point of view. When we comment on how much we like or dislike a particular person, object, or circumstance, we are saying as much—if not more—about our own tastes, preferences, and meanings as we are about the intended focus of our evaluation.
- Because message sending and message receiving are ongoing and inevitable, there can be no "breakdowns in communication" in the sense of communication stopping. Even silence or the refusal to negotiate are messages. Their impact will depend on factors beneath the surface of easily observable activity.
- To those who have not thought much about human communication, the process appears to be very simple and easy to understand and predict: Send a message and people will behave as intended. From this perspective, "communication problems" are seen as the exception to the rule. When they do occur, it is assumed that the mes-

sage simply needs to be re-sent or refined: "If they didn't get the message, we'll tell them again, and this time we'll say it louder."

- Those who have studied human communication recognize that it is very complex and is difficult to understand and predict: Send a message and anything can happen! Sometimes we have the impact we intend; often we do not. From this perspective, "communication problems" are no surprise. In fact, we may even take notice when problems don't occur. When they do, we assume very little about the factors involved. The "problem" could be that the message needs to be re-sent or refined. Perhaps our message wasn't heard. More than likely, however, the difficulty can be found in factors that operate below the level of observable experience. It may be that others have different meanings for the words we used, or perhaps cultural barriers are operating. If they didn't get our message—and it is sometimes quite difficult to determine whether they did or not—we want to first determine what may have happened, and then strive to develop strategies that may help to overcome the difficulty.

- We can see people, symbols, and technologies when they are present. These are the observable aspects of a complex process. Most of what makes communication work occurs below the surface of observable experience and is invisible. We cannot see meaning, learning, subjectivity, negotiation, or culture at work. We don't see interacting levels of analysis, self-reference, self-reflexivity, ethics, or inevitability. However, each plays a monumental role in the communication process and its outcomes. It is the effort to understand these fundamental but largely invisible characteristics—and their consequences—that makes the study of human communication so intriguing, so vital, and so complex.

Summary

This chapter has examined visible and invisible characteristics that are fundamental to human communication. Visible characteristics include people, symbols, and media. We create and use symbols and symbolic language. A language, in the most general sense, is a set of characters, or elements, and rules for their use in relation to one another. Symbols are characters, letters, numbers, words, objects, people, or actions that stand for or represent something besides themselves. Through the use of technology, symbols have the potential for permanence and portability. For most animals, visual, tactile, olfactory, gustatory, and auditory signals are transitory in nature. Human symbols have significance apart from the situation in which they were originally used and may have a virtually unending existence and use.

Invisible characteristics include meaning, learning, subjectivity, culture, interacting levels and contexts, negotiation, self-reference, self-reflexivity, ethics, and inevitability. Human communication involves meaning. In order to use symbols in communication, their significance and the responses to them must be created. Learning is another characteristic. Animals are born with the knowledge of the meanings to attach to the signals necessary for their survival; humans must learn communication patterns and meanings. The characteristics of words and the sounds of their spoken pronunciation comprise a symbolic code that is useful only to those who have learned to decipher it.

Human communication is subjective. The symbols used in human communication will not necessarily mean the same things to those who create and send messages as they do to those who receive them. People relate to messages in a particular way as a product of their experiences. No two individuals have precisely the same experiences, and no two people attach precisely the same meaning to the messages in the environment.

Negotiation is another characteristic of human communication. When we engage in communication with others, we negotiate a shared culture. Generally, our meanings mesh reasonably well with others' meanings, because others' meanings are learned through social interaction. In this social communication process, symbols and their meanings become shared and standardized—intersubjectified.

Human communication operates in various contexts and at various levels. It is the lifeblood of individuals, relationships, groups, organizations, and societies, and there is interplay between contexts and between levels.

Self-reference is another characteristic of human communication. The meanings we learn to attach to the symbols we use reflect our own experiences. As a result, things that we see in or say about other people, messages, and events in the environment are always autobiographical—they say as much about the person offering the description as they do about the objects being described.

Another related characteristic of human communication is our capacity for self-reflexiveness. Because of our symbol-using capacity we are able to reflect upon ourselves and our actions, to set goals and priorities, to have expectations.

Ethical choices are a very fundamental aspect of everyday communication dynamics. Key ethical considerations include fostering dialogue, valuing diversity, tolerating disagreements, and valuing integrity. Finally, human communication is inevitable. "We cannot not communicate." Our verbal and nonverbal behaviors are ongoing sources of information for others; and, in turn, we are continually and unavoidably processing information about the people, circumstances, and objects in our environment, and about ourselves.

Notes

1. See discussion of human uniqueness and symbols in Anatol Rapoport, "Man, The Symbol User," in *Communication: Ethical and Moral Issues.* Ed. by Lee Thayer (New York: Gordon and Breach, 1973), especially p. 27.

2. The painting was completed to illustrate this concept. It appeared on the cover of the first edition of *Communication and Human Behavior.*

3. The example and discussion of the runner and gazelle is based upon an illustration provided by Jacob Bronowski, *The Ascent of Man* (Boston: Little, Brown, 1973), pp. 3–36.

4. Geoffrey Vickers, "The Multivalued Choice," in *Communication: Concepts and Perspectives.* Ed. by Lee Thayer (New York: Spartan Books, 1967), p. 272.

5. Ben Shahn, *The Shape of Content* (Cambridge, MA: Harvard University Press, 1967), pp. 130–131.

6. William B. Gudykunst, *Bridging Differences* (Newbury Park, CA: Sage, 1991), p. 44.

7. Geert Hofstede, *Culture's Consequences* (Beverly Hills, CA: Sage, 1980).

8. A. Waterman, *The Psychology of Individualism* (New York: Praeger, 1984), p. 4.

9. S. Saleh and P. Gufwoli, "The Transfer of Management Techniques and Practices: The Kenya Case," in *Diversity and Unity in Cross-Cultural Psychology.* Ed. by R. Rath et al. (Lisse, The Netherlands: Swets & Zeitlinger, 1982), p. 327.

10. Richard W. Budd and Brent D. Ruben, *Beyond Media,* 2nd ed. (New Brunswick, NJ: Transaction Books, 1987), p. 109.

11. Richard L. Johannesen, *Ethics in Human Communication,* 4th ed. (Prospect Heights, IL: Waveland, 1996).

12. Johannesen, 1996, p. 59.

13. William B. Gudykunst, *Bridging Differences: Effective Intergroup Communication* (Newbury Park, CA: Sage, 1991), p. 21.

14. Fern Johnson, "Feminist Theory, Cultural Diversity, and Women's Communication," *Howard Journal of Communications,* Vol. 1, No. 2, 1988, p. 40.

15. Paul Watzlawick, Janet H. Beavin, and Don D. Jackson, *Pragmatics of Human Communication: A Study of Interactional Patterns, Pathologies, and Paradoxes* (New York: Norton, 1967), pp. 48–49.

6

Information Reception

In this chapter

Why . . .

- The reception of information is at least as complex and important as message sending.

- You can listen to two conversations at once at a party.

- A receiver's needs have a major impact on communication outcomes.

- The absence of a message can itself be a powerful message.

- Grocery stores often place the most popular items farthest from the door.

Information reception involves attending to and transforming environmental messages into a form that can be used to guide behavior. This process is an active one, consisting of three elements—*information selection, interpretation,* and *retention.* We will discuss each of these in detail in the pages ahead, beginning with an illustration.

Ed awoke this morning at 7:30 to a grey sky and light rain. He noticed the weather almost immediately, because it was a Saturday and he had looked forward all week to a chance to get outside. He chatted with his wife, Jane, about a variety of topics while he dressed and ate breakfast. He began to ponder his options as to how to spend the day, given that he was stuck inside. Ed left the breakfast table and walked down the hallway.

He glanced in the study and saw the piles of pages strewn about his desk. "I should work on the report due next month," he thought to himself. "My annual review will depend on how well that's received."

He continued into the family room where he noticed his children, Robert and Ann, sitting in front of the television set. He reflected to himself on how fast time goes by, and decided that he really ought to spend more time with the kids. "Maybe a computer game or some sort of craft project that we could work on together . . ." He exchanged a few brief words with his children, and it seemed that Elmo was of more interest to the kids than he was, so he turned his attention to a stack of newspapers and magazines lying across the room on a table. As he looked at the pile of reading material, he thought about how he had spent only a few minutes with the mail, newspapers, and magazines all week. "I really should go through them today," he thought. "No . . . the report has got to come first!"

He made his way back to the study, turned on the receiver, and searched for a station that played the kind of music he liked as "background." Ed situated himself at the desk and began to shuffle through the materials before him. He came across a book he had been using as a primary source in his report, picked it up, and began rereading sections of the text and leafing through the illustrations.

The FM station kept fading in and out, and the occasional interruptions for news were annoying him. He walked over to a nearby CD rack, and picked several jazz instrumentals, which he thought would be enjoyable, but not distracting.

As he walked back to the desk, Ed happened to glance out the window. Incredible! The grey skies had cleared, the rain had stopped, and the sun was shining brightly. Ed heard the distant whine of a neighbor's lawn mower and glanced almost instinctively at his own lawn. "My yard really does need to be mowed . . . And the car is dirty," he thought to himself. "I could do both jobs tomorrow, if the weather holds."

He turned the FM on again and scanned for a local station and the weather report. "Clearing this afternoon, highs in the low 80's."

"I'll wash the car today, so it will be clean for the weekend, and put off mowing the lawn until tomorrow," he decided. "This grass might still be a bit wet now, anyway . . . But what if the weather report is wrong? *If* it's wrong? It's always wrong. If I put off mowing until tomorrow, and it rains, I might not be able to mow until next weekend; and by then the grass will be so long it would take most of two days to mow."

"How ridiculous this is!" he concluded. "The lawn is ruling my life. It's amazing how one's priorities evolve by default. Back to the report!"

The foregoing vignette reveals a good deal about Ed's communication habits, values, orientations, and, at the same time, helps to illustrate how communication works. For analytic purposes, let's briefly reconstruct the scenario, paying particular attention to the cues Ed attended to, the meanings he attached to them, and the manner in which these meanings guided his behavior.

There are a number of things Ed might think about upon waking on a given day. On this particular day, he was primarily concerned with the day of the week and the weather—*Saturday* and *rain*. That he chose to be interested in these particular things and not others had largely to do with the meanings each had for him. Saturday was a special day, one he had looked forward to all week. Grey clouds and rain meant it would be impossible for him to pursue some of the activities he had hoped and planned for. Together, *Saturday* and *rain* signified plans ruined, nothing more, nothing less.

Despite this reality, Ed moved through the sequence necessary to the activities he had come to think of as essential to the start of each day: taking a shower, shaving, selecting clothes, dressing, making his way to the kitchen, sitting down at the table, talking to his wife Jane, eating breakfast, and so forth.

As he chatted with Jane, new messages were introduced into his environment. These provided an opportunity for him to overcome the "plans ruined" aura, which to that point had been the dominant theme in his information processing.

In talking to his wife—and himself—Ed determined that there was little to be gained by stewing over one set of plans ruined. There were, after all, a number of plans one might have that *Saturday + rain* would not ruin. As he began to attach new meaning to the situation, his attention was directed toward information sources and possible interpretations he was unaware of only minutes earlier.

Because Ed was ready to consider options as to how to spend the day, the stack of printed pages from his report was singled out from other potential sources of information in the environment. At some level of awareness, those pages meant a variety of things to him at that point, including *job unfinished, frustration, guilt,* and *challenge.* None of these meanings were compelling enough, however, to lead him to undertake work on the report at that instant.

In the family room, his children almost instantly became prominent communication sources. They triggered a variety of meanings—*affection, enjoyment, responsibility, concern.* As with the significance of the report, these meanings were central to his self-concept and sense of what matters, and as a result they commanded his interest and receptivity.

In passing, he also attended momentarily to the television show they were watching. He recognized at some slightly-less-than-conscious level that the messages generated by the cartoon were performing very different functions for Robert and Ann than for him. In some sense, Ed was competing with Elmo for his children's attention.

The presence of the week's mail, magazines, and newspapers became additional sources of communication. In the context of his own life they signified *knowledgeability, credibility, enjoyment,* and *responsibility.* Ed was also aware of a need to be familiar with the "news" in order to be current in discussions with his friends and colleagues.

Though these meanings were also important to his definition of himself, they were not, at that instant, as critical as the meanings related to the report. Ed "decided"—again, in a less-than-wholly-aware manner—to reject these and other options in favor of returning to work on the report.

The communication process continued as he selected a particular information source—FM radio—and a specific frequency on the dial with a message set he had learned to associate with that station. His unstated objective in so doing was to control the background cues in the immediate environment.

In looking through the materials on his desk, his eyes fell upon a book that had been significant earlier in his work. It became a primary object of attention for several minutes, as he recalled its contents and his reaction to them. Noise resulting from the fading of the radio station became another unavoidable information source, and he acted to replace the messages from FM with others from CDs, which he assumed would better meet his needs.

On glancing out the window, the clearing skies and sun were especially meaningful cues. They signified "original plans O.K.; no need to pursue the present options, unless you want to." As his attention shifted to the environment outside, Ed noted the whine of a lawn mower, which triggered a variety of meanings, each of which required attention and resolution—the lawn, the car, and so on.

In examining the alternative meanings called up from memory, he inadvertently began a self-reflexive thought process. As he reflected on his own information processing, this time quite consciously, he decided to execute more control over himself and his surroundings and pursue what he had determined to be the most "logical" alternatives for use of his time.

In returning his attention to work on the report, Ed, in effect, decided to attach less value to messages related to the physical environment external to his study—the lawn, cars, and so on. He chose instead to focus on information sources that were pertinent to his report. The act of selecting the option he did also had the effect of reaffirming his priorities.

Many interesting facets of communication are illustrated in even a commonplace situation such as the one just described. As simple and automatic as such events may seem, they involve an array of factors operating in the very active processes of information selection, interpretation, and retention.

Selection

At any instant in time we are surrounded in our environment by persons, objects, and circumstances that are sources of messages vying for our attention and interest. In the foregoing sequence, Ed's FM receiver, CD player, wife and children, the pages of his report, the outdoors, the lawnmower, and the weather were each potential communication sources that were competing for his attention, as illustrated in Figure 6.1.

Predictably, in such circumstances we select certain information sources to attend to and disregard others. Even in a simple situation we make a number of elaborate decisions, and we are unaware of many of them. Ed "decided" to give attention to the weather, the day of the week, his children, and the report rather than to other information sources in his environment—such as a room that needed painting, clothes that were to be taken to the cleaners, an unopened package on the table, the expressions on his children's faces when they exchanged words, and so on.

This selection process operates similarly in all situations. Consider a circumstance where we pause in a hallway to chat with an acquaintance. First, the very act of noticing the other person involves selection of particular communication sources. Triggered by the constellation of factors associated with the appearance of the other person, and perhaps some verbal cue—"Hi"—we begin focusing ourselves on the other person and on things that we believe will be necessary to the interchange that will follow. In so doing, we ignore other potential cues—the temperature, the color of the carpeting, the appearance of other persons who may pass by, the noise of a nearby copy machine, or the thunderstorm

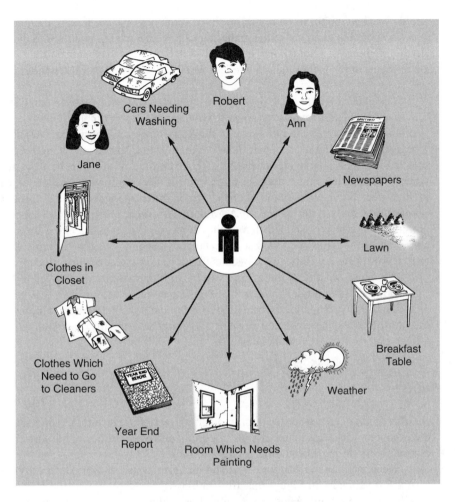

FIGURE 6.1   At any one point in time we are surrounded by a large number of people, events, objects, and circumstances that are communication sources competing for our attention.

outside—through a complex selectivity process that has occupied the attention of many scholars over the years.[1]

The classic illustration of *selective attention* is provided by large parties and similar social gatherings. During such events, one finds that it is not at all difficult to carry on a series of perfectly intelligible discussions without being overly distracted by other conversations. It is even possible to tune in to an exchange between several other persons a good distance away, without shifting one's position and while appearing to be deeply engrossed in conversation with a person close at hand. In that same setting, we are able to tune out the entire external environment, periodically, in order to concentrate on our own feelings, decide what we ought to be doing, or think about how we are being perceived by others. It is also possible to attend to the gathering as a whole, paying attention to the level, pitch, rhythm, number of interactions, and level of activity, as a basis for making some general assessments of the gathering as a whole—whether it is sedate or wild, winding up or down, and so on.[2]

Given these examples, it may seem as though selection operates much like a filter, letting in some sounds, images, or smells, while screening out others.[3] However, the process is often more complex than this way of thinking implies. For instance, we know that even when we have "tuned in" to a particular communication source and "tuned out" others, the selected-out messages may, nonetheless, be taken note of. This is the case, for instance, when a honking horn interrupts our attention in a discussion with a colleague while crossing the street, or when the sound of one's own or a friend's name is heard "through" the otherwise unintelligible din of a party.[4] Additionally, there is evidence to suggest that it is possible to take note of and attach meaning to messages even when one is unaware of doing so.[5] And some studies suggest that under hypnosis we may be able to remember information that we were not fully aware of selecting for attention in the first place.[6]

An understanding of the complexity of the attention process has led to the adoption of a "modified filter model" as a way of thinking about selection.[7] It is thought that we assign priorities to competing information sources and allocate attention among them, while monitoring other messages and perhaps even attending to still other sources that are unknown even to the individuals involved.

Interpretation

Interpretation occurs when we assign meaning or significance to a cue or message in the environment—whether to regard it as important or trivial, serious or humorous, new or old, contradictory or consistent, amusing or alarming.

Depending on the way we select and interpret messages, very different consequences result. For example, in Figure 6.2, Illustration A, if we are drawn first to the large white portion, we see a skull. Attention to subtleties of the drawing in black, however, reveals a lady seated at a dressing table staring into a mirror. In Illustration B, we count either 3 or 5 cubes depending on which cues we define as pertinent to interpreting the figure.

Again, depending on message selection and interpretation, Figure 6.2, Illustration C either appears to be a stylish young lady with a feather in her hat or an older, haggard woman with a wart on her nose, staring downward in apparent depression.

At first glance, Illustration D may appear to be a weather satellite photo, a highly magnified bacterial organism, or simply a random, nonsense image. Once our attention is directed to particular elements of the photo, however, the nonsense image becomes the image of a cow. Interestingly, once we see a cow, it becomes virtually impossible to see it any other way.

Even our reaction to a simple, "Hi, how are you?" will depend, among other things, on whether the person is male or female (and the significance we attach to each), whether we regard the individual as attractive or unattractive, whether the person is a family member or a stranger, how the person is dressed, where the event takes place, and how we interpret the other person's motives.

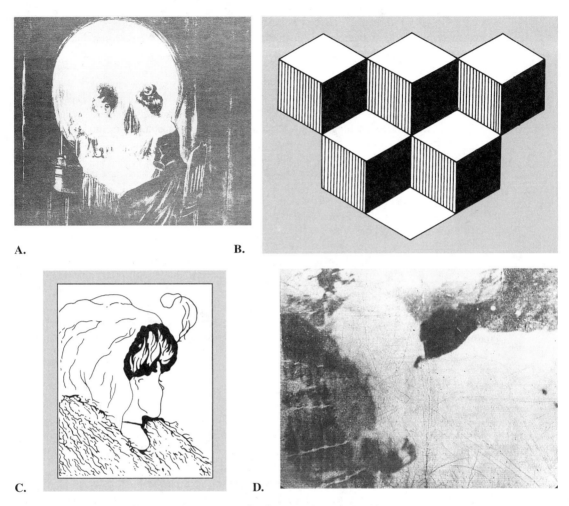

A.   B.
C.   D.

FIGURE 6.2 *Interpretation—The Construction of Meaning*

Retention—Memory

From the preceding discussion, it should be apparent that memory plays an indispensable role in the interpretative process. We are able to store and actively use an incredible amount of information, and we can locate and use it with an efficiency and ease of operation that is astounding.[8]

We have little difficulty accessing the information we need in order to go about our daily routine—to locate the bathroom, closet, and kitchen; to select appropriate clothing and to dress; to start and operate an automobile; or to find the way to the bus or train. In a split second, and with a high degree of accuracy, we can answer questions like "Who was the first president of the United States?" or "What is the name for the sound frequently heard following lightning?" These certainly seem like "simple" questions. But think how long it would take to answer these questions in a book, library, or electronic database using a table of contents, index, or other search technique. Or a quick electronic search may turn up incorrect information.

As Morton Hunt notes:

> Although every act of thinking involves the use of images, sounds, symbols, meanings, and connections between things, all stored in memory, the organization of memory is so efficient that most of the time we are unaware of having to exert any effort to locate and use these materials. Consider the ranges of kinds of information you keep in, and can easily summon forth from, your own memory: the face of your closest friend . . . the words and melody of the national anthem . . . the spelling of almost every word you can think of . . . the name of every object you can see from where you are sitting . . . the way your room looked when you were eight . . . the set of skills you need to drive a car in heavy traffic . . . and enough more to fill many shelves full of books. . . .[9]

These are examples of *recall*—active, deliberate retrieval of information from memory, a capability that may well be unique to humans. We share with other animals the capacity to use information for *recognition*—recognizing objects, places, circumstances, and people when in their presence.[10] See Figure 6.3.

Much effort has been directed to understanding the complex processes by which memory operates, particularly in the area concerned with identifying stages of information processing.[11]

Short-Term and Long-Term Memory

Information enters the system through one or several communication modes. In selecting and attending to particular messages, we begin to attach meaning to those symbols following rules we have learned and frequently used.[12] A good deal of sensory information can be processed within the system at any one time. If, for example, you looked through the newspaper to determine what movie was playing at a particular theater, not only that information but also information relative to other items in the paper, such as other movies and other theaters, would also be processed at some level of awareness. The information other than that being sought would be lost and would decay very rapidly—probably within a second or so.[13]

Information that is to be further used becomes a part of what is called *short-term memory* and is available for a relatively restricted period of time—perhaps fifteen seconds.[14] Our short-term memory capacity is limited under normal circumstances to a few pieces of information only—a phone number, an e-mail address, or a string of several letters or words. Most of us have had the experience of looking up a number or an address, only to forget it by the time we walked across the room to get the phone or computer. This forgetting illustrates how rapidly information is lost from short-term memory. Through recitation or rehearsal, however, we can extend the time available to use information. Thus, if we repeat a phone number to ourselves several times as we walk across the room, the likelihood of remembering it for the needed time period greatly increases.

FIGURE 6.3 Memory plays an important role in the processing of information at any point in time. A quick glance at either of the two triangles leads us to conclude that the sentences are "Once in a lifetime" and "Paris in the spring." These two phrases are familiar to most of us and we expect such phrases to follow the normal rules of grammar we have learned. Thus, the repeated "A" and "THE" are easy to miss. Looking at Illustration C, we have little trouble determining that the image is that of a "dog." Actually, very little detail is provided in the illustration. Were it not for substantial previous experience in selecting and interpreting messages relative to "dog," we would have great difficulty making sense of this image.

Some of the information is further processed and elaborated to become a part of our *long-term memory*. Generally, the longer time information is available to us in short-term memory, the greater the chance it will become a part of our long-term memory. Therefore, a phone number looked up, rehearsed, and dialed several times over the period of an hour because of a busy signal, is far more likely to be remembered than a number successfully reached on the first try. Phone numbers that are dialed often become a part of an individual's long-term memory naturally, or actively, through memorization. Of course, if we use autoredial or store the number in a cell phone, we don't get the chance to learn it through practice.

Recall and recognition exemplify the two general classes of human memory: (1) relatively slow retrievals that require conscious processing, and (2) relatively fast retrievals that require no conscious processing. Some of the other characteristics of these two retrieval processes include:[15]

Slow Retrievals	*Fast Retrievals*
Nonautomatic	Automatic
Conscious	Unconscious
Controlled	Uncontrolled
Indirect access	Direct access
Voluntary	Involuntary

Semantic and Episodic Memory

Our general knowledge of the people, places, and things in the world is called *semantic memory*. *Episodic memories* relate to recollections and retrieval of information regarding personal happenings, particular objects, people, and events experienced by an individual at a specific time and place.[16] *Autobiographical memories*—memories of oneself—are considered to be episodic.[17] While this distinction is a useful one, scholars also point out that the two types of memory are related: Semantic knowledge is derived from episodic memory, and episodic memories are organized and categorized based on semantic categories.[18]

In the summary of his book, *Memory in the Real World,* Gillian Cohen provides the following list of characteristics of memory:

- Memory is an overloaded system—there is more to be remembered than can possibly be managed by the brain.
- Memory must be selective—decisions must be made as to what to remember and what to ignore.
- Memory must be dynamic—adjustments must be made to changes in the world around us.
- Memory must link past, present, and future—memory provides for continuity of meaning across time.
- Memory must be able to construct hypothetical representations—imagination, creativity, and consideration of possibilities are necessary characteristics of memory.
- Memory must store both general and specific information—generalized and specialized knowledge are both required in human activity.

- Memory must store information implicitly—information must be easily and automatically stored and organized for retrieval. Often this is done in terms of categories, time periods, and level of generality/specificity.
- Memory processes must be complex—elaborate information sorting and organizing processes are necessary to integrate new information with past experience.
- Memory retrieval strategies are critical—retrieving information becomes more critical and difficult as memories proliferate.
- Memory retrieval must utilize spontaneous and deliberate retrieval—memories must be able to be retrieved spontaneously as well as deliberately.[19]

As useful as the foregoing view of information processing is, it is important to be aware of the limitations of what has been termed the sequential-stage model. Researchers remind us that information processing is an extremely complex operation. It is often difficult to distinguish between its various stages. The distinction between selection, interpretation, and episodic and semantic memory can be fuzzy. Further, a sequential-stage model could imply that the individual plays a passive role in information processing. Clearly this is not the case; complex interactions between the individual and environment are fundamental to the ongoing dynamics of information reception.

Receiver Influences

For each of us, a complex set of influences works together to influence our decisions as to which messages we will attend to and how we will interpret and retain the information that results. Many of these have to do with the nature of the *receiver.*

As children we adapt to a world in which we are highly dependent upon parents and other adults for the satisfaction of our needs, wants, and desires. That dependence carries with it a particular set of information-reception tendencies for most of us, in which our parents, relatives, and, gradually, peer relations are highly significant.

Needs

Among the most crucial factors that play a role in reception are what are commonly termed *needs.* Scholars generally agree that our most basic needs, like those of other animals, have to do with our physiological well-being—food, shelter, physical well-being, and sex.[20] Basic needs can be potent forces in directing our behavior. When needs are not met, our efforts to satisfy them are important guiding forces in information reception and processing. To the individual who hasn't eaten for several days, for example, few message sources are likely to be as noteworthy, or *salient,* as those relating to food. A knowledge that unsatisfied needs often increase the salience attached to particular messages has led nutritionists to suggest that a good way to save money and diet is to shop for groceries after eating, rather than before.

The same pattern occurs with regard to our health. A headache or upset stomach, which is readily dismissed by persons who believe themselves to be well, may become the focus of great attention and concern for persons who believe they may be ill.

Other needs or motives, including social contact, reality exploration and comprehension, socialization, diversion, entertainment, and play, have to do with our spiritual,
psychological, social, and communicative well-being.[21] Perhaps the most basic of these
needs has to do with maintaining and developing our identity and self-concept.[22] All of us
want to be seen positively, as worthy, desirable, competent, and respectable. There are, of
course, differences between us as to the particular qualities for which we wish others to
value us. Some of us aspire to be seen as creative, intelligent, professionally competent,
and an occupational success. Being seen as religious, honest, honorable, or empathetic may
be more important to others. Some of us would prefer to be admired for our leadership capacity; others wish to be respected for their loyalty as followers, and so on.

Personal, social, and communicative needs play an important role in selection, interpretation, and retention. Their role has been highlighted by scholars who focus on the
"uses and gratifications" of mass media.[23] This work helps substantiate the view that there
can be a direct relationship between particular unsatisfied, or ungratified, needs and resulting patterns of exposure to mass media programs and other message sources.

Attitudes, Beliefs, and Values

The attitudes, preferences, and predispositions one has about particular topics, persons, or situations also play a critical role in information-receiving activities and outcomes. For instance,
people will generally attend to and be favorably disposed toward messages, sources, and interpretations that support their present views before they consider nonsupportive messages,
sources, or conclusions.[24] The person who supports candidate X for a particular elective office is likely to pay far more attention to articles and political ads and sources of new information about that candidate than he or she will to items about candidate Y or Z. And such a
person is also likely to spend time talking politics with others who share his or her view.

Values is a term used to refer to basic principles that we live by—our sense of what
we ought and ought not do in our relations with the environment and one another. As with
attitudes and beliefs, values influence selection, interpretation, and retention. Individuals
who are opposed to abortion, for instance, are likely to take notice of and have strong reactions to those who advocate a "pro-choice" position.

There are instances where messages that are likely to be interpreted as inconsistent
and nonsupportive of our attitudes, beliefs, or values can lead to *more,* rather than *less,* attention and interest. We may devote attention and effort to converting individuals who es-
pouse beliefs or values that differ from our own. Following a similar logic, we sometimes
spend more time reflecting upon people and events that trouble us than on those that reas-
sure and comfort us, perhaps because we have come to take the latter for granted.

Goals

Most of us are at best only partially aware of our needs, attitudes, beliefs, and values. In
contrast, we consciously set our *goals.*

When an individual decides to pursue a particular plan, career, personal relationship,
or personal challenge, that goal serves to direct his or her attention toward certain information sources and away from others, as suggested in Figures 6.4 and 6.5.

FIGURE 6.4 At any point in time, one's goals have a direct and profound effect on information selection, interpretation, and retention.

If a woman has the goal of driving from Princeton, New Jersey, to JFK Airport in New York City to catch a specific flight, this objective plays a major role in guiding information selection, interpretation, and retention. On the way to the airport, she must process messages concerning the location, direction, and rate of speed of her car and other vehicles in the vicinity. She must also attend to, interpret, and remember the road markings and signs that provide pertinent information and those that indicate the way to the airport. The gauges, instruments, and other controls of the car must also be monitored. Additionally, the driver must take account of weather conditions, time remaining before arrival at the final destination, location of the long-term parking area, the proper terminal, the flight number, the seat assignment, and so on. Until the goal is achieved and the individual is comfortably seated aboard the airplane, a substantial amount of the person's information-receiving effort is influenced by the commitment to the self-determined goal of catching a plane. See Figure 6.5.

When an individual sets the goal of achieving certain competence in an area such as athletics, this objective shapes not only the messages to which the individual attends but also the interpretations of them that he or she makes. First, the goal increases the likelihood that the individual will expose himself or herself to communication sources

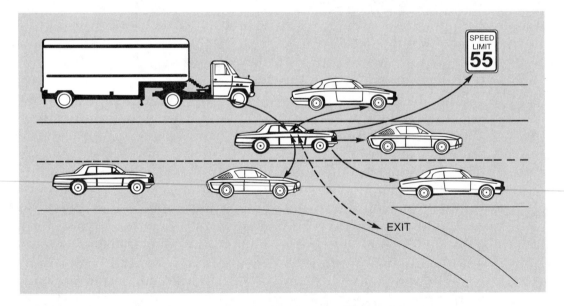

FIGURE 6.5 Even a relatively simple goal, like driving from point A to point B, makes incredible demands on one's information selection, interpretation, and retention skills. Information must be gathered and processed as to the location and rate of speed of other vehicles, and projections must be developed as to where nearby vehicles will be at future points in time. Road signs, gauges in one's own car, and remembered information as to which exit to take, what lane to be in, and so forth, must also be utilized. In time, this complex information processing task becomes so natural that one can listen to a CD, plan a speech, or replay the day's events while driving.

and situations that pertain to athletics in general and his or her sport in particular. Secondly, the goal may well increase the individual's contact with other people interested in a similar activity, and this will have an additional influence on information reception. The demands of physical fitness may also play an important role in determining how information about food, drinking, smoking, health, and drugs will be attended to, interpreted, and remembered.

In a similar manner, a decision to pursue a particular career—to become a medical doctor, for instance—directs one's attention toward certain messages and away from others. The aspiring doctor is influenced by his or her goal toward knowledge based in physiology, anatomy, and chemistry and away from information pertinent to students of engineering, business administration, and journalism. Acquiring appropriate interpretations for these information sources is a priority until the goal is achieved or revised. A change of goals often also implies a change in information processing.

Capability

Our level of intelligence, previous experience with a particular topic area, and facility with language have an important impact on the kinds of messages we attend to and the manner in which we interpret and retain them. The probability of a person who speaks only English spending much time listening to Spanish radio broadcasts, watching French television programming, or reading Russian publications is naturally very low, simply because he or she lacks the capability of meaningfully processing the information. By the same token, it is unlikely that an individual who has no quantitative or research background will read articles in technical or scholarly journals. While the individual may possess the intellectual potential, his or her lack of familiarity with research and with the technical language used in the publications affects potential interest and comprehension, not to mention retention.

Use

We attend to and devote effort to understand and remember messages we think we will need or be able to use. The learning of language offers an excellent example. It is a virtual certainty that children will learn to speak the language of those around them. For the most part, this learning occurs irrespective of whether there are efforts at formal instruction. We attend to, learn to interpret, and retain messages about how to use spoken language because it is essential to our participation in most human activities.

In school we attend to and retain a large quantity of information on a variety of topics that may have no immediate personal relevance. Were it not for the opportunities and requirements to "rehearse" and "use" this retained knowledge to demonstrate course mastery on exams and quizzes, much less information would be remembered.

The same principle operates in many other domains. To the individual who is thinking about purchasing a new automobile, statistics such as safety ratings, estimated miles per gallon, and price suddenly become much more salient and far easier to remember than they were prior to the decision to shop for a new car.

Communication Style

Communication style can influence information reception in two ways: first, depending on our habits and preferences, we may be drawn to or may actively avoid the opportunity to deal with other people. People who are shy or apprehensive about engaging in verbal communication in a group setting, for example, may avoid such circumstances whenever possible.[25] Such an individual might prefer to watch a television show on health or consult an Internet site for information on a particular illness, rather than ask a doctor for information. Even when a person with this style of communication makes an effort to take part in interpersonal situations, he or she may be uncomfortable. This discomfort may well affect the way he or she attends to, interprets, and retains information.

A less direct influence of our communication style on information reception has to do with the manner in which we present ourselves to others. The way we "come across" to those with whom we interact can have a substantial impact on the way they react to us, and this will influence both the quality and quantity of information they make available. People who are highly talkative, for instance, often have less verbal information available to them than they otherwise might, because the people with whom they converse are often limited in their interest and in the time available to speak. Various aspects of our interpersonal style—our greetings, tone, word choice, level of openness, dress, and appearance—also have an impact on the messages other people make available to us, and this, in turn, has a direct bearing on our selection, interpretation, and retention.

Experience and Habit

Many of our information reception tendencies develop as a result of our experiences. These "communication habits" are no doubt the major guiding influence in how we select, interpret, or retain messages at any moment in time. Whether one thinks of reading a daily newspaper, watching a particular television show, exchanging pleasantries with an acquaintance on the way to work, checking our e-mail or cell phones throughout the day, or arguing with a friend or family member, our previous experiences, and the communication patterns we have developed as a result of these experiences, have a definite influence on our message reception. See Figure 6.6.

Message (Information) Influences

In addition to factors associated with *receivers,* characteristics of the information, or *message,* also have a major impact on selection, interpretation, and retention. Five particularly important considerations are origin, mode, physical character, organization, and novelty.

Origin

Some of the messages we attend to have their origins in our physical environment. When we select an item on which to sit, identify a landmark as a guide to navigation, pick out an apartment in which to live, decide whether the temperature in our room is too high, or de-

FIGURE 6.6 Glance at the items in the illustration above for five to ten seconds, close the book, and list the items that you can remember on a sheet of paper. When you compare the resulting list with the picture, it is obvious that many items were forgotten and others were perhaps never noticed in the first place. Further study of those things noticed and remembered, and those not, can underscore aspects of the information reception process, the impact of memory on selection and retention of new information, and the complexity of information processing. Generally speaking, in any situation what we notice and remember directly reflects our past experiences. Sometimes an item is taken note of precisely because we cannot relate to and identify it. In any case, those things noticed and remembered and those forgotten in any situation generally say as much or more about us—our past xperiences, interests, priorities, hobbies, and so on—as they do about the actual information sources present in the environment.

velop a theory of why apples fall from trees, we do so using information based on the objects, events, relationships, or phenomena in the physical environment.

We also make use of information we create ourselves through *intrapersonal* communication. When we listen to and think about what we have said to someone else, try to recall our knowledge about a particular topic, talk to ourselves, or look at ourselves in a mirror before leaving for an important engagement, we are dealing with information of which we ourselves are the source. We also use messages we ourselves create to assess our own internal feelings. Our sense of illness, fear, happiness, frustration, confusion, excitement, pain, and anxiety result from information that originates in our own physiological functioning.

Certainly the great majority of information of significance to us in our environment arises either directly or indirectly from the activities of other persons—through *interpersonal communication.* Often these messages originate in face-to-face interaction with others. Other interpersonal messages are the product of the activities of people separated from us in either time or space or both, transported to us by means of various communication media. A favorite television program, the evening news, an e-mail, or a text message from a friend, a best-selling novel, the morning paper, a cherished painting, or the latest CD by a favorite group can satisfy some of the same needs as face-to-face encounters, though the originator and receiver of the information are separated from one another physically.

In many circumstances we are limited as to which of these message sources we can use. If, for example, we wish to find out the temperature in Tokyo last night, we have little choice but to rely on messages provided by other people through technology. If we want to know how we feel about some situation facing us tomorrow, we rely on information we create ourselves. If we need to determine the exact temperature of our bath water, that information can be best derived by placing a thermometer in water.

There are many other instances in which we can choose among these sources. We can seek an answer to the question, "Is it hot in here?" using any of these sources: We can make a determination based on our personal "feelings"; we can ask the opinion of one or several other people; or we can use a nearby thermometer. A similar situation occurs when we undertake a project such as figuring out how to set up a new computer. We may choose to tackle the chore ourselves making use of the manufacturer's instructions. We could seek the assistance of a friend, or we may "dig right in" without consulting the instructions, relying on our own resources and prior experience with similar projects. Or, we can use a combination of these information sources.

The availability or lack of availability of various message sources has an obvious and direct impact upon the way in which we attend to, interpret, and retain information. Individuals may vary in terms of their preferences for particular types of sources; however, when there is a choice many of us rely on "self-created" messages first. That is, if we think we already have the information necessary in a particular circumstance, we may go no further. When we feel we lack the internal resources to make sense of or handle a particular situation on our own, we turn to other sources. For instance, when we enter an electronics store to shop for particular items, we will probably go directly to the shelves where we expect to find them. If, however, the store is an unfamiliar one, or the items are not where we expected, we are likely to look around for signs to help us navigate or to ask a clerk for assistance.

Mode

Information reception varies depending upon whether visual, tactile, auditory, gustatory, or olfactory modes are involved. In any number of situations, a touch or reassuring embrace will be taken note of and interpreted in quite a different way than spoken words of encouragement. In such an instance, actions may speak louder than words. Likewise the smell of decaying garbage may be a much more poignant message than a newspaper story about the consequences of a garbage strike or a description of the odor from a friend who witnessed the accumulating trash. In other circumstances, however, words may be extremely important, such as in a brainstorming session, a term paper, a letter to a friend, a legal brief, or a debate.

Physical Characteristics

Physical characteristics such as size, color, brightness, and intensity can also be important to information processing. In general, symbols, actions, objects, or events that are large or prominent attract more attention than those which are not. A bright light is more salient than a dim light; large type is more noticeable than small type.

Actions and circumstances that have major consequences for large numbers of people—a fire, natural disaster, or international conflict for instance—are more likely to be taken note of than less important events of less widespread impact. These events appear on the front page of the newspaper or as lead stories on the evening news. The extent of their impact is a major factor in the information-reception processes of reporters and editors, who recognize that readers and viewers are also likely to attend to and be interested in these events.

Other things being equal, messages that have vivid color, brightness, or intensity are more apt to be noticed and taken account of than those lacking these characteristics. A four-color advertisement, a brightly colored dress or jacket, or a high intensity light are likely to be attended to before objects lacking these attributes. The intensity of potential visual or verbal messages can also be an important consideration in message reception.

Organization

A good deal of research in the area of persuasion has been directed toward determining the way in which the ordering of ideas or opinions affects reception. Research suggests that when we are presented with a series of items, we devote greatest attention to the items listed first. As a result, this information has the greatest likelihood of becoming a part of our long-term memory.[26] When asked to recall items from a list after it has been completed, individuals do best with those things presented near the beginning (primacy) and those near the end (recency). The items at the end are thought to be recalled because they are still a part of one's short-term memory, while those at the beginning are remembered because the information can be retrieved from long-term memory.[27]

The significance of organization on information reception is evident in a variety of settings. Within a picture or a report the arrangement of elements can have a substantial impact on the overall impression created. The ordering of material within a database is also an important factor in whether and how that material will be used. Even the arrangement of foods at a grocery store often has an impact on the communication process. How many times do we pick up grocery items we hadn't intended to because we noticed them while on our way to the place in the store where bread or milk were shelved?

Novelty

Information that is novel, unfamiliar, or unusual stands out, "grabbing our attention" if only for the moment. While we may generally devote very little attention to the color of

RESEARCH PROFILE

The Stories Television Tell Us • Nancy Signorielli

Does television reflect the reality we live in everyday? Does it influence our perception of our environment? Does televised violence affect us? Professor Signorielli's research provides answers to these and other important questions about the influence of television on our lives.

• • •

My research focuses on television as the world's primary storyteller. But what is important about television is that its stories are told by commercial institutions, rather than parents, the church, or the school. In order to understand the effects of this phenomenal medium, I look at images in media content and how exposure to television's messages is related to audience beliefs and behaviors.

I study the basic set of images to which most people are exposed on a daily basis. Television programming, whether seen through broadcast or cable programming provides a rather stable set of images about life. For example, for the last thirty years the demography of the television world has consistently underrepresented women. Moreover, while in more recent years, the numbers of black characters have come to reflect their numbers in the U.S. population, other minorities, such as Hispanics, are extremely underrepresented. Notions of under- and overrepresentation are extremely critical in our understanding of the world. Daily viewing of a medium that overrepresents some groups at the expense of others provides subtle messages of who is important. Another outcome is that television does not provide diverse role models for children.

The other part of my research, called cultivation analysis, has focused on how these images contribute to people's ideas about the world or their conceptions of social reality. For example, children's beliefs about nutrition often reflect the nonnutritious messages about food they see on television. Similarly, studies have shown that television's abundance of messages about violence are related to viewers believing that the world is a mean and dangerous place and overestimating their chances of being involved in violence. Overall, this research has shown, in many different venues, that television viewing plays an important role in people's understanding about the world, its peoples, and how things work.

automobiles, a bright pink or yellow car is likely to "catch the eye" of even the most preoccupied motorist.

The same principle applies in other areas such as dress, language, appearance, or greetings, to which we may devote little conscious attention unless these message sources dramatically violate what we have come to expect. An unfamiliar foreign language, unusual dress, or a normally tidy room in disarray often become very salient to us. Other examples are provided in Figures 6.7 and 6.8. Though we are typically only somewhat aware when we engage in a ritualistic handshake greeting, we certainly do take note when the other person squeezes our hand too firmly, too loosely, or continues to shake long after the conventional number of pumps.

Source Influences

Some of our most interesting and complex information-reception decisions involve interpersonal sources. Why do we listen to and believe some people more than others? Why are

FIGURE 6.7   People, objects, events, or patterns that are unique or novel often grab our attention far more than the usual, commonplace, or predictable. Barbara Cartland reports, for example, that during the two years after the Mona Lisa was stolen from the Louvre in Paris in 1911, more people came to stare at the place in the museum where the famous painting had hung than had come to see the actual painting during the 12 previous years.

Niagara Falls provides another interesting case in point. One of the first things that strikes most visitors to the falls is the pervasive sound created by the pounding of the falls to the river below. To residents of the area, however, the noise goes generally unnoticed. Ironically, it was the sudden absence of the thundering falls during a hard freeze in the winter of 1936 and previously in 1909 that reportedly awoke the residents.

Source: Barbara Cartland, *Barbara Cartland's Book of Useless Information.*

we more influenced by some people than others? Our decisions depend on a number of factors including: *proximity, attractiveness, similarity, credibility, authoritativeness, motivation, intent, delivery, status, power,* and *authority.*

Proximity

Our distance from a source can have a major influence on the likelihood of our attending to particular messages. We are more likely to be exposed to sources that are close at hand

FIGURE 6.8 Unusual objects, events, individuals, or actions often command attention and interest.

than to those that are farther away.[28] The closer we are, the less time, effort, and money that must be expended to engage in communication.

For example, if we walk into a library to find a reference and must pass by the librarian, we may decide to ask his or her advice simply because of proximity. For this same reason, we are far more likely to attend to the actions and reactions of a next-door neighbor or colleague at work than to those of persons who live a block away or work in the next building.

The significance of distance as a factor in communication is highlighted by considering the function of technology. By means of television, radio, newspapers, magazines, books, cell phones, and the Internet, information from thousands of miles away becomes available without leaving the comfort of one's home. It is, in fact, the ease of access to television, e-mail, online services, phones, and other technology that has helped to make these technologies and the information they transport such a central part of our lives.

Physical and Social Attraction and Similarity

The way in which we engage in interpersonal communication often has a great deal to do with how attractive we believe a particular message source to be. Particularly when we first meet an individual, we react largely to his or her general appearance. If, based on first impressions, we are attracted to the person, it is likely that we will pay increased attention to, remember, and attach special significance to his or her words. In this way, attraction plays a significant, though often subtle, role in influencing the nature of communication.

Though we tend to think of attractiveness primarily in physical terms, we often find people appealing for other reasons as well. An individual who appears to be friendly, warm, empathetic, and concerned, and who expresses interest in or respect for us, may be quite attractive to us as a social companion. Like physical attractiveness, *social attractiveness* also can be an important influence in information reception.

Similarity is another factor of significance in communication. The more like a source we are, or believe ourselves to be, the more likely we are to pay special attention to that person and what he or she says.[29] Sometimes similarities that interest us in others are basic characteristics such as gender, level of education, age, religion, ethnic background, hobbies, or language capacity. In other instances, we are drawn to people because they share our needs, attitudes, goals, or values.

The influence of similarity on reception is vividly illustrated by the great impact of our peer group, beginning in our early school years. Our peers play a significant role in shaping our reactions to clothing, movies, music, school, books, various occupations, and also to our parents, friends, and acquaintances. Preferences for persons with similar cultural, religious, racial, occupational, political, and educational backgrounds continue to influence communication throughout our lifetimes.

Credibility and Authoritativeness

We are likely to attend to and retain information from sources we believe to be experienced and/or knowledgeable.[30] Certain people—or groups—may be viewed as credible and authoritative, regardless of the topic. Information provided by medical doctors, clergy, or professors, for example, may be regarded as more noteworthy than messages from people with other vocations, even on topics that are outside the professional's areas of expertise. Similarly, many of us afford actors, television personalities, politicians, and other people who are in the public eye particular attention and credibility. Thus, the actor speaking on politics or the medical doctor lecturing on religion may be given more than the usual level of attention by receivers.

In some instances, the attention and credibility accorded a particular person depends upon the topic in question. Other things being equal, we are more likely to attend to and retain information on international affairs presented by a network news commentator than to messages on the same topic offered by our next-door neighbor. When the topic is insurance, however, we may well attach more weight to the views of a neighbor who has twenty-five years' experience working in that field than to reports provided on television.

Motivation and Intent

The manner in which we react to a particular interpersonal message source also depends on the way we explain his or her actions to ourselves.[31] Depending on what motives we attribute to an individual, our response may vary substantially. If we assume a person intends to inform or help us, we are likely to react in quite a different way than if we believe the intention is to persuade or deceive us.

Delivery

The manner in which a source delivers a message can be an important influence in information reception. Among the factors that come into play in delivery of spoken messages are volume, rate of speaking, pitch, pronunciation, and the use of pauses. Other visual factors, such as gestures, facial expressions, and eye contact may be significant.

Status, Power, and Authority

The presence or lack of *status*—position or rank—can also be important in determining how likely it is that an information source or message will be selected and acted on. The *power* or *authority* of a source—the extent to which the source is capable of dispensing rewards or punishment for selecting, remembering, and interpreting messages in a particular way—is also influential in communication.

Generally speaking, parents, teachers, employers, supervisors, or others who have status, power, or authority relative to us have a better than average chance of obtaining our attention to their messages. The significance we attach to their role directs our attention to their words and actions in an effort to be aware of their opinions or to seek their favor. To the extent that we can be rewarded or punished through grades, money, favors, or praise for interpreting their messages in particular ways, we may be especially attentive.

Technological and Environmental Influences

Beyond the *receiver, information,* and *source, technology* and the *environment* also have a substantial impact on communication.

Technology

The technology, or channel, through which messages reach us can be a significant factor in information reception. Differences, such as whether messages are presented via print or electronically, film or videotape, radio broadcast or the spoken words of a friend, can have a direct, and in some cases obvious, influence. Simply in terms of availability, some technologies provide a greater likelihood of exposure to information than others. More people watch television than participate in chat rooms, and the size of both of these is much larger than the group that reads scholarly journals.

Of the various mass media, television has traditionally received the most attention among scholars. This interest is not surprising given the central role of television in the lives of most Americans. Even as early as the 1950s, families viewed television on the average of four and one-half hours a day. That number jumped to over five hours in the 1960s, over six hours in the 1970s, nearly seven hours in the 1980s.[32] Current figures indicate that White households view an average of 7.2 hours of television each day and African American households 10.7 hours per day.[33]

In terms of exposure to messages alone, television is clearly a major force in the lives of most Americans. As noted in the classic summary of a National Institute of Mental Health report, *Television and Behavior,* television is an influential source of information processing.

> The simplest representations (on television) are literal visual and auditory pictures of something in the real world, for example, a car moving along a highway. To process this information, children probably depend on the same perceptual and cognitive skills they use in processing information in the real world. . . . At the next level are the forms and conventions that do not have real-world counterparts. Some of them are analogs of real-world experiences. . . . For example, a "zoom in," in which the object in front of the camera seems to get larger and more focused, is similar to moving closer to something in real life. But some effects, for example, slow motion, do not appear in the real world, and children—and others who are unfamiliar with television—must learn what they mean.
>
> Once they are learned, these media conventions can be used by people in their own thinking. For example, children may learn to analyze a complex stimulus into its smaller parts by watching the camera zoom in and out. The forms can take on meaning, sometimes as a result of associations seen on television.[34]

The report also indicates that the rapid movement and visual and audio contrasts presented by television are particularly salient to very young viewers, who often become "passive consumers of audio-visual thrills."[35] Much of what can be said of television in this connection can be applied also to other technologies that use screens to display information.

Ten years ago, e-mail, Web pages, chat rooms, online vendors and auctions, and the many other services now afforded by the Internet were unheard of. In 1997, 18.6 percent of U.S. homes had computers with active Internet connections. By 2003, that number had grown to 54.6 percent. With this remarkable growth has come a significant new communication medium—one that is capable of providing personalized and specialized information to meet user needs.

RESEARCH PROFILE

Mobile Communicating • James Katz

Have you ever seen two people having dinner in a restaurant talking to other people on their cell phones? Professor Katz's research on mobile communication explores the implications of the public use of new communication technologies.

• • •

We often do not realize how dramatically ordinary technologies like the telephone can affect our lives. Yet they give us powers of communication that would seem superhuman to those who lived in earlier eras. Just think for a moment about the way mobile phones make a difference in people's lives. This question is the focus of my research.

The mobile phone has improved the lives of many people. But one communication process, known as the "actor–observer" paradox, leads to some uncomfortable moments when people use mobile phones around their friends. The person who wishes to use the mobile phone (the actor) may do so despite being with someone else because she or he feels that the call is important. That is, the caller feels that she or he has a good and necessary reason to make or take the call, and does so with the expectation that others should understand and accept this necessity. On the other hand, the people around the user (the observer) will view the situation differently. Observers may feel that the mobile phone user is being selfish and self-indulgent, and is failing to respect the moral conventions of polite society.

The public use of mobile phones is likely to remain a source of normative conflict since the sources of irritation are not merely conventional. Instead, they seem to go to the core of human cognitive processes. The result could be that as mobile phone users pursue their private pleasures of conversation there will be a reduction in the *civility* and *personal engagement* in public. The enjoyment of being in public space, or having an evening with friends, could be diminished to the detriment of all. By using research, we can understand just how big a problem this is and what might be done about it. Think about these issues the next time you answer your phone!

The Environment

Context. The manner in which a particular person or event is reacted to depends on whether we are at home or on vacation, at work or at school or engaged in a leisure activity. It will depend also on whether the messages are received in an office, a church, a bedroom, a classroom, or an auditorium. It is not difficult to think of examples of how the same message would be interpreted very differently depending on the context in which it was encountered. See Figure 6.9.

The presence of others often has a very direct bearing on how we select as well as interpret and retain information. How we want to be seen, how we think other people see us, what we believe others expect from us, and what we think they think about the situation we are in are among the considerations that shape the way we react in social situations.

If we are in the company of colleagues or friends, we may pay particular attention to the people, events, and circumstances they attend to. In our effort to decide how well we liked a particular movie, lecture, painting, or person, the reactions of other persons are often of major significance to our own judgments. Sometimes, we conform our own in-

FIGURE 6.9 The context or setting in which potential information sources are encountered can be an important factor influencing whether and how messages are selected, interpreted, and remembered.

formation processing to that of others for appearances only; in many other instances the influence is more subtle and far-reaching.

Repetition. We are likely to take into account and remember messages that are repeated often. Advertising slogans and jingles, lyrics of popular songs, multiplication tables, and birth dates of family members stand out in our minds, in part because they have been repeated so often. Repetition also contributes to our learning our native language, our parents' and friends' opinions, the slang and jargon of our associates, and the accent of our geographic region.

Consistency and Competition. When a person has been exposed over a long period of time to one religious orientation, one political philosophy, or one set of values, there is a likelihood that the individual will come to select and accept messages consistent with that position. *Brainwashing* is the extreme example of this sort of communication phenomenon. In such circumstances, the individual is bombarded with messages that advocate a particular position, and information supporting alternative points of view is systematically eliminated from the environment. When coupled with the promise of reward (or absence of punishment) and consistency, the lack of competitive messages becomes a powerful shaping force influencing the probability of message selection and the manner of interpretation and retention.

In considerably less extreme forms, the educational process makes use of these same principles. Math, language, reading, and spelling are taught not only through repetition but also through consistency. The arrangement of classroom furniture and the use of examinations, lectures, books, and homework assignments are among the strategies typically used to minimize the influence of competing messages.

An Active and Complex Process

Selection, interpretation, and reception are basic to message reception, and reception is fundamental to communicating. These activities are influenced by any number of the factors discussed in this chapter, making information processing one of the most active and complex facets of human communication. Morton Hunt makes this point eloquently in discussing the opening sentence of Gibbon's *Decline and Fall of the Roman Empire:*

> "In the second century of the Christian era, the Empire of Rome comprehended the fairest part of the earth, and the most civilized portion of mankind."

> A reader who finds this sentence perfectly intelligible does so not because Gibbon was a lucid stylist but because he or she knows when the Christian era began, understands the concept of "empire," is familiar enough with history to recognize the huge sociocultural phenomenon known as "Rome," has enough information about world geography so that the phrase "the fairest part of the earth" produces a number of images in the mind, and, finally, can muster a whole congeries of ideas about the kinds of civilization that then existed. What skill, to elicit that profusion of associations with those few well-chosen cues—but what a performance by the reader! One hardly knows which to admire more. . . .[36]

Without doing any injustice to Hunt's intent, we could extend the point to apply equally to the impressive accomplishments of a listener in a personal, group, technologically mediated, or public setting, or to the observer of visual images in an art gallery, a baseball game, or a television program.

Implications and Applications

- Reception is a fundamental aspect of our communication behavior—an aspect to which we often pay little attention.
- Listening and observing are our primary means for gathering information about the people, events, problems, and opportunities in our environment.
- Listening and observing involve selection. While we attend to and attach importance to some people, circumstances, and objects, we inevitably ignore others.
- Our selections, interpretations, and memories of messages are subjective and are influenced by what we, personally, bring to the situation, as well as by available information, sources, technology, and environmental influences.

- Our personal characteristics, previous experiences, and habits have a major influence on what we see, hear, understand, believe, and remember.
- Competence in listening and observing requires conscious effort, an awareness of factors influencing the process, and an understanding of ourselves and our own capabilities, needs, attitudes, values, and goals.

Summary

In this chapter, our focus has been on the nature of information reception, and the processes involved in sensing and making sense of the people, objects, and circumstances in our environment. Individuals play an active role in this process though they may have little awareness that it is taking place.

Selection, interpretation, and retention are primary facets of information reception. Collectively, they are the processes by which we create, transform, and use information to relate to our environment and one another.

Selection involves the selective attention to particular environmental information sources from all those to which an individual is exposed. Interpretation consists of the transformation of those messages into a form that has value and utility for the individual. Retention involves short- and long-term, semantic and episodic, memory. In actual operation, selection, interpretation, and retention are very much interrelated activities.

A number of factors influence selection, interpretation, and retention. Many of them have to do with the receiver and his or her needs, attitudes, beliefs, values, goals, capabilities, uses, style, experience, and habits.

Other factors that influence information reception have to do with messages—their origin, mode, physical characteristics, novelty, and organization. Sources also have an impact on reception, through their proximity, attractiveness, credibility, motivation, intention, delivery, status, power, and authority. Message reception may also be affected by factors related to technology and the environment.

Notes

1. See Stuart M. Albert, Lee Alan Becker, and Timothy C. Brock, "Familiarity, Utility, and Supportiveness as Determinants of Information Receptivity," *Journal of Personality and Social Psychology,* Vol. 14, 1970, pp. 292–301. D. E. Broadbent, "A Mechanical Model for Human Attention and Immediate Memory," *Psychological Review,* Vol. 64, 1957, pp. 205–215. Robert T. Craig, "Information Systems Theory and Research: An Overview of Individual Information Processing," in *Communication Yearbook 3.* Ed. by Dan Nimmo (New Brunswick, NJ: Transaction, International Communication Association, 1979), pp. 99–120. D. Deutsch and J. A. Deutsch, "Attention: Some Theoretical Considerations," *Psychological Review,* Vol. 70, 1963, pp. 80–90. Lewis Donohew and Philip Palmgreen, "An Investigation of 'Mechanisms' of Information Selection," *Journalism Quarterly,* Vol. 48, 1971, pp. 624–639. Lewis Donohew and Philip Palmgreen, "Reappraisal of Dissonance and the Selective Exposure Hypothesis," *Journalism Quarterly,* Vol. 48, 1971, pp. 412–420. Anne M. Treisman, "Strategies and Models

of Selective Attention," *Psychological Review,* Vol. 76, No. 3, 1969, pp. 282–299. Sally Planalp and Dean E. Hewes, "A Cognitive Approach to Communication Theory: Cognito Ergo Dico?" in *Communication Yearbook 5.* Ed. by Michael Burgoon (New Brunswick, NJ: Transaction, 1982), pp. 49–78. Klaus Krippendorff, "The Past of Communication's Hoped-For Future," *Journal of Communication,* Vol. 43, 1993, pp. 34–44.

2. Samuel L. Becker, "Visual Stimuli and the Construction of Meaning," in *Visual Learning, Thinking and Communication.* Ed. by Bikkar S. Randhawa (New York: Academic Press, 1978), pp. 39–60.

3. Broadbent, 1957.

4. Craig, 1979, p. 102.

5. See Norman F. Dixon, *Preconscious Processing* (London: Wiley, 1981).

6. The issue of *what* is recalled under hypnosis and drugs is relatively controversial. While it was long believed that the information remembered was in its "original, unaltered" form, recent studies have suggested that often it is a transformed, elaborated, and often distorted version, changed by time and circumstance. For a discussion of these issues, see Elizabeth Loftus, *Memory* (Reading, MA: Addison-Wesley, 1980), pp. 54–62.

7. Craig, 1979, p. 103.

8. Morton Hunt, *The Universe Within* (New York: Simon & Schuster, 1982), p. 85.

9. Hunt, 1982, p. 86.

10. Hunt, 1982, p. 86.

11. For a more detailed description of information-processing stages and dynamics see Geoffrey R. Loftus and Elizabeth F. Loftus, *Human Memory: The Processing of Information* (Hillsdale, NJ: Lawrence Erlbaum), 1976; and Peter H. Lindsay and Donald A. Norman, *Human Information Processing* (New York: Academic, 1977).

12. Hunt, 1982, p. 104.

13. G. Loftus and E. Loftus, 1976, p. 8. The authors provide a useful overview and model of information processing and memory in their "Introduction." See also Hunt, 1982, especially Ch. 3, and Elizabeth Loftus, 1980, especially Ch. 2.

14. G. Loftus and E. Loftus, 1976, p. 8.

15. George Mandler, *Cognitive Psychology: An Essay in Cognitive Science* (Hillsdale, NJ: Lawrence Erlbaum, 1985), pp. 92–94. Lists of distinguishing characteristics are presented here in shortened form.

16. E. Tulving, *Elements of Episodic Memory* (Oxford, England: Oxford University Press, 1983). See discussion in Mandler, 1985, pp. 106–107; and Gillian Cohen, *Memory in the Real World* (Hillsdale, NJ: Lawrence Erlbaum, 1989), pp. 114–115.

17. Cohen, 1989, pp. 114–115.

18. Cohen, 1989, pp. 114–115.

19. Based on a listing and discussion by Cohen, 1989, pp. 217–221.

20. One of the most widely cited classifications in recent years was provided in the writings of Abraham Maslow, "A Theory of Human Motivation," *Psychological Review,* Vol. 50, 1943, pp. 370–396. The framework differentiates between basic biological needs and "higher order" psychological and social needs.

21. Maslow, 1950.

22. Maslow, 1950.

23. See Elihu Katz, Jay G. Blumler, and Michael Gurevitch, "Utilization of Mass Communication by the Individual," in *The Uses of Mass Communications,* Jay G. Blumler and Elihu Katz, eds. (Beverly Hills, CA: Sage, 1974), pp. 22–23; and Alan M. Rubin, "Audience Activity and Media Use," *Communication Monographs,* Vol. 60, 1993, pp. 98–105.

24. Lawrence R. Wheeless, "The Effects of Attitude, Credibility, and Homophily on Selective Exposure to Information," *Speech Monographs,* Vol. 41, April 1974, pp. 329–338.

25. Cf. Philip Zimbardo, *Shyness* (Reading, MA: Addison-Wesley); James C. McCroskey, "Oral Communication Apprehension: A Summary of Recent Theory and Research," *Human Communication Research,* Vol. 4, 1977, pp. 78–96; Gerald M. Phillips and Nancy J. Metzger, "The Reticent Syndrome: Some Theoretical Considerations about Etiology and Treatment," *Speech Monographs,* Vol. 40, 1973; James C. McCroskey, "The Communication Apprehension Perspective," in *Avoiding Communication: Shyness, Reticence, and Communication Apprehension.* Ed. by John A. Daly and James C. McCroskey (Beverly Hills, CA: Sage, 1984), pp. 12–38

26. Loftus, 1980, pp. 24–25.

27. Loftus, 1980, pp. 24–25.

28. Nan Lin, *The Study of Human Communication* (New York: Bobbs-Merrill, 1973), pp. 44–46.

29. Wheeless, 1974.

30. Carl I. Hovland and W. Weiss, "The Influence of Source Credibility on Communication Effectiveness," *Public Opinion Quarterly,* Vol. 15, 1951, pp. 635–650; for a discussion of the role of credibility in communication see James C. McCroskey, *An Introduction to Rhetorical Communication* (Englewood Cliffs, NJ: Prentice Hall, 1986), especially Ch. 4.

31. The way we explain behavior to ourselves is the focus of work in an area called *attribution theory.* See David R. Seibold and Brian H. Spitzberg, "Attribution Theory and Research: Formalization, Review, and Impli-

cations for Communication," in *Progress in Communication Sciences,* Vol. 3. Ed. by Brenda Dervin and M. J. Voight (Norwood, NJ: Ablex, 1981), pp. 85–125.

32. "What Is TV Doing to America?" *U.S. News and World Report,* August 2, 1982, p. 29.

33. Bill Carter, "Two Upstart Networks Getting Black Viewers," *New York Times,* Oct. 7, 1996, p. c16.

34. *Television and Behavior: Ten Years of Scientific Progress and Implications for the Eighties,* Vol. 1: Summary Report (Rockville, MD: National Institute of Mental Health, 1982), p. 24.

35. *Television and Behavior,* 1982, p. 26.

36. Hunt, 1982, pp. 119–121.

7 Verbal Messages

In this chapter

Why . . .

- Language and reality are sometimes mistaken for one another.

- We follow rules when we engage in conversations.

- Stereotypes about which gender is most talkative are misleading.

- Verbal messages say as much about our relationships as they do the topic of conversation.

- Metacommunication is important.

Message Production

Producing messages is as fundamental to our lives as receiving them. Virtually every aspect of our behavior—our language, tone of voice, appearance, eyes, actions, even our use of space and time—is a potential source of information that may be selected for attention, interpreted, remembered, and acted upon by others.

An Illustration

As a way to introduce the topic of message production, consider the following scenario involving a job interview:

It's time to get serious about finding a job. A friend calls your attention to an advertisement online for a position that sounds interesting at a company whose name you recognize. You prepare a resume and send it off with a cover letter.

Several days later you get a call and an interview is scheduled.

You decide that it's wise to spend time preparing. You gather some information on the organization and plan what you'll say if they ask why you want the position and why you are not working now. You also make up a list of questions you would like to ask them and give some thought to the kind of impression you would like to create.

When the day of the interview arrives, you dress well and arrive a few minutes early. You feel well-prepared and are ready to make a good impression. When the interviewer arrives, you greet her enthusiastically with "Hello. How are you?", shake her hand, and take a seat next to the desk. You take a deep breath, hoping that will help you relax.

As the questions begin to come, you try to respond in a way that will lead the interviewer to see you as comfortable yet not overly informal, interested but not overly assertive, composed yet spontaneous, self-assured but not arrogant, interested in the job but not desperate.

After what seems like about an hour, she says she has no more questions, and asks if you do. You inquire about starting salary, opportunities for advancement, and benefits—questions you selected because they would yield information you needed, while creating the impression of competence and alertness.

After brief responses, she thanks you for coming, and indicates that she will be in touch with you as soon as all the applicants for the position have been considered. You respond, "Thanks," get up, and leave.

Now let's examine the situation from the organization's point of view: The task of finding a qualified person was initiated long before the interview, with the collection of information and the preparation of the job description and advertisement. In a more general sense, the recruitment process actually began with the firm's advertising and public relations efforts over the years.

After screening many applications, the list of people to be interviewed was finalized. The goal of the interview itself was to create a positive, yet realistic, impression of the organization and the job and to evaluate candidates' suitability for the position.

Questions were asked from a standardized interview guide. They were designed to help probe candidates' technical qualifications, while giving the interviewer a sense of how much "homework" applicants had done to prepare for the interview, how composed and confident they were, how they approached problems, how they dealt with people, and how they felt about themselves. Typical interview questions include:

- How did you learn about the position?
- How much do you know about the company?
- Where did you go to school?
- What was your major? Why did you select that field?
- What experience have you had that is relevant to this job?
- What are your greatest strengths and weaknesses?
- What are you looking for in this position?
- What questions do you have about the job?
- What are your long-term career objectives?

Encoding and Decoding

In a situation such as the one described, each party is putting forth a good deal of effort to provide information and to create particular kinds of impressions. The individuals involved have specific goals in mind and communicate in ways designed to achieve them. This process—converting an idea into a message—is termed *encoding.* Some of the messages that become significant for others are intentionally encoded. Our hope is that the individuals for whom our messages are prepared will *decode* them—translate the message into an idea—more or less as we intend.

Even in circumstances like the job interview discussed previously—where participants have a clear idea of the meaning they want to convey through their messages—they are also likely to communicate information that is unintended. This happens no matter how well we plan or rehearse. An inappropriate greeting, evasiveness in answering a question, a shaky voice, an abrupt change of topic, a misused word, a poorly constructed phrase, the lack of eye contact, or a sweaty brow can easily have as much—or more—impact as the messages we try to encode intentionally.

The messages we produce fall into two broad categories: verbal and nonverbal. In this chapter, we will examine verbal messages in some detail. Nonverbal messages are the focus of the next chapter.

Process- versus Meaning-Centered Models of Communication

As we discussed in Chapter 3, many of the major models of communication emphasize the process of communication. These models focus on message transmission and are concerned with the channel, sender, receiver, noise, and feedback. Such models, and some of our discussion of verbal messages, focus on sending and receiving a message. Looking at communication in this way has several advantages. The models allow us to examine how messages may get lost or distorted in the communication process and how receivers may miss the message sent. For example, the phrase "brick red" may be used by someone interested in fashion. Someone uninterested in fashion may differentiate red from orange, but not attach specific labels to distinct shades of red. If someone uses a very specific color label, he or she may be greeted by a blank stare from others who are not concerned about this type of distinction.

Another view of communication focuses on communication as the generation of meaning. John Fiske describes this model by saying:

> For communication to take place I have to create a message out of signs. This message stimulates you to create a meaning for yourself that relates in some way to the meaning that I generated in my message in the first place. The more we share the same codes, the more we use the same sign systems, the closer our two "meanings" of the message will approximate.[1]

Note that this definition relies on concepts such as signs, codes, and meaning. In this view, messages are constructed of signs which produce meaning in interaction with receivers.[2]

Codes are the systems into which signs are organized. This view emphasizes the meaning while the process model emphasizes the sender and receiver.

The theories we discuss in this chapter are examples of both the process and meaning-centered views of communication. Both viewpoints contribute to our understanding of the phenomenon of communication.

The Nature of Language

Verbal messages make use of alphanumeric language, one of humanity's most impressive accomplishments. About 10,000 distinct languages and dialects are in use today, and each is unique in some respects.[3] There are also a number of commonalities among languages. All spoken languages, for instance, make use of a distinction between vowels and consonants, and in nearly all languages the subject precedes the object in declarative sentences.[4] Every language has an identifiable pattern and set of rules relative to:

- *Phonology.* The way sounds are combined to form words
- *Syntax.* The way words are combined into sentences
- *Semantics.* The meanings of words on the basis of their relationship to one another and to elements in the environment
- *Pragmatics.* The way in which language is used in practice

Physiological Factors

Some general similarities among languages may be the result of a common ancestry. Major similarities, however, appear to be more the result of human physical and mental capacities. Although a number of animal species can produce auditory messages, even primates with their ability for vocalization lack the basic physiological capacity of humans.

As shown in Figure 7.1, the human larynx located at the upper end of the trachea or windpipe is strengthened by cartilage that supports the vocal cords. When air from the lungs passes over the vocal cords with a greater force than occurs during normal breathing, the cords vibrate. The vibrations that result are called *voicing.* As the vocal cords are tightened, the pitch of the voice rises; as they are loosened, the pitch lowers. The position of the tongue provides additional variation in sound production. As the air is projected with voice-producing force, it is affected by the vocal cords and the tongue, as well as by the lips, mouth, teeth, and jaw.

The position of the tongue, lips, and jaw are the primary factors involved in the creation of the vowel sounds in English. When the out-flowing breath creates friction against the teeth, lower lip, or the upper parts of the mouth or tongue, sounds such as the American English pronunciation of f, v, s, z, th, sh, and zh are produced. If the breath is stopped momentarily by movement of the lower lip or some part of the tongue, another sort of friction results, creating sounds such as that of p, b, t, d, k, and g. When the breath is rapidly and intermittently stopped, trills or flips result, which are associated with the pronunciation of rr in Spanish, and tt in words such as butter or letter in English. If the breath stream is stopped in the mouth such that it is forced through the nasal passages, the result is a nasal

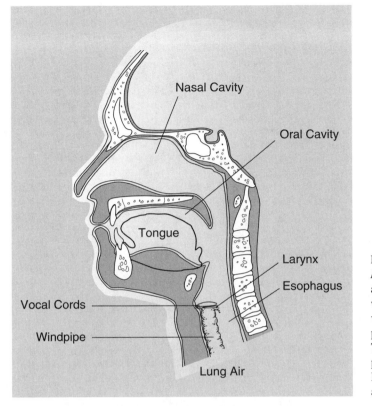

FIGURE 7.1 *Human Sound Production* The larynx is located at the upper end of the trachea or windpipe. Air passing through the vocal cords causes vibrations that produce human voice patterns. Tightening of the vocal cords produces high-pitched sounds; loosening the cords results in a lower pitch.

sound common to French and to the English pronunciation of b, m, d, n, and g.[5] Sounds of letters are combined to form words, and words to form phrases and sentences.

Cognitive Factors

Human physiology only partially explains the workings of the communication process. Controlling these mechanisms are the brain and nervous system, which enable us to sense, make sense of, and relate to our environment and one another. Here, the differences between humans and other animals are striking.

One example will help to illustrate this point. Studies of chimps and gorillas who have been taught American sign language indicate clearly that primates can be taught to use language. However, the total vocabulary of the most successful of these "students" was four hundred words. In contrast, the average human has a vocabulary nearly two hundred times that large.[6]

Findings from neurophysiological research have pointed to the importance of particular areas of the brain for linguistic functioning. Especially important in this regard are *Broca's Area* and *Wernicke's Area,* both of which are located in the left half or hemisphere of the brain.[7] See Figure 7.2. Research suggests that ideas or feelings that an individual

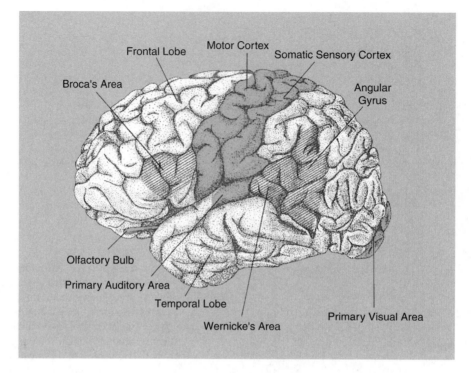

FIGURE 7.2   *Left Hemisphere of the Human Brain*

wishes to vocalize are translated into an appropriate auditory pattern in Wernicke's Area and then transmitted to Broca's Area, which activates the electrical impulses needed to mobilize the voice-producing mechanisms and to create the intended vocalization.[8] This conclusion is supported by studies that have shown that damage to Broca's Area of the brain disturbs the production of speech but has much less impact on comprehension, whereas damage to Wernicke's Area disrupts all aspects of language use.[9]

Language Acquisition

A good deal of attention has been devoted to determining precisely how and when we first develop competency in the use of language. Some linguists contend that the basic structure of language is innate in humans and that a child needs to learn only the surface details of the language spoken in his or her environment. Others see language acquisition as a part of the general development of the individual.[10] Both groups agree that interaction between the individual and the environment is essential to linguistic competence. Studies have demonstrated that without the capacity and opportunity to talk with others, no language capability develops.[11]

There are two broad perspectives on language development—the psycholinguistic approach and the sociolinguistic approach:[12]

1. *The psycholinguistic approach.* Early utterances—*protowords* (the forerunners of words) and words themselves—are based on a child's personalized understanding of the world. Language is a means for the expression of meanings he or she has learned.
2. *The sociolinguistic approach.* Language development occurs when a child experiences a need to communicate. Language is learned through social interaction and is a means for accommodating the demands of social life.

Studies of the first few months of life suggest that language acquisition begins with random "coos" and "giggles" in the presence of family members and other familiar persons, as illustrated in Figure 7.3. At age six to nine months, the "coos" and "giggles" are replaced by babbling sounds; and by eighteen months, most children can form a few simple words—dada, papa, mama, or nana.[13]

The speech patterns of others in the environment are important during this stage and throughout language acquisition. Generally, the speech of those who care for and speak to a child differs from adult language use. Vocabulary is simplified; intonation patterns are exaggerated; sentences are simple; frequent questions are asked by mothers; and frequent assertions are made by fathers.[14] This phenomenon is known as child directed speech.[15]

During the earliest stages of language development children use single words to label, assert, or question.[16] In addition to describing an important person, for example, "mama" may be used as an assertion. "Mama!" may mean, "I want you!" or "I need you, now!" Posed as a question, "Mama?" is a way of saying, "Where are you?" or "Will you come help me?" or "Is that you?" By the time most children reach the age of two, they are able to use language to express any number of meanings such as:[17]

- *Nomination.* Naming
- *Recurrence.* Acknowledging recurrence or reappearance
- *Denial.* Rejecting an idea
- *Nonexistence.* Acknowledging the absence or disappearance of something or someone
- *Rejection.* Preventing an activity or appearance of something or someone
- *Location.* Specifying the relationship between two objects
- *Possession.* Associating an object with someone or something
- *Attribution.* Relating objects to one another
- *Experience + experiencer.* A living thing affected by an event
- *Action + actor.* A living thing receives the force of an action
- *Action + object.* An object affected by an action or activity

As illustrated in Figure 7.3, when a child reaches the age of two and beyond, he or she begins to form two-word sentences: "The two-word stage is a time for experimenting with many binary semantic-syntactic relations such as possessor-possessed ("Mommy sock"), actor-action ("Cat sleeping"), and action-object ("Drink soup").[18]

Although the child's vocabulary is growing, words are being used primarily to define specific, concrete actions and objects. A "car" may be understood as "a way to go to the store," and a "jack-in-the-box" is "what plays music and pops up." From this point on, a child's vocabulary and ability to form sentences progresses rapidly. Before youngsters are three, most are able to use their three-hundred to four-hundred word vocabularies to create well-formed sentences of three, four, and more words.[19]

Child's Age	Coordination		Language
4 months		 Holds head up.	Coos and chuckles when people play with him/her.
6 to 9 months		 Can sit alone and pull himself/herself up into a standing position.	Babbles continually, sounding like this: "gagagag; yayayaya; dadadada."
12 to 18 months		 First stands alone, then walks along furniture, and, finally, walks alone.	Uses a few words, follows simple commands, and knows what "no" means.
18 to 21 months		 Walking looks stiff and jerky, sits in a chair, can crawl down stairs, and throw a ball (clumsily).	Understands simple questions and begins to put two or three words together in sentences.
24 to 27 months		 Runs well, but falls when making a quick turn. Can also walk up and down stairs.	Uses short sentences composed of words from a 300–400 word vocabulary.
30 to 33 months		 Has good hand and finger coordination and can manipulate objects well.	Vocabulary increases in size, and three and four word sentences are prevalent; language begins to sound adult like.
36 to 39 months		 Runs smoothly and negotiates sharp turns; walks stairs by alternating feet; can ride a tricycle, stand on one foot (briefly), and jump twelve inches in the air.	Talks in well-formed sentences, following rather complex grammatical rules; others can generally understand what he/she is talking about.

FIGURE 7.3   *The Development of Language Skills*

Source: "The Development of Language Skills" from Frank Smith and George A. Miller (eds.), *The Genesis of Language.* Copyright © 1966 by the MIT Press. Reprinted with permission.

As a child grows older, his or her phonetic, syntactic, semantic, and pragmatic skills develop. Words are used in increasingly more abstract ways. Whereas "dog" to the toddler meant "my dog Spot," to the youngster it may refer to "my dog Spot and John's dog Rusty." And in later stages of development, "dog" becomes "a kind of pet" and later "a specific kind of four-legged animal."

What began as the use of words and sentences to refer to things that are immediate and tangible gradually evolves to a capability for referring to ideas and objects that are abstract or distant. Thus, as a child develops increasing skill in the use of language, the linkage between his or her words and the particular events of the immediate surroundings becomes progressively more remote. For an adult, any word's meaning is an abstraction based on a lifetime of experiences.

Language is an incredibly powerful tool. We use language not only in vocal but also in written form, not only in single sentences but in lengthy documents and databases, not only face-to-face but also in situations involving communication technologies. We can classify the major everyday uses of language into three categories: (1) Representation; (2) Conversation; and (3) Social and Public Communication.

Representation

Language and Reality

At the most basic level, language enables us to name and symbolically represent elements in our world. Ferdinand de Saussure, a noted linguist, maintains that the relationship between the word (the "signifier") and the object it represents ("the signified") is an arbitrary one. With the exception of a few onomatopoeic words like "whoosh" and "clang," there is no intrinsic connection between the objects and the "signs" we use to refer to them. Some of the labels refer to the tangible and concrete—friends, teachers, books, courses, reading, and writing. Language also provides the means through which we represent abstract concepts—friendship, learning, love, knowledge, freedom. Through language, we are able to manipulate symbols in our thinking. We can create, test, and refine our theories or understandings of the world.

The relationship between language and the "reality" it represents is complex.

In the Middle Ages, for example, the word *Abracadabra* was believed to be capable of curing fever. Apparently, the first prescription for its use came from a poem on medicine by Quintus Serenus Sammonicus, a doctor who accompanied the Roman Emperor Severus on an expedition to Britain in 208 AD. The word was to be written on a triangular piece of paper. The sheet of paper was to be worn on a piece of flax around the patient's neck for nine days and then thrown backwards over the shoulder into a stream that ran eastward. Presumably, when the word disappeared, so would the ills of the patient.[20]

The words and concepts we have available to represent experience guide us toward particular ways of understanding reality. In English, a common arrangement of nouns and verbs is:

subject → verb → object

RESEARCH PROFILE

Studying Everyday Conversation • *Jenny Mandelbaum*

Conversations are important aspects of our day-to-day activities. Professor Mandelbaum illustrates a systematic way to study these often taken-for-granted interactions and demonstrates how complex our conversations actually are.

• • •

It is often pointed out that we are so immersed in communication that it is hard for us to see it objectively or analytically. This is especially the case with everyday conversation, even though in many ways it is the "currency" of our daily lives. Once we begin to take a close look at ordinary conversation though—both the things we say, and the ways we say them with our words, voices, and bodies—we may begin to revise our taken-for-granted views of communication. Close examination of everyday conversations in a variety of settings can be accomplished by collecting audio- and videotape recordings, transcribing them in detail, and then using the transcripts as guides while analyzing the tapes in detail. Close looking and listening of this kind reveal a number of unexpected features of our everyday communication practices. Describing and revealing these taken-for-granted but often unnoticed patterns of communication in ordinary interaction is the focus of my research.

For instance, we commonly believe that we communicate in order to exchange information, and that this is a major function of our everyday encounters. It turns out, though, that even simply exchanging information (something that we rarely do, in fact), is fraught with concerns of self-presentation and identity (e.g., how do I seem to the person I am talking with? What are they making of what I'm trying to do?); and relationship (e.g., do I appear to be "acting superior" by telling them this? Am I being respectful? or respected?). That is, any communicative action that we engage in shapes, and is shaped by, identity and relational concerns. We may not always be completely aware of this, but looking closely at the interactional practices we use to "put together" different actions in conversation can help us understand first of all how these actions are accomplished, and second, how concerns about identities and relationships are inextricably implicated in the ways in which we engage in everyday communication.

Two examples are: "Bill hit Mary," or "You make me mad." The pattern is "one person or thing causing another person or thing." Implicit in the form is a sense of one-way causality—the subject (noun) causes (verb) the outcome in the object (noun). Patterns of representational language use are more than just ways of talking. They imply and encourage ways of thinking—in this instance, they encourage us to see things in terms of "this" causing "that."

According to the *Sapir–Whorf hypothesis,* language "is not merely a reproducing instrument for voicing ideas but rather is itself the shaper of ideas. . . . We dissect nature along the lines laid down by our native language."[21] For example, although colors occur on a continuous spectrum without natural divisions, we classify this spectral band into discrete sections (such as blue versus green). Everyone who speaks the same language agrees on these labels. While many languages classify colors in the same way English does, some languages divide the spectrum differently. A person's ability to remember a particular color correlates to the codeability of a word for that color in the speaker's language.

Although the language system available to us has a major impact on our perceptions, our ability to understand external reality is not controlled entirely by our language.[22] The realities which confront us have a great impact on our language and the patterns we develop and use. In a society in which people's survival depends upon fishing, for instance, the language will include many words and phrases that capture subtleties of weather, the sea, boats, and fishing. These subtleties are absent in the common language of more technologically-oriented societies in which computer and electronics terminology abound. Similarly, the language used by an engineer to describe the structures of the world may be difficult to comprehend by a friend who is a lawyer or a psychologist.

The use of language is such a basic and subtle aspect of human life that its representational and "artificial" nature are often overlooked. This is especially so when particular language use patterns are widely shared. As long as others seem to share our meaning, we believe that representation and "reality" are the same. Unfortunately, there are many instances where we *assume* our words are being understood and their meanings shared when they may not be. Researchers have shown that even terms like "always," "often," and "rarely," when used by health professionals in the context of laboratory reports, are subject to a wide range of interpretation. A study of physicians and health care administrators in several settings showed that estimates of the meaning of "always" varied from 60 percent to 100 percent. For "sometimes," estimates ranged from 0 to 90 percent; and for "rarely," meanings varied from 0 to 95 percent.[23]

Generally, language seems to work "as if it were real." Most often, when we ask someone to pass the salt, their arm extends, grasps a salt container, and, without much difficulty at all, places the salt container in front of us. But there are also a number of circumstances in life which remind the reflective person that an uncritical belief in the "reality of language" can lead to difficulties. Getting a message through to someone who should quit smoking, lose weight, drive more carefully, or "turn over a new leaf" is a much more difficult proposition.

Similarly, a man saying that he is "in love" may not tell us all that much about the way he feels, how he will behave, or what he really thinks about the concept and the person to whom his words refer. We use the words "I do," for example, to seal the bonds of marriage. Although these two words have great symbolic value to the parties involved at that moment, the stability of the marriage will depend not upon the words but upon the behaviors and ideologies to which they refer.

Beyond the problems that arise from confusing words with the people, behaviors, actions, or ideas to which they refer, additional complexity in language results because in actual use words seldom represent the same things to two different people. As noted earlier, the meanings each of us attaches to words and phrases depend on our experiences. As a consequence, the meanings of words are subjective and, to some extent, unique to each individual. The following exchange illustrates the point:

Lynn: (9:00 in the morning) Marty, I need that breakdown on the Johnson deal that you've been working on for this afternoon's meeting.

Marty: Okay, Lynn, you'll have it soon.

Marty: Sally, that memo for sales has got to go out this morning.

Sally: I'll get it right out.

Lynn: (4:30 that afternoon) Marty, where's that information you promised to get me this afternoon?

Marty: You should have had it this morning. I asked Sally to get it right over to you.

Lynn: Well, it's not here and you know this isn't the first time something like this
has happened . . .

As a result of the day's events, Marty has accumulated more evidence that Sally is incompetent. Lynn has decided once and for all that she simply can't count on Marty, and
Sally is convinced that Marty is always looking for a reason to criticize her. Although all of
these conclusions may be justified, it is also quite possible that at least a partial explanation
of what occurred is to be found in the words and phrases each person used and how they were
interpreted. Initially, Lynn indicated to Marty that she needed the information for the afternoon meeting. Marty told Sally that it had "to go out this morning." But what did "go out this
morning" mean? To Sally, who sent it out at 11:00 A.M. through the interoffice mail system—
it meant *go out* this morning. To Lynn and Marty it meant *be delivered* this morning.

The same kind of difficulties arise in many other settings. For instance, hour after
hour is spent in labor negotiations, arguing over the precise terminology to be used in a
contract. Seemingly innocent words like "should," "will," "are," or "may" can become very
problematic in these circumstances. See Figure 7.4.

Limitations of Language for Representation

Although language functions successfully in many interactions, a group of scholars known
as general semanticists caution that several characteristics of language limit its usefulness.[24]

The Principle of Nonidentity (A is not A).   The principle of nonidentity reminds us that
words are not the same order of "stuff" as the "realities" to which they refer. The world is
constantly changing, while the language available for making sense of it may not. The reverse may also occur when language changes but the reality it refers to doesn't.

A dramatic illustration of the representational limitations of language—and the manner in which these limitations can be overcome—is provided by the New Revised Standard
Version of the Bible. The 1990 version was an update of the 1952 version, both of which
are descendents of the 1611 *King James Bible.* Changes in this edition aim to make language clearer, more contemporary, and more gender- and racially sensitive, as shown in
Box 7.1 (p. 138).[25]

As another example: who would have imagined fifty years ago that advances in electronics would mean that words like *floppy disk, mouse, DVD, CD,* or *MP3* would become
household terms for so many of us?

The Principle of Non-Allness (A is not all A).   The principle of non-allness asserts that
"the map is not the territory"—our language can never represent all of the object, event, or
person to which we are referring. As Anatol Rapoport explains:

> . . . no matter how good a map you make, you cannot represent all of the territory in it.
> Translated into terms of language, it means that no matter how much you say about some
> "thing," "event," "quality," or whatnot, you cannot say all about it.[26]

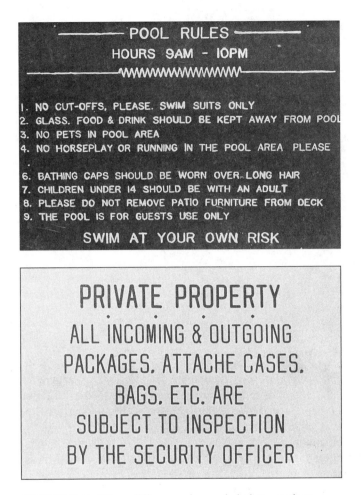

FIGURE 7.4 Minor differences in word choice—such as "should" versus "are" in the signs shown—may have a substantial impact on the significance a message will have.

The Principle of Self-Reflexiveness.   The principle of self-reflexiveness calls attention to the problems that can arise when we use language to talk about our use of language. When we use concepts to talk about concepts, we become increasingly abstract and move progressively into the world of words and away from the world of the tangible.

For example, our self-reflexive capability allows us to label ourselves "successes" or "failures" as if these were actual characteristics that have an existence apart from our representations of them. We may easily forget that one cannot *be* a success or failure but can only be *seen* or *interpreted* as such by someone.

BOX 7.1 • *Changing Language in the Bible*

Mathew 4:4
  1952 Version: "Man does not live by bread alone."
  1990 Version: "One does not live by bread alone."
II Corinthians 11:25
  1952 Version: "Once I was stoned."
  1990 Version: "Once I received a stoning."
Song of Solomon 1:5
  1952 Version: "I am very dark, but comely."
  1990 Version: "I am black and beautiful."

Source: Ari L. Goldman, "New Bible: 'He' Goes the Way of All Flesh," *New York Times*, Sept. 28, 1990, p. A10.

Conversation

Negotiation of Meanings

As we noted at the beginning of this chapter, we can also look at language from a social and interactional perspective. Through language we are able to coordinate our own activities with those of others, to undertake joint projects, to discuss and solve problems, and to share in the pursuit of personal and social needs.

From an interactional perspective, language is a tool for the negotiation of meanings between and among individuals. When we create a spoken or written message, our language serves as the medium to convey our representations. It is our means of projecting ourselves and our ideas into the environment.

As we have discussed previously, the messages we encode are based on meanings influenced by our own experiences, needs, and goals; and, to some extent at least, we are each unique in these terms. When others decode our messages, they do so in terms of the meanings our words have for them—based on their experiences, needs, goals, and capabilities. When people talk about their feelings about "dogs," they, of course, are using the word *dog* to refer to the "dogs-of-their-experience" as they are relevant to the current conversation. When we decode the message, we do so in terms of the "dogs-of-our-experience." See Figure 7.5.

Thus, in any conversation (or written exchange), language serves as a medium through which individuals: (1) code and externalize meanings, and (2) decode and internalize meanings. As the interaction continues, language serves as the channel through which interactants may: (3) discover discrepancies and/or similarities in their meanings, and (4) negotiate a mutuality of meaning appropriate to the purposes at hand. In some circumstances, we may be able to get along fine in a discussion about dogs if one person is

FIGURE 7.5   In everyday usage, we speak and hear based on the meanings words have for us.

thinking of a poodle and the other person is thinking about a pit bull. In other situations, a greater level of mutual understanding would be essential.

Rules and Rituals

Do you get out your cell phone as soon as you leave class? We take our ability to converse with others very much for granted, so much so that it may seem like quite a simple activity. Clearly, this is not the case. As communication researcher Margaret McLaughlin indicates, our ability to engage in conversation presupposes that we have and can use an incredible amount of knowledge:

> . . . not only what we might call *world knowledge* (that groceries cost money, that parents love their children, that dogs bite, etc.), but also more specific knowledge bases, such as the rules of grammar, syntax, etiquette, and so on, as well as specifically *conversational rules* such as "When someone has replied to your summons, disclose the reason for the summons," and "Before saying good-bye to a telephone caller, reach agreement that all topical

talk is completed." What is fascinating about conversation is that the ordinary person rarely reflects upon the vastness of the knowledge store that is required to carry it on.[27]

A *rule* is a prescription, regulation, or requirement. Some rules are obvious and explicit—like the rules of tennis, traffic regulations, or the requirements for membership in a formal group or organization. Other rules are implicit and subtle, like tennis etiquette, or the informal norms and practices expected of members of a group or organization. *Conversational rules* are those largely implicit and subtle regulations that guide our behavior in verbal interaction. They describe how one must, should, or should not behave in interactions with others.[28] Conversational rules facilitate cooperative effort, help to structure and regularize interaction, provide a basis for predicting patterns of communication, and guide us in interpreting the actions of others.

Communication scholars have identified a number of rules that guide our behavior in conversations. We can group these rules into the following categories:[29]

- *Cooperativeness.* Be sincere and make your contributions reasonable, given the agreed-on purpose of the conversation.
- *Informativeness.* Make your contributions as informative as possible or necessary.
- *Responsiveness.* Take account of and be responsive to the informational needs of others.
- *Interactiveness.* Share responsibility with other interactants for guiding and managing the conversation.
- *Conformance.* Know and follow accepted conversational practices. Inform others when you violate a rule.

Cooperativeness.   Without some degree of cooperativeness and willingness to commit to interaction, conversation is impossible. H. Paul Grice, an important contributor to our understanding of conversational rules, called this general rule the *cooperative principle,* out of which flows other maxims of cooperation:[30]

- Don't state the obvious, or restate what others already know.
- Don't be superfluous—don't say too much.
- Make your comments relevant to the topic at hand.

Informativeness.   Conversation also normally involves a commitment to be informative:

- Don't knowingly mislead or say something you believe is false.
- Don't exaggerate or say more than you know.
- Don't withhold or say less than you know.

Responsiveness.   The obligation to be aware of and accommodating to the needs of other interactants involves inferring and responding to other's knowledge and beliefs, responding to questions and requests for information, using a manner and tone that takes account of the needs of other interactants, being clear, being courteous, and avoiding excessive boasting and self-promotion.

Interactiveness. Interactiveness also refers to rules governing the management of the conversation. These commitments have to do with conversational sequences and rituals, including:

1. *Initiating interaction.* Initiating conversations and/or responding to the initiation efforts of others. If, for example, I say: "How are you?" the expectation is that you will participate in the initiation ritual by responding and will do so along the lines of: "Fine, and you?"
2. *Establishing a conversational agenda.* Participating in the process of setting the agenda for discussion such as in a meeting. If, for example, I say: "I guess our main topic of discussion today is how to update our advertising," the expectation is that you will either agree with the agenda as defined and allow it to guide the conversation or disagree and take the lead in suggesting another agenda.
3. *Turn taking as the conversation progresses.* Sometimes called *interaction management.* This is the expectation that people will "take turns" in speaking as a conversation progresses, avoiding monopolizing the discussion and nonparticipation.
4. *Topic shifting.* Changing topics and/or responding to the topic changes of others. The expectation is that topic changes are suggested and agreed to or explicitly negotiated, rather than unilaterally imposed. If you are in the middle of an enthusiastic description of a recent trip to Europe, it is expected that the other person will not interrupt in the middle of your statement and begin talking about a course he or she is thinking of taking. Rules call for the other person to work to produce a gradual, "natural" transition in the topic or to wait until a natural break in the conversation occurs or to introduce a transition that is responsive to you. Thus, he or she might say: "Your talking about the trip reminds me of a new course I learned about while you were away. I really want to tell you about it. It sounds interesting."
5. *Closing.* Terminating conversations and responding to termination initiatives by others—sometimes called *leave-taking.* The expectation is that leave-taking occurs by mutual agreement. That is, it is expected that someone will not get up and walk away while you're in the middle of talking about your trip. As with openings, there are a number of conversational rituals and conventions associated with conversational closings. Thus, a closing like, "OK, then, take care," and a response, such as, "You, too!" serve to signal the desire of the initiator to terminate conversation and provide a standardized way of dealing with what would otherwise be an ambiguous and potentially awkward circumstance.

Conformance. Conformance refers to our obligation to adhere to conversation rules or to provide an explanation when a violation occurs. The expectation is that we will follow rules in our conversations. When violations occur, the consequences are frequently negative. They may include confusion, frustration, misunderstanding, a loss of trust or friendliness among conversants, or a reinterpretation of the value and goals of the conversation by one or more of the parties involved.

There are any number of circumstances in which we violate rules. We may shift a topic abruptly, get up to leave in the middle of a conversation, exaggerate or understate, or say things we don't mean. There may be good reasons for these actions. When rule violations occur, we are expected to explain the reason for the violation. For instance, when you must interrupt or exit a conversation abruptly, an explanation that you just realized you're late for class, together with an apology, will help to excuse the rule violation.

One of the most blatant examples of rule violation happens when one interactant knowingly engages in deception. In such a circumstance, the informativeness rule and, hence, the sharing of information, have been undermined. When all other rules are followed, efforts to deceive may be quite successful. For instance, we may find ourselves persuaded by a cooperative, responsive, and interactive salesperson, even when some of the information provided about a product is incorrect. One of the reasons this occurs, of course, is that we are often better able to make accurate judgments about whether conversational rules are being followed than whether we are being told the truth. If deception is detected, it is likely to have a substantial impact on the conversation and the meanings which result. The consequences of an attempt at deception will depend on the topic, the nature of the relationship between conversants, and the situation.

In some situations, individuals may say things that are untrue, but without the goal of deception. For example, we may say, "That dress looks great on her," but if we are being sarcastic and don't intend our message to be taken literally, we can indicate this through tone of voice or facial expressions.

Rules and the significance of rule violations depend a lot on the situation or context. Our expectations may differ depending on whether we are talking with an intimate friend or a stranger, a child or an adult, a member of the same or opposite sex, a salesperson or a member of the clergy, one other person or several others. Thus, contextual, gender, ethnic, racial, and cultural differences may all have an impact on conversational protocol.

Language and Gender

In most cultures, individual communication behaviors are used by both men and women. For example, men and women may smile to indicate pleasure or raise their voices to indicate anger. According to one estimate, men and women overlap in their communication actions 99 percent of the time.[31] On the other hand, there are scholars who believe that men and women learn to speak differently and that men and women have internalized different norms for conversation.[32] According to this view, men tend to adopt a more competitive style in conversation while women tend to adopt a more cooperative mode. Because gender is the social construction of masculinity and femininity within a culture, these differences may vary by culture. The areas in which differences have been noted by some researchers include: initiation, conversational maintenance and question asking, argumentativeness, and lexical and phonological characteristics.[33]

Initiation.   Women generally spend more time initiating conversations than men. However, topics introduced by men are more likely to be taken note of and carried on by other interactants. The following exchange at a restaurant illustrates a familiar pattern:[34]

> *Maureen:*   What are you going to order?
>
> *Tom:*   The bacon burger.
>
> *Maureen:*   That sounds good. I think I'll have the chicken salad.

RESEARCH PROFILE

Flaming, Politeness, and Netiquette • Ulla Bunz

An increasing number of our verbal messages are exchanged via e-mail. Professor Bunz's research reminds us of the significance of language usage in electronic communication.

• • •

The field of computer-mediated communication has traditionally focused on the interaction between two human beings with the help of or through a communication technology. One example for such an interactive communication technology is electronic mail or e-mail. Since the 1990s, much research has been conducted on negative or hostile language used in e-mail, including flaming. Flaming is described as an intentional personal attack at another person in the online environment, including verbal aggression, the spreading of false information, and public ridicule. At the same time, many handbooks were and still are being published on netiquette—etiquette, or appropriate behavior, on the Internet. These handbooks provide guidelines such as using appropriate address in e-mail, using proper grammar and spelling, or the expected timeframe until one should have responded to an e-mail. However, a very limited number of academic research studies exist related to e-mail courtesy. Rather than focus on hostile behavior like flaming, research on e-mail courtesy focuses on creating and eliciting favorable impressions through language choices.

My research has shown that e-mail messages written with a certain level of politeness usually result in a response which shows an equal level of politeness. Simple linguistic cues, such as a greeting at the beginning of the e-mail, set the tone for a message, and are accommodated by others. Similarly, relationship status in an interaction—such as writing to a potential employer as opposed to a friend—is conveyed by language and the choice of universally recognized phrases. For example, the word "sincerely" is considered to be a formal expression between people of different status, while "could you let me know" is a polite expression in family interaction, and "hey" is a friendly expression among peers. While most people are aware of social situations and the behavior and language choice these require in an off-line environment, people don't always consider their language choice and the impression they will make due to the choice in their e-mail interactions. Research on e-mail courtesy shows that just by including a few seemingly innocuous words one can set a positive tone for the interaction and create the desired impression in the other person's mind.

After the order is taken, and a moment of silence. . . .

> *Maureen:* I went to the mall yesterday to look for a dress for my sister's wedding.
> *Tom:* Yeah?
> *Maureen:* But I couldn't find anything I liked. I guess I'll have to keep looking around.
> *Tom:* (No response.)

As Lea Stewart and colleagues explain: "This example illustrates one way that men may inhibit conversations with women, by giving minimal responses such as 'yeah' or 'oh' to topics introduced by women."[35]

Conversational Maintenance and Question Asking. Women generally spend more time and effort facilitating the continuation of conversation, as is well illustrated in the restaurant dialogue discussed previously. Researchers have also found that when they analyzed tapes of actual conversations, 70 percent of the questions asked by interactants were posed by women.[36]

Argumentativeness. *Argumentativeness* is defined as a stable trait that predisposes an individual in communication situations to advocate positions on controversial issues and to verbally attack the positions that other people take on these issues.[37] In general, men score higher on measures of argumentativeness than women.[38] Although women are able to use this communication strategy when appropriate, they are more likely to believe that arguing is a strategy for dominating and controlling another person.[39]

Lexical and Phonological Characteristics.   Not surprisingly, studies show that women use a larger vocabulary to discuss topics about which they have greater interest and experience. And, conversely, in areas where men have greater expertise, their vocabularies are broader. There are also differences in the adjectives used by the two sexes. Robin Lakoff has noted that words like *adorable, charming, sweet,* and *lovely* are more likely to be used by women, while men are more apt to use terms such as *nice, good,* or *pretty.*[40] Studies suggest that women use intensifying adverbs more than men—for example, "I *really* enjoyed the book," or "I'm *so* disappointed."

Content and Relationship

Whether we use our words in a planned, intentional way or in a less systematic, unintentional fashion, verbal messages provide potential information of two types: (1) information about *content*—the topic under discussion, and (2) information about *relationships*—about the source and how the source regards the intended recipient(s).[41] A written or spoken presentation designed to convince us to vote for a particular candidate, for instance, includes *content* about the candidate, his or her qualifications, campaign promises, and potentials. Also, the presentation provides messages as to the level of preparation, interest, education, intelligence, attitudes, beliefs, mood, and motives of the speaker. And the speech may provide clues as to how the speaker regards the intended audience. Does the speaker "look down" on the audience? Does he or she consider them to be powerful, authoritative, educated? Does he or she fear or resent them?

To further clarify this distinction, consider the following statement:

Marge: Carol is an incompetent and uncaring person!

From a content point of view, Marge is indicating that there are some things about Carol that bother her. Beyond that, Marge may also be providing some clues about herself. She seems to feel quite strongly about Carol. Perhaps she is a fairly outspoken individual. Perhaps she is judgmental and intolerant of individual differences. Perhaps she is just jealous or envious of Carol.

In her communication about Carol and herself, Marge may also be providing clues to how she regards the person to whom she is speaking. It is likely that Marge sees herself as being, or wanting to be seen as being, closer to the person she's talking to than she is to

Carol. It is also probable that Marge assumes the listener is closer to her than to Carol. One could also infer that she trusts the listener, that she simply doesn't care who knows how she feels about Carol, or that she is pursuing a specific personal motive. At the least, we can safely assume that Marge has some reason for wanting to share her reaction with the listener. No matter what her intent is, however, her message has both a content and relationship component.

Consider two more examples:

1. ***Daddy:*** (Following the sound of breaking glass) Marc.

   Marc: Daddy, I didn't do it. Honest.

2. ***Ed:*** Mary, I want to talk to you.

   Mary: Ed, I know what you're going to say. I'm sorry, I never intended for you to get hurt . . . It just happened.

In all respects except the content, these two exchanges are quite similar. In each instance the first speaker is really saying very little from a topical point of view. In fact, in both cases, the individuals that initiate the conversation provide no information that identifies a topic for discussion. The second speakers, however, provide the basis for a number of inferences. Both Marc and Mary seem to assume they are being asked about a particular act, even though this is not necessarily the case. They respond *defensively*—as though they have been attacked. Their responses, perhaps motivated by guilt, fear, or both, are messages from which one could infer something about their feelings and attitudes. Their messages also provide the basis for inferences as to how they feel about the other person. Both Marc and Mary are concerned about their relationships, by necessity or choice. For whatever reasons, both seem to see themselves in a "one-down" or inferior position, in which they must justify, explain, and/or seek forgiveness or approval from Daddy or Ed.

Let's examine a slightly more complicated situation:

Bill: My wife and I are really excited. We've got a chance to go to Las Vegas this weekend on a special half-price package on the Internet. It wasn't really the time we had picked to go, but we just can't pass it up . . . Doubt we'll ever have a chance to go so cheaply again.

Todd: I considered going, but with my job the way it is, I decided it's not smart to spend money on travel this year.

In the brief exchange, Bill is providing information about the prospect of an upcoming trip. He's also explaining that it will cost only half the normal amount. The fact that Bill is talking about the trip at all may suggest that he's the type of person who enjoys sharing his excitement. Or he may be boasting; perhaps he is seeking attention or recognition.

By explaining that he got a special price, Bill may provide a clue that he wishes to be seen as clever, shrewd, or economical. Or, alternatively, his message may suggest that he is the kind of person who feels the need to justify or apologize for his good fortune. The decision to share his plans with Todd suggests that Bill cares about or values Todd, or that he wants to impress Todd, or to solicit support or encouragement.

Todd says that he does not think it is a smart time to spend money on a trip. Beyond this, his response may provide a clue that he is unwilling to share in Bill's excitement. He may be jealous. Or he may fail to detect Bill's excitement. Todd's response also may suggest that he wishes to be seen as more rational than Bill—at least in this instance. From a relationship perspective, it seems that he feels no obligation to acknowledge or contribute to Bill's excitement and has no particular interest in providing an audience for further discussion of Bill's trip.

While the content aspect of an utterance is generally fairly straightforward to discern, it may be harder for interactants to be confident about their understanding of the relationship aspect. Nonetheless, all utterances can be, and generally are, understood at both content and relationship levels.

Thus, language not only communicates something *about* a relationship, it also helps to create the relationship. For example, we are more likely to feel close to someone who discloses a very personal feeling to us. That person trusts us enough to share a hidden feeling, and we reciprocate by deepening our friendship.

Metacommunication

Sometimes we engage in conversations about our conversation; or to put it differently, we communicate about communication. This is termed *metacommunication*.[42]

1. *Brenda:* Matt, let's go to a movie tonight.
2. *Matt:* Oh, I don't know, Brenda. Can we talk about it later?
3. *Brenda:* That's becoming a pattern around here, Matt. You never want to carry a discussion through to a conclusion.
4. *Matt:* The pattern *I see* is the one where you refuse to end a conversation until you've gotten the decision you want.
5. *Brenda:* Same old story. You can't handle any negative feedback. One small criticism, and you get so defensive.

In the first exchange above—(1) and (2)—Matt and Brenda are discussing the possibility of going to a movie. With Brenda's response (3), there is a shift from talking about the movie to talking about the way Matt responded. In his next response (4), Matt comments on Brenda's communication. Brenda continues the process of metacommunication as she replies (5), carrying forth a fairly common pattern of communication.

Of course, metacommunication can be used in a positive way in a relationship, too. Consider this conversation:

1. *Sally:* Jim, let's go to a movie tonight.
2. *Jim:* Oh, I don't know, Sally. Can we talk about it later?
3. *Sally:* That doesn't really sound like you, Jim. Is everything okay?
4. *Jim:* I got some bad news at work today and don't feel like going out.
5. *Sally:* What's wrong? Can I help?

In this instance, Sally and Jim begin by discussing going to a movie (1 and 2), but Sally interprets Jim's reply as atypical and asks him about it (3). This metacommunication leads Jim to disclose his bad news (4), and then Sally asks for more information (5).

Social and Public Communication

Production and Distribution of Social Realities

Language is the primary means used for social and public expression. We are confronted by public speeches on all topics, as well as by news, entertainment, advertisements, e-mail, and public relations messages. These messages are a pervasive part of the environment in which we live. Messages and meanings which are widely distributed and popularized through public communication become accepted realities. As communication scholar Lee Thayer explains:

> What is uniquely characteristic of human communication . . . is the fact that (human) . . . sophistication . . . has made possible the emergence and evolution of a purely communicational environment or reality . . . i.e., an environment or reality comprised of anything that can be and is talked about. Whatever can be talked about comprises a reality in the sense that it must be adapted to and dealt with in much the same way as that reality which is subject to sensory validation (the physical environment).[43]

Thus, it is largely through social and public communication that the shared realities of language and meanings are created, perpetuated, reaffirmed, or altered. The familiar story of "The Emperor's New Clothes" (Box 7.2) gives us insight into the powerful and pervasive nature of the basic process by which this happens. Messages are produced, distributed, believed, used, socially accepted, and eventually take on an objective reality that is seldom questioned.

Implications and Applications

- Language is the primary means of recording information for ourselves, and for producing and transmitting messages for others.
- Our use of language provides messages from which inferences are drawn about our interest in a particular topic, attitudes, education, mood, motives, age, personality, concepts of ourselves, and our regard for our listeners, readers, or viewers.
- Verbal messages may be either oral or written. Written messages (whether in print or electronic formats) are well-suited to situations in which we desire a high degree of control and predictability over the message that is produced and transmitted, or in which a document or record of communication is required. However, compared to oral communication, written message sending and feedback require more time; and it is sometimes more difficult to change one's position once it has been committed to writing. Oral messages create a sense of spontaneity and provide for instantaneous feedback and adjustment of one's position or approach. They leave no document behind, which can be an asset in some circumstances and a liability in others.

BOX 7.2 • *The Emperor's New Clothes*

In the great city in which he lived many strangers came every day. One day two rogues came. They said they were weavers, and declared they could weave the finest cloth anyone could imagine. Their colors and patterns were unusually beautiful, they said, and explained that the clothes made of the cloth possessed the wonderful quality that they became invisible to anyone who was unfit for the office he held or was not very bright or perceptive.

"Those would be most unusual clothes!" thought the Emperor. "If I wore those, I should be able to find out what men in my empire are not fit for the places they have; I could tell the clever ones from the idiots." He asked the men to begin weaving immediately.

They put up two looms, and pretended to be working. They at once demanded the finest silk and the costliest gold; this they put into their own pockets, and worked at the empty looms till late into the night.

After a few weeks passed, the Emperor said to himself, "I should like to know how far they have got on with the cloth." But he felt quite uncomfortable when he thought that those who were not fit for their offices could not see it. He believed, of course, that he had nothing to fear for himself, but he preferred first to send someone else to see how matters stood.

"I will send my honest old Minister to the weavers," thought the Emperor. "He can judge best how the cloth looks, for he has sense, and no one understands his office better than he." So the good old Minister went out into the hall where the two rogues sat working at the empty looms.

"Mercy!" thought the old Minister, and he opened his eyes wide. "I cannot see anything at all! Can I indeed be so stupid? Am I not fit for my office? It will never do for me to tell that I could not see the cloth."

"Haven't you anything to say about it?" asked one of the rogues, as he went on weaving. "It is charming—quite enchanting!" answered the old Minister, as he peered through his spectacles. "What a fine pattern, and what colors! Yes, I shall tell the Emperor that I am very much pleased with it."

The Emperor soon sent another honest officer of the court to see how the weaving was going on, and if the cloth would soon be ready. He fared just like the first: he looked and looked. "Isn't that a pretty piece of cloth?" asked the two rogues; and they displayed and explained the handsome pattern which was not there at all.

"I am not stupid!" thought the man. "Yet it must be that I am not fit for my office. If that is the case, I must not let it be noticed." And so he praised the cloth which he did not see, and expressed his pleasure at the beautiful colors and charming pattern. "Yes, it is enchanting," he told the Emperor.

All the people in the town were talking of the gorgeous cloth. The Emperor wished to see it himself while it was still upon the loom. With a whole crowd of chosen men, among whom were also the two honest statesmen who had already been there, he went to the two cunning rogues.

"Isn't that splendid?" said the two statesmen, who had already been there once. "Doesn't your Majesty approve of the pattern and the colors?" And they pointed to the loom, assuming that the others could see the cloth.

"What's this?" thought the Emperor. "I can see nothing at all! That is terrible. Am I stupid? Am I not fit to be Emperor?" He said aloud, "Oh, it is very beautiful! It is our highest approval." He nodded in a contented way, and gazed at the loom. . . .

The fable of "The Emperor's New Clothes" provides an excellent, though exaggerated, illustration of the process by which our realities are created through language.

- Our words and concepts are our tools for labeling the people, objects, and events around us.
- There are many circumstances in life which remind us of the dangers of reacting to words as if they were the objects, people, or events to which they refer.
- Our representations are seldom, if ever, neutral or value free. They are influenced by our ways of thinking, and, in turn, they guide our thinking. Sometimes the influence is liberating; sometimes it constrains us. For instance, when we use sentences in which the structure is noun → verb → noun, we are more likely to think about the world, and communication, in cause-and-effect terms.
- The labels we use for ourselves—such as intelligent, attractive, poor, or unhappy— direct our thinking about ourselves down particular paths and not others. Likewise, the labels we use for other people—rich, uncaring, friendly, or aggressive, for instance— also guide our ways of thinking about people in particular ways, while discouraging other ways of viewing them.
- In our conversations we expect others to follow a number of rules and rituals— regarding social initiation, turn taking, agenda setting, topic shifts, and leave-taking, for instance. We tend to think little about conversational rules until they are violated. When rules are broken, they often have a great impact on the conversation, on our impression of the rule breaker, and on our concept of the relationship.
- In some instances, women and men use language differently, as a consequence of different patterns of experience. Women are more forthcoming as conversation initiators, question askers, and conversation maintainers. Men may be more argumentative and may work harder to maintain control of conversations.
- Our verbal messages to others, and theirs to us, do two things simultaneously: (1) they relate specific content; and (2) they establish, comment on, reinforce, or alter relationships.
- As we engage in social or public communication, we take part in creating, distributing, reinforcing, or altering the meaning of language and the rules for its use.

Summary

Through our words, sentences, tone, appearance, actions, and other behaviors, we produce messages that are potentially significant sources of information for others. Some of the messages we encode intentionally, others more by accident. Decoding occurs when our messages are attended to and interpreted.

Most of our purposefully-created messages involve the use of language. Languages are similar to one another in several respects. All have rules relative to phonology, syntax, semantics, and pragmatics. Still more basic similarities result from the physiological and cognitive capacities of humans. The physiology of human speech is more advanced than that necessary for vocalizations in other species, and the differences between human mental abilities and those of other animals are even more pronounced. Particular areas of the brain—*Broca's Area* and *Wernicke's Area*—both of which are located in the left hemisphere, are thought to be critical to language use.

Our capacity for language develops from the time we are infants through a progressive series of stages. As adults, we use language not only to refer to the immediate environment as does the child, but also to record, describe, assert, express emotion, question, identify ourselves, entertain, defend, and accomplish a number of other purposes.

Language plays a central role in human interaction in terms of representation, conversation, and social and public communication. At the most basic level it is our means for representing and labeling elements of our environment and one another.

By means of language we negotiate understandings through conversation. Understanding the nature of conversation requires an awareness of the influence of rules and rituals, language and gender differences, content and relationship messages, and metacommunication. Additionally, language provides the medium through which social and public communication take place and the means through which shared communication realities are created.

Notes

1. John Fiske, *Introduction to Communication Studies* (New York: Methuen, 1982), p. 43.

2. Fiske, 1982, p. 3.

3. William S-Y Wang, "Language and Derivative Systems," in *Human Communication: Language and Its Psychobiological Basis.* Ed. by William S-Y Wang (San Francisco: Freeman, 1982), p. 36.

4. Wang, 1982, p. 36.

5. Harold Whitehall, "The English Language," in *Webster's New World Dictionary of the American Language* (Cleveland: World, 1964), pp. xv–xxix.

6. Morton Hunt, *The Universe Within* (New York: Simon and Schuster, 1982), pp. 36–37.

7. What is named Broca's Area is based on the pioneering research by Paul Broca during the late 1800s. Wernicke's Area is named for German neurologist Karl Wernicke, who is acknowledged as the first to discover that damage to that section of the left hemisphere would lead to difficulties in speech comprehension. For a detailed discussion of the history and significance of this work to neurophysiology and speech, see *Left Brain, Right Brain,* by Sally P. Springer and George Deutsch (San Francisco: Freeman, 1981); "Specializations of the Human Brain," by Norman Geschwind in *Scientific American* (September 1979); Ross Buck, "Spontaneous and Symbolic Nonverbal Behavior and the Ontogeny of Communication," in *Development of Nonverbal Behavior in Children.* Ed. by R. S. Feldman (New York: Springer-Verlag, 1982), pp. 29–62; and an overview provided by Hunt, 1982.

8. Norman Geschwind, "Specializations of the Human Brain," in Wang, 1982, pp. 113–115.

9. Geschwind, 1982, p. 112. Also see discussion in Hunt, 1982, pp. 33–36.

10. Breyne Arlene Moskowitz, "The Acquisition of Language," in Wang, 1982, p. 122.

11. Moskowitz, 1982, p. 123.

12. Judith Coupe and Juliet Goldbart, *Communication before Speech* (London: Croon Helm, 1988), pp. 20–21.

13. The summary of stages in language acquisition is based upon an in-depth discussion provided in Barbara S. Wood, *Children and Communication* (Englewood Cliffs, NJ: Prentice Hall, 1976), pp. 24–27, adapted from Eric Lenneberg, "The Natural History of Language," in *The Genesis of Language.* Ed. by Frank Smith and George A. Miller (Cambridge, MA: MIT Press, 1968), p. 222. See also, Moskowitz, 1982.

14. Moskowitz, 1982, p. 123.

15. Jean Berko Gleason, "Sex Differences in Parent–Child Interaction," in *Language, Gender, and Sex in Comparative Perspective.* Ed. by S. U. Philips, S. Steele, and C. Tanz (Cambridge, England: Cambridge University Press, 1987), p. 191.

16. Wood, 1976, pp. 112–113.

17. Adapted from Coupe and Goldbart, 1988, p. 25. Based originally on L. Leonard, "Semantic Considerations in Early Language Training," in *Developmental Language Intervention.* Ed. by K. Ruder and M. Smith (Baltimore: University Park Press, 1984).

18. Moskowitz, 1982, p. 125.

19. Wood, 1976, pp. 25–26.

20. Richard Cavendish, *Man, Myth, and Magic, Volume 1* (New York: Marshall Cavendish, 1970).

21. Benjamin L. Whorf, *Language, Thought and Reality* (Cambridge, MA: MIT Press, 1956), p. 206.

22. Peter Farb, *Word Play* (New York: Bantam Books, 1978), p. 213.

23. William O. Robertson, "Quantifying the Meanings of Words," *Journal of the American Medical Association,* Vol. 249, No. 19, 1983, pp. 2631–2632.

24. See discussion by Richard Budd in "General Semantics," in *Interdisciplinary Approaches to Human Communication.* Ed. by Richard W. Budd and Brent D. Ruben (Rochelle Park, NJ: Hayden, 1979). Reprinted by Transaction Books, New Brunswick, NJ.

25. Ari L. Goldman, "New Bible: 'He' Goes the Way of All Flesh," The *New York Times,* Sept. 28, 1990, p. A10.

26. Anatol Rapoport, "What Is Semantics," in *The Use and Misuse of Language.* Ed. by S. I. Hayakawa (New York: Fawcett, Premier Books, 1962), pp. 19–20.

27. Margaret McLaughlin, *Conversation: How Talk Is Organized* (Newbury Park, CA: Sage, 1984), pp. 13–14.

28. Adapted from Susan Shiminoff, *Communicative Rules: Theory and Research* (Beverly Hills, CA: Sage, 1980); see discussion in McLaughlin, 1984, p. 16.

29. Adapted from Mark Ashcraft, *Human Memory and Cognition* (Glenview, IL: Scott, Foresman, 1989), pp. 447–467, especially the framework presented on p. 459. Based on the framework developed by H. Paul Grice, "Logic and Conversation," in *Syntax and Semantics, Vol. 3: Speech Actions.* Ed. by P. Cole and J. L. Morgan (New York: Seminar Press, 1975), pp. 41–58. And D. A. Norman and D. E. Rumelhart, *Explorations in Cognition* (San Francisco: Freeman, 1975); Ronald Wardhaugh, *How Conversation Works* (Oxford, England: Blackwell, 1985); and McLaughlin, 1984.

30. Grice, 1975; see discussion in Stephen W. Littlejohn, *Theories of Human Communication,* 5th ed. (Belmont, CA: Wadsworth, 1996), p. 91.

31. D. J. Canary and K. S. Hause, "Is There Any Reason to Research Sex Differences in Communication?", *Communication Quarterly,* Vol. 41, 1993, p. 129.

32. Jennifer Coates, *Women, Men and Language* (New York: Longman, 1986); Deborah Tannen, *You Just Don't Understand: Men and Women in Conversation* (New York: William Morrow, 1990).

33. The framework and research summary presented in this section is based on Lea P. Stewart, Pamela J. Cooper, Alan D. Stewart, and Sheryl A. Friedley, *Communication and Gender,* 4th ed. (Boston: Allyn and Bacon, 2003), pp. 37–61. See also discussion in John Pfeiffer, "Girl Talk—Boy Talk," *Science,* Vol. 6, No. 1, Feb. 1985, pp. 58–63.

34. Based on dialogue provided Stewart, et al., 2003, p. 49.

35. Stewart, et al., 2003, p. 49.

36. P. M. Fishman, "Interaction: The Work Women Do," *Social Problems,* Vol. 25, pp. 397–406, 1978, discussed in Pfeiffer, 1985.

37. D. A. Infante and A. S. Rancer, "A Conceptualization and Measure of Argumentativeness," *Journal of Personality Assessment,* Vol. 46, 1982, pp. 72–80.

38. D. A. Infante, "Inducing Women to Be More Argumentative: Source Credibility Effects," *Journal of Applied Communication Research,* Vol. 13, 1985, pp. 33–44.

39. A. M. Nicotera and A. S. Rancer, "The Influence of Sex on Self-Perceptions and Social Stereotyping of Aggressive Communication Predispositions," *Western Journal of Communication,* Vol. 58, 1994, pp. 283–307.

40. Robin Lakoff, *Language and Woman's Place* (New York: Harper & Row, 1975).

41. Paul Watzlawick, Janet H. Beavin, and Don D. Jackson, *Pragmatics of Human Communication* (New York: Norton, 1967), pp. 51–52.

42. Watzlawick, et al., 1967, pp. 53–54.

43. Lee Thayer, "Communication—Sine Qua Non of the Behavioral Sciences," in Budd and Ruben, 1979. Reprinted by Transaction Books, New Brunswick, NJ.

8 Nonverbal Messages

In this chapter

Why . . .

- Nonverbal messages are often more important than verbal ones.

- Most of us know so little about nonverbal communication.

- Paralanguage can be more influential than language.

- Eye contact is influential in relationships.

- Your seating position in a classroom may predict your grade.

Kim walks over to a row of unoccupied chairs, places the briefcase and purse she is carrying on the seat to her right, and situates a bag with a picture of Mickey Mouse near her on the floor. She begins to leaf through the pages of *The Wall Street Journal,* glancing periodically at her watch and the monitor listing incoming flights. She checks her cell phone and sighs.

After about five minutes have passed, a middle-aged man dressed in a three-piece suit with a carry-on bag over his shoulder walks over and takes a seat directly across from her. As Kim glances up, her eyes catch his. He smiles, and she looks away. Kim concentrates her attention on the newspaper in front of her, but senses that the man is still staring. Finally, she notices him get up and walk away.

Several minutes later he reappears, walks over to the seat next to her and sits down without saying a word. Seconds later, Kim picks up her briefcase, the newspaper, and shopping bag and walks rapidly toward the concourse. Shortly thereafter, the man gets up and heads off in the same direction.

Though no words are spoken in this scenario, the individuals' appearance, facial expressions, dress, actions, use of space and time provide important cues that are interpreted and acted upon. Based on the man's smile, eye contact, and physical movement, Kim concludes that the onlooker is taking more than a casual interest in her and removes herself from the situation.

You have probably also formed initial impressions of the two individuals based on nothing more than the sparse description of their nonverbal behavior. For instance, you may have concluded that Kim is

- Carrying items she purchased at a Disney store or theme park
- Very conscious of the time
- Waiting for a plane
- Employed in a professional position

The man in the three-piece suit, you may assume to be

- Traveling
- Interested in initiating contact with Kim
- Employed in business or a profession

The formation of your reactions to the characters—and theirs to one another—based on nonverbal cues is not unique to this situation. Particularly in circumstances where we are forming first impressions, or where there are conflicts between words and actions, nonverbal messages are often far more influential than verbal ones. In fact, researcher Albert Mehrabian suggests that where we are confused about how we feel about another person, verbal messages account for only 7 percent of our overall impression and the rest are accounted for by nonverbal factors.[1] Thus:

Total Feeling = 7% Verbal Impact + 38% Vocal Impact + 55% Facial Impact

Although some researchers disagree with these numbers, it is clear that nonverbal codes are very influential. A great many nonverbal factors contribute to the global impressions people form. Sometimes impressions are accurate; often they are incorrect, exaggerated, or incomplete. In the situation just described, our first impressions may be correct. However, a number of other interpretations are possible. The Mickey Mouse bag may have been given to Kim to carry several reports from her office. The frequent glances at her watch could have simply been a nervous gesture, and she may have been leafing through

The Wall Street Journal for no better reason than she found it on the chair next to her. She might have been passing time before going to work at one of the shops in the airport. Or perhaps she was a plainclothes airport security guard.

The man in the suit may have been interested in establishing a personal relationship or simply a friendly person with no intentions that involved Kim. His actions may have been a response to hers, or any apparent connection could have been coincidental. Or, *he* may have been a member of the security staff with questions about the contents of the Disney bag and growing suspicions about Kim's very nervous behavior.

Even from this simple example, three important characteristics of nonverbal communication are apparent:

1. A number of factors influence nonverbal communication.
2. Nonverbal messages generally have a variety of meanings.
3. The interpretation of nonverbal communication depends on the nonverbal messages themselves and also on the circumstance and the observer.

Similarities between Verbal and Nonverbal Communication

Rule-Governed

Rules can be identified in nonverbal, as well as in verbal, messages. Some of these patterns pertain to the production of nonverbal messages and to the ways in which emotions are displayed. Still others are necessary to comprehend the significance of messages.

Rules associated with the creation of many nonverbal behaviors—a handshake, for instance—are similar to phonetics. Rules prescribing the appropriate sequence of nonverbal cues relative to one another—in meeting someone for the first time, for example—are a type of syntax. There are also general semantic patterns for many nonverbal behaviors that can be identified, and there are conventions as to when and how particular cues are to be used—a kind of pragmatics of nonverbal communication.

As with verbal messages, some nonverbal patterns are common to the behavior of all individuals. In facial expressions, for instance, studies suggest that there is a predictable relationship among emotions such as happiness, sadness, anger, disgust, surprise, or fear, and distinctive movements of facial muscles regardless of a person's personal and cultural background.[2] Gestures, such as head nodding, which we associate with "yes" and "no," as well as crying or laughing also seem to be universal, though their precise meanings may not be. But there are a great many more patterns that are unique to particular individuals, groups, regions, occupations, or cultures.

Intentionality

Most often, language is consciously used by people for the purpose of sending messages. This is the case in spoken, and especially written, communication. This is also often the case with nonverbal communication. We may consciously use particular facial expressions, gestures, and dress on a first date, job interview, or a group meeting, with the intention of creating a desired effect.

Both verbal and nonverbal messages may also be produced and transmitted unintentionally. Unintentional cues, like lowering your eyebrows and tightening your lips in anger when trying to appear kind and understanding of a friend's rudeness, can have as much information value as poor word choice or confusing sentences.

Common Message Functions

Verbal or nonverbal behavior may bear any one of several relationships to one another:[3]

- Messages may be *redundant* and duplicate one another, as when a person says, "I am going to sit down," and then walks over to a chair and sits.
- They can also *substitute* for one another, as when a handshake substitutes for "Hello, it's nice to meet you."
- Verbal and nonverbal messages may be *complementary,* as when an individual smiles and says, "Come in, I'm glad to see you."
- A verbal or nonverbal code may also be used to add *emphasis* to the other, such as making a fist to underscore a point being made verbally.
- Verbal and nonverbal codes can also be sources of *contradiction,* as would be the case if we were told how interested another person was in hearing our thoughts, while the "listener" stared across the room at a member of the opposite sex.
- Both types of codes can be used for *regulation*—controlling the communication process, determining who will speak, for how long, and even when changes in topic will occur.

Differences between Verbal and Nonverbal Communication

Awareness and Attention

During the last several decades nonverbal communication has emerged as an area of extensive scholarly study and a topic of popular articles and books. But verbal communication continues to receive more attention.

This emphasis is most apparent when we consider the manner in which training in the two areas is handled in schools. Proficiency in communicating information through verbal messages is, in fact, considered to be so important that it is regarded as one of "the basic skills"; and great effort is expended to ensure that we are taught rules of pronunciation, syntax, semantics, and pragmatics as a part of our formal education. Theory and practice in the written and oral use of language are provided at virtually all educational levels.

By comparison, nonverbal skills receive little attention in most schools. Music, art, and physical education are generally included as part of the curriculum. However, no pro-

RESEARCH PROFILE

Nonverbal Communication in the Real World • *Mark Frank*

The study of nonverbal communication is an important part of the discipline of communication today. Professor Frank (whose face is featured in Figure 8.4) traces his research heritage back to Charles Darwin and demonstrates the relevance of detecting interpersonal deception in today's world.

• • •

The terrorist attacks of September 11th left laypeople and professionals alike wondering how the nineteen hijackers eluded detection by law enforcement personnel. This speculation in turn raises other questions of direct interest to communication scholars, such as what happens verbally and nonverbally when someone tells a lie, whether people can recognize these clues if they appear, and in particular whether those in law enforcement—whom we as a society entrust to catch criminals and terrorists—are able to do so.

As a social scientist who is interested in understanding nonverbal communication in the real world from one of the strongest and most enduring traditions of scholarship in communication, namely that of Charles Darwin and the well-known developments and extensions of Darwin's emotion and expressive communication work pioneered by Paul Ekman, I am intrigued by all those questions. My specific interests are in the basic questions of how people's internal states communicate—either intentionally or unintentionally—information to others through our facial expressions, tone of voice, and hand, leg, head, or body movements. Interpersonal deception is particularly interesting in that it is a phenomenon where a person's internal, unintentional communication may compete or conflict with their intentional communication. Think of a situation where you find something very funny, yet the situation you are in calls for serious demeanor. You may find yourself struggling to control your facial expression and voice tone because of a powerful urge to smile. Or think of a situation where you commit a *faux pas*, but you don't want others to know you've done so, yet despite your efforts you still blush.

The study of nonverbal communication provides insight into the real essence of human beings through identifying how our thoughts, feelings, and interactions with others are expressed as well as interpreted by others. Moreover, applying this knowledge to real-world situations like deception may help educate law enforcement, health care, and other professionals to understand what information they can and cannot tell about people based on their nonverbal communication; information that we can hope will facilitate the accuracy of their judgments to make a better and safer world.

ficiency training comparable to composition, literature, or public speaking is provided for the nonverbal competencies that are so vital to human communication.

At home, attention is paid to dress, personal habits, and other forms of nonverbal messages that would get someone labeled as unpopular, dangerous, or even unappealing. However, most of these nonverbal "lessons" learned at home have to do with avoiding these negative attributions.

Overt and Covert Rules

One of the explanations for the relatively greater emphasis placed on verbal communication is that in all cultures there are *overt rules* and structures for language and language use. As a result, this information is provided in various sources. Nothing comparable exists for nonverbal communication. There are no nonverbal dictionaries or style manuals. And, other than books on etiquette, fashion, and body language, there are no guides to nonverbal usage.

We learn the *covert rules* of nonverbal communication more indirectly, through observation, and subtle—and sometimes not so subtle—patterns of reward and punishment.[4] Thus, we "know the rules" for greeting and expressing affection to others nonverbally—when to shake hands, for how long, how hard to squeeze the other person's hand, and when hugs and kissing are appropriate—but these rules are covert and not as universally agreed on. Few of us are conscious of their role in governing our behavior or are able to articulate the rules involved.

Control

While we devote considerable attention to managing our nonverbal communication in some situations, we are often more successful in controlling our verbal messages. If the goal is to convey our competence or grasp of a situation, for example, most of us are better able to control the impression we create verbally than nonverbally. Through planning and rehearsal, we will probably be able to gain predictability regarding the messages we will send verbally. However, despite our best efforts to manage our nonverbal behavior, nervousness or embarrassment may be quite apparent through *nonverbal leakage* (nonverbal behavior that contradicts our verbal messages)—a trembling voice or sweaty palm, for instance.

Public versus Private Status

Language usage patterns have long been regarded as a topic that is appropriate for public discussion and scrutiny. Teachers, parents, or friends are generally quite willing to ask us questions when they don't understand what is being said or to comment when they disagree. However, matters relating to our appearance, gestures, mannerisms, and body positions are generally considered private, personal, and even taboo topics, and are therefore far less likely topics of open discussion, analysis, or critique.

Recently the rules for discussing appropriate nonverbal behaviors have changed, especially for public figures. A great deal of attention is paid to various parts of movie stars' bodies or wardrobes. And everything is being "made over" from faces to hips to houses.

Hemispheric Specialization

Another major difference and a topic of scholarly interest is the location in the brain in which nonverbal activities are centered. As we noted, the left hemisphere of the brain is thought to play a predominant role in language processes.[5] Other activities which require the sequential processing of information, such as mathematics, seem also to rely heavily on the left hemisphere. The right hemisphere is of special significance in the recognition of faces and body images, art, music and other endeavors where integration, creativity, or imagination are involved.[6]

Studies show that some individuals with damage to the right hemisphere have difficulty with location and spatial relationships, recognition of familiar faces, or recognition of scenes or objects. Other research, which argues convincingly in favor of right-hemisphere specialization, has shown that even where damage to the language centers in the left hemisphere is so severe that the patients may have difficulty speaking, the ability to sing is often unaffected.[7] People with severe stutters can often sing without difficulty, too.

In the remainder of this chapter, we will examine four channels of nonverbal cues:

- Paralanguage
- Face
- Body
- External cues—space and time

Paralanguage

We've all heard the phrase, "It's not what you said, but how you said it." What we say—using words, phrases, and sentences—is obviously important to communication. However, the way we use language can be even more important than our words as sources of information. *Paralanguage* refers to any message that accompanies and supplements language. Technically speaking, any supplemental nonverbal message can be viewed as an instance of paralanguage.

Vocalic Forms

One focus of our discussion of paralanguage will be on *vocalics*—auditory messages, other than words, created in the process of speaking.[8] Vocalics, which include pitch, rate of speech, rhythm, coughs, and giggles, nasality, pauses, even silence, are very significant sources of impressions in face-to-face communication.[9] Recall that Mehrabian found that when an individual is confused in his or her feelings about another person, vocal messages accounted for 38 percent of the impression that is formed.[10]

Long before children develop skill in language use, they have a familiarity with the tonal pattern of the language in their surroundings. Studies suggest that from the tonal contours of the babbling, it is possible to identify the language environment in which a child lives, even as early as the second year of life.[11] The paralinguistic patterns acquired by children reflect not only the language patterns of the region in which they are being raised but also the unique patterns of family and friends.

With spoken language, paralinguistic cues such as loudness, rate of speaking, tone, interjections, pitch variation, and use of pauses can have a major influence on whether and how one reacts to the individual and his or her verbalizations. On the basis of pitch, for example, we are able to determine whether a particular utterance is a statement or a question, a serious comment, or a sarcastic barb. Whether the word *really* spoken orally is interpreted as "Really?" or "Really!" is determined through paralanguage rather than through the word itself. In the same way, we decide whether, "That's beautiful," is to be taken literally or to mean quite the opposite.

Pitch is also the difference between whether "Can I help you?" creates a positive or negative impression. Spoken with a raised pitch at the end of the sentence, the sense is one of politeness and genuine interest. The same words, spoken in a monotone are likely to be taken as rudeness and disinterest.

Interjections (*nonfluencies*)—such as "like," "a," "huh," "so," or "you know"—and stuttering may also have an impact upon the way an utterance is interpreted. Remember the teacher who inserted "um" between every other word? Consider the potential difference in the impressions and likely impact created by each of the following:

Sam: Like do you want to like go now or like later?

Shawna: Do you want to go now or later?

Although the words used are essentially the same, the meanings we would attach to these two messages, and the inferences we would draw about their sources, are likely to be very different. Based on first impressions, would you rather hire Sam or Shawna to represent your company to the public? Who would you prefer to date?

As suggested by previous examples, paralanguage provides a basis for inferences about a speaker, as well as having a potential influence on the impact of the content of the message. Rate of speed and accent, for example, can provide the basis for inferences as to nationality, the region of the country in which the person was raised, and other characteristics associated with stereotypes about the geographic locale. The stereotypical linguistic patterns of the "fast-talking New Yorker" or "the slow-speaking Southerner," are often associated with behavioral, as well as geographic, characteristics. Paralanguage can also provide the basis for assumptions about the speaker's educational level, interest in the topic, and mood. Moreover, tone, pitch, rate of speech, and volume provide clues as to an individual's emotional state.

In some languages, paralanguage is even more essential to communication than it is in English. In Chinese, tones determine the meaning of words, as illustrated in Figure 8.1. Standard Chinese has only four tones: falling, rising, level, and dipping (or falling and then rising).[12] The drawings on the right show the voice pattern as the words are spoken. Changing the tone has the same kind of effect on the meaning of a word as changing a vowel or a consonant would in English.

Written Forms

Up to this point we have been discussing paralanguage as it relates to *spoken* language. The form of a word or statement is also important to interpretation in *written* language use. The visual appearance of written materials, in terms of punctuation, spelling, neatness, the use of space for margins and between words, whether the document is printed or handwritten, and even the color of ink are likely to influence the reader's reaction to the words and its source.

In written language, paralinguistic cues serve as a basis for generalized inferences as to how educated, careful, respectful, or serious a person is, and may provide clues as to his or her mood or emotions at the time of writing. See Figure 8.2. These in turn, may affect the way others think about and relate to the author.

The use of paralinguistic cues is evident in the conventions developed for appropriate communication via e-mail. For example, using capital letters is considered SHOUTING.

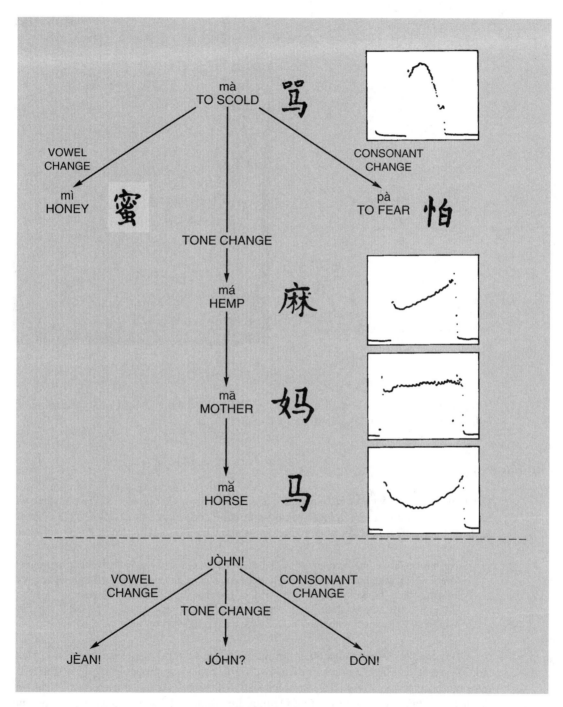

FIGURE 8.1 *Paralanguage Is Essential to Language Use in Chinese*

Source: William S.-Y. Wang, "The Chinese Language," *Scientific American* (February 1973), p. 56.

FIGURE 8.2 Anger or frustration may be apparent in paralinguistic cues in written messages.

Emoticons are useful in e-mail and text messaging. Combinations of punctuation marks indicate smiling :-) or winking ;-), for example.

The Face

Generally speaking, we react to a person's face holistically. See Figure 8.3. That is, when we look at someone's face, we get an overall impression and seldom think of the face in terms of its distinctive features. Yet as nonverbal communication researcher Mark Knapp explains

> The human face comes in many sizes and shapes. Faces may be triangular, square, and round; foreheads may be high and wide, high and narrow, low and wide, or protruding; complexions may be light, dark, smooth, wrinkled, or blemished; eyes may be close or far apart, or bulging; noses may be short, long, flat, crooked, "hump-backed," or a "ski slope"; mouths may be large or small with thin or thick lips; and cheeks can bulge or appear sunken.[13]

Beyond their significance in contributing to one's overall appearance, facial expressions serve as message sources in their own right, providing probably the best source of information as to an individual's emotional state—happiness, fear, surprise, sadness, anger, disgust, contempt, and interest.[14] Our feelings are often, as the adage suggests, "written all over our faces." It has been estimated that our faces are capable of creating 250,000 ex-

FIGURE 8.3   Could these children look any happier?

pressions. Nevertheless, we don't actually show that many. Researchers estimate there are only about 44 distinct ways in which facial muscles move (see Figure 8.4).

Researchers also believe that the role of the face in relation to emotion is common to all humans. Describing what has been called a "neurocultural theory of facial expression," Paul Ekman explains: "What is universal in facial expressions of emotion is the particular set of facial muscular movements when a given emotion is elicited."[15] The specific events and circumstances that *trigger* emotions vary from one individual and culture to another.[16] And the customs and rules guiding the *display rules* of particular emotions also may vary from person to person, and culture to culture. Yet, for any emotion, exaggeration, understatement, and masking (deception) may occur.[17] An employee might exaggerate or mask an emotion of disappointment with a smile, for example, when learning that a promised "generous raise" only amounts to 25 cents per hour.

Eye Gaze

Probably the most influential features of the face in terms of communication are the eyes. As Ellsworth notes:

> Unlike many nonverbal behaviors having a potential cue-value that is rarely realized, such as foot movements, [or] subtle facial or postural changes, a direct gaze has a high probability of being noticed. For a behavior that involves no noise and little movement, it has a remarkable capacity to draw attention to itself even at a distance.[18]

As significant as eye behavior is to human communication, most of us are relatively unsophisticated in our awareness of eye behaviors and our ability to characterize them with

FIGURE 8.4   In addition to contributing to overall appearance, one's face provides the basis for inferences as to one's emotional state, age, mood, interest level, personality, and reaction to events and people.

any precision. Among those who study this facet of our nonverbal behavior, a number of terms have been advanced that assist in description:[19]

- *Face contact.* Looking at a person's face
- *Eye contact (or eye gaze).* Looking at a person's eyes
- *Mutual gaze.* Mutual gazing by two individuals at one another's face
- *One-sided gaze.* One person looking at another's face, but the behavior is not reciprocated
- *Gaze avoidance.* One person actively avoiding another's eye gaze
- *Gaze omission.* One individual failing to look at another, but without the intention of doing so

As children, we have heard many times that "it's not polite to stare"; and, as adults, there are frequent reminders of the "rule." If one stops at a traffic light, and the person in the next car looks interesting, one may "steal a glance"; but one is careful not to appear to stare. Similarly, while waiting in line at a grocery store, or sitting in a restaurant or other public place, we may casually glance at the people around us, but at the same time we should try to appear as though we are not noticing the other people at all.

Actually, the rule that we apply as adults is, "It's not polite to stare at people you don't know very well, unless you can do so without having them notice you." When and if we are noticed, we pretend not to have been looking, unless the intent is to violate the other's expectations.

The rules for eye contact with friends and acquaintances are quite different from those for strangers. When conversing verbally with even a casual acquaintance, some degree of mutual eye gaze is customary. "Looking" may help in grasping the ideas being discussed and is an indication of attention and interest. Among close friends, extended eye contact is not only acceptable, but is expected. In the case of intimate friends and lovers, prolonged glances may be exchanged periodically even when no accompanying words are spoken.

There are a number of other situations where eye glances are optional. For instance, when a speaker such as a teacher asks a question of a large audience, each member of the group may choose to engage or avoid the glance of the speaker. Generally, the likelihood of being called on to answer a question is considerably greater if one looks at the speaker than if one looks away.

At what and whom we look, for how long, under what circumstances, whether the gaze is one-sided or mutual, and whether we are engaged in gaze omission or gaze avoidance, provide the basis for inferences as to our focus of attention, interests, intentions, and even attitudes. Looking may be a matter of observing, orienting, inspecting, concealing, avoiding, or searching for pacification.[20]

Researchers have demonstrated that a primary function of eye gaze, or the lack thereof, is to regulate interaction. Eye contact serves as a signal of readiness to interact, and the absence of such contact, whether intended or accidental, tends to reduce the likelihood of such interaction.[21] Other studies suggest that eye gaze also plays an important role in personal attraction. Generally speaking, positive feelings toward an individual and high degree of eye contact go together. Perhaps for this reason, we often assume that people who look our way are attracted to us. Studies indicate, further, that individuals who engage in high levels of eye gaze are typically seen as more influential and effective in their dealings than others.

A number of factors have been shown in research to be related to the extent of eye gaze, including distance, physical characteristics, personality, topic, situation, and cultural background.[22] Based on this research, one can predict that, generally, more eye contact will occur when one is physically distant from others, when the topic being discussed is impersonal, and when there is a high degree of interest in the other person's reactions. Greater eye contact also occurs when one is trying to dominate or influence others, comes from a culture that emphasizes eye contact during conversation, is generally outgoing, striving to be included, listening rather than talking, or when one is dependent on the other person.[23]

One would expect less gazing between people who are physically close, when intimate topics are being discussed, when there are other relevant objects or people nearby, or when someone is not particularly interested in another's reactions or is embarrassed. Similarly, if an individual is submissive, shy, sad, ashamed, attempting to hide something, or of higher status than the person with whom he or she is talking, less eye contact is also likely.[24] Obviously, these are generalities which may not apply in a given circumstance.

Eye gaze is one area of nonverbal communication in which there are many cultural differences. For example, a student from Greece commented that in his culture it is considered polite to maintain direct eye contact while listening to someone talk. His North American friends continually ask him if something is wrong because they feel he is "staring at them." In some cultures, it is considered respectful to look down when a person in authority is speaking. In North America, however, parents often criticize their teenagers for not listening to them if they are not looking at them.

Pupil Dilation

The pupils of the eye can be an indication of interest or attraction. See Figure 8.5. As we look at people or objects that are seen as appealing, the pupils tend to enlarge; and, in at least some experimental settings, there is evidence that pupil size can be a factor in judgments of a person's attractiveness. In these studies, pictures of females with enlarged pupils were consistently rated as more attractive by males than were those of women with small pupils.[25]

The extent to which pupil size is actually a useful source of information is still a question. Particularly in a culture such as ours, in which we stand so far apart during most conversations, it is difficult to discern the size of another person's pupils, even when making an effort to do so. In Middle Eastern cultures, however, where the standard distance separating people during conversations is much smaller, information based on pupil size may be more usable.[26]

The Body

It is said that "Beauty is only skin-deep," and "You can't judge a book by its cover." However, there is little doubt that, particularly when other sources of information are lacking, "surface-level" information plays a critical role in human communication.

Appearance is probably the single most important information source in the formation of initial impressions. Perhaps the most dramatic evidence of the importance of appearance comes from studies of dating preferences, in which perceived attractiveness was more important than such factors as religion, race, self-esteem, academic achievement, apti-

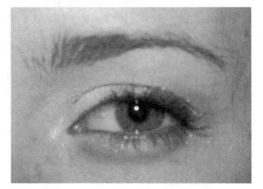

FIGURE 8.5 Research suggests that when we look at an individual or object that is of interest or is seen as attractive, our pupils dilate.

tude, personality, or popularity, in determining how well individuals would like one another. Evidence from other studies suggests that physical attractiveness is not only important to dating preferences but also is often a predictor of how successful, popular, sociable, sexually attractive, credible, and even how happy people are.[27]

A number of factors contribute to appearance, among them one's *hair, physique, dress, adornment,* and *artifacts.*

Hair

Hair and beard length, color, and style also are important nonverbal message sources. These factors contribute to overall attractiveness and may also serve as the basis of inferences as to one's personality, age, occupation, attitudes, beliefs, and values.

Physique

Physique includes body type, size, and shape. Studies have suggested, for example, that inferences may be drawn about personality based on *somatype*—body shape and size. People who appear to be "soft," "round," and overweight (endomorphs) may be assumed to be affectionate, calm, cheerful, extroverted, forgiving, kind, soft-hearted, or warm. People who appear to be muscular, bony, and athletic-looking (mesomorphs) may be stereotyped as active, argumentative, assertive, competitive, confident, dominant, optimistic, or reckless; and people who are tall and thin in appearance (ectomorphs) may be assumed to be aloof, anxious, cautious, cool, introspective, meticulous, sensitive, or shy. Although most studies find a match between particular physical traits and people's *perceptions,* there is little correlation between somatypes and actual behavioral characteristics.

One's height alone may also provide the basis for stereotyping. For males in our culture, greater height is often associated with positive qualities, while, beyond a certain point, the opposite is the case for females. Where these biases operate, they may be a consequence of primitive, subconscious reactions. Height plays an interesting role in politics and other aspects of society, for example:[28]

- All U.S. presidents except for James Madison (5 foot 4) and Benjamin Harrison (5 foot 6) have been taller than the average height of men of their time.
- Richard Nixon was perceived by his supporters to be taller than John F. Kennedy. Kennedy's supporters believed he was taller. Both men were actually six feet tall.
- Every inch taller a man is than average equates to an average of $600 more per year in salary.
- In 1973, the U.S. Civil Service Commission eliminated height and weight requirements that discriminated against women applying for police, park service, and fire fighting jobs.

Dress and Adornment

Dress fulfills a number of functions for us as humans, including decoration, physical and psychological protection, sexual attraction, self-assertion, self-denial, concealment, group identification, and display of status or role.[29] Cosmetics, jewelry, eyeglasses, tattoos, hair weaves, false eyelashes, and body piercings serve many of these same ends.

Nonverbal communication scholar Dale Leathers writes: "Our social identity and image is defined, sustained and positively or negatively modified by communication through appearance."[30] Dress is the major facet of appearance through which we can exercise control over communication. We generally assume that people make conscious choices about what they wear and therefore take their dress to be an important source of information about them.[31]

Dress and adornment are noteworthy and often utilized as the basis for judgments as to gender, age, approachability, financial well-being, social class, tastes, values, and cultural background. See Figure 8.6.

Badges of various kinds also provide information about a person's identity, status, or affiliations. Often dress serves as an occupational badge, as is generally the case with police officers, nurses, doctors, clergy, military personnel, and members of particular athletic teams. In such instances, the "costume" people wear is designed, standardized, and used to make their occupation easy to determine. The "uniforms" of college students, businesspeople, or factory workers may serve much the same function, though they are not necessarily intended to do so.

FIGURE 8.6   In addition to providing a source of basic information such as age, gender, occupation, and group affiliation, dress also often plays a critical role in first impressions.

Other badges are hats, shirts, sweatshirts, or jackets that bear the name of an individual, school, employer, manufacturer, favorite auto, or musical performer. Specialized jewelry such as a fraternity or sorority pin, a wedding or engagement ring, or a necklace with a name or religious symbol, may also serve to provide information as to one's identity, status, group, or organizational affiliation.

In an interesting study, nonverbal researchers Mark Frank and Thomas Gilovich found that what we wear influences not only others' behavior but also our own.[32] They discovered that, reflecting the notion that "bad guys wear black," professional football and ice hockey teams that wear black uniforms were penalized more. Teams that changed their uniforms to black had an increase in penalties. Judges rated the same behavior as "more illegal" when performed by a player in a black uniform. Finally, when students put on black uniforms they chose to play more aggressive games than when they put on white uniforms.

Artifacts

We surround ourselves with artifacts—toys, technology, furniture, decorative items, and so on. Our cars and homes are also artifacts—objects—that provide additional messages from which others may draw inferences about our financial resources, aesthetic preferences, personality, status, or occupation. A particular credit card, briefcase, or a business card may serve as artifactual cues to which people react as they form impressions based on our appearance.

Gestures—Kinesics

Movements of body, head, arms, legs, or feet—technically labeled *kinesics*—also play an important role in human communication. Studies suggest that we progress in the development of our capacity for gesturing through four basic stages.[33] In the first stage, from birth to three months, irregular, jerky movements of the entire body indicate excitement and distress. In the next stage, three to five months, the infant is able to move the entire body more rhythmically, in patterns associated with anger and delight. In the third stage, five to fourteen months, children develop specialized gestures such as making faces, head turning, and poking. Between the ages of fourteen and twenty-four months, the child is able to express affection for particular people, as well as joy and jealousy, through contact movements such as poking, hitting, and caressing.

Gestures, as well as other cues, may either be *purposeful*—messages which are intended to achieve a particular purpose—or *incidental* and *unintended*. Some gestures may be used as complements for language, such as if we shake our head back and forth while saying "no," when asked a question. In other instances we use gestures in place of words. A shrug of the shoulders, for instance, is used to indicate confusion or uncertainty, a frown and slow horizontal back-and-forth motion of the head to indicate frustration or annoyance, or the circle sign made by the thumb and the forefinger to mean "OK."

Inherited, Discovered, Imitated, and Trained Actions

Desmond Morris, an anthropologist, suggests that gestures are acquired through *inheritance, discovery, imitation,* and *training.*[34] Examples of actions that are inborn include the sucking response of the baby and the use of body contact gestures as a part of courtship.

Some gestures we discover as we identify the limitations and capabilities of our bodies. The way people cross their arms is an example. There is little variation from one culture to another, but there are differences between individuals within any one culture, and each individual tends to be fairly consistent over time. Some of us fold left hand over right, and others right over left. Regardless of which we have become accustomed to, it is difficult to reverse the pattern without considerable effort, as shown in Figure 8.7.[35]

We acquire many of our gestures unknowingly from the people around us as we grow up. The typical handshake, for instance, is acquired through imitation, as are many other greeting forms and cultural and subcultural mannerisms.

Actions such as winking, playing tennis, jumping on one foot, whistling, or walking on one's hands, require active training in order to master. The wink, for example, taken so much for granted by the adult, is a formidable challenge for a child. Like other trained actions, substantial observation and systematic effort is required to master it.

Origins of Gestures

It is interesting to speculate on the origins of human gestures. Some gestures displayed by adults seem to be carried over from our activities as children. Smoking, pencil chewing, nail biting, candy and gum chewing, and "emotional eating" may well have their roots in our early feeding experiences when oral satisfaction was associated with safety and security.

Other gestures may have cultural origins. Kissing may have its roots in the feeding habits of our ancestors. At early points in human history, mothers apparently fed their young by chewing food in their mouths first and then passing the food to their child's mouth in a gesture which very much resembles the tongue-kissing of adult lovers today.[36]

Another gesture, the horizontal head shaking which we use to say "no," may well have its origins in the infant's side-to-side head shaking gesture indicating he or she wants no more milk from the mother's breast, a bottle, or a spoon.[37]

FIGURE 8.7   Folding one's arms can be considered a *discovered action.* Cross your arms. Now reverse them. How does that feel?

Source: Desmond Morris, *Manwatching* (New York: Abrams, 1977).

Types of Gestures

There are many ways of classifying gestures. An extensive list provided by Morris includes the following.[38]

Baton Signals and Guide Signs. One type of gesture, the *baton signal,* is used to underscore or emphasize a particular point being made verbally. Examples of baton signals include a downward clipping motion of the hand, a forward jabbing movement of the fingers and hand, and the raised forefinger. Another similar kind of gesture is the *guide sign,* by means of which we indicate directions to others, as when we point, direct, or beckon another person nonverbally.

Yes–No Signals. *Yes–no signals* are another category of gesture. Movements of the head are the primary means for creating these signals. While many gestures are unique to one or several cultures, the vertical, "yes" head nod appears to be fairly universal. Even though we might assume that the meaning of the "yes" nod is fairly specific, there are a number of variations:

> *The acknowledging nod.* "Yes, I am still listening."
> *The encouraging nod.* "Yes, how fascinating."
> *The understanding nod.* "Yes, I see what you mean."
> *The agreeing nod.* "Yes, I will."
> *The factual nod.* "Yes, that is correct."[39]

The "no" gesture, of course, consists of a horizontal movement of the head. In many parts of the world a side-to-side swaying of the head is also used to say "maybe yes, maybe no." In addition to the head, the hand and fingers can also be used to express yes–no signals. For instance, in North American culture a shaking of the forefinger from side to side is a way of saying "no." Similarly, forming a circle with the thumb and forefinger can often mean "yes," or "ok," though this meaning varies from culture to culture. See Figure 8.8.

Again it is important to recognize the existence of cultural differences. For example, a quick upward nod of the head can mean "no" in Greece.

Greetings and Salutation Displays. The most familiar greeting forms are the handshake, embrace, and kiss by which we signal our pleasure at someone's arrival or the significance of their departure.

There are several stages in the greeting or salutation process. The first phase is the *inconvenience display:*

To show the strength of our friendliness, we "put ourselves out" to varying degrees. We demonstrate that we are taking the trouble. For both host and guest, this may mean "dressing up." For the guest it may mean a long journey. For the host it may entail a bodily shift from the center of [the] home territory. The host may make an effort to meet a guest like when a head of state formally welcomes another head of state at an airport or

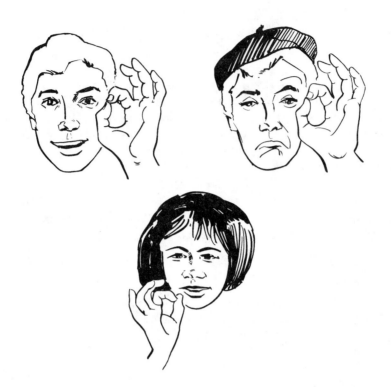

FIGURE 8.8   A circle sign made with the thumb and forefinger illustrates
how the significance of a single gesture can vary substantially from one
culture to another. In England and North America, the sign means, "okay."
For the French, it signifies "okay" when the gesture is made while smiling. If
it is accompanied by a frown, it is taken to mean "worthless" or "zero." In
Japan, the same sign is often used as a sign for "money."

Source: Desmond Morris, *Manwatching* (New York: Abrams, 1977).

when a brother drives to the airport to greet his sister returning from abroad. This is the
maximum form of bodily displacement that a host can offer. From this extreme there is a
declining scale of inconvenience, as the distance traveled by the host decreases.[40]

The second stage is the *distant display.* From the moment the guest and host see
each other, they can indicate the other's presence by several other gestures including a
smile, eyebrow flash, head tilt, wave, and sometimes an outstretching of arms indicating
an upcoming embrace. As the two individuals approach one another, they signify pleasure
at the other's presence by hugging, squeezing, patting, kissing, or pressing their cheeks
together, perhaps with extended eye contact, laughing, smiling, or even crying. The particular greeting used depends on a number of factors including the nature of the relationship, the situation in which they are meeting one another, the length of time that has

passed since they have seen one another, and the extent of change in either person's status since they were together.

Tie Signs. The *bonding* or *tie sign* is a category of gesture through which individuals indicate that they are in a relationship. In much the same way that wedding rings, fraternity or sorority pins, or matching clothing suggest the existence of a relationship between two or more people, certain gestures serve the same purpose. Handholding, linked arms, a single drink shared by two people, close physical proximity when sitting or walking, and the simultaneous sharing of objects of all kinds provide cues about the individuals and the nature of their relationship. See Figure 8.9.

Isolation Gestures. Other common gestures are body positionings such as crossing arms or legs, through which we conceal or block portions of the body from view. In some instances, *isolating gestures* may serve as intentional messages, though more often they are less purposeful. These and other gestures, including hugging oneself, supporting the chin or cheek with an arm, or touching one's mouth, may signal discomfort or anxiety, even though we may be unaware of these feelings.[41] According to Paul Ekman, these adaptors or manipulators tend to increase with anxiety.

Other Gestures. Gestures also play a major role in courtship, mating, and sexual affairs. In addition to hand holding, kissing, petting, and forms of sexual contact, *preening behavior*— for instance, stroking one's hair, adjusting makeup or clothing in the mirror, or stroking one's own arms or legs—can also play a role in sexual attraction.[42]

FIGURE 8.9 Even when no words are spoken, nonverbal cues often provide clues as to who "goes with" whom in any given situation.

In religion, gestures have significant functions. Kneeling, standing at appropriate times, bowing, and folding one's hands in prayer are symbolic means through which people participate in the central rituals of any faith.

Touch—Haptics

When a gesture is extended to the point where physical contact is involved, tactile messages are created. For humans the significance of tactile messages, also known as *haptics,* begins well before birth in the prenatal contact between mother and infant. From the first moments of life, touch is the primary means by which children and parents relate to one another. Through this tactile mode, feeding takes place and affection is expressed.

During the early years of our development, touch continues to be the central means for expressions of warmth and caring among family members and close friends. Beginning with the preschool and elementary years, physical contact also takes on a role in play and sports and, particularly among boys in our culture, fighting. During this period, we also learn the significance of tactile messages in greeting rituals such as the handshake, hug, and kiss.

In the teenage and preadult years, touching takes on increasing significance in expressions of warmth, love, and intimacy. Tactile messages are important in athletic endeavors, in the actual activity of the sport, and in the pats and slaps of assurance and encouragement among players and coaches. For some, the role of touch in aggression continues during this period. Among adults, most physical contact is associated with (1) informal greetings and gestures of departure between friends and colleagues, (2) expressions of intimacy and sexual activities, and (3) expressions of hostility and aggression.

Two of the interesting facets of tactile messages are their power and their inherent ambiguity. In health care settings, one of the sources of discomfort for many patients is the fact that examinations and treatment involve being touched by relative strangers in a manner that we normally associate with intimate relations.

Recent innovations in technology have helped to link our sense of touch with our ability to communicate verbal messages. For example, the tactile graphic display allows Web surfers with vision impairment to feel images from the Internet much in the same way words can be represented in Braille.[43]

Levels of contact and comfort with touching vary to some extent from one culture to another. In some Asian or African cultures, for example, male friends may walk down the street hand-in-hand as they talk. In Middle Eastern cultures, casual acquaintances stand so close together when talking that North Americans may assume they are intimates. By comparison, the United States is a low-contact culture. In general, North Americans go to great lengths to avoid touching whenever possible. In an elevator or crowded shopping mall, for instance, we generally touch strangers only when absolutely necessary and then often with discomfort.

Depending on the circumstance, people involved, and the culture, touch may lead us to react with considerably more intensity than we would to verbal or other nonverbal cues. Touching another person without his or her consent is regarded in many societies as far more disturbing than verbal abuse or obscene gestures.

Space—Proxemics

The use of space, *proxemics,* plays an important role in human communication. To some extent the intensity of tactile messages occurs because we have well-defined expectations as to how much personal space we will have around us. When our *personal space,* the *portable territory* we carry with us from place to place, is invaded, we respond. Being bumped unnecessarily in an elevator, having a beach towel walked across or practically shared by a stranger, or being unnecessarily crowded while shopping generally cause us discomfort for this reason. Our response is to readjust our own position to regain the amount of space we think we need. Research suggests that in some instances the extreme violation of personal space over time, such as occurs in hysterical crowds and very high density neighborhoods, can lead to extreme reaction, frustration, and even aggression.

Edward Hall has done much to broaden our understanding of the way space is used during face-to-face conversations.[44] Hall found that the distance between interactants varied predictably depending on the setting and the content of conversation:

- *Public conversations.* 12 feet to the limits of visibility
- *Informal and business conversations.* 4 to 12 feet
- *Casual conversations.* 1½ to 4 feet
- *Intimate conversations.* 0 to 18 inches

Fluctuations in each category depend on a number of factors: the culture in which the conversation takes place, the ages of the interactants, topic being discussed, setting, nature of the relationship, attitudes and feelings of the individuals, and so on.[45] See Figure 8.10.

The use of space and position is also important in seating. In a group situation, for instance, certain positions are more often associated with high levels of activity and leadership than others. Being in front of a group, separated more from the group as a whole than are any of the individual members from one another, affords the isolated individual a position of distance and authority. Examples are a teacher in front of a class, a judge in front of the court, a religious leader at the front of the church, and so on.

A person's position within a large room—a classroom, for example—can also have an influence on verbal behavior. In typical classes, over 50 percent of the comments are initiated by class members located in the front and center positions within the room, referred to as the "participation zone." For many individuals, position is the most influential factor explaining their participation.[46] In smaller groups, particularly where furniture is involved, the head of the table is traditionally a position of leadership, honor, respect, and power. See Figures 8.11 and 8.12. In a conference room, a similar association often exists with the person sitting at the head of a table. Some researchers have found, for instance, that in experimental jury deliberations, the person sitting at the head of the table was chosen much more often as leader than people in other positions.[47] Our positions relative to others, whether in silence or active conversation, standing or sitting, can be a significant factor in shaping communication and in contributing to others' impressions of us and ours of them.

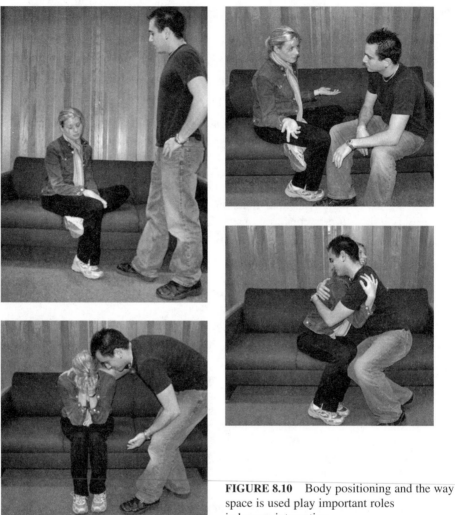

FIGURE 8.10   Body positioning and the way space is used play important roles in human interaction.

The Physical Environment

Our buildings, furniture, decor, lighting, and color schemes are the result of human decision making. In addition to providing shelter and housing, and facilitating our various activities, the man-made elements of our physical environment also serve a number of informational functions—some intentionally, many by accident.

Whether one thinks of the arrangement of furniture and the selection of wall hangings in one's own apartment, the design and furnishing of an elegant restaurant, the layout of a shopping mall, or the architecture of a massive airport complex, all have much in common in terms of communication.

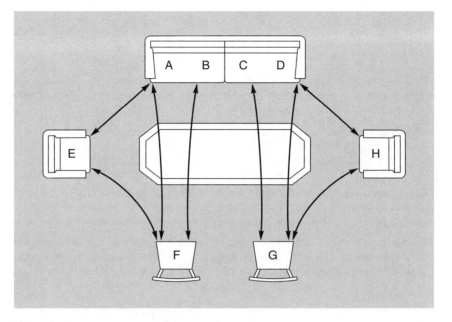

FIGURE 8.11   The arrangement of furniture and seating patterns play an important role in the level and direction of conversation. All other things being equal, the pairs marked by arrows would engage in the most frequent conversation. Those persons seated on the couch would be least likely to engage in interaction.

From *Public Places and Private Spaces: The Psychology of Work, Play and Living Environment* by Albert Mehrabian. Copyright © 1976 by Basic Books, Inc. Reprinted by permission of Basic Books, a member of Perseus Books, L.L.C.

Directing Behavior.   Each environment with its furniture, decor, and color serves as a source of information that may have an impact on the people present. Some of the information is "designed-in" by the architect or designer to shape the way the environment or its parts are used. Sidewalks in a park, for example, direct our movement as we walk about. Similarly, chairs used in some fast-food restaurants are designed to be comfortable for only a short period of time and may well influence our decisions about how long to remain in the environment.

Provide Symbolic Value.   Structures and their contents, by virtue of their size, shape, use of space, and decor, may also have symbolic significance for us. Religious buildings and their contents, for example, are often symbolic by their very nature. Large rooms with high ceilings, stained glass windows, dimly-lit interiors, deep colors, and sacred books and objects, each have information value to those who use the environment.

The symbolic properties of houses of worship have their parallels in shopping malls, parks, restaurants, as well as in the structure and decor of homes and apartments. The differences, for instance, between dining in a candlelit room with elegantly upholstered

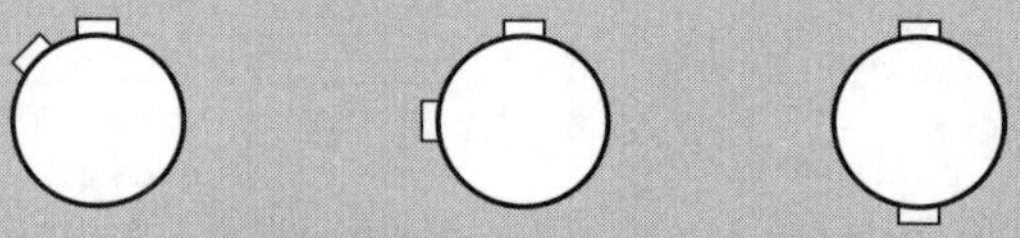

Conversation	60%	27%	13%
Cooperation	68	13	19
Co-action	18	32	50
Competition	12	23	65

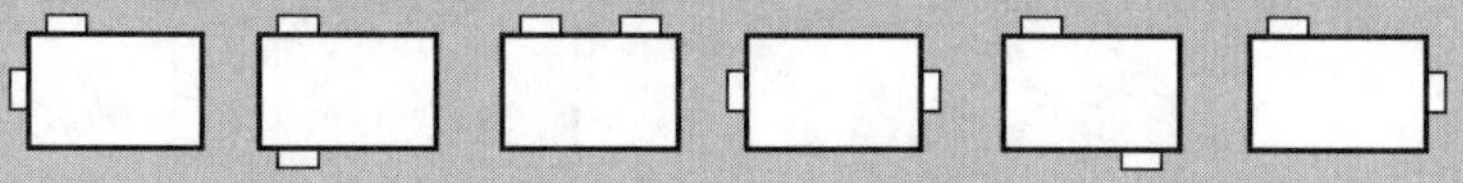

Conversation	45%	36%	12%	1%	4%	2%
Cooperation	23	13	42	8	10	4
Co-action	8	8	10	21	34	19
Competition	6	22	7	40	19	6

FIGURE 8.12   In studies of relationships and seating preference, Robert Sommer and M. Cook asked students to indicate how they would prefer to situate themselves for each of the following situations:

(1) *Conversation:* Casual discussions for a few moments before class.
(2) *Cooperation:* Sitting and studying together for a common exam.
(3) *Co-action:* Sitting and studying for different exams.
(4) *Competition:* Competing to see which person would be first to solve a series of puzzles.

Students were asked to indicate their preferences for round and rectangular tables, each with six possible seating positions. The results of the two studies are shown under the diagrams.

Source: Mark L. Knapp and Judith A. Hall, *Nonverbal Communication in Human Interaction,* 5th ed. (Belmont, CA: Wadsworth, 2002), p. 164.

armchairs and soft dinner music compared to the experience of having dinner at the counter of a truck stop or diner are quite substantial. See Figure 8.13.

Regulating Interaction.   Environments may also provide the basis for information that regulates—encourages or discourages—interaction. The study carrels of the library, for example, serve to separate and isolate their users, discouraging interaction, while a business office with no private offices or partitions encourages interchange. In a similar sense, a classroom with permanently attached chairs contributes to "one-way" message flow. Robert Sommer provides the following description of the typical classroom and its impact.

> The American classroom is dominated by what has been called the rule of two-thirds—two-thirds of the time someone is talking and two-thirds of the time it is the teacher, and two-

FIGURE 8.13 The objects of our physical environment also serve as nonverbal information sources, providing clues as to how they are to be understood, related to, and whether and how they are to be used.

thirds of the time that the teacher is talking, she is lecturing, giving directions or criticizing behavior. Movement in and out of classrooms and the school building itself is rigidly controlled. Everywhere one looks there are "lines"—generally straight lines that bend around corners before entering the auditorium, the cafeteria, or the shop. . . . The straight rows tell the student to look ahead and ignore everyone except the teacher, the students are jammed so tightly together that psychological escape, much less physical separation, is impossible. The teachers have 50 times more free space than the students with the mobility to move about. . . . The august figure can rise and walk among the lowly who lack the authority even to stand without explicit permission. Teacher and children may share the same classroom but they see it differently. From a student's eye level, the world is cluttered, disorganized, full of people's shoulders, heads, and body movements. [The student's] world at ground level is colder than the teacher's world. [The teacher] looms over the scene like a helicopter swooping down to ridicule or punish any wrong-doer.[48]

Time—Chronemics

The use of time and timing—*chronemics,* as it is technically designated—is another critical, and often overlooked, factor in communication. In fact, the reactions to our words and deeds may depend far more on *when* we speak or act, than on the content of the action.

Timing

Timing plays a role in interaction at two levels of analysis: (1) micro and (2) macro. Micro-conversational time-use characteristics include the speed at which we talk, the number and extent of pauses and interruptions, our "talk-to-silence" ratio, and our patterns of conversational "turn taking." These factors can play an important role in terms of message transmission, reception, and interpretation; and each also serves as a basis for the formation of impressions about the individuals involved. Too little talking, for instance, can be read as disinterest, shyness or boredom, whereas too much can be construed as aggressiveness, self-assuredness, presumptuousness, overconfidence, or rudeness.

At the macrolevel are our more general decisions as to whether to even engage in conversation at a particular point in time. It comes as no surprise to anyone who has ever asked for a raise or to borrow the family car that there are certain times that are better than others for presenting ideas or suggestions. The decisions people make about when to speak and when to be silent, when they have said too much and when too little, when to "speak their piece" and when to "keep it to themselves" are among the most critical decisions they make relative to communication.

Timeliness

Sayings like "Time is money," "Never put off until tomorrow what you can do today," "A stitch in time saves nine," and "The sooner the better" reflect the common North American view that time is a precious commodity. The faster we can get something done, the less time we "waste."

Our "time-is-money" philosophy shows up in a great many of our activities. We find ourselves rushing to meet deadlines, keep appointments, avoid waste, and increase productivity. We drive as fast as we legally can, so we'll get where we're going quicker. When we have an appointment with someone, we like to get business transacted in as little time as possible so we can move on to the next task. We want to leave work "on time" whenever possible to hurry home. En route every red light, wait at a pedestrian crossing, or slow-moving car is an annoyance as we rush home. We want to get home quickly to relax and enjoy our "leisure time."

Given the significance of time in our daily lives, it is not surprising that our use of it can have an important impact on behavior. Being "early" or "late" is a message. The meaning provided by such messages varies depending on a number of factors, including the amount of time we are early or late, the purpose of an appointment, the length of the relationship between the people involved, the relative status of the parties involved, and the orientation toward time of each of the individuals.

Being fifteen minutes late for a job interview can lead to the cancellation of the appointment, while being fifteen minutes late for a party may result in being embarrassingly "early." Being late for a business meeting carries different consequences than being late for a social engagement. Arriving an hour late—even with a good reason—for a first date will probably be reacted to differently than being as late for dinner with one's spouse. In such circumstances, timeliness and the use of time—being on time, late, or early—may be as significant a source of information to other persons as whatever one does or says after arriving.

There are very significant intercultural differences in the use of time. In Latin America and the Middle East, one can arrive at a time that a North American or Canadian would consider "late," and still be considered "on time" or even "early." Business executives and travelers must learn about, understand, and respect these cultural differences when in other countries.

Messages and Meanings: MS ≠ MR

We have seen how verbal and nonverbal behaviors play a pervasive role in human communication. Individuals create verbal and nonverbal messages that can and often do become significant to others. Sometimes the behaviors are intentional, as with a planned speech or the wave of a hand. Often they are accidental, as with a blush or an avoidance of eye contact in embarrassment.

The process of verbal, and especially nonverbal, message making seems automatic. Both occur as a natural and basic part of human activity. The nonverbal and verbal behaviors of any one individual can be seen as contributing to the vast array of information in the symbolic environment that surrounds us at any point in time.

It is important to keep in mind that the presence of particular verbal or nonverbal messages in the environment provides little or no assurance that they will be attended to or interpreted in a particular way. Bill tells Mary "I love you." Mary says, "I love you, too." Each has heard the verbal message provided by the other, and the words each are saying are the same. Can we assume the message has the same meaning for both Bill and Mary? Not necessarily. Whether we think in terms of ourselves as "senders" or "receivers" of messages in a relationship, group, organization, society, or mass audience, messages sent (intentionally or not) do not necessarily equal messages received. Common messages do not necessarily result in shared interpretation. Maybe Bill and Mary have the same meanings in mind. Or, perhaps, Bill means he wants to get married, while Mary means she wants to go out only with Bill.

The same distinction between message and meaning is important in the realm of nonverbal codes: Eye engagement intended as a sign of interest by one person may be read as aggressiveness by another; a gesture interpreted as an isolation gesture by one person may be regarded as a way of keeping warm in a cold room to others. Verbal and nonverbal behaviors are *sources* of meaning, but they are not, in and of themselves, meaningful, with the possible exception of facial expressions that accompany emotions.

Situational and topical considerations can also be important. Nonverbal communication researcher Mark Frank explains that people often prefer to receive admissions of affection in person rather than in a letter or on the phone. In a face-to-face situation, we can see how the other person "really" feels because we can observe their nonverbal behaviors. The same principle applies to relationship breakups, too.[49]

The meanings of verbal and nonverbal messages depend not only on the messages that are available but also on our individual ways of processing information and on our social interactions with others. Whether we regard a particular person as attractive or intelligent will depend minimally on: (1) the nonverbal and verbal behaviors of the person in question; (2) the way we personally attend to and interpret those behaviors; and (3) the social interactions with our peers and other members of our society that have helped to define and shape our notion of what constitutes attractiveness or intelligence.

To determine the meanings of particular messages, we have to look beyond the verbal and nonverbal messages to the processes involved in information reception. We must look also to the relationships, groups, organizations, cultures, and societies, which provide the contexts in which verbal and nonverbal messages are created, shared, and interpreted.

Implications and Applications

- Paralanguage, appearance, gestures, touch, space, and time are important sources of information in a wide range of situations.
- Our nonverbal behaviors are governed by rules we have learned through experience over the course of our lifetime.
- We are largely unaware of the rules that guide our nonverbal behaviors and our reactions to them.
- When others violate nonverbal rules, we generally have global, overgeneralized, sometimes emotional reactions. For instance, a person may be perceived to be a wimp if he or she doesn't squeeze firmly enough while shaking hands, or we may feel angry when someone is continually late for appointments.
- We are generally aware of only a small percentage of the nonverbal messages we create and convey in any situation.
- Some facets of nonverbal communication, such as dress, greetings, and time, we can easily manage if we choose to do so. Others, like paralanguage, eye contact, gestures, and the use of space can be managed with effort and practice. Still others—a blush of embarrassment or a nervous gesture—we may be unable to control.
- Nonverbal competence requires awareness of and attention to the patterns of communication, and conscious effort to be sensitive to the impact of our nonverbal behavior on others.

Summary

Nonverbal behavior plays an important role in human communication. There are a number of similarities between verbal and nonverbal communication. They: (1) are rule-governed;

(2) make possible the production of unintended, as well as purposeful messages; and (3) share a variety of message functions in common.

There are also key differences: (1) Compared to language, there has been a lack of awareness and attention to nonverbal cues and their impact on behavior; (2) nonverbal communication involves rules which are primarily covert rather than overt; and (3) verbal message processing is thought to occur primarily in the left hemisphere of the brain, while the right hemisphere is essential for processing information related to nonverbal activity.

Paralanguage, appearance, gestures, touch, space, and time are six primary sources of nonverbal messages. Appearance plays an important role in interpersonal relations, particularly in initial impressions. Dress, adornment and physique are facets of appearance that serve as potential information sources. The face is a central aspect of one's appearance, providing the primary source of information as to one's emotional state. Hair is also a message source.

The eyes are perhaps the most important component of the facial system in terms of communication. Based on direction and duration of eye gaze, or the absence thereof, cues are provided that serve as the basis of inferences as to interest, readiness to interact, and attraction. Pupil size may also be important.

Gestures are potential sources of information. Among the most common types of gestures are: baton signals and guide signs, yes–no signals, greetings and salutation displays, tie signs, and isolation gestures.

Touch is another source of messages that plays a central role in greetings, the expression of intimacy, and acts of aggression. The intensity of reactions to tactile cues is suggestive of the importance of space in communication. When our personal space is invaded in other than intimate relationships, discomfort—and often a "fight or flight" reaction—results.

The significance of spatial cues is also apparent in seating patterns. Certain seating positions may be associated with high levels of participation and leadership. The nature and placement of elements in the physical environment—furniture, decor, lighting, and color schemes—also generate messages that are potentially significant to behavior. They often provide cues that influence their use, symbolic value, and interaction patterns.

Time, timing, and timeliness can also be significant in the communication process. The way time is shared in conversations, for instance, can be a source of information that is even more influential than the content of those discussions. Timeliness—being "late" or "early"—can itself be a potential information source. Substantial cultural variations exist.

Our verbal and nonverbal behaviors—some intentionally enacted—create a pool of messages that is part of the environment that surrounds us. The presence of verbal and nonverbal messages provides no assurance that they will be attended to or be of particular significance to individuals within that environment. Messages sent (intentionally or not) do not equal messages received.

Notes _____

1. Albert Mehrabian, *Silent Messages* (Belmont, CA: Wadsworth, 1971), pp. 42–47; and *Nonverbal Communication* (Chicago: Aldine-Atherton, 1972), pp. 181–184.

2. See Paul Ekman, Wallace Friesen, and P. Ellsworth, *Emotion in the Human Face: Guidelines for Research and an Integration of the Findings* (New York:

Pergamon Press, 1972); Paul Ekman, "Universal and Cultural Differences in Facial Expressions of Emotions," in *Nebraska Symposium on Motivation.* Ed. by J. K. Cole (Lincoln: University of Nebraska Press, 1972), pp. 207–283; and the discussion of these and other related works in Robert G. Harper, Arthur N. Wiens, and Joseph D. Matarazzo, eds., *Nonverbal Communication: The State of the Art* (New York: Wiley, 1978), p. 212.

3. For a detailed discussion on functions of nonverbal cues, on which this summary is based, see Judee K. Burgoon and Thomas Saine, *The Unspoken Dialogue: An Introduction to Nonverbal Communication* (Boston: Houghton Mifflin, 1978), pp. 10–14.

4. We are indebted to Valerie Manusov for suggesting the distinction between covert and overt rules in discussing nonverbal and verbal communication.

5. Robert E. Ornstein, *The Psychology of Consciousness* (San Francisco: Freeman, 1977), pp. 20–21. See more detailed discussion in Sally P. Springer and George Deutsch, *Left Brain, Right Brain* (San Francisco: Freeman, 1981), and Norman Geschwind, "Specializations of the Human Brain," *Scientific American,* September, 1979, pp. 180–182.

6. Springer and Deutsch, 1981.

7. Springer and Deutsch, 1981, p. 15.

8. Burgoon and Saine, p. 80.

9. See discussion in Burgoon and Saine, 1978, pp. 80–84.

10. Mehrabian, 1972, pp. 181–184.

11. William S-Y Wang, "The Chinese Language," in *Human Communication: Language and Its Psychobiological Bases* (San Francisco: Freeman, 1982), p. 58.

12. Wang, 1982, p. 58.

13. Mark L. Knapp and Judith A. Hall, *Nonverbal Communication in Human Interaction,* 5th ed. (Belmont, CA: Wadsworth, 2002), p. 305.

14. Knapp and Hall, 2002, p. 308.

15. Ekman, Friesen, and Ellsworth, 1972, p. 50.

16. Ekman, 1972, p. 216.

17. See discussion in Harper, et al., 1978 pp. 98–105; and Ekman, 1972.

18. P. C. Ellsworth, "Direct Gaze as a Social Stimulus: The Example of Aggression," in *Nonverbal Communication of Aggression.* Ed. by P. Pliner, L. Krames, and T. Alloway (New York: Plenum, 1975), pp. 5–6.

19. Harper, 1978, p. 173.

20. G. Nielsen, *Studies of Self-Confrontation* (Copenhagen, Denmark: Munksgaard, 1962).

21. An excellent summary of research findings on the functions and perceived impact of eye gaze is provided in Harper, 1978, pp. 181–215.

22. See discussion in Knapp and Hall, 2002, pp. 349–355.

23. Knapp and Hall, 2002, p. 361.

24. Knapp and Hall, 2002, pp. 355–358.

25. A discussion of research on pupil dilation by E. H. Hess, *The Tell-Tale Eye* (New York: Van Nostrand Reinhold, 1975); and E. H. Hess, A. L. Seltzer, and J. M. Shlien, "Pupil Responses of Hetero- and Homosexual Males to Pictures of Men and Women: A Pilot Study," *Journal of Abnormal Psychology,* Vol. 70, 1965, pp. 587–590. A useful summary is provided in Knapp and Hall, 2002, pp. 366–369, and Desmond Morris, *Manwatching* (New York: Abrams, 1977), pp. 169–172.

26. Edward T. Hall, "Learning the Arabs' Silent Language," *Psychology Today,* August 1979, pp. 47–48.

27. Knapp and Hall, 2002, pp. 180–181.

28. John S. Gillis, *Too Tall, Too Small* (Champaign, IL: Institute for Personality and Ability Testing, 1982); and Kim Painter, "How Bush, Dukakis Measure Up in '88," *USA Today,* Vol. D4, Sept. 22, 1988.

29. Knapp and Hall, 2002, p. 208.,

30. Dale G. Leathers, *Nonverbal Communication Systems* (Boston: Allyn and Bacon, 1976), p. 96.

31. Valerie Manusov, unpublished notes on nonverbal communication, January 1991.

32. Mark G. Frank and Thomas Gilovich, "The Dark Side of Self and Social Perception: Black Uniforms and Aggression in Professional Sports," *Journal of Personality and Social Psychology,* Vol. 54, 1988, pp. 74–83.

33. A discussion of research and writings on the development of nonverbal capabilities in children is provided in Barbara S. Wood, *Children and Communication* (Englewood Cliffs, NJ: Prentice Hall, 1976), pp. 194–200.

34. Morris, 1977, pp. 17–23. The term *imitated actions* is used to refer to what Morris has labeled *absorbed actions.*

35. Morris, 1977, pp. 16–17.

36. Morris, 1977, p. 52.

37. Morris, 1977, pp. 68–69.

38. The discussion of baton signals, yes–no signs, guide signs, salutations displays, tie signs, and isolation gestures is based on the work of Morris, 1977, pp. 56–100.

39. Morris, 1977, p. 68.

40. Morris, 1977, p. 79.

41. See Morris' discussion of "barrier signals," 1977, pp. 133–135, and "auto contact behaviours" pp. 102–105.

42. Knapp and Hall, 2002, p. 229.

43. "New Device Enables Blind to 'Feel' Electronic Images," *Education USA,* Vol. 44 (23), November 11, 2002, p. 12.

44. See discussion of personal space provided in *The Silent Language,* Edward T. Hall (New York: Doubleday, 1959), especially Chapter 10.

45. A useful discussion of the work of Edward Hall and others in the area of personal space is provided in Knapp and Hall, 2002, pp. 152–161, and Burgoon and Saine, 1978, pp. 92–97.

46. A summary of research on position and participation is provided in Knapp and Hall, 2002, pp. 109–114.

47. F. Strodtbeck and L. Hook, "The Social Dimensions of a Twelve Man Jury Table," *Sociometry,* Vol. 24, 1961, pp. 297–415.

48. Robert Sommer, *Personal Space* (Englewood Cliffs, NJ: Prentice Hall, 1969), p. 99.

49. Mark G. Frank, unpublished notes on nonverbal communication, December 1996.

9 Media

In this chapter

Why ...

- Human tool-making has been important to the evolution of communication.

- Information overload is inevitable, and media literacy is critical.

- Media make synthetic experience reality.

- New media increase receiver control of communication.

- Higher quality media may not result in higher quality communication outcomes.

6:15 A.M. Clock radio clicks on. "Hostilities continue in the Middle East . . . Dow-Jones closed up 30 in light trading . . . lows in the mid 50s, possibility of showers early this evening. . . ." Check e-mail. Up and at 'em. Get into jogging gear, grab the IPOD, and out the door.

7:00 A.M. Back from running. Check answering machine. Pick up the newspaper. Glance at the headlines, turn on the TV, and grab a quick bite to eat.

7:20 A.M. Set the car radio to the station with the "Eye-in-the-Sky" traffic reporters: "Overturned truck causing delays on I-380; otherwise, traffic conditions normal . . ." Off with the radio, in with the CD. Almost forgot! Return rented DVDs. Take out the bank card and pull in next door to the ATM.

7:30 A.M. On the way again. Meant to call Rick before leaving home. Better call him now on the cell phone. Check for messages first.

7:45 A.M. Arrive at work. Check my schedule for the day on my PDA. Turn on the computer. Check voice mail and e-mail.

8:00 A.M. Contracts arrive from client via fax. Sign and fax copy back.

And, so it goes.

The Tool-Making Animal

Beyond our capacity for creating and using messages for communication, one of our other basic human skills is the capacity to create tools.

This capability has aided us greatly in our efforts to adapt to our environment. It has given us great advantages over other animals in terms of our capability to grow food, build shelters, and carry out the many other activities necessary for our basic survival.

Our tool-making facility has given us another unique advantage over other animals—the ability to create communication *media*—technological devices that extend our natural ability to create, transmit, receive, and process visual, auditory, olfactory, gustatory, or tactile messages. In this chapter, our focus is on media and *mediated communication*—communication which occurs when media intervene, or *mediate*, between message sources and receivers.

Media and Their Functions

At first consideration, tools like telephones, pencils, CD players, answering machines, and computers may not seem to have much in common. However, on further reflection, it becomes apparent that in one way or another each of these extends our ability to engage in human communication.

Without basic communication technologies, such as writing instruments and surfaces on which to write—or electronic substitutes—there would be no way to preserve messages, nor to move them from one place to another. And, if there were no printing presses, telegraph, telecommunication, or the Internet, it would be impossible to rapidly distribute a single message to a number of distant points on the globe. Without tools like computers, copying machines, fax machines, DVD players, and MP3 players, we would be severely limited when it comes to copying, organizing, storing, and retrieving information for future use. Media extend human communication by enhancing (1) message production and distribution, and (2) information reception, storage, and retrieval.

Production and Distribution

When we examine the communication media that we take so much for granted, we find that one of the most basic functions they perform is to extend our ability to produce and distribute information at great distance in space or time from the point of origin. *Production* involves the creation of messages using communication media. *Distribution* has three components:

1. *Transmission.* Moving messages
2. *Reproduction and amplification.* Duplicating, amplifying, or multiplying messages
3. *Display.* Making messages physically available once they arrive at their destination

Spoken language is our most basic means of vocal message production. Telephones, CDs, MP3s, audio cassette tapes, beepers, and other recording devices facilitate message production, and especially, distribution. Included in the long and diverse list of visual media that make message production and distribution possible are the alphabet, pens and pencils, computers, the Internet, billboards, signs, and message-bearing articles of clothing. A number of devices combine audio and visual capabilities, among them film and videotape, DVDs, television, cable systems, and the World Wide Web (WWW). Braille is an example of a message production and distribution technology that involves tactile codes. See Table 9.1.

Reception, Storage, and Retrieval

Media that aid in production, distribution, reproduction and/or amplification also play an important role in reception in that they serve to make messages accessible. As noted in Table 9.2, tools such as radio and TV receivers, magnifying glasses, radar, and telescopes, assist with the reception of visual information, while earphones and hearing aids expand capabilities for receiving auditory messages.

Though we are unaccustomed to thinking of written documents as communication media, they also serve very basic functions in extending our information storage and retrieval efforts. Certainly the most noteworthy information-recording tools to be developed in recent years are computers, with their enormous capacity to code, store, manipulate, and retrieve information.

Types of Media

Communication media may extend any form of communication, including face-to-face. We use media in this way when we call a friend on the phone, write a letter to a relative, leave a message on an answering machine, or interact with a colleague or friend via e-mail. See Box 9.1.

Mass Media such as newspapers, magazines, books, radio, and television multiply, duplicate, or amplify messages for distribution to a large audience.

TABLE 9.1   *Message Production and Distribution Media*

Auditory Media	
Spoken Languages	Satellite Radio
Musical Instruments	Telephones
Amplifiers	Telegraphs
"Walkie-Talkies"	"Beepers" (Paging Devices)
Phonograph Recording	CB Radios
Audio and Video Duplication	CD and DVD players and Media
AM, FM, Other Band Radios	Audiocassettes

Visual Media	
Alphabet	Bumper Stickers
Internet	Skywriting
Smoke Signals	Print Media
Cave Drawings	Billboards
Hand and Arm Signals	Typewriters/Printers
Pens and Pencils	Reprography/Copying Equipment
Carbon Paper	Ribbons and Badges
Lanterns	Blackboards
Artists and Graphics Materials Signs	Signs
Photography and Photographic Equipment	Message-Bearing Articles of Clothing
Flags	Satellite Dish Systems
Pins	

Auditory-Visual Media	
World Wide Web (WWW)	Cable Systems
Cinematography and Films	Digital Video Disks
Broadcast Television	Video Cassettes
Projection Systems	Electronic Games
Microwaves	Fiber Optics
Teleconferencing	

Tactile Media	
Braille	Medical Palpation

Group and organizational media extend or enhance communication processes among individuals in groups or organizations.

Communication media that assist in exchanges between two or among several people in this way are *interpersonal media*. They are being used to enhance interpersonal communication. By means of interpersonal media, time and space may be overcome in our interactions with others. These and other media are also used to expand our capabilities for communication within and between groups, organizations, and societies.

Media can be thought of as *intrapersonal communication media* when they expand our ability to produce, store, or retrieve messages of which we ourselves are the source.

TABLE 9.2 *Examples of Information Reception, Storage, and Retrieval Media*

Auditory Reception Media	
Hearing aids	Radio Receivers
Earphones	Stethoscopes

Visual Reception Media	
Eyeglasses	Cameras
Mirrors	Sonograms
Contact Lenses	CRT (Cathode Ray Tube)
X-ray Systems	Digital Scanners
Microscopes	Medical Imaging Devices (MRI, CAT Scan)
Magnifying Glass	Telescopes
Binoculars	Periscopes
Radar	

Storage and Retrieval Media	
Diaries	CDs
Wills	Microfiches and Microfilms
Appointment Calendars	Magnetic Disks
Personal Data Assistants (PDAs)	CD-ROMs
Flight Recorders	Scrolls
DVDs	Audio and Video Recorders
Files	Written Documents
Audio and Audio/Video Disks	Computers and Software
Books	Film
MP3s	

BOX 9.1 • *Types of Media*

- Mass Media: tools used to transmit messages to large audiences. *Examples:* television, newspapers, magazines, books.
- Group and Organizational Media: tools used to extend group and organizational communication capabilities. *Examples:* telephones, Internet, intercoms, paging systems, computers.

- Interpersonal Media: tools used to extend interpersonal communication capabilities. *Examples:* letters, greeting cards, e-mail, telephones.
- Intrapersonal Media: tools used to extend intrapersonal communication capabilities. *Examples:* tape recorder, home video, personal data assistants (PDAs), diary, mirror.

Evolution of Communication Media: From Smoke Signals to the Internet

It was about 20,000 B.C. when early humans first carved symbols on the walls of caves and used drums and smoke to signal one another. While smoke signals and cave drawings served their intended purposes well, they lacked the capacity for making messages permanent or portable.

By about 1000 B.C., early hieroglyphic and pictographic drawings had given way to systems of writing that made use of an alphabet.[1] Paper was invented around A.D. 100, and the oldest-known printed work is a Sutra printed in Korea in A.D. 750. Writing extended the natural human capacity for memory by providing a means for creating a lasting record of our messages.

The ancient Greeks built a series of high walls stretching across the countryside from which messages were relayed using fire and smoke. The Persians and Romans had postal systems; official correspondence was carried by horseback between stations on a more or less regular basis.

By 1500 Johannes Gutenberg had completed the printing of a Bible using movable type. Although printing as it is known today began in Germany during the mid-fifteenth century, Chinese, Japanese, and Koreans actually had developed the process much earlier. Printing made it possible to rapidly duplicate and transmit messages, as shown in Figure 9.1. Together, writing and printing had a revolutionary impact on communication and on virtually all facets of life—education, government, commerce, and religion.[2]

Newspapers appeared in their present-day form in the 1600s. It was during this period that regular mail service was established to link major cities in Europe, and by the 1700s postal services were operating in many countries. The mid-1800s brought the advent of the telegraph and the Morse code, and with them the introduction of electronic media, which greatly increased both *range* (distance) and *immediacy* (shortness of delay between message transmission and message reception). See Figure 9.1.

Prior to Marconi's development in 1895 of the wireless telegraph—radio, as it is commonly called today—the source and the destination had to be physically connected by wire. With a means for sending coded signals and later voice through the air, many new alternatives became available. As shown in Figure 9.1, these advances paved the way for the introduction of television in the 1930s.

There were a number of other notable advances in the 1800s. In 1866, cable was laid across the seabed of the Atlantic, further extending the capability for rapid message transmission. The telephone—a medium that has come to play an incredibly pervasive role in human communication—was patented during the same period.

The 1950s saw the widespread adoption of television. In 1950, only 10 percent of U.S. households had television sets; ten years later that figure had jumped to a remarkable 89 percent. Communication satellites were developed in the 1960s. See Figure 9.2.

In the decade that followed, a number of new communication media became widely available, including miniaturized transistor radios, stereophonic audio equipment, home movie systems, photocopiers, and cassette audio recorders.

Developments in the more recent past include new and hybrid media such as digital photography, audio and video recording and playback, and the diversified uses and increasing popularity of cellular telephony.

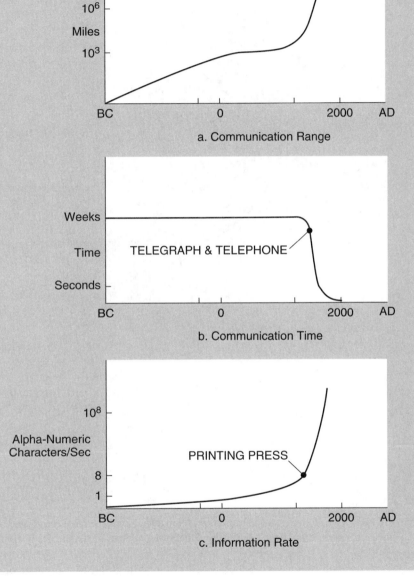

FIGURE 9.1 *The Evolution of Communication Technology in Terms of* **Range, Time,** *and Information* **Transmission Rate**

Source: Don L. Cannon and Gerald Luecke, *Understanding Communication Systems.* Copyright © 1980. Courtesy of Texas Instruments.

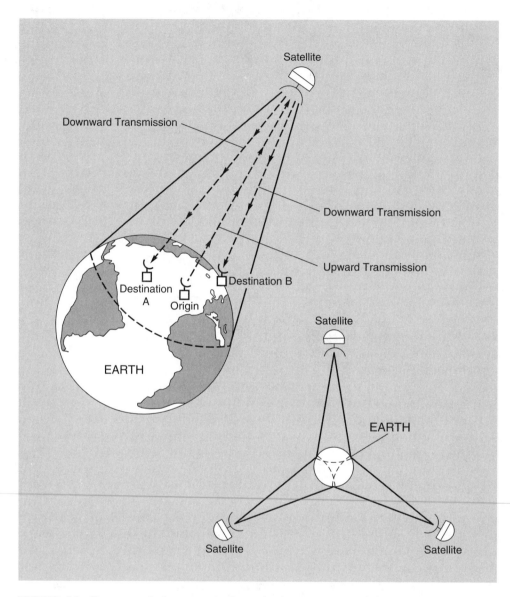

FIGURE 9.2 By means of telecommunication technology, messages originated at one point on the earth's surface can be relayed via satellite to any number of remote destinations and back again.

In 1985 there were 340,213 cell phones. In 2004, that number of cell phone subscribers rose to more than 160 million in the United States. Interestingly, among those 60 to 69, cell phone ownership (60 percent) is nearly the same as for those in the 18- to 24 year-range (66 percent). Highest are 30- to 49-year-olds (76 percent). Ownership is an amazing 32 percent among those in the 80 and older age bracket.[3] See Box 9.2.

Certainly the most dramatic changes involve computer-mediated communication and the Internet.[4] In 1995, roughly 30 million people used the Internet worldwide. Today,

BOX 9.2 • *The Case for—and Against—Cell Phones*

The arguments for cell phone ownership and use are well known: they increase productivity for real-estate agents, repair and service personnel, some managers and others who travel frequently or who work away from an office. They are also vitally important for doctors and other healthcare workers, police and fire personnel, and other first responders. And they keep us connected anytime, anywhere to friends, family, and colleagues.

Critics of cell phones argue, however, that for most of us the liabilities outweigh the benefits.

Cell phone conversations make private affairs public, distract drivers, encourage wasteful communication, and perhaps most importantly, cause a further breakdown of the distinction between work and leisure. Cell phones may seem to increase your freedom, but they actually rob you of it. As Robert Samuelson has noted, "People so devoted to staying interconnected are kept in a perpetual state of anxiety, because they may have missed some significant memo, rendezvous, bit of news or gossip. They may be more plugged in and less thoughtful."

Source: Robert J. Samuelson, "A Cell Phone? Never for Me," *Newsweek,* August 18, 2004.

estimates place the total number of Internet users, world wide, at approximately 800 million—12.5 percent of the world population—more than double the number of users in the year 2000. The ten countries with the highest number of users, in order, are the United States, China, Japan, Germany, the United Kingdom, South Korea, Italy, France, Canada, and Brazil. In terms of penetration—the percentage of the population using the Internet—the ten leading countries are Sweden, the United States, Hong Kong, Australia, Iceland, Netherlands, Canada, Denmark, South Korea, and Switzerland. In all of these countries, more than 60 percent of the population uses the Internet.[5]

Impact of Media on Contemporary Life

We are living today in the *Information Age,* an era when communication media have become central to nearly all that we do. Our tools for sending, transmitting, and receiving information have always occupied an important place in human activity. Now, more than ever before, communication technology has a pervasive impact on our personal and professional lives, our groups and organizations, our own society, and the world community.

Evidence of the impact of new media is all around us. Consider the proportion of the space in department stores and shopping malls allocated to communication and information technology—television, stereo systems, audio and video disk players, video games, copiers, cellular telephones and pagers, photographic equipment, home telephones and answering machines, desktop and laptop computers, and a variety of other technologies. This is the *hardware*—the physical tools—of the Information Age. Additional space is devoted to *software* such as CDs, DVDs, tapes, computer programs, video game cartridges, and a number of magazines and books that relate to the use of these media.

New media appear in nearly all facets of contemporary social and professional activity. In the entertainment industry, cable television, telecommunications, video-gaming, Internet services, and recording and playback devices have greatly broadened the number of leisure outlets available to us. Increasingly, portable video and audio devices provide greater flexibility as to when, where, and how we are entertained.

At work, word-processing systems, desktop publishing, networking, photocopying equipment, voice messaging and e-mail, fax machines, cellular phones and pagers, the Internet, and other media are the accepted standard even for small businesses. Within larger organizations, management information systems (MIS), corporate video, and computer conferencing provide decision makers with access to vital information at the touch of a key.

New media are also used in medicine to aid in data collection and record keeping. They facilitate patient diagnosis, care, and treatment. With computers, all medical information about an individual—medical histories, data on prescribed medications, lab test results, copies of all X-rays—can be transmitted electronically or stored on a portable disk. This information can be moved physically or electronically from one physician or hospital to another.

In the news media and the publishing industry, technology has changed the way information is collected, processed, and distributed. Writers and editors have access to a variety of databases to supplement information gathered through interviews and other means. Articles are written, revised, edited, and arranged on screen. The finished product—newspaper, magazine, or book—may be printed in a traditional manner or transmitted via satellite or cable to remote printing sites, as is the case with newspapers like *USA Today* and *The Wall Street Journal.*

Libraries are also being transformed by the new media. The concept of the library as a building where people come to read and check out books and copy articles is giving way to the view of a service institution that aims to serve the diverse information needs of its clients. In addition to print materials, patrons at a number of libraries have access to textual databases, voice and video files, and a full range of Internet sources. New information systems allow users at remote stations to review and access documents that were formerly available only in print form in a single or few copies, and were unavailable to others once checked out. Devices like CD-ROMs also offer great potential for reducing the space necessary for data storage and for increasing ease of access to documents once stored.

Technological Convergence

At the heart of these advances is the convergence of media that were once distinct in their forms and uses. Newspapers, for example, historically provided their audience with the summary of daily events. Television, radio, and film were primarily entertainment media. Telephones were used socially and in business contexts, typically as a substitute for short, face-to-face conversations. Today, many of these traditional distinctions are becoming obsolete. Cable television allows us to select shopping, music, religious programming, weather, comedy, foreign, and adult movies, and to access the Internet.

Similarly, the video screen and telephone line connected to a computer and the Internet becomes a mail system, a newsstand for newspapers and magazines, a game room, an auction, a collection of reference books, catalogues for consumer goods, a community bulletin board, a job placement agency, an airline reservation service, a place to meet and chat with electronic acquaintances, and a variety of other things. See Figures 9.3 and 9.4.

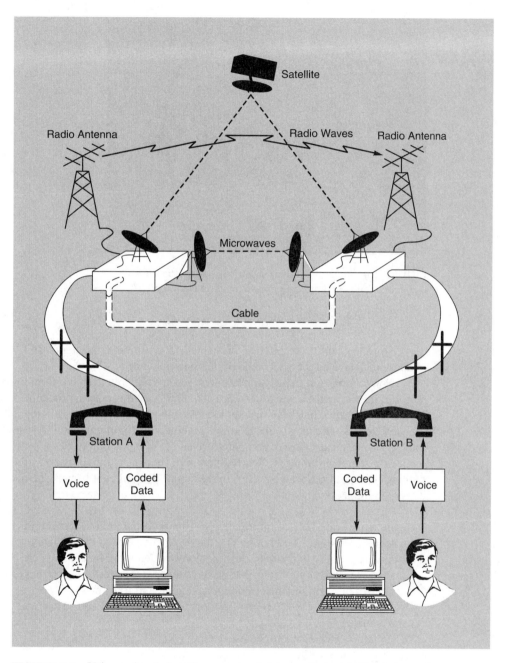

FIGURE 9.3 Voice and coded auditory or visual data can be transmitted between home, office, or production studios via satellite, radio wave, microwave, or cable.

Source: Don L. Cannon and Gerald Luecke, *Understanding Communication Systems.* Copyright © 1980. Courtesy of Texas Instruments.

FIGURE 9.4   In terms of their functions, transportation
technology and communication have much in common.

Similarly, the convergence of cameras, computers, printers—and now cellular
phones—has created a broad range of photographic options.

Commenting on these various developments, Everett Dennis, former executive director of the Gannett Center for Studies at Columbia Universities, proclaimed that technological convergence has been the single most important development in the media field in
the past several decades—"the coming together of communication devices and forms
into . . . electronically-based, computer-driven . . . systems that retrieve, process and store
text, data, sound and images. Nearly thirty-five years ago, Edwin Parker observed the beginnings of this trend, which he saw as particularly significant because he recognized that
it would ultimately lead to:

1. Increased amounts of information available to the public, and increased efficiency,
   since everything need not be distributed to everyone in the audience
2. Greater variety in the ways information packages can be constructed
3. Receiver selection of information (both in content and timing) as opposed to source
   control of information selection, packaging, and transmission
4. Improved "feedback" capability (since the individual subscriber can "talk" to the
   system)
5. Greater convenience to the user[6]

In the field of law, computers and telecommunications systems are used in the storage and retrieval of information regarding legal decisions, regulations, and statutes. Word
processing also facilitates the "personalized" preparation of standardized documents, such
as wills and contracts, in a fraction of the time that was required when each legal docu-

ment had to be created from scratch. For scientists, scholars, inventors, and engineers, improved communication media leads to broader access, with greater ease and in less time, to better organized information.

Additionally, advances in media have created a growing number of entirely new jobs in information management, information services, and communication and information policy. See Box 9.3.

By the end of the year 2004, the average person in the United States spent more than ten hours a day with information and entertainment media. This was an increase of an hour per day over the average of less than five years earlier. The increased usage is also accompanied by a shift away from traditional news and entertainment media such as newspapers, magazines, broadcast television, and radio, in favor of convergent digital media—a trend that seems certain to continue.[7]

Increasing Number of Messages and Media

Each new technological advance, particularly those with the capability of multiplication, amplification, or duplication, brings an increase in the volume of messages and the number of media available to us. By some estimates, the total number of words available from all media in the United States has more than quadrupled in the last quarter century.[8] Unfortunately, our own ability to select, interpret, and retain this information has not increased at a similar rate. With access to more media and messages, the problem of *information overload*—the availability of more messages than can be effectively utilized—becomes more critical. As this occurs, the real challenge facing humans will shift from "how to get it" to "what to do with

---

BOX 9.3 • *Information Brokering*

Information brokers, offering a wide range of services that are often otherwise unavailable to small companies and individuals, are playing an increasingly important role in our information-intense economy. Though the field is believed to have developed in the 1940's, the dramatic growth of information brokering is directly attributable to the explosion of computerized information services. Now, with no more than a computer and a modem, familiarity with computerized databases, and an enterprising approach, one or several individuals can begin their own information service.

Potential customers for information brokers exist throughout our economy. Large corporations generally maintain their own information centers and archives. Smaller organizations and companies cannot justify this expense, yet they have dramatic information needs. And, even the most highly educated among them usually have no idea how to get the information that their tasks require. The information broker who is willing to work with individuals or small business can find an enormous untapped market in this country. As a service business within our service economy, information brokering has gained importance.

Source: Excerpted and adapted from: "Information Brokering" by Karen Smalletz in *Bulletin of the American Society for Information Science*, April/May 1988, p. 28.

it." How many telephone messages do we want to answer? Is there a limit to how much information we can use on any one topic? How many CDs and MP3s can we listen to, and how many videocassettes or DVDs can we watch? How many newspapers, magazines, and books are we able to read? How many Web pages can we review regularly?

Because the number of messages and media grows larger while our abilities to use them remain more or less constant, we are actually less fully informed about what is available in our environment now than we were ten or twenty years ago.

New human competencies are needed to deal more effectively with an increasing number of media and messages. These skills include

- Identifying available media and assessing their attributes
- Diagnosing information needs
- Accessing and retrieving useful and valid information
- Organizing, classifying, and managing information

RESEARCH PROFILE

Escaping Television • *Robert Kubey*

Is television addicting? Professor Kubey's research demonstrates the importance of media literacy, especially for young people.

● ● ●

When I was in my first year of college, I wrote a paper entitled "Psychoanalysis of the Filmgoer." Without knowing it, I was embarking on what is now nearly 35 years of thinking and research about how audiences use the media. My early research demonstrated that people concentrated less, and used less mental energy, watching television than most any other daily activity. I also found that people gravitated to the tube, partly, as an escape from negative feelings experienced earlier in the day. Later my work focused on whether or not television viewing can be considered an actual "addiction." I have concluded that heavy television use can be compared, in many ways, to actual substance abuse although, with television viewing habits, there appears to be no actual biological dependency as there is with addictive drugs. Otherwise, the similarities in how heavy television viewing develops, and is sustained as a habit, are remarkably similar to other habits that sometimes get out of control. Furthermore, obsessive and excessive use of other media, from

videogames to the Internet, can similarly become very habit forming and can sometimes interfere with the pursuit of other critical social, familial, work, and recreational activities.

This may sound as if I think television viewing is bad or even dangerous. I do not. I love a great many programs that appear on television and have done research and recently published a book on how they are created. The way I reconcile my work on media is to do research on, and advocate for media literacy education in our schools. It's my view, and that of a growing number of educators and researchers, that people must be educated in how to access, analyze, evaluate, and produce media in all their forms. Some of my recent research has focused on why media literacy education has been slower to develop in the United States than in every other English-speaking country in the world. Australia and Canada, for example, now mandate media education for all students in public schools. I have also done research on which approaches to delivering media education work best. In sum, my research points to the importance of understanding how the media communicate; how we can be misled by things we read, see, and hear; and also that our media habits need to be kept under some degree of personal control.

- Using computers and other communication technologies
- Assessing the value and importance of information
- Selecting, ignoring, and resisting messages when appropriate

Substituting Communication for Transportation

There has always been an interesting relationship between the functions of transportation technology and communication technology. Even with the earliest media this relationship was apparent. Instead of delivering a message in person, one could send it on horseback or by ship via courier. It was not necessary to deliver a message personally, if the information could be transported.

Moving messages across time and space can be an effective, efficient, and economical alternative to moving things or people. As Mark Aakhus notes:

> In thinking about the fast-paced changes in the area of communication and information technology, the prevailing idea is that "communication is the sharing of minds and that technology should make possible 'perpetual contact' that overcomes time and space barriers."[9]

Business conferences may be held between individuals across the continent using telephones and video hook-ups. Using telephone lines, doctors at a hospital monitor the vital signs of a patient miles away; and with similar technology, medical personnel also have access to current research findings in their efforts to diagnose and treat illness. Lawyers can search through the equivalent of whole libraries to find key cases or legal opinions, when connected to a nationwide network and computerized database, without leaving their offices. Moreover, AOL, Yahoo, Google, eBay, and Amazon.com offer access to a variety of services. And yet, as we shall discuss later, this capability can be a mixed blessing.

Evolving Concepts of Office and Home

With the capabilities of today's communication media, concepts of home and office have become far less distinct than they once were. For most of us, *work* has traditionally been a place away from home. However, because of new media, work is increasingly becoming less "a place" and more "an activity." The idea of an office filled with individuals conversing face-to-face about social and business matters is being joined by an understanding of *office* that includes an individual at home in leisure attire, engaged in telework—conducting business via phone, computer, or fax machine. As one home-worker comments: "You can work in your pajamas if you want to. There's no dress code to worry about. And there are perks that come from being in your own house, such as easy access to your favorite coffee and being able to position your desk so that you have a view."[10]

In discussing how new and converging technology will affect people's work lives, James Katz notes first-, second-, and third-order effects. First-order effects consist of the potential for increased productivity and better control over resources—time, people, and dollars. Multitasking, quick response time, mobile access, and better connectivity of all kinds help to make these outcomes possible. Second-order effects include reduced costs of starting new businesses, the potential for economic growth, and potentially, more efficient and effective relations with clients. Finally, Katz lists organizational control of workers as a third-order effect. Technology makes it easier to track, monitor, and measure productivity and activity—an asset, given some perspectives and purposes, and probably a liability given others.[11]

Increasing Value of Information as a Commodity

The economics of communication and information refers to the *value* associated with communication technology, products, and services. The evidence of value is the willingness of individuals, groups, organizations and societies to pay for these media and information products or services. Researchers point to an increasing number of individuals within the U.S. whose occupational roles involve information production or use; and the production of communication media and messages are central to a great many of the largest and most significant corporations.[12] As communication scholars Jorge Schement and Leah Lievrouw explain:

> Information has been exchanged in the marketplace since ancient times. But before the twentieth century it was rarely sold as a commodity in its own right, and, when it was, it was always treated as an exceptional good. Now it is exchanged as routinely as "ordinary" commodities . . . [13]

Information products, unlike many other products, can often be easily duplicated and are generally not consumed when they are used. Several pages of an article or songs on a CD can be copied without detracting from the value of the original product. Moreover, a book or CD can be passed along from one person to another, with each person deriving equivalent value. The fact that this is possible is a growing concern to authors, artists, composers, and production and distribution companies. This is not an issue with products like foods or fuels which cannot be easily copied and lose their value as they are consumed.

As scholar Alfred G. Smith noted: "Today our primary resource is information. Today knowledge is the primary wealth of nations and the prime base of their power. Today the way we trade messages and allocate information is our information economy."[14] In the case of media, use requires the purchase, lease, or rental of hardware. Typically, when first introduced, technologies are not widely affordable. As sales and production increase, costs generally drop, and an increasing number of consumers can afford the media.

However, even with economies resulting from production, contemporary communication technologies carry a substantial price tag, and many people cannot afford them. Beyond the cost of media hardware, there are costs associated with maintenance, software, and use (such as cable and online service subscription costs) by both producers and consumers. Often the one-time cost of buying equipment is small compared to costs of continued use and "upgrading" as the technology is refined.

For individuals, organizations, and societies alike, the potential of the Information Age is most readily available to those who can afford the necessary hardware and software. Because resources are unevenly distributed, advantage goes to those who can afford to acquire these products and services. Thus, it may be argued that rather than narrowing the gap between the information rich and poor, as so many had hoped would happen, advanced media of the Information Age may further increase that gap.

Increasing Availability of Synthetic Experience

Communication media often present messages that may be unlike any we experience first hand. As Ray Funkhouser and Eugene Shaw note:

> Until the nineteenth century, for most people actual experience was limited to events occurring within the 'natural sensory envelope'—the limits of the human nervous system to detect physical stimuli, governed by natural, physical processes.[15]

Today, communication media increasingly enable us to experience what may be termed a "synthetic reality." Funkhouser and Shaw list the following as examples:

- Altered speeds of movement, either slow or fast motion
- Reenactments of the same action (instant replay)
- Instantaneous cutting from one scene to another
- Excerpting fragments of events
- Juxtaposing events widely separated in time or space
- Shifting points of view, via moving cameras, zoom lenses, or multiple cameras
- Combined sight from one source and sound from another (e.g., background music, sound effects, dubbed dialogue)
- Merging, altering, or distorting visual images, particularly through computer graphics techniques and multiple-exposure processing
- Manufacturing "events" through animations or computer graphics[16]

Thus, communication media not only extend our capability to experience the realities available to our senses but actually add a number of "artificial" experiences as well.

The International Scene

Communication technology has always served to broaden our horizons and extend the range of information available to us. Now, with new and hybrid technologies, global communication on a scale that was only a fantasy a couple of decades ago has become a reality. TV satellite services, cell phones, and the Internet have had a dramatic impact on the international scene. Moreover, newspapers are printed and distributed at various geographic sites around the world via satellite, and the international distribution of books, CDs, DVDs, and computer software has become commonplace.

Media Characteristics

Asynchronous–Synchronous

In some communication situations, there is a substantial time lag between message production and consumption; with others there is little or no gap. In face-to-face communication, for instance, there is little or no time or space gap. Our verbal and nonverbal behaviors

RESEARCH PROFILE

Media, Race, and Crime • *Mary Beth Oliver*

African American men, in particular, are often portrayed on television as perpetrators of crimes. Professor Oliver's research explores the important implications of this stereotyping.

• • •

My research pertaining to race and the media has focused on the ways in which media portrayals associate crime, violence, and aggression with African Americans and African American men, in particular. For example, this research has examined the nature of portrayals in reality-based police programming, showing that African Americans are overrepresented as criminal suspects and underrepresented as police officers. African American criminal suspects are also more likely to be the victim of police aggression than are white suspects. Hence, these types of crime programs imply that not only are African American men particularly likely to be involved in crime, the types of crimes for which they are wanted are depicted as particularly dangerous or worthy of police use of force. Given these patterns, it is not surprising that subsequent research suggests that these types of shows are more appealing to and more frequently viewed by individuals reporting higher levels of racial prejudice.

More recently my research has focused on the ways in which viewers' memories of race and crime reported in news stories may serve to intensify or sustain stereotypes of African Americans. Specifically, my recent work on viewers' responses to news stories reveals a tendency for viewers to mistakenly remember seeing (and then identifying) African American men as individuals pictured in crime stories (and particularly violent stories) when these individuals were never actually featured. In addition, these mistaken and stereotyped memories appear to happen across all individuals, regardless of their self-reported racial attitudes. Consequently, this pattern of results suggests that these sorts of biases may be examples of implicit stereotyping and, therefore, are outside of viewers' awareness or ready control.

Given that, as a society, we often learn about other people and groups by how they are portrayed in the media, research on stereotyping and crime suggests that media portrayals of this sort should be carefully scrutinized. Furthermore, the importance of viewers' responses to these sorts of portrayals imply that greater attempts to enhance critical viewing skills and media literacy may be very important steps in attempting to diminish potentially harmful effects attributable to media consumption.

create messages which may be instantaneously attended to by other interactants. In such a situation, communication is *synchronous*. In other situations, the creation and transmission of messages is not synchronized in time with message reception and use. There may be a delay of seconds, minutes, hours, days, or even years—as, for example, between the printing of a book and its being read in different regions or countries. In such a circumstance, communication is *asynchronous*.

We can think of a continuum of situations in which communication media are involved, ranging from virtually synchronous to extremely asynchronous. At one extreme are communication situations involving media such as books, films, CDs, or DVDs; at the other are face-to-face interaction, concerts, and events involving "live" media like television, radio, instant messaging, and telephones. Nearer the center of the continuum are e-mail, voice messaging, and telephone answering machines.

Generally speaking, new media provide greater flexibility in bridging time and space than many of the earlier media. Depending on the specific application and the needs of interactants, media like fax, e-mail, teleconferencing, computers, and answering machines can be used in ways that either minimize or expand the gap in time between production and consumption.

Low Interactivity–High Interactivity

Communication media vary in the extent to which message content and timing are controlled by the source rather than by the user. With mass media such as books, television, newspapers, and magazines, content and timing of production and distribution are source-controlled. Audience members engage in active decision making about whether to give attention to particular mass media offerings and, in many instances, can actively and consciously choose *how* to use the information received. Consumer decisions—as well as letters to the editor and other forms of feedback—have an impact on content, but the influence is delayed and often indirect. In the short-term individuals have no way to interact with or control message content or timing. Such media have limited potential for *interactivity.*

Other media, such as telephones, e-mail, fax, VCRs, DVDs, home video, and many computer applications, are more interactive. They permit receivers to exert greater control over the content, timing, and locale. CDs, for example, can be played at whatever time of day or night we choose to listen to them. And we may choose to play these CDs at home, at work, in the car, or while walking or jogging. We can "fast-forward" through selections we don't care for, "pause" for interruptions, and "pause" or "rewind" to repeat segments that we particularly like. Similarly, voice mail, e-mail, and inexpensive home answering machines provide a high level of user control. See Box 9.4.

Communication researcher Carrie Heeter provides the following list of dimensions of interactivity that may be used to classify media.[17]

- *Complexity of choices available.* How much choice users have regarding content and timing of utilization.

BOX 9.4 • *Television Viewers Become Producers*

Technological advances promise to make broadcast television a far more interactive, user-controlled medium. For about the price of a movie channel, cable system subscribers are able to play a direct and active role in creating sports and news coverage. With such systems, viewers may select from among four different views of the event on four different channels. In the case of sporting events, one channel provides the traditional "wide angle" coverage. Other channels offer close-ups of players, while yet another provides continuous instant replays. For news programs, the system allows viewers to break away from the standard newscast at various points to receive more in-depth information on a news story of particular interest and later to return to the "standard" broadcast. Other applications are being developed and market tested.

- *Effort users must exert.* How the activity required by the user compares to the activity level of the medium.
- *Responsiveness to users.* How actively a medium responds to users; the degree to which media are "conversational"—that is, operate like human conversations.
- *Monitoring information use.* How able a particular medium is to monitor behaviors of users and adjust its operation based on this feedback.
- *Ease of adding information.* How easily users are able to create and distribute messages for other user audiences. Based on this criterion, broadcast television has very low interactivity, call-in radio has moderate, and computerized bulletin boards have very high levels of interactivity.
- *Facilitation of interpersonal communication.* How difficult interaction is between specific and known interactants.

Low Social Presence–High Social Presence

In some circumstances, we may have a sense that a communication event is quite personal, sociable, and warm. In other situations, the process seems impersonal, unsociable, and cold.[18] When the former occurs, the event is described as high in *social presence;* the latter is considered to be low. Not surprisingly, face-to-face communication is generally regarded as higher in social presence than mediated communication. There are also differences between media in terms of social presence, as shown in Table 9.3.

A primary difference between face-to-face and mediated communication that affects social presence is nonverbal communication. In all mediated situations some communication modes are restricted in this regard. In the case of written media, cues related to oral paralanguage, appearance, eye gaze, kinesics, proxemics, and haptics are absent. In the case of audio mediation, visual and tactile cues are missing, and so on.

Moreover, many of the conversational cues that are so important in face-to-face interaction may be missing in mediated situations. Researchers point out however, that, depending on the goals, the situation, and the relationship between interactants, the limitations on social presence may be unimportant. And, with care and attention, the social presence of any medium can be enhanced. See Box 9.5.

TABLE 9.3   *Social Presence Rating of Five Media*

Communication Mode	*Social Presence Rating**
Face-to-face	0.81
Television	0.24
Multispeaker Audio	−0.18
Telephone Audio	−0.52
Business Letter	−0.85

*Social presence scores range from +0.9 to −0.9.

Source: J. Short, E. Williams, and B. Christie, *The Social Psychology of Telecommunications* (New York: Wiley, 1976), p. 71.

BOX 9.5 • *The Need to Be "In Touch"*

A study published by the Office of Technology Assessment found that nearly half of those surveyed believed it was important to be in touch with other people.

Study findings include the following:

- 48.8% of those surveyed agreed with the statement: "My responsibilities require me to be easily reachable."
- 48.4% agreed that, "People need to contact me about important matters."

- 44.8% agreed that, "There are often times when I urgently need to get through to another person."
- 48.9% agreed that, "I 'stay in touch' even when I am on vacation."

The survey was conducted in 1994, which probably means the results understate the current needs people feel to be connected.

Source: James E. Katz, *Connections,* New Brunswick, NJ: Transaction, 1999, pp. 19–26.

Mediated Communication: A Mixed Blessing

Mediated communication extends the basic capacities of human communication. We generally think of this expansion in very positive terms, pointing to the capability of media to traverse time and space in a manner and at a pace that would otherwise be impossible. However, mediated communication is a mixed blessing, on the one hand enhancing and enlarging the potential of message sending and receiving, while on the other hand limiting and constraining communication or human experience.

Limited Communication Modes

One potential limitation imposed by media is the reduction of the range of potential modes of communication available. In face-to-face encounters, an individual has the potential for processing visual, auditory, tactile, olfactory, and gustatory modes. Communication media limit the number of these modalities and, hence, the *richness* of the information they provide.[19] In the case of telephone, radio, or print, one mode is involved. Television or film utilize two.

In one sense, of course, any restriction on the number of available modes can be seen as limiting the richness of human communication. For some purposes, however, one or two communication modes may be quite adequate. A newspaper or magazine account of an event in the Middle East certainly may provide consumers with an overview of noteworthy events that have transpired during the period in question. However, even with the most sophisticated communication media, many of the sights, sounds, and smells that were present for the reporter are unavailable to audience members.

At times, this limitation is not a liability but is, in fact, a positive and desirable characteristic. A case in point is a work of fiction. In reading a novel, it is often the absence of fully-functioning face-to-face communication modes which both requires and allows readers to play a very active role in creating the visual images themselves. In such an instance, it can be argued that the media constraint actually enhances the richness of the communication experience.

Decreased Control

In contrast with the typical face-to-face communication situation, the receiver or audience member in mediated communication often has much less influence on the content and directions of interaction. As suggested previously, this is particularly the case in mass-mediated situations in which the only option available to an audience member who wishes to alter the content of communication is to "turn off" the message—an option that at times we might wish were available in interpersonal situations!

New technologies, such as e-mail, answering machines, TiVos, and VCRs, have lessened the significance of this limitation of traditional media. This attribute helps to explain the popularity of many of these newer communication technologies.

It is important to note that from a source's perspective, mediated communication situations often afford *more,* rather than *less* control. A videotaped speech, prerecorded television program, or written correspondence may be revised many times before being released. In contrast, all face-to-face communication is "live," meaning that messages are produced and transmitted in the same act. There are no opportunities for rewriting, editing, reshooting, retouching, or lip-synching.

Anonymity and Depersonalization

In mediated communication situations, interactants often have no direct knowledge of one another. In many mass communication situations, for instance, audience members may know the producer, reporter, or author by name but may have little broader knowledge of the individuals involved. Despite this relatively limited information, it is interesting that audience members often think of themselves as "knowing media personalities."

The problem of anonymity and depersonalization is particularly apparent from the perspective of mass media sources. If mass communication producers know their audience members at all, it is generally in terms of their aggregate market characteristics such as age, gender, occupation, political orientation, or brand preferences.

While this limitation may seem to be a liability, there are a number of instances in which mediated communication serves as well as it does for the very reason that interactants do not know one another personally. The success of listener call-in radio programs can be partly attributed to the anonymity afforded by the medium. One need not identify himself or herself in order to share an opinion about a controversial topic or seek advice on a personal problem. In such instances, mass communication provides a vehicle for mediated therapeutic communication.[20] The attraction of 900 number "dial-a-date" or Web-based equivalents for some people can, similarly, be traced to the anonymity afforded by media.

It is important to remember that, in a sense, face-to-face interaction is also often mediated—by makeup, perfume, clothing, furniture arrangement, eyeglasses, scarves, and so on. Human encounters may also be mediated by shyness and apprehension, and these barriers are often less limiting in situations where technology is mediating than in face-to-face situations. It can certainly be argued that an encounter with a van Gogh portrait is more "personal" and less "anonymous" than one with a state trooper in mirrored sunglasses.

Decreased Responsibility and Accountability

The decreased control, anonymity, and depersonalization that sometimes occur in mediated communication situations can foster a sense of detachment, increased passivity, and a decreased sense of responsibility for directing the communication process and its outcomes. To a greater extent than in face-to-face encounters, the sense that we are actively engaged in a human communication act can be lost.[21] Because interactants are removed in time and space from one another, the dynamic nature of the process is obscured. These consequences can "spill over" to nonmediated situations, encouraging passivity and a lack of responsibility for one's role in the communication process generally.

Decreased Sense of Place

In 1985, Joshua Meyrowitz began a dialogue regarding electronic technology and one's "sense of place."[22] The discussion may have even greater relevance to everyday experience now than it did then. Essentially, the issue is that communication media—most especially the newer mobile technologies such as cell phones, laptop, and hand-held computers allow a user to be *physically,* in one time or place, but *communicationally,* at another point in time or place. To illustrate, you may be sitting on the beach surrounded by sunbathers while talking to a friend miles away. Or, you may be traveling in Europe, but using your free time to exchange e-mails with the office, family, and friends back home. Or, you may be visiting relatives, but spending much of your time working on a paper that will be due when you return from the trip. Or, you may be walking through a museum while listening to your favorite MP3s.

In these and other such instances, technology quite literally transports a person from the present place and moment to another time and place. While this was always a possibility to some extent through reading newspapers or books, watching television, or listening to music using conventional media, the possibilities are greatly magnified using portable technologies. No doubt, the ability to be in control of the media and messages to which one is exposed is comforting and probably contributes to one's sense of being in control, being in familiar circumstances, and so on. At the same time, it has the potential to lessen the possibility of having novel or unpredictable experiences or of meeting new and unfamiliar people. As the use of portable technologies increases, the possibility of finding ourselves increasingly in the past or future, or somewhere other than where we actually are—rather than in the present moment—seems an increasingly likely prospect, and an increasingly interesting topic for reflection.

Media and the Quality of Life

Media Forms

Over the course of human history, the forms of communication media have changed in dramatic, complex ways. Our first messages using communication tools were fashioned from

sticks, rocks, smoke, and fire. We have progressed today to the point where we are surrounded by a wide variety of machines and electronic devices that extend our information-
processing modalities incredibly. The advent of television made it possible to view as well
as listen to local and national programming for the first time. We now have cable television, projection television, and even television sets that double as telephones. While people
once made program selections from among a handful of stations, we are now able to choose
among any number of offerings in most locales in the country. And, with videocassettes,
we are not limited in our selections to programs being broadcast to us. In effect, we are
able to create our own programming with such luxuries as rewind, slow motion, stop-ac-
tion, fast-forward, and stereo sound.

Further advances in computers, cable, and telecommunication networks provide still
other options. Using relatively inexpensive computers and software, it became possible to
send and receive acoustically coded alphanumeric data through telephone lines. With this
medium, the user gained access to a number of large data bases that contained current
newspapers, airline schedules, and a variety of games. Using this same equipment, it became possible to bank, shop, bid for auction items, make restaurant reservations from
home, order "hard" printed copies of desired materials, and "converse" via computer.

As impressive as these home technologies are, there is little doubt that they will seem
elementary compared to the home communication centers to which we will become accustomed in the years ahead.

Nicholas Negroponte lists the following changes which will ultimately result from
the new media of the information age—some of which are already becoming reality.[23]

- *Place without space.* The limitations of geography are being eliminated. Life will depend less and less on being at a particular place at a particular time. Your e-mail address, for instance, is portable, and rather than being a physical location as is the case
  with postal addresses.
- *Being asynchronous.* With asynchronous media, our time-management capacity
  greatly increases. We respond to voice messages and e-mail, and watch videotapes
  of television programs when it's convenient for us, rather than when it is convenient
  for someone else.
- *Demanding on demand.* With new media, it will be increasingly possible to shift from
  "broadcasting" to "broadcatching"—from accepting standardized programming that is
  broadcast to mass audiences to having programming selected, sorted, and organized in
  a customized manner that meets our individualized needs. As Negroponte notes, on-
  demand information will come to be the accepted standard in new media.[24]

Media Functions

For all the obvious changes in the *forms* of our communication media over the years, it is
important to question the extent to which their *functions* have also changed. There can be
little doubt that communication media today are quicker and more flexible than ever before. To what degree, however, have these changes led to an improvement in the quality of
human communication or the quality of life? In any given day, how much more do we know

as a result of all the technology we have available? Are people more satisfied in their jobs? How much better entertained are we by all the new media? Are we better organized, or happier? Do we have better relationships? Do people understand each other better? Is the promise of improved international relations becoming a reality?

Questions such as these remind us that communication media are only extensions of our own communication abilities and liabilities. They can do little more than transport, store, duplicate, amplify, or display the messages *we* create. The nature and significance of messages and the uses to which they are put will depend, in the final analysis, on us and not on our media.

Implications and Applications

- Media play a pervasive role in our personal, social, and occupational activities.
- Through mediated communication we are able to overcome natural limitations of space and time.
- Mediated communication also provides a means for supplementing human memory by expanding our capacity for storing, arranging, and retrieving information.
- Increasingly, we need the capacity to analyze media and messages to determine their quality, value, and appropriateness for particular purposes. We need to know when and how to select particular media and messages and when and how to *deselect*—disregard, distrust, or ignore—media and messages. This implies that we must also develop skills for assessing our own and others' communication needs and goals.
- There are many circumstances in which mediated communication can be substituted for—and may be more effective than—face-to-face communication. In such situations, we must be able to determine the trade-offs between these two types of communication—as sources and receivers.
- As our forms of personal, organizational, and mass media become increasingly sophisticated, it is easy to conclude that the qualities of human communication and of human life are advancing at a similar pace. Changes in media forms, however, do not necessarily result in corresponding changes in function. More news sources, channels, watts, remote controls, CDs, video games, and Web sites do not necessarily result in our being better informed, better entertained, happier, or more successful. A critical question is: as individuals in relationships, groups, organizations, and societies, are we using mediated or face-to-face communication in a way that can fulfill the desired functions?

Summary

Our tool-making facility has given us the ability to create communication media—technological devices that extend our natural ability to create, transmit, receive, and process visual, auditory, olfactory, gustatory, or tactile messages. The basic functions media serve involve: message production and distribution, and reception, storage, and retrieval.

Communication media have had major impacts on contemporary life. These include an increase in the number of messages and media, an increase in the capacity for information storage and retrieval, a substitution of communication media for transportation technology, the initiation of new concepts of office and home, the changed uses of media, an increase in the value of information as a commodity, and the increasing availability of synthetic experience. Characteristics of media include their degree of synchronicity, interactivity, and social presence.

Over the course of human history, the forms of communication media have changed in dramatic ways. For all the changes in the *forms,* it is important to question the extent to which their *functions* have also changed. Have these changes led to an improvement in the quality of human communication or in the quality of life? Questions such as these remind us that the nature and significance of messages and the uses to which they are put will depend, in the final analysis, on us and not on our media.

Notes

1. For detailed discussions of the history of communication media see George N. Gordon, "Communication," in *World Book Encyclopedia* (Chicago: World Book, 1981), Vol. 4, pp. 711–723; and Colin Cherry, *World Communication: Threat or Promise? A Socio-Technical Approach* (New York: Wiley, 1971). See also Jorge Reina Schement and Daniel A. Stout, Jr., "A Time-Line of Information Technology," in *Information and Behavior: Volume 3. Mediation, Information, and Communication.* Ed. by Brent D. Ruben and Leah Lievrouw (New Brunswick, NJ: Transaction, 1989), pp. 395–424.

2. Anthony Smith, *Goodbye Gutenberg: The Newspaper Revolution of the 1980s* (Oxford: Oxford University Press, 1980), p. 3.

3. Robert J. Samuelson, "A Cell Phone? Never for Me," *Newsweek,* August 18, 2004. Statistics provided by the Cellular Telecommunications & Internet Association (CTIA) and Pew Research Center.

4. Nicholas Negroponte, *Being Digital* (New York: Vintage Books, 1995), pp. 5–6.

5. Internet World Stats, http://www.internetworldstats.com/stats.htm, August 19, 2004.

6. Edwin Parker, "Information Utilities and Mass Communication," in H. Sackman and Norman Nie, eds., *The Information Utility and Social Choice* (Montvale, NJ: AFIPS Press, 1970), p. 53.

7. See discussion in John V. Pavlik and Shawn McIntosh, *Converging Media,* Boston: Pearson, 2004, based on statistics provided by Veronis Suhler Releases 15th Annual Communications Industry Forecast, May 15, 2002, http://www.veronissuhler.com/publications/forecast/highlights2001.html.

8. Ithiel De Sola Pool, Hiroshi Inose, Nozomu Takaski, and Roger Hurwitz, *Communication Flows: A Census in the United States and Japan* (New York: North-Holland Press, 1984), p. 44. Based on data covering 1960 to 1980 for radio, television, cable television, records, tapes, movies, classroom education, newspapers, books, direct mail, first class mail, telephone calls, telex, telegrams, mail grams, fax, and data communication.

9. Mark Aakhus, "Understanding Information and Communication Technology and Infrastructure in Everyday Life," in *Machines That Become Us,* James E. Katz, ed. New Brunswick, NJ: Transaction, 2002, p. 27.

10. "Running Your Business from Home," *Aide Magazine,* Feb. 9, 1991, p. 10.

11. For a detailed discussion of these effects, see James E. Katz, *Connections.* New Brunswick, NJ: Transaction, 1999, pp. 19–26.

12. Further discussion of these issues is provided in Todd Hunt and Brent D. Ruben, *Mass Communication: Producers and Consumers* (New York: Harper-Collins, 1992), Chapter 20; and Jorge Reina Schement and Leah Lievrouw, *Complex Visions, Complex Realities: Social Aspects of the Information Society* (Norwood, NJ: Ablex, 1987).

13. Schement and Lievrouw, 1987, p. 3.

14. Alfred G. Smith, "The Cost of Communication," Presidential Address, International Communication Association, 1974. Abstracted as "The Primary Resource," *Journal of Communication,* Vol. 25, 1975, pp. 15–20.

15. Ray Funkhouser and Eugene F. Shaw, "How Synthetic Experience Shapes Social Reality," *Journal of Communication,* Vol. 40, No. 2., 1990, p. 78.

16. Funkhouser and Shaw, 1990, p. 79.

17. See listing, discussion, and review of additional writings on this topic by Carrie Heeter, "Implications of New Interactive Technologies for Conceptualizing Com-

munication," in *Media Use in the Information Age: Emerging Patterns of Adoption and Consumer Use.* Ed. by J. L. Salvaggio and J. Bryant (Hillsdale, NJ: Lawrence Erlbaum), pp. 217–235; Ronald E. Rice, "New Media Technology: Growth and Integration," in *The New Media.* Ed. by R. Rice and Associates (Beverly Hills: Sage, 1984), pp. 33–54; and William Paisley, "Computerizing Information: Lessons from a Videotex Trial," *Journal of Communication,* Vol. 33, No. 1, 1983, pp. 153–161.

18. See Ronald E. Rice, "Computer-Mediated Communication System Network Data: Theoretical Concerns and Empirical Examples," *International Journal of Man-Machine Studies,* Vol. 32, 1990, pp. 627–647; Ronald E. Rice and Gail Love, "Electronic Emotion: Socioemotional Content in a Computer-Mediated Communication Network," *Communication Research,* Vol. 14, No. 1, 1987, pp. 85–108; and Rice, 1984, pp. 57–62, for a detailed discussion.

19. See discussion and review of literature on information richness in Ronald E. Rice and Associates, "Task Analyzability, Use of New Media, and Effectiveness: A Multi-Site Exploration of Media Richness," *Organization Science,* 3(4), 1991, pp. 475–500.

20. Gary Gumpert and Sandra L. Fish, eds., *Talking to Strangers: Mediated Therapeutic Communication* (Norwood, NJ: Ablex, 1990), provide an excellent collection of articles examining therapeutic uses of communication technologies.

21. See Kubey and Csikszentmihalyi, 1990, for a discussion of the impact of television viewing on passivity.

22. Joshua Meyrowitz, *No Sense of Place.* Cambridge: Oxford University Press, 1986.

23. Negroponte, 1995, pp. 185–191.

24. Negroponte, 1995, p. 169.

10 The Individual

In this chapter

Why . . .

- We know how to sit on chairs and say hello to people.

- Making sense of our world involves playing with toys and talking to others.

- Becoming is important.

- Stress can be good for us.

- A window can help us understand our interpersonal communication.

Reaction, Action, and Interaction

Earlier we discussed message reception, verbal and nonverbal communication, and the nature and role of communication media and technology in some detail. When we examine these separately, we "freeze" and dissect the communication process in order to gain a better understanding of its components. The chapters in this section extend this framework to consider the role of communication in the ongoing activities of individuals, relationships, groups, organizations, cultures, and societies. We begin with a focus on the individual and the role communication processes play in our everyday lives and in our long-term development.

Through message receiving and sending we *sense, make sense of,* and *act toward* the people, circumstances, and objects in our environment. As we process visual, auditory, tactile, olfactory, or gustatory messages, we are *reacting* to our environment. When we initiate verbal and nonverbal communication, we are *acting*. We are *interacting* when we are involved in message-sending/message-receiving exchanges with other interactants.

Reacting, acting, and interacting are the most basic activities of human communication. They are essential to basic functions like navigation, parent–child relations, and

215

courtship, and are equally vital to interpretation, cognitive development, self-development, self-expression, and self-reflexiveness.

Interpretation

In the ongoing dynamics of human life, we must not only select, interpret, and remember messages, but we must also use the resulting information as the basis for the decisions that guide our behavior. Our decision making occurs in what may be termed an *information-use environment.* We can distinguish four general types of information-use environments.[1]

- *Geographical.* Defined by physical or geographical limits. Examples: a room, building, neighborhood, city, state, region, or country.
- *Interpersonal.* Defined by the presence of other individuals in face-to-face situations. Examples: ritual greeting situations, riding with others on an elevator, an interview, a conversation, or a date.
- *Group or organizational.* Defined by the presence of individuals in a group or organizational unit formed for a specific purpose. Examples: a club, a fraternity or sorority, a religious organization, a corporation, a public institution.
- *Cultural or societal.* Defined by the presence of individuals who may be personally unknown to each other, but who are linked by a common cultural, ethnic, or national affiliation. Examples: Latino, African American, Canadian.

We carry out decision-making activities in any of these circumstances by employing an *information-use sequence* through which messages are used as the basis for interpretation and action. See Figure 10.1.

In nearly every circumstance, a primary interpretive use of a message is to *describe:* to determine the nature, characteristics, or appearance of an object, situation, or person. Description is necessary for the most basic communication functions like navigation, food finding, and courtship, as well as in relationships, groups, organizations, or societies.

Based on our descriptions, *classification* is possible. When we classify, we compare our new observations with information stored from previous experience to see where a person, object, or event "fits."

Through *evaluation* we identify the range of possible relationships between ourselves and the objects, situations, or persons in our environment, and determine what, if any, actions or reactions are appropriate and/or necessary.

A fourth step in the message-processing sequence is carrying out particular verbal or nonverbal actions, based on our descriptions, classifications, and evaluations. Then, after *acting,* we often gather information as "feedback" to monitor and assess the impact of those actions. In so doing, we are once again involved in the description, classification, and (re)evaluation and action sequence. See Figure 10.2.

Let's illustrate this sequence by considering a very simple activity. Imagine for a moment that you have just left a classroom and stepped out into the hallway looking for a place to relax, check your phone messages, and spend ten minutes before your next class.

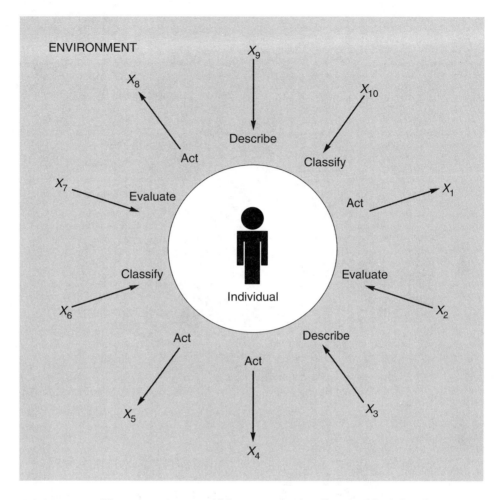

FIGURE 10.1 We use messages to which we react to describe, classify, and evaluate the objects, people, and circumstances in our environment. When we *act* based on our reactions, we *create* messages, completing the information-use sequence.

As you begin to move through the hallway, you notice a chair ahead of you. Actually, of course, you don't notice a chair. Instead, you see a physical object from a particular point of view. Based on the visible characteristics of that object, you infer the existence of portions of it that you cannot see. You may only be able to make out two legs, for instance, connected by what appears to be a one-inch-thick horizontal plane. Given your observation that the object is standing evenly on the floor, however, it seems safe to conclude that there are probably two additional legs which are not visible because of your position relative to the object. See Figure 10.3.

As you continue to interpret information, you eventually classify the object as a chair, by which you mean "something to sit on." In the split second that this information-use

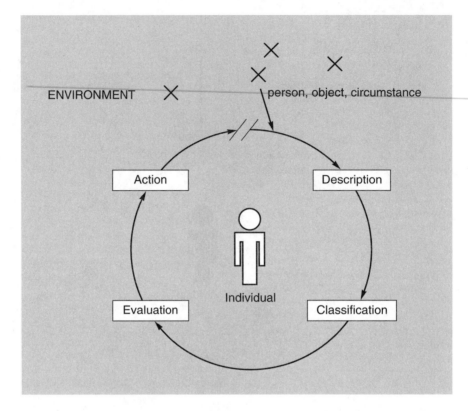

FIGURE 10.2 *Information-Use Sequence*

sequence requires, you observe it, walk over, and sit down, in full confidence that the object will support your weight.

With only a slight change in circumstance, the outcomes of the interpretive process might be quite different. If, for example, the hallway were crowded with people and you were in a hurry, your attention might well be focused on *avoiding* rather than using the chair. In such a situation, the objective would be to maneuver past the object, perhaps without ever giving a thought to it as "something to sit on." The chair would be a "stationary object to be avoided," and you would act to move rapidly past it.

From the perspective of interpretation, the way we process information about people, circumstances, and objects is similar. If you noticed someone walking toward you in the hallway, his or her appearance, expressions, eye movements, actions, use of time and space would serve as message sources in the same way as did the properties of the chair. His or her nonverbal (and perhaps, verbal) behavior would serve as the basis for information as to age, gender, race, attractiveness, and perhaps even willingness to talk to you.

If, from your description, classification, and evaluation the person seemed friendly, interesting, and receptive, you might exchange glances, smile, or speak. If, however, you were in a hurry to get to your next class, it is likely that you would relate to the individual

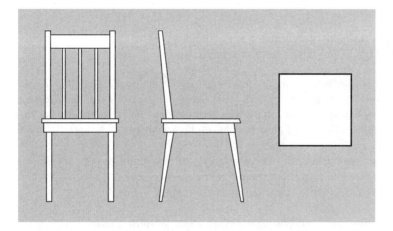

FIGURE 10.3 In observing an object such as a chair, we infer—based on past experience—elements, properties, and characteristics that we often cannot actually see.

in the hallway precisely as you would to the chair in the previous example. He or she would be classified essentially as "something to be avoided," with the major difference between a person and a chair being that the former is "mobile" and the latter "stationary." Thus, whether the message sources that matter to us in a particular situation are people, objects, or circumstances, we go through a similar process of describing, classifying, evaluating, and then acting. Because of differing goals, needs, habits, and other factors, however, the outcomes of this sequence may vary greatly from one situation to another.

When the information being processed involves other people, the process of reacting to and acting often gives rise to a process of *interacting*. In such a circumstance the interpretive activities of each person are contingent on the behavior of the other. As we will see in the next chapter, relationships are developed by means of interpersonal communication and reciprocal interpretation and action.

Cognitive Development

As psychologist O. J. Harvey noted: "That the individual will come to structure or make sense of the personally relevant situation is one of psychology's most pervasive tenets."[2] During each instant, we are involved in reacting to, acting toward, and interacting with our environment and the people in it. At the same time we are engaged in a far more subtle activity with major long-term consequences for us. As we routinely process information and develop interpretations, we are also developing internalized representations of our world that allow us to think and comprehend what we experience around us. These personal theories or representations—which are variously called *images, mental models, cognitive maps,* and *semantic networks*—provide our means for relating to the environment and to one another.[3]

Learning

Our images develop over time in a very complex manner. The process begins early in life. As Jose Delgado and others have observed:

> The newborn baby is not capable of speech, symbolic understanding, or directing skillful mobility. It has no ideas, words, or concepts, no tools for communication, no significant sensory experience, no culture. The newborn baby never smiles. He (or she) is unable to comprehend the loving phrases of his (or her) mother or to be aware of the environment.[4]

Helped and limited by the physiological potentialities we inherit—our "cognitive hardware"—we begin to learn about our environment and our relation to it and to develop our personalized theories—our "cognitive software."

> For some time . . . (the baby) see(s) just a mass of shifting shapes and colors, a single, ever-changing picture in front of (him or her). . . . The picture . . . is not made up, as it is for us, of many separate elements, each of which we can imagine and name, by itself, and all of which we can combine in our minds in other ways.
>   When we see a chair in a room, we can easily imagine that chair in another part of the room, or in another room, or by itself. But for the baby the chair is an integral part of the room he (or she) sees. . . . This may be the reason, or one of the reasons, why when we hide something from a very young baby, it ceases to exist for him (or her). And this in turn may be one of the reasons why peek-a-boo games are such fun for small babies to play, and may contribute much to their growing understanding of the world.[5]

The infant's awareness of mother, father, food, and objects as potential sources of satisfaction represents perhaps the first elements of the child's lifelong cognitive map-making enterprise. Gradually, the infant's world view expands to take account of the rapidly changing environment of his or her experience. The fascination and attention to fingers, hands, and mouth broadens to toys in and around the crib and to the physical environment itself. The map continues to expand to define more and more detail of the child's room, other rooms in the dwelling, the neighborhood, the community, and eventually, the country and world. At the same time, the child is developing the verbal and nonverbal communication rules necessary for making sense of and relating to his or her social environment—first family, then friends, relatives, acquaintances, teachers, peers, colleagues at work, and so on.

As children grow, they select, interpret, and retain information, and they begin to learn about the physical and social environment and their relationship to it. The physical and social world provides an extensive menu of message sources, as the developing human individual embarks on a life-long quest to make sense of and cope with the situations he or she encounters. See Figure 10.4.

As suggested earlier, much remains to be learned about the ways in which selected environmental cues are transformed into interpretable information and stored in a way that makes it quickly and easily accessible to us. It is thought by scholars working in this area that much of the information is processed and stored in long-term memory in what cognitive psychologists call a *semantic network,* whereby incoming messages are linked systematically to previously stored information based on common characteristics.

FIGURE 10.4 As we respond to the many circumstances, objects, and persons in our environment, we are developing our internalized theories of the world.

A *canary,* for instance, might become significant to an individual through a process of comparing its properties to those of previously observed and classified objects. That it "has wings," "flies," and is "quite small" suggests it is similar to other animals we have learned to call *birds*—about which information has been previously processed and retained. That this *bird* "sings" and is "in a cage in a friend's house," suggests that while this canary has much in common with other birds, it also is different in some respects. A *canary* is a special kind of bird—a *pet bird.* See Figure 10.5.

As Morton Hunt explains metaphorically:

> New material is added to this network by being plunked down in a hole in the middle of an appropriate region, and then gradually . . . tied in, by a host of meaningful connections, to the appropriate nodes in the surrounding network.
>
> Thus, although remembered information is arranged by categories of subject matter, the arrangement is far less orderly and regular than in reference works or libraries. But also far more redundant: we have many ways of getting to something filed in long-term memory, many cues and routes to the item we are seeking. When no cue or route takes us directly to it, we can guide ourselves to the general area and then mentally run through the items in that area until we come across the one we're looking for.[6]

Our personal theories and representations are the long-term informational consequence of our efforts to adapt to the messages with which we are confronted over the course of our lifetimes.[7] They are not simply the result of an accumulation of messages to which we have been exposed, though these messages certainly play an important role.[8]

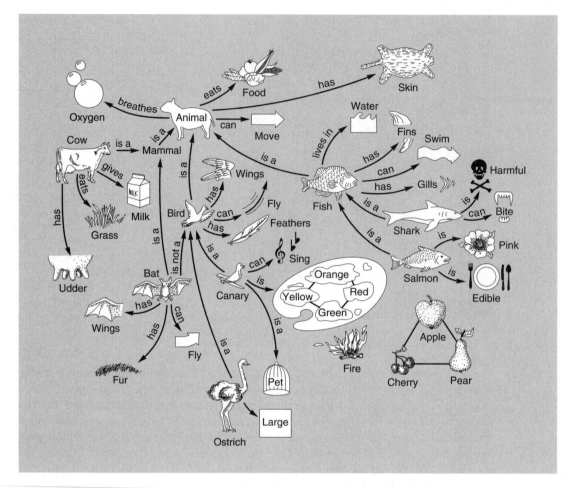

FIGURE 10.5 Humans interpret, store, and retrieve information according to the associations and meanings the objects, phenomena, and events of their experience have for them.

Source: Adapted from Roy Lachman, J. L. Lachman, and E. C. Butterfield, *Cognitive Psychology and Information Processing.* Copyright © 1979 by Lawrence Erlbaum Associates. Reprinted with the permission of Roy Lachman and Lawrence Erlbaum Associates, Inc.

Mediated Communication and Development

Mediated communication plays a critical role in the developmental process. In our culture, television often is the first medium to which children are exposed, and it rapidly becomes a noteworthy part of their lives.[9] Studies indicate that by four years of age, many children have become regular viewers.[10] Researchers have found that television use begins even earlier for some children, based on observations that babies six to twelve months old respond visually and verbally to TV for one to two hours daily.[11]

Books, and later newspapers and magazines, begin to take on significance during the grade school years. Studies find that one-third of six- to eight-year-olds have read a newspaper. The percentage increases to 61 percent for nine- to eleven-year-olds, 75 percent for twelve- to fourteen-year-olds, and more than 80 percent for fifteen- to seventeen-year-olds.[12]

A similar pattern occurs for radio and recordings. One-third of six- to eight-year-olds listen to radio or recordings on a daily basis; the figure increases to 60 percent of fifteen- to seventeen-year-olds.[13] The availability of computers, DVDs, portable CD players, and online services has further extended the role of mediated communication in the daily routines of children.

Children and adolescents spend lots of time playing electronic games such as video and computer games. Researchers Jeanne Funk and Debra Buchman examined the game-playing behavior of seventh- and eighth-grade students.[14] Not surprisingly, they found that boys report spending more time than girls playing electronic games both at home and in arcades. Girls are more likely to favor fantasy violence games, and boys are more likely to favor human violence games. Although these researchers note that there is no indication that playing electronic games causes major adjustment problems for most players, they did find that girls who spend more time playing electronic games also had a more negative self-concept. Self-concept and game-playing behavior was not correlated for boys. The researchers note that game-playing habits may be a warning sign that could be used to identify adolescents who are at risk for adjustment problems.

Characteristics of Personal Representations

Through a subtle self-programming process, as a consequence of communication, we acquire the personal theories and mental models and associations that direct our behavior in any given situation. Whether we are aware of it or not, our mental models and decision rules guide us about what to say, when to say it, how to act in this and that circumstance, how to tell one kind of circumstance from another, what to pay attention to and what to ignore, what to value and what to dislike, what type of people to seek out and which to avoid, what and whom to believe, and so on.

These representations are our means for navigating in our symbolic and physical environments and the basis for our functioning as human beings. They enable us to act and react and to carry our knowledge of our environment forward in time. Without them, each experience would be totally new and potentially bewildering.

The significance of these theories is clear when we consider an illustration such as the simple act of putting a key in a lock or opening a door. Our image of keys and doors and our rules for door opening tell us how to locate and use the handle and whether to pull or push the door in order to open it. Without this stored knowledge, each door opening would be a wholly novel and very time-consuming experience.

Models are also invaluable in dealing with interpersonal aspects of our environment. Standardized greetings such as a handshake and "Hi, how are you?" and "Fine, thanks, and you?" are easily accomplished. This is the case because we have categorized a particular situation as being like certain other situations in the past, for which we have learned a particular conversational pattern. Our models also guide us in deciding when "Hi! How are you?" is simply a request for a "routine" acknowledgement, and when the person wants more detailed information about our physical or mental health.

In emphasizing the obvious assets and values of our internal theory-building capability, it is quite possible to overlook some of the shortcomings and dysfunctions of this capacity. Primary among these liabilities is the fact that once our internal representations become fairly well defined, they take on an objective quality and sometimes become rigid. Often, they seem so real to us that we lose sight of their representational nature and forget that they are in many senses our own personal creations. We seldom give a second thought, for instance, to whether a paper dollar has buying power, or to the meaning of symbols like "dog" or "mother," "Democrat" or "Republican," "man" or "woman." We have so thoroughly internalized our images of "dollars," "mother," or "dogs," that we may behave as if our representations were, in fact, identical to the persons, objects, situations, or ideas to which they refer.

This kind of problem comes about for several reasons:[15]

1. The environment is constantly changing while our representations are relatively fixed.
2. Any representation is necessarily incomplete.
3. Representations are personal and subjective.
4. Representations are social products.
5. Representations are resistant to change.

Changing.   Like a paper map and the territory it characterizes, there can never be a point-for-point correspondence between our cognitive map and our environment. General semanticists, who developed the map-and-territory analogy, point out several reasons why this match between our internal maps and external physical and symbolic reality is never complete. The first has to do with the process-like nature of the environment. The environment is ever-changing.[16] Our symbols and symbolic images are not always changing in the same way or at the same rate of speed as the environment. For instance, long after we have moved a clock or wastebasket to a new location, we persist in looking for it where it used to be because of our well-learned maps. As another example, some older people are still surprised when they visit a doctor's office and discover that she is a woman.

The usefulness of our representations is often time-dependent. Images and models appropriate at one point in time may be useless, even harmful at other times. For example, many fathers today would like to take advantage of the paternity leave policies of their employers, but they continue to be told (however subtly) that taking time off from work will jeopardize their careers. The world and the behavior of its inhabitants may change substantially from one time to another, and there is unfortunately no guarantee that our maps will be sensitive to these changes. If for no other reason, we should perhaps be grateful that our memories are imperfect, since forgetting contributes to the potential for change in our maps.[17]

Incomplete.   A second reason for mismatches between our maps and the environment is that our representations are always less complete and comprehensive than what they symbolize. Details are invariably left out. Much as a highway map highlights some features of the landscape and ignores others, our personal images are also selective. They are generalizations that categorize or stereotype selected aspects of the environment for our convenience. See Figure 10.6.

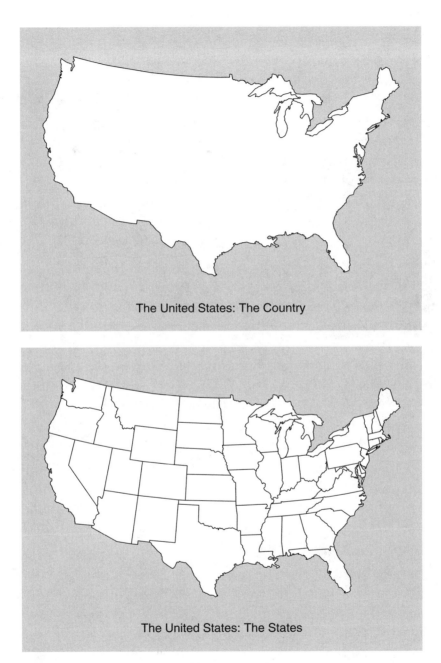

The United States: The Country

The United States: The States

FIGURE 10.6 Our maps, like physical maps of geographic territories, are necessarily selective. Maps highlight some characteristics of a territory and obscure others. These maps also exclude two important parts of the U.S. What are they?

(continued)

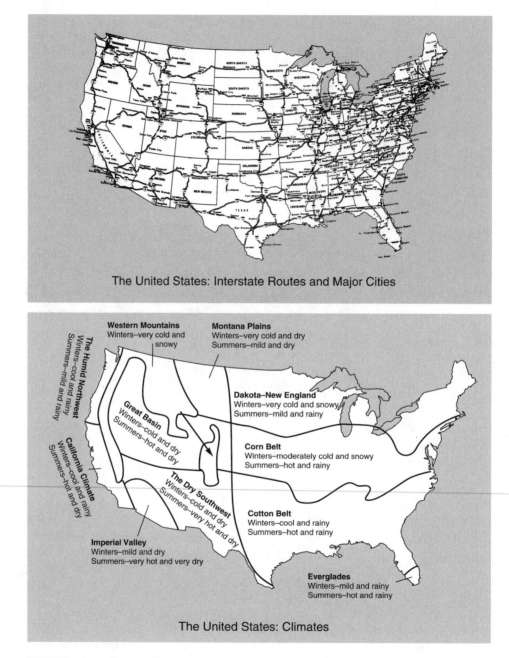

The United States: Interstate Routes and Major Cities

Western Mountains
Winters–very cold and snowy

Montana Plains
Winters–very cold and dry
Summers–mild and dry

The Humid Northwest
Winters–cool and rainy
Summers–mild and rainy

Dakota–New England
Winters–very cold and snowy
Summers–mild and rainy

Great Basin
Winters–cold and dry
Summers–hot and dry

Corn Belt
Winters–moderately cold and snowy
Summers–hot and rainy

California Climate
Winters–cool and rainy
Summers–hot and dry

The Dry Southwest
Winters–cold and dry
Summers–very hot and dry

Cotton Belt
Winters–cool and rainy
Summers–hot and rainy

Imperial Valley
Winters–mild and dry
Summers–very hot and very dry

Everglades
Winters–mild and rainy
Summers–hot and rainy

The United States: Climates

FIGURE 10.6 *Continued*

The symbol "dog," to which we have previously referred, illustrates this point. Each person has a different image of the animal to which the word refers. When we think of dog, our images are based on our own personal experience, which bears an arbitrary relationship to the four-legged animal we refer to as "dog." Further, our personal meaning of "dog" is very likely to be far less comprehensive than the collective standardized definitions of the word.

Stereotypes tend to reduce individual differences to generalizations about a group in ways that may be damaging to people.[18] In addition, stereotypes generally have an evaluative dimension—they are seen as either negative or positive.[19] For example, the negative stereotype that women are passive and indecisive was used in the past as an excuse to keep women out of positions of political power. The success of women such as Supreme Court Justices Sandra Day O'Connor and Ruth Bader Ginsberg demonstrate the limitations of this stereotype.

Personal and Subjective.   As we know, our images develop in our effort to adapt to the situations that confront us in our lives. We are not all confronted with the same situations, and the images and rules we develop as a result of our experiences vary greatly from person to person.

An exchange between two characters in the classic film *Eye of the Beholder* makes this point. The scene takes place on a sidewalk in an urban area. A landlord (Copplemeyer) and his artist tenant (Michael Garrard) gaze across the street at a passing woman:

> *Garrard:*   Do you see that woman over there? She isn't real.
>
> *Copplemeyer:*   That woman over there isn't real, huh? I made her up from my imagination?
>
> *Garrard:*   Yes, exactly. One man looks and sees nothing, another looks and falls in love. Today I will put on a canvas what I see in a woman. To me the painting will be as real as that woman. To you it will be only a painting.
>
> *Copplemeyer:*   The painting will be as real as that woman?
>
> *Garrard:*   Yes, Copplemeyer, yes! Do you understand?
>
> *Copplemeyer:*   I understand you are a lunatic!
>
> *Garrard:*   (laughing) You see, Copplemeyer, you prove my point. The man you see in me does not exist.[20]

This dialogue clearly illustrates that we each create our own images.

Social Product.   Whether one considers a child striving to make sense of a toy jack-in-the-box, a physicist trying to integrate a new observation into his or her theory, or a salesperson trying to make a sale, the influence of others is unmistakable. From our earliest days, parents, family, and previous generations play a role in determining the messages and experiences to which we will be exposed. Even the language we use is a product of our having developed the necessary knowledge and skills through social learning.

We are influenced not only by these informal, developmental experiences but also by our formal education and training. These social processes direct our attention in a highly selective fashion, highlighting certain phenomena and situations while minimizing others, shaping our representations in a host of subtle and not-so-subtle ways through the course of our lifetime.

For example, many families celebrate important religious or civic holidays in ways that have been handed down through several generations. Specific decorations may be used. Particular prayers may be said by specific family members or "meaningful" foods may be eaten. The importance of these traditions can be seen when two people from different cultural traditions have to negotiate the "right way" to celebrate a particular event. Giving up a cherished tradition (like hearing a relative recount a familiar family story) may be difficult.

Stable and Rigid.   After our images are fairly well established, new messages generally produce very little fundamental change. After we have developed a preference for one political party, for instance, it is unlikely that a single or even several advertisements or news articles will lead us to change our affiliation. Similarly, once we have decided we don't care for a particular job, television program, or individual, it is seldom that any single exposure to potentially contradictory information will change our minds.

Our maps and force of habit tend to guide us toward messages and message sources that are generally consistent with the representations we have developed. In most instances, our tendency is to ignore or distort information that contradicts or disconfirms our image.

Like the scholar who has great difficulty discarding a particular theory or scientific paradigm even in the face of seemingly disconfirming information, we part reluctantly with elements of our personal paradigms—our representations of reality. Nonetheless, in some instances, changes in our models do occur. Sometimes the weight of accumulating evidence, the influence of people who are important to us, or critical incidents in our own lives lead to fundamental changes in our ways of acting, reacting, and interacting. Even a single incident can have a rather dramatic impact. Sometimes, for instance, a car accident, illness, disappointment, or a particular achievement can be a trigger for significant change.

Self-Development

Becoming is a term coined by Gordon Allport to capture the dynamic process by which we as humans develop, modify, and refine our personal identity—our "self" and our concept of ourself.[21] The role of communication in this "becoming process" can be viewed as beginning with the very act of conception, at which instant the information necessary to the blueprint of growth for the offspring begins its work. The potentials we inherit are nurtured and shaped by our life experiences in our physical and communicational environment. Collectively, these experiences exert a subtle yet pervasive influence on us.

We know that our self-development is very much shaped by our earliest interactions with those who care for us as infants and children. For the most part, our care givers create and control the environment to which we are exposed and with which we must cope.

As we grow, our care givers are our models for how we are to act and how we are to think and feel about ourselves.

Psychologist Carol Gilligan believes that the way children experience their early social environment is different if they are male or female. She contends that since the primary caretaker in the first three years of life for both sexes is usually female (a mother or other female adult), "the interpersonal dynamics of gender formation are different for boys and girls."[22] According to this theory, girls experience themselves more like their mothers and fuse the experience of attachment with the process of gender development. Boys, on the other hand, experience themselves unlike their mothers in some ways and are more likely to be comfortable with separation. Given this initial developmental experience, women are more likely to see problems in terms of conflicting responsibilities and their impact on relationships with others (called the ethics of care), while men are more likely to base their judgments on a hierarchical set of principles determining what is right and wrong (called the ethics of justice).

As we grow and become mobile, the number and diversity of shaping influences increase. As shown in Figure 10.7, encounters with family members are supplemented by face-to-face dealings with peers, and by broadening experiences in relationships, groups, organizations, and society. The impact of these interactions is sometimes quite dramatic. We come to use the same "buzz words" and slang phrases as friends and family members, and we often share their values, opinions, occupational preferences, outlooks, and political preferences. We may adopt similar styles of dress and even develop the same gestures. Some of these shaping influences have a fundamental and lasting impact on our development, others much less so.

Mass communication and communication technologies also play a role in our self-development in that they provide us with a wealth of information relative to such facets of life as masculinity and femininity, age, race, occupation, consumption, violence, health, and family and interpersonal relations. People are increasingly turning to the Internet as a source of health information, for example.

An important part of self-development is our self-esteem or sense of self-worth. People with a high sense of self-esteem generally have a positive attitude toward themselves.[23] They are satisfied with themselves, believe they have a number of good qualities, feel they have much to be proud of, and respect themselves.

Self-esteem affects our communication behavior. For example, people with high self-esteem are more flexible in the way they respond to situations.[24] They may be able to cope better with a difficult situation because they are more relaxed and are able to accept themselves as they are. Judy Pearson and her colleagues contend that self-esteem is so important that similarity in self-esteem may be a factor in selecting a person to date or have a relationship with.[25]

Stress and Growth

Self-development is an ongoing process of adjusting and readjusting to the many influences, challenges, and opportunities we encounter. As such, it is necessarily a stressful process.

From a biological point of view, the *stress-adjustment cycle* we go through directly parallels that of other living things, whose day-to-day existences are also fraught with continual

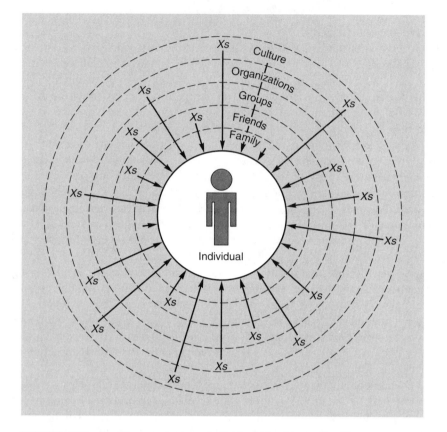

FIGURE 10.7   To a large extent our individual identities and self-concepts are a consequence of having adapted to information from our family and the relationships, groups, organizations, and culture of which we have been a part.

threats and challenges to their growth and development.[26] However, in terms of the origins of the stress, and the means available for dealing with it, we are quite unlike other animals. Most animals detect and react to threats and challenges in their environment in a direct, reflex-like manner. For instance, when a deer hears a loud noise, it instinctively begins to run away from the source of the noise. It detects a challenge to its well-being, comfort, or safety, and it flees. This instinctive reaction to stressful situations is known as the *fight-or-flight response.*

Human stress is usually the consequence of a second-order information-processing event involving symbolic meaning. Many of the situations that are stressful for us threaten our psychological, rather than physical, well-being. The threat of rejection by a loved one, a heated argument with a colleague, the prospect of failing an important exam, or the pressure of an approaching deadline for an incomplete project are frequently potent stressors for us. Positive events, like marriage, can be stressors, too. Other common stresses are listed in Box 10.1. These symbolic threats are capable of triggering the same hormonal,

BOX 10.1

Health Educator Fern Walter Goodhart has adapted Holmes and Rahe's Life Events Scale (also called the Social Readjustment Rating Scale) to measure stress levels. To determine your stress score, circle the number adjacent to each event that has occurred to you in the past six months. Add up the numbers. Under 150 is a "reasonable" level of stress. If your score is above 150, you have an elevated risk of stress-related health changes. Scores above 300 indicate a 50 percent chance of serious health change in the next two years.

Event	*Points*
Death of a spouse/partner	100
Unwed pregnancy (if you are female)	92
Death of a parent	80
Male partner in an unwed pregnancy	77
Divorce	73
Death of a close family member	70
Death of a close friend	65
Parents' divorce	63
Jail term	61
Major personal injury or illness	60
Marriage	55
Fired from a job	50
Loss of financial support from college	48
Failing grade in an important or required class	47
Sexual difficulties	45
Serious argument with significant other	40
Academic probation	39
Change in major	37
New love interest	36
Increased academic workload	31
Outstanding personal achievement	29
First term in college	28
Serious conflict with an instructor	27
Lower than expected grades	25
Change in college (transferring to a new school)	24
Change in social activities	22
Change in sleeping habits	21
Change in eating habits	19
Minor violation of the law (e.g., traffic ticket)	15
Total	

Source: From http://health.rutgers.edu/stress/stressed_out.asp. Adapted from T. Holmes and R. Rahe, "Social Readjustment Rating Scale," *Journal of Psychosomatic Research, 2* (1967), p. 214.

muscular, and neural reactions that for other animals are associated only with physical threats to their safety and well-being.

Unlike other animals, we do not generally cope with challenge by physical fleeing or fighting; we have learned that physical combat and running away are not regarded as "civilized" ways for us to deal with problems. Because of this learning, we hold our bodies in check and usually react by "fight" or "flight" only in a symbolic sense. For example, we might spend a large portion of a boring class looking out of a window day-dreaming about our plans for the weekend. Although we control our urge to physically flee from the situation, our mind has taken flight.

Though stress and adjustment are normal aspects of human life, evidence suggests that chronic and accumulated stress can have serious physical, as well as emotional, consequences, as suggested in Box 10.1. Research indicates that stress lowers our resistance to illness and can play a contributory role in diseases of the kidney, heart, and blood vessels, as well as contributing to high blood pressure, migraine and tension headaches, gastrointestinal problems such as ulcers, asthma, allergies, respiratory diseases, arthritis, and even cancer.[27]

Though there are a number of negative consequences of stress, it is an inevitable part of the process of life and of becoming. It may also be a very positive force in the sense that stress presents opportunities for personal and social growth and change.[28] Ultimately, the consequences of stress for us depend on the ways in which we take advantage—or fail to take advantage—of the opportunities environmental challenges provide.

This duality is expressed clearly by physician M. Scott Peck in *The Road Less Traveled:*[29]

> What makes life difficult is that the process of confronting and solving problems is a painful one. Problems, depending upon their nature, evoke in us frustration . . . grief . . . sadness . . . loneliness . . . guilt . . . regret . . . anger . . . fear or anxiety. These are uncomfortable feelings . . . often as painful as any kind of physical pain. . . .
>
> Yet it is in this whole process of meeting and solving problems that life has its meaning. . . . It is only because of problems that we grow mentally and spiritually.

Becoming is not a passive process. In reacting to, acting upon, and interacting with these influences, we provide the fuel for the becoming process. Each encounter builds on the last, as we negotiate our way through the demands and opportunities around us and as we fashion our identities. In a very real sense, we become what we live. Whatever we are, have been, and will be—whether dominant or submissive, withdrawn or outgoing, self-confident or insecure, rigid or flexible, passive or assertive—is very much influenced by the communication experiences we have had up to that point and the ways we have adapted to them.

Self-Expression

Although we are discussing the concepts of self-development and self-expression separately, they are inextricably intertwined. Our sense of self is developed in interaction with others; therefore, our ability for self-expression is a crucial component of the relational process of communication. Self-expression is a fundamental facet of human activity. Whether it involves speaking, writing, painting, singing, or engaging in other forms of performance, the process is one of communication.

In a wide range of communication situations, a great deal of our energy is expended not only "making statements," but also "making a statement." "Making statements" serves *instrumental* communication functions. In the case of instrumental communication, we have information we want to convey or receive, and our efforts are directed toward ensuring the clarity of our messages and accuracy of meanings. In contrast, "making a statement" has to do with *expressive* functions of communication. Here, our concerns may be more with impression, tone, and mood.

In his classic book, *The Presentation of Self in Everyday Life,* sociologist Erving Goffman makes a similar distinction. He notes that there are two kinds of communication: expressions *given* and expressions *given off.*[30] Goffman describes self-expression using a theatrical metaphor in which individuals are actors on a stage, presenting themselves to an audience. In this perspective, people encounter one another in face-to-face engagements and take turns presenting dramas or telling stories to one another. In distinguishing between instrumental and expressive forms of communication, Goffman says

> . . . often what talkers undertake to do is not to provide information to a recipient but to present dramas to an audience. Indeed, it seems that we spend most of our time not engaged in giving information but in giving shows. And observe, this theatricality is not based on mere displays of feelings of faked exhibitions. . . . The parallel between stage and conversation is much, much deeper than that. The point is that ordinarily when an individual says something, he is not saying it as a bold statement of fact on his own behalf. He is recounting. He is running through a strip of already determined events for the engagement of his listeners.[31]

Thus, if the goal of instrumental communication is exchanging information, *impression management* is the goal of expressive communication. But it is important to note that expressive communication is not necessarily an intentional process, as suggested by Figure 10.8. Through verbal and nonverbal behaviors, we create the basis for impressions—and form impressions of others—whether we intend for this to occur or not.

Kenneth Burke also believed that people see the world in terms of a drama.[32] He developed the *Dramatistic Pentad* to analyze the language individuals use for self expression. The five elements are

1. *Scene* (the place where the action occurs). People who focus on the scene are *materialists.* They believe that changing the scene or environment will change people. For example, a couple having problems in their relationship might go to a romantic location to see if they can improve their relationship.
2. *Act* (the action that occurs). People who focus on the act are *realists.* They process and record information and believe that a mixture of causes directs human affairs. They support the status quo.

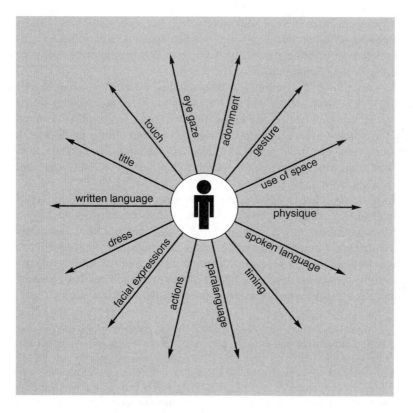

FIGURE 10.8   Every facet of our behavior is a potential source of instrumental and expressive communication.

3. *Agent* (the actor who acts out the action or plot). People who focus on the agent are *idealists.* They believe that people control their own destiny. Persuaders who focus on the agent would encourage people to join self-help programs.
4. *Agency* (the tool actors use to accomplish their ends). People who focus on agency are *pragmatists.* They search for the most speedy and immediately practical solutions. They might support putting up a stop sign at a dangerous intersection, for example.
5. *Purpose* (the reason why people do what they do). People who focus on purpose are labeled *mystics.* They believe a power or focus beyond them directs human destiny. They would support religious or patriotic ideas.[33]

Burke argued that people were more likely to use whichever element corresponded to their view of the world. Thus, individuals who are pragmatists, for example, would be likely to argue that a particular restaurant was a good place to eat because it is inexpensive and in a convenient location. A realist, on the other hand, might say, "We always eat at the Pizza Palace on Wednesday nights. Why change?"

FIGURE 10.9 Individuals express themselves in a variety of ways including clothing and hairstyle.

It is important to understand our usual mode of self-expression and to determine if we want to modify or alter it to fit the needs or expectations of a particular audience. See Figure 10.9 for an interesting example of self-expression.

Emotional Intelligence

One of the keys to interpersonal competence in relationships is to effectively manage our emotions—what Daniel Goleman and others refer to as emotional intelligence or EI. Most fundamentally emotional intelligence has to do with the way in which we understand and regulate our emotional reactions. Scholars identify several critical facets of EI:

- *Self-awareness.* The ability to recognize and understand our own moods, emotions, and drives, and their effects on others
- *Self-regulation.* The capacity to control our impulses and moods, and to think before taking action
- *Motivation.* A passion for work and a propensity to energetically and persistently pursue goals
- *Empathy.* The capacity to understand others' emotions and reactions
- *Social skills.* Competency in building and maintaining interpersonal networks and building rapport[34]

Emotional intelligence is displayed through communication. It is through our verbal and nonverbal behavior in social interaction that our orientation of emotion becomes apparent to others and, at the same time, influences interpersonal dynamics and relationships.

Self-Awareness

Self-Reflexiveness and Self-Monitoring

As we discussed in Chapter 5, the capacity for self-reflexiveness is one of the fundamental characteristics of human communication. Our self-reflexive capability allows us to look upon and analyze ourselves, our thoughts, and our actions. It also permits us to turn our attention inward in order to examine our own communication behavior. Through self-reflexiveness, we can replay and think about our actions, reactions, and interactions. Similarly, we can examine our own self-development and self-expression. We also can reflect on our interpretive processes, cognitive development, and self-development.

When we engage in any of these forms of self-reflexiveness, we do so by means of *intrapersonal communication*—the processing of messages of which we, ourselves, are the source. By means of intrapersonal communication and self-reflexiveness, we are able to engage in *self-monitoring*—the analysis and adjustment of our actions in order to achieve a particular communication goal (or goals). We are engaged in self-monitoring when we analyze our communication behavior in a public speaking situation, in a job interview, on a date, or in exchanges with colleagues. Although we all analyze our communication behavior to some extent, people who are high self-monitors are more likely to behave in a way they think is required in a social situation, while low self-monitors are more likely to act in a way consistent with their values, attitudes, and beliefs.[35] In each of these cases and so many others, we have one or more communication goals we want to achieve. If we are aware of our goals and understand the nature of communication, we can monitor and adjust our communication behavior, our goals or both.

As we noted earlier, it is difficult to discuss self-awareness without referring to interaction with others. One way to think about our understanding of ourself as part of the communication process is by using the Johari Window. The *Johari Window* provides a useful way to think about the dynamics of self-awareness of behavior, feelings, and motives. Shown in Figure 10.10, the *Johari Awareness Model,* as it is also known, includes four quadrants:

- Quadrant 1, the open quadrant, refers to behavior, feelings, and motivation known to self and others.
- Quadrant 2, the blind quadrant, refers to behavior, feelings, and motivation known to others but not to self.
- Quadrant 3, the hidden quadrant, refers to behavior, feelings, and motivation known to self but not to others.
- Quadrant 4, the unknown quadrant, refers to behavior, feelings, and motivation known neither to self nor to others.[36]

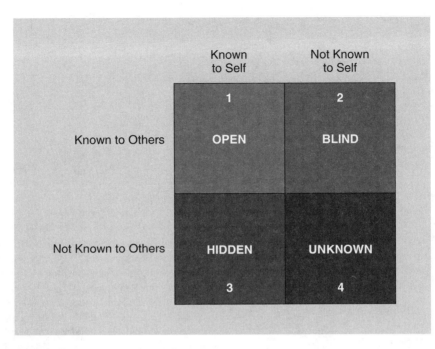

FIGURE 10.10   *The Johari Model*

Source: "The Johari Model" from *Group Process,* 3rd edition by Joseph Luft. Reprinted by permission of The McGraw-Hill Companies.

In discussing the model, Joseph Luft contends that we should strive to increase self-awareness by reducing the size of Quadrant 2—our blind area. Quadrant 2 is an area of vulnerability in that it includes what others know about our behavior, feelings, and motivation that we are unaware of, or choose to ignore or deny. Decreasing our blind area also has the effect of increasing Quadrant 1—the open area—and this in turn holds promise for improving interpersonal relationships as well as self-awareness. Luft offers a number of suggestions for how one can enhance self-awareness:

- Threat tends to decrease awareness; mutual trust tends to increase awareness.
- Forced awareness (exposure) is undesirable and usually ineffective.
- Interpersonal learning means a change has taken place so that Quadrant 1 is larger, and one or more of the other quadrants has grown smaller.
- Sensitivity means appreciating the covert aspects of behavior, in Quadrants 2, 3, and 4 and respecting the desire of others to keep them so.[37]

Self-reflexiveness and self-monitoring provide us with a means of assessing our actions, reactions, and interactions, understanding ourselves, benefiting from experiences,

RESEARCH PROFILE

Self-Talk in Intrapersonal Relationships • *Linda C. Lederman*

The relationship we have with ourself can be as important as the relationships we have with other people. Professor Lederman describes how this relationship is created, maintained, and changed over time.

• • •

For a number of years I was aware of how much I affected my own feelings about any given day by the kinds of things I said to myself about myself, like "Your hair's too short" or "Great decision you made." I started to wonder whether this was true for other people, too. And that began my study of self talk, and of what I came to refer to as *intra*personal relationships.

I based my conceptualization of *intra*personal relationships both on my own initial interviews with others about their self talk and other exploratory studies. My studies provided me with information about people's internal dialogues with themselves about themselves. A review of the *inter*personal literature helped provide ways for me to interpret that information by analogy. It suggested to me how it was possible to study relationships that are not observable. I discovered that cues to *intra*personal relationships could be found in what people can tell you about what they say to themselves, such as "I said to myself, 'Look, fella, ya gotta get with the program' " or someone reporting that she said to herself, "Hey, babe, you look so cool."

By examining intrapersonal relationships using the same kinds of considerations used in the exploration of interpersonal relationships, I was able to explain intrapersonal communication as including intrapersonal relationships. I also became sure that all of us could improve our relationships with ourselves, just as we can improve our relationships with others. When we talk in encouraging, supportive ways (including appropriate criticism), we create more positive relationships with our friends, family, and others. The exact same thing is true when we talk constructively to ourselves about ourselves. No one would have a good day if he or she were followed around all day by a "friend" who was continually putting her or him down. And none of us have good days when our internal voices are giving us a hard time, either. Listening to our internal conversations with ourselves and learning to talk in constructive ways to ourselves about ourselves is a guaranteed way to enhance our relationships with ourselves, to feel a sense of self-worth and well being, and to create a relationship on which we can always count: our relationship with ourselves.

enhancing our interpersonal effectiveness, learning from our failures as well as our successes, and growing as human beings. They can be incredibly powerful tools, providing some of our most important opportunities for applying our understanding of communication and human behavior to the betterment of our own lives.

Self-Talk

One of the ways to increase self-awareness is to focus our attention periodically on how we talk to ourselves. Many of us spend time analyzing how we talk to others and how they talk to us, but how often do we think about how we talk to ourselves? How do we talk to ourselves when we have failed at something? When we have succeeded? Are we as supportive and forgiving of ourselves as we would be of others?

Self-talk provides clues as to the kind of relationship we have with ourselves.[38] As much as our relationships with others can typically benefit from care and attention, so too can our relationships with ourselves.

Implications and Applications

- A basic communication need is to make sense of the situations we encounter.
- We use messages to make decisions about the physical environment, and we also use them to make decisions about the human and social environment.
- Over time, the consequences of our individual interpretations form patterns. These patterns form the basis for the personal theories, or representations, that guide our ways of sensing, making sense of, and acting toward the people, objects, and circumstances we encounter.
- Personal representations are mixed blessings. On the one hand, they are invaluable as guides to orient ourselves in what would otherwise seem like a forever new and unpatterned world. On the other hand, our personal representations may also allow us to mislead ourselves because they may not correspond well to the changing world in which we live, and because they are necessarily incomplete, personal, subjective, socially-based, and resistant to change.
- Throughout our lives, we develop as individuals through communication encounters in a variety of relationships, groups, organizations, and culture. We are very much influenced by these communication experiences; in a sense, we are created by them.
- The phrase "no pain, no gain" is one way to express the relationship between stress and growth—both of which are inevitable aspects of communication. When we experience the pain of failure, fear, or loss, it is extremely difficult to see the experience as positive. However, the raw material for intellectual and emotional growth is present in such circumstances.
- Impression management is one of the major communication activities in which we engage as individuals. We want to be seen and thought about in particular ways; and most of us devote substantial time, money, and energy to achieve this communication goal.
- Self-reflexiveness can be very beneficial in enhancing our ability to understand and use our communication knowledge. It is this capacity that allows us to make plans and set goals for ourselves. And it is self-awareness and self-monitoring that later allow us to assess our own performance, evaluate it against our goals, and identify ways to improve our performance the next time.
- Self-talk can be one of the most important forms of human communication.

Summary

We have examined a number of uses and consequences of communication from an individual perspective. By sending and receiving messages, we react to and act toward the people, objects, and events in our environment. It is also through communication that we interact and negotiate meanings with others.

Interpretation is a fundamental process in which communication plays an important role. In making interpretations, we use messages to describe, classify, evaluate, and act in information-rich environments.

Communication is also basic to cognitive development. Through message processing we learn and develop the personalized theories and representations of the world that guide our behavior. These representations have limitations because they may fail to keep pace with changes in the environment. Additionally, they are incomplete, subjective, socially-influenced and sometimes overly rigid.

"Becoming" is a term coined to refer to the process of self-development. The role of communication in development continues throughout our lives, as we adjust to a variety of individuals, influences, and circumstances.

In the developmental process, we undergo stress in our efforts to adapt to the challenges and opportunities that present themselves. Many of the stressors to which we react are symbolic and themselves the product of communication. Through communication, we identify these stressors; and message processing is a primary means by which we react to and cope with such circumstances.

Self-expression is a fundamental part of human activity. Whether it involves speaking, writing, painting, singing, or engaging in other forms of performance, the process is one of communication. Communication serves instrumental and expressive functions. Instrumental communication involves conveying information; expressive communication involves impressions.

Self-awareness involves reflecting on and monitoring our own behavior. Awareness involves intrapersonal communication—the processing of messages of which we ourselves are the source. By means of self-reflexiveness and self-monitoring, it is possible to adjust our communication behaviors to achieve particular goals. Analysis of "self-talk" provides insight into the kind of relationship we have with ourselves. Self-awareness gives us an important opportunity to apply our understanding of communication on our own behalf.

Notes

1. Adapted from Robert S. Taylor, *Value-Added Processes in Information Systems* (Norwood, NJ: Ablex, 1986), p. 35.

2. O. J. Harvey, *Motivation and Social Interaction* (New York: Ronald, 1963), p. 3.

3. The term *map* is drawn from the writings of general semantics. See Richard W. Budd, "General Semantics," in *Interdisciplinary Approaches to Human Communication,* 2nd. ed., Ed. by Richard W. Budd and Brent D. Ruben (New Brunswick, NJ: Transaction, 1988), for a discussion of the history of the term. *Image* was first used in the present context by Kenneth Boulding in *The Image* (Ann Arbor, MI: University of Michigan Press, 1956). The phrase *semantic network* comes from cognitive psychology. See Morton Hunt, *The Universe Within* (New York:

Simon & Schuster, 1982), for a general discussion of the origin and uses of the term.

4. Jose M. R. Delgado, *Physical Control of the Mind* (New York: Harper, 1969), p. 45. See also "Neurophysiology" in Budd and Ruben 1988, p. 126. Parenthetical material added.

5. John Holt, *How Children Learn* (New York: Pitman, 1969), p. 61. Parenthetical material added.

6. Morton Hunt, *The Universe Within* (Simon & Schuster, 1982), pp. 107–108.

7. See George Kelley, *A Theory of Personality* (New York: Norton, 1963), for a discussion of a similar notion that he refers to as *personal constructs*. See also the discussion of schemata in Edward E. Jones, David E. Kanouse, Harold H. Kelley, Richard E. Nisbett, Stuart Valins, and Bernard

Weiner, *Attribution: Perceiving the Causes of Behavior* (Moorestown, NJ: General Learning Press, 1971).

8. See Kenneth Boulding, "General Systems Theory—The Skeleton of Science," *General Systems,* Vol. 1, 1956, p. 15.

9. An excellent overview of this topic is presented by Ellen Wartella and Byron Reeves in "Communication and Children," in *Handbook of Communication Science.* Ed. by Charles R. Berger and Steven H. Chaffee (Newbury Park, CA: Sage, 1987), pp. 619–650.

10. D. Roberts and C. Bachen, "Mass Communication Effects," in *Mass Communication Review Yearbook.* Ed. by D. Charles Whitney and Ellen Wartella (Newbury Park, CA: Sage, 1982), pp. 29–78.

11. Hollenbeck and R. G. Slaby, "Infant Visual Responses to Television," *Child Development,* Vol. 50, 1979, pp. 41–45.

12. Newspaper Advertising Bureau, 1980.

13. Newspaper Advertising Bureau, 1980.

14. Jeanne B. Funk and Debra D. Buchman, "Playing Violent Video and Computer Games and Adolescent Self-Concept," *Journal of Communication,* Vol. 46, No. 2, 1996, pp. 19–32.

15. See Budd, 1979. See also Wendell Johnson, *People in Quandaries* (New York: Harper, 1946).

16. Johnson, 1946.

17. See discussion of adaptive function of forgetting in Hunt, 1982, p. 111, and Elizabeth Loftus, *Memory* (Reading, MA: Addison, 1980), p. 19.

18. Lea P. Stewart, Pamela J. Cooper, Alan D. Stewart, and Sheryl A. Friedley, *Communication and Gender,* 4th ed. (Boston: Allyn and Bacon, 2003), p. 158.

19. E. Seiter, "Stereotypes and the Media: A Reevaluation," *Journal of Communication,* Vol. 36, No. 2, pp. 14–26.

20. Dialogue based on *The Eye of the Beholder,* Stuart Reynolds Productions.

21. Gordon Allport, *Becoming* (New Haven, CT: Yale University Press, 1955).

22. Carol Gilligan, *In a Different Voice* (Cambridge, MA: Harvard University Press, 1982), p. 7.

23. For an excellent discussion of self-esteem see Morris Rosenberg, *Conceiving the Self* (New York: Basic Books, 1979).

24. William B. Gudykunst, Stella Ting-Toomey, Sandra Sudweeks, and Lea P. Stewart, *Building Bridges: Inter-personal Skills for a Changing World* (Boston: Houghton Mifflin, 1995), p. 40

25. Judy C. Pearson, Lynn H. Turner, and William Todd-Mancillas, *Gender and Communication,* 2nd ed. (Dubuque, IA: Wm. C. Brown, 1991), p. 67.

26. See Hans Selye, *The Stress of Life,* rev. ed. (New York: McGraw-Hill, 1976).

27. Thomas H. Holmes and Richard H. Rahe, "The Social Adjustment Rating Scale," *Journal of Psychosomatic Research,* Vol. 11, 1967, pp. 213–218; a review of research and a discussion of the relationship between stress and illness is provided by Kenneth R. Pelletier, in *Mind as Healer, Mind as Slayer* (New York: Delacorte, 1977), pp. 117–188.

28. See Brent D. Ruben, "Communication and Conflict: A System Theoretic Perspective," *Quarterly Journal of Speech,* Vol. 64, No. 2, 1978, pp. 202–210.

29. M. Scott Peck, *The Road Less Traveled* (New York: Simon & Schuster, 1979), p. 17.

30. Erving Goffman, *The Presentation of Self in Everyday Life* (Garden City, NY: Doubleday, 1959), p. 4.

31. Erving Goffman, *Frame Analysis: An Essay on the Organization of Experience* (Cambridge: Harvard University Press, 1974), p. 508. See overview in Stephen W. Littlejohn, *Theories of Human Communication* (Belmont, CA: Wadsworth, 1988), pp. 106–108.

32. Kenneth Burke, *A Grammar of Motives* (Berkeley: University of California Press, 1970). For an excellent discussion of Burke's principles see Charles U. Larson, *Persuasion: Reception and Responsibility,* 6th ed. (Belmont, CA: Wadsworth, 1992), pp. 126–129.

33. Larson, 1992, pp. 126–127.

34. Daniel Goleman, "What Makes a Leader?," *Harvard Business Review,* 1998, November–December.

35. Gudykunst et al., 1995, p. 179; see also Mark Snyder, *Public Appearance/Private Realities* (New York: W. H. Freeman, 1987) for an extensive discussion of this concept.

36. Joseph Luft, *Of Human Interaction* (Palo Alto, CA: Mayfield, 1969).

37. Luft, 1969.

38. Linda C. Lederman, "Intrapersonal Communication," in *Encyclopedia of Communication and Information.* Ed. by Jorge R. Schement (New York: Macmillan, 2002), pp. 490–492.

11 Relationships

In this chapter

Why . . .

- People riding on elevators are engaged in interpersonal communication even if they don't speak.

- Both short- and long-term relationships have advantages.

- Breaking up isn't always hard to do.

- Intimate communication is important to health.

- Pets make good relationship companions.

Interpersonal Communication and Relationships

Types of Relationships

- Dyadic and Triadic Relationships
- Task and Social Relationships
- Short- and Long-Term Relationships
- Casual and Intimate Relationships
- Dating, Love, and Marital Relationships
- Family Relationships

The Evolution of Relationships

- Stage One: Initiation
- Stage Two: Exploration
- Stage Three: Intensification
- Stage Four: Formalization
- Stage Five: Redefinition
- Stage Six: Deterioration

Relational Patterns

- Supportive and Defensive Climates
- Dependencies and Counterdependencies
- Progressive and Regressive Spirals

Factors That Influence Patterns

- Stage of Relationship and Context
- Interpersonal Needs and Styles
- Power
- Conflict

Implications and Applications

Summary

For months you have wanted to get together to try to work things out. You think your ex feels the same way. What's needed is calm and rational conversation. You want to make clear how much the relationship matters and to try to recapture what's been lost. Minutes into the encounter, another argument begins. Your ex thinks he or she is right; you are convinced you're right. He or she yells; you yell back even louder, as each of you tries—in vain—to get one another to understand.

Participation in relationships with friends, family members, intimates, roommates, siblings, employers, and peers is basic to life. Situations like the one above are, unfortunately, not all that uncommon. They remind us that productive relationships are as challenging to develop and maintain as they are important to us.

Communication is the basic ingredient in social life, and an understanding of it can be a very powerful tool for fostering positive and productive relationships of all kinds.

The concepts of *communication* and of *relationship* are intertwined in several basic ways. First, as we have seen, one of the most fundamental outcomes of human communication is the development of social units; and no such units are more central to our lives than relationships. Second, our relationships—with parents, relatives, friends, intimates, and colleagues—are essential to our learning, growth, and development. Third, it is within relationships of one sort or another that most of our purposeful communication activities take place.

Interpersonal Communication and Relationships

What is a *relationship*? Sometimes the term *relationship* is used as a way of talking about a friendship we regard as particularly significant. Relationships may involve emotional or sexual intimacy. Relationship is also used more generally to refer to other one-to-one social units, such as those composed of a teacher and student, parent and child, employer and employee, or doctor and patient.

Although most people agree that friendships, intimate arrangements, or other social groupings qualify as relationships, few people would use this term to describe passengers riding on an elevator or strangers passing on a crowded street. From the point of view of communication, however, these also can be thought of as relationships, and analyzing these units provides valuable insights into other, more complex, human relationships.

In the most basic sense, a *relationship* is formed whenever reciprocal message processing occurs: that is, when two or more individuals mutually take account of and adjust to one another's verbal or nonverbal behavior. This reciprocal message processing, which we can call *interpersonal communication*, is the means through which relationships of all types are initiated, develop, grow, and sometimes deteriorate.

One of the simplest relationships is that created by people passing one another on a crowded sidewalk. In order for two individuals to negotiate past each other without bumping, each must process information relative to the other's presence, location, direction, and rate of movement. The individuals involved must use this information to guide their action in order to pass without colliding. In this simple situation all the essential elements of any relationship are in operation.

A slightly more complex example is provided by people riding on an elevator, as depicted in Figure 11.1. When alone in an elevator, most of us stand to the rear, often in the center. Typically, as a second person enters, we move to one corner or another, leaving the remaining corner for the newly arriving passenger. In so doing, we initiate a simple relationship as we take note of and adjust our behavior—movements, gestures, and position—relative to one another. With little conscious awareness, reciprocal message processing and mutual influence have taken place, as we define and redefine the territory available for our use.

As a third person enters the elevator, further adjustments are likely to occur as the social unit shifts from a two-person relationship to one composed of three individuals.

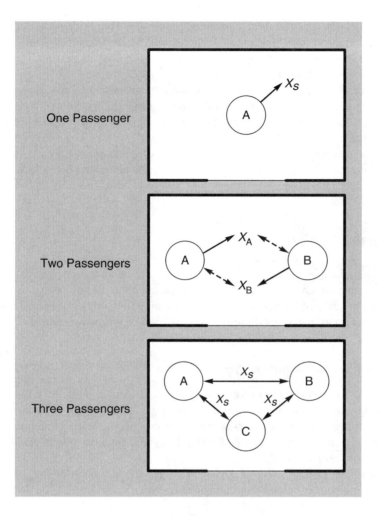

FIGURE 11.1 In a very basic sense, a relationship is formed among passengers on an elevator as the individuals adjust their behavior relative to one another, based on an awareness of one another's presence.

Readjustments of this kind provide observable evidence that reciprocal message processing is taking place and that a relationship has been formed.

Whether our point of reference is strangers passing on the street or an intimate, enduring friendship, the basic dynamics involved in the formation and evolution of relationships are quite similar. In each circumstance, we enter the relationship behaving toward other people on the basis of the personal theories and representations we have acquired through previous experience. As relationships develop, a mutual influence occurs as we adopt or create *joint, or relational, communication rules.* These rules guide, shape, and, in a sense govern the particular social unit from its initiation through the various stages of development to its eventual termination, in much the same ways as personal representations guide an individual's behavior.

In the case of strangers passing on the street, the information-processing rules the individuals use are relatively simple; and the relationship itself is short-lived. By contrast, intimate relationships between people who have lived or worked together for many years can be exceptionally complex.

We are unaware of many of the relationships of which we are a part. Very often, we are taking account of and being taken account of, influencing and being influenced, without awareness or intention.

Types of Relationships

In this chapter, the primary focus of our discussion will be on those relationships of which we are aware and which we intentionally form and maintain. Relationships of this kind can be classified in terms of a number of factors, including the number of people involved, the purpose of the relationship, its duration, and the level of intimacy attained.

Dyadic and Triadic Relationships

The vast majority of our relationships are *dyads*—two person units. As children, our first contacts with others are dyadic, and it is not until we reach the age of six to twelve years that we are able to engage in conversation with several people at the same time.[1] As adults, we are members of a large number of different dyads, such as roommates, best friends, spouses, or co-workers.

As William Wilmot notes in *Dyadic Communication,* each of the many dyads in which we participate is unique in a number of respects.[2]

1. Every dyadic relationship fulfills particular ends. The functions served by a teacher–student relationship, for instance, are generally quite different from those of a husband–wife relationship; and both are distinct from those served by doctor–patient or employee–employer relationships.
2. Each dyad involves different facets of the individuals who participate in them. The demands placed on an individual as a student in a teacher–student relationship are different from those placed on that same person as a wife in a husband–wife relationship or as a supervisor in a work relationship. No two dyads in which we participate make precisely the same demands on us or present the same opportunities.
3. In any dyad, unique language patterns and communication patterns develop that differentiate that relationship from others. Slang and "in-phrases" among friends, terms of endearment between intimates, and ritualized greetings and work place jargon among colleagues are the result of these ongoing communication dynamics within relationships.

Although the majority of the relationships in which we participate involve two people, we also often find ourselves in social units composed of three or four people, and these relationships may get very complex, as the popular television show *Will and Grace* demonstrates.

Triads—three-person relationships—differ from dyads in several respects, particularly in their complexity. In dyads, reciprocal message processing takes place between two people. With triads, there are six possible message-processing pairings: person 1 with person 2, person 1 with person 3, person 2 with person 3, persons 1 and 2 with person 3, persons 1 and 3 with person 2, and persons 2 and 3 with person 1.[3]

Beyond the increased complexity resulting from more possible pairings, triads differ from dyads in several additional respects. One of these is intimacy. While it is possible for members of triads (or larger groups) to develop very close relationships, there is generally a greater potential for intimacy when interaction is limited exclusively to two people.

Intimacy is a difficult concept to define, however. Traditionally, communication scholars have discussed intimacy in terms of amount and depth of self-disclosure. For example, a friendship was seen as intimate if the individuals told each other their most personal secrets. More recent evidence suggests that intimacy may result from participating in activities together as well as from disclosing highly personal information.[4] Intimate relationships based on mutual participation in activities may be particularly important for males. Although many men may enjoy doing things together while many women may enjoy talking together, this does not mean that men do not confide in each other and that women do not share activities.

Second, in relationships of more than two people, differences of opinion can be resolved by voting to determine the majority opinion. In dyads, negotiation is the only means of decision making available. A further distinction is that triads and larger groups have somewhat more stability than dyads. When only two people are involved in a relationship, either party has the power to destroy the unit by withdrawing. In triads, and larger social units, the withdrawal of one party may have a marked impact on the unit, but it will not necessarily lead to its termination.

FIGURE 11.2 Sometimes our closest relationships are with inanimate objects.

Finally, it is rare that triads operate such that all parties are equally and evenly involved. Typically, at any point in time, two members of the relationship are closer to one another or in greater agreement than the other party or parties. The result is often the formation of coalitions, struggles for "leadership," and sometimes open conflict. Because of this, some authors have argued that there is actually no such thing as a triadic or quadratic relationship, but rather that such units are better thought of as a dyad plus one, or two dyads.[5]

Task and Social Relationships

In addition to thinking about relationships in terms of the number of people involved, we can also look at the primary purpose for their formation. Many relationships are developed for the purpose of *coordinated action*—completion of a task or project that one individual could not manage alone. A simple example of this type of relationship is one person holding on to a board while another person saws off a piece.

The relationships created between a taxi driver and passenger or between an athletic trainer and athlete, provide other illustrations of two individuals working together to accomplish a specific task.[6] Social units composed of colleagues at work, employer and employee, leader and follower, doctor and patient, teacher and student, therapist and patient, are additional examples of *task relationships* that play a major role in our lives.

In some situations, accomplishing a task is of secondary importance or perhaps of no significance whatsoever. In such circumstances, *personally-* or *socially-oriented goals* take precedence. Making a new acquaintance, having coffee with a friend, and spending time chatting periodically with a co-worker during lunch serve a number of important functions, even though they are not essential to the completion of a task. *Social relationships* can provide a means of diversion, recreation, intimacy, or companionship. They may also be a way of avoiding isolation or loneliness, confirming our own sense of worth, giving and receiving affection, or comparing our views and opinions to those held by others.[7]

Individuals may be willing to devote more or less time, energy, and commitment to a relationship, depending on whether they see it as essentially task or socially oriented. As a result, the communication patterns that develop will often vary substantially depending on how the members regard their purpose for participating in a given relationship in the first place.

Short- and Long-Term Relationships

Longevity is another factor that has a significant bearing on the nature of relationships. Most of us are engaged in at least several *long-term relationships* with members of our immediate families, relatives, intimates, and friends. We also participate in the formation and/or maintenance of any number of *transitory relationships*—an exchange of smiles and glances while walking down a hallway, a wave and hello to a familiar face in the neighborhood, or an exchange of pleasantries with a clerk in a store.

Between these two extremes are relationships of varying duration. In general, the older a relationship, the more the investment we have made in it, and the greater the in-

FIGURE 11.3   Friendships serve important functions in our lives.

vestment we are willing to make in order to preserve it. A substantial investment in long-term relationships makes us willing to maintain them with investments that are greater than those we would make in a newly formed relationship.

With short-term relationships there is little history, generally fewer personal consequences should the relationship not progress, and relatively little personal involvement. In such circumstances, we are far less locked into particular identities, and much less constrained by past actions and the images others may have of us. In many instances, short-term relationships can be attractive and functional precisely because they are seen as allowing greater personal flexibility and requiring less investment, commitment, and follow-through. See Figure 11.4.

Casual and Intimate Relationships

Relationships can also be characterized in terms of their "depth" or level of intimacy. At one extreme are relationships between acquaintances. At the other extreme are relationships between intimates. Casual relationships between friends and colleagues fall near the center between these two extremes.

In general, relationships between acquaintances are characterized by impersonal and ritualized communication patterns. The following exchange of pleasantries is typical of such relationships:

Eric: Hello. How are you?

Pam: Fine, thanks, and you?

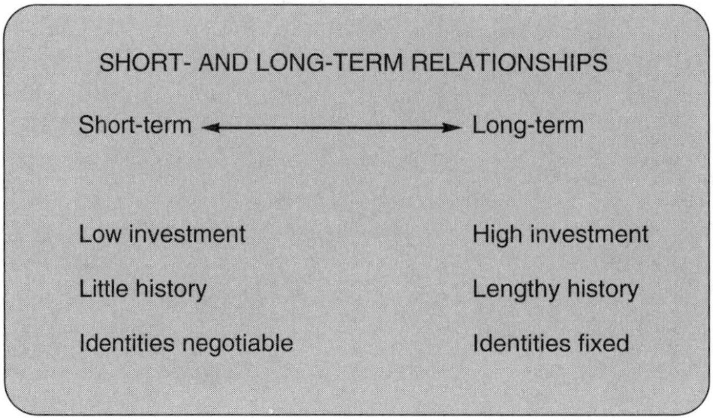

> **SHORT- AND LONG-TERM RELATIONSHIPS**
>
> Short-term ◄───────────► Long-term
>
> Low investment   High investment
>
> Little history   Lengthy history
>
> Identities negotiable   Identities fixed

FIGURE 11.4

> *Eric:* Good.
> *Pam:*   It's a beautiful day today, isn't it?
> *Eric:* Sure is.
> *Pam:*   How's the family?
> *Eric:* Everyone is fine. How's yours?
> And so on.

Disclosure.   The specifics of the exchange are impersonal and ritualized in the sense that either person could—and probably would—make the same remarks to anyone. There is little that suggests the uniqueness of the relationship to either individual. Further, in such a conversation, there is a lack of *self-disclosure, other-disclosure,* or *topical disclosure.*[8] That is, neither person is disclosing much information about his or her own opinions or beliefs at other than a surface level, and there is an obvious absence of personal feeling being expressed.

In more intimate relationships, individuals may share some of their private concerns about life, death, illness, and their feelings about other people and themselves. An exchange between people who have attained greater intimacy would contrast markedly with the previous exchange:

> *Eric:* Hello. How are you?
> *Pam:*   Not that great, to be honest.
> *Eric:* What's the matter?
> *Pam:*   I went for a routine check-up last week, and the doctor found a tumor.
> *Eric:* How serious is it?

Pam: They don't know yet. The test results aren't back, but I'm really afraid.

Eric: I don't blame you. It scares me even hearing about it. Do you want to talk?

Pam: I really think I need to, if it's O.K.

Eric: Of course it's O.K. . . .

And so on.

Contrasted with the earlier example, this exchange is neither ritualized nor impersonal. A high degree of topical-disclosure, other-disclosure, and self-disclosure is involved. The interaction is also distinctive. It seems unlikely that either person would be participating in precisely the same kind of discussion with many other individuals, which suggests the uniqueness of this relationship.

A good deal of research has been conducted on self-disclosure. Findings include:[9]

- Disclosure increases with increased intimacy.
- Disclosure increases when rewarded.
- Disclosure increases with the need to reduce uncertainty in a relationship.
- Disclosure tends to be reciprocated.
- Women disclose more to individuals they like.
- Men disclose more to individuals they trust.
- Disclosure is regulated by rules of appropriateness.
- Attraction is related to positive disclosure but not to negative disclosure.
- Negative disclosure occurs with greater frequency in highly intimate settings than in less intimate ones.
- Relationship satisfaction is greatest when there is moderate—rather than a great deal of or very little—disclosure.

Relationships of different levels of intimacy have varying values for us. As Erving Goffman and other writers have noted, the ritualized exchanges that characterize casual acquaintances permit us to maintain contact with a large number of individuals with a minimum of effort and conscious attention. Such exchanges are a way of saying: "Hello, I see you. It seems to me it is worth acknowledging you. I want you to know that. I hope you feel the same way, too." Ritualized conversation is also important because it is generally the first step in developing closer relationships.

Intimate relationships, by contrast, require a substantial investment of time and effort. They can, however, provide opportunities for personal and social growth that may well be impossible to derive in any other way. They afford a context of trust in which individuals can express themselves candidly. Intimate relationships also encourage a greater degree of continuity and honesty than in other relationships, and allow us to openly explore and apply the insights gained over a period of time.

Intimate relationships may have physical benefits as well as emotional ones. In his book, *The Broken Heart: The Medical Consequences of Loneliness,* James Lynch cites research that indicates that the absence of intimate relationships can have negative medical consequences. Studies have shown that a continual state of loneliness, the absence or death of parents during the early years of childhood, or the loss of a loved one are significant factors contributing to the likelihood of premature death. This work vividly underscores the critical role of intimate relationships in our lives.[10]

Some studies suggest that having a relationship with a pet may serve the same beneficial role as significant human attachments in times of stress, providing not only a source of companionship but an aid to health and relaxation.

Are all pet relationships equally effective in this regard? Apparently not. Dogs seem to make better relationship partners than cats or birds. Studies show that dog owners with high levels of stress visited their physicians less frequently than similarly stressed people without dogs. This result did not occur for the owners of cats and birds.[11]

What is it, exactly, that dogs do in relationships that apparently makes them such ideal partners? Some dogs provide protection. But this is certainly not the case with the majority of pet dogs. Even if they lack the ability to protect their owners, they may still be wonderful companions. They exhibit a number of the qualities that are highly valued in human companions. Dogs are perceived by their owners to be attentive, interested, trusting, loyal, and tolerant. They are nonargumentative and seem, at times, able to demonstrate compassion and empathy. Some dogs are even masters of good eye contact. Collectively, these are many of the characteristics we value in friends and human companions; such behavior provides a sense of security and reassurance and confirms our sense of worth.

Dating, Love, and Marital Relationships

Communication obviously plays a very important role in dating, love, and marital relationships. The initial attraction and encounters that lead to dating, love, and marriage begin as casual contacts and develop through stages of increasing intimacy.

As Edwin Thomas explains:

> Talking is one of the primary activities marital partners engage in together and most couples spend enormous amounts of time talking to each other. Communication between marital partners is vitally important for individual well-being and mutual harmony. It reflects difficulties and strengths in the marriage and in other areas of life and sets the stage for future marital satisfaction or discord.[12]

Communication researcher Michael Beatty points out that early in the development of dating and love relationships, couples often overlook or avoid discussions of potential problems and conflicts.[13] They may assume that conversing about problems and the expression of conflict or anger will necessarily be destructive. As difficulties become great, pressure to address these issues increases. Couples lacking a tradition of disclosure and openness in dealing with one another and their relationship may decide that breaking up is the only logical alternative.

On the other hand, couples who are willing and able to converse with one another about their relationship, its evolution, and its problems may achieve more satisfying and effective relationships. Through conversation:

RESEARCH PROFILE

Disclosure of Personal Information • *Kathryn Greene*

People disclose information in a variety of contexts including interpersonal relationships and healthcare settings. Professor Greene's research demonstrates the importance of disclosing information about relevant topics such as HIV/AIDS.

• • •

Many college students are exploring relationships in the process of dating and meeting many new people. One issue that arises in dating or meeting new people generally is what information to share with this person, especially as it relates to health. My research focuses on the area of privacy and disclosure of HIV diagnoses. This work examines how people balance competing needs to disclose and protect privacy. Overall, my research indicates that people choose to disclose an HIV diagnosis to those they feel close to, when they expect a positive response to sharing the information, when they need support, and only after they have adjusted to the diagnosis. These decisions to disclose to family members, children, and partners are especially difficult.

Some of my research examines attitudes toward privacy, and other work examines disclosure behavior or intentions to disclose. For example, I conducted interviews with African American pregnant teenage women with HIV about how they choose to share their diagnosis. This research on disclosure and health also provides added understanding about how risk decisions are made, for example the roles of stigma, relational variables, and the family. My most recent project in this area is described in a co-authored book, *Privacy, Disclosure of HIV/AIDS in Interpersonal Relationships: A Sourcebook for Researchers and Practitioners* (Lawrence Erlbaum, 2003). This particular line of research is expanding to include examination of the role of stigma in health decision making. Other emerging research focuses on the role of social and personal relationships in the context of health conditions. My research explores factors such as social support, coping, and disclosure in relationship management.

The value of this research examining privacy, disclosure, and stigma is particularly apparent in the application to HIV and AIDS. Because people with HIV need support and also can transmit the virus to partners, studying disclosure has potential benefits in multiple ways. Disclosing can help people access support, can possibly protect someone from contracting HIV, yet it is risky to tell others. To help apply the knowledge gained through research, I work with various local and regional HIV service organizations and several school districts and health departments on issues related to communication and disclosure.

- Partners are able to anticipate or deal with potential problems at an early stage.
- Partners have the benefit of knowing how each other perceives and feels about the relationship, its development, and each other's contribution to it.
- Partners have the opportunity to work together to meet challenges and solve problems.
- Partners can monitor the relationship, and that process will provide an additional source of intimacy and commonness between them.

Family Relationships

Families, and our images of families, are based on, formed, and maintained through communication. Family members and family relationships simultaneously influence and are influenced by each other.[14]

Historically, families have been defined from three perspectives: structural, psychosocial task, and transactional.[15] *Structural* definitions are based on the presence or absence of certain family members (for example, parents and children) and distinguish between families of origin, families of procreation, and extended families. *Psychosocial task* definitions are based on whether groups of people accomplish certain tasks together (for example, maintaining a household, educating children, and providing emotional and material support to each other). *Transactional* definitions are based on whether groups of intimates through their behavior generate a sense of family identity with emotional ties and an experience of a history and a future.

Communication scholars Ascan Koerner and Mary Ann Fitzpatrick argue that some families exhibit a *conversational orientation* in which they create an atmosphere in which all family members are encouraged to voice their opinions about a wide range of topics. These families believe that open and frequent sharing of information is essential to an enjoyable and rewarding family life. Families exhibiting a *conformity orientation* create a communication climate that is characterized by homogeneity of attitudes, values, and beliefs. This type of orientation is usually associated with a more traditional family structure.[16]

These orientations toward lead to four different types of families:[17]

- *Consensual* families are high in both conversation and conformity orientation. Their communication is characterized by an interest in open communication and exploring new ideas as well as a desire to preserve the existing hierarchy within the family.
- *Pluralistic* families have a high conversation orientation and low conformity. They are more likely to engage in open, unconstrained discussion among all family members about a variety of topics.
- *Protective* families are low on conversation orientation and high on conformity orientation. Their communication is more likely to emphasize parental authority with parents believing they should make all the decisions for their children.
- *Laissez-faire* families are low in both conversation and conformity orientations. They have relatively little interaction among family members. Parents exhibit relatively little interest in their children's decisions and do not appear to value communicating with them.

The relationship between mass media and family communication is highly interdependent and complex.[18] Communication researcher Barbara J. Wilson reminds us how family life may be organized, structured, and defined in part by the mass media, particularly television. In many families, the architecture of the house, meal times, and even conversations are structured around television. Television and other media, such as the Internet, have the potential to enhance family interaction if, for instance, they bring families together in a shared social space and foster a feeling of togetherness. In this way, as families structure their activities around the media, the technologies themselves become part of how family members negotiate their social reality. Media also play an important

FIGURE 11.5 Nonverbal cues provide information about the nature of relationships.

role in shaping one's beliefs and expectations of family life. On the other hand, family conflict can also arise over mass media, for example, when family members argue over the remote control or who will have access to the computer to check their e-mail.

Communication within families is influenced by many factors including culture, race, and ethnicity. Research based on European American families does not necessarily. generalize to non–European American families.[19] But ethnicity is a good predictor of family communication only when we study people who identify with their ethnic groups and maintain ethnic cultural practices. Given the increasing number of blended families, traditions common to members of particular groups are being adopted by others, which creates more diverse communication patterns for many families.

The Evolution of Relationships

Whether relationships are dyads or triads, task or socially oriented, short- or long-term, casual or intimate, the dynamics by which they are initiated, develop, and eventually deteriorate and terminate are quite similar in terms of communication.[20]

Stage One: Initiation

The initial stage in the formation of any relationship involves *social initiation* or *encounter.* In this phase, two or several individuals take note of and adjust to one another's behavior.

Often the initial messages to which the individuals adjust are nonverbal—a smile, glance, handshake, movement, or appearance. Should the relationship continue, progressive reciprocity of message processing occurs. One person notices the other's actions, position, appearance, and gestures. The second person reacts, and those reactions are noted and reacted to by the first person, whose reactions are acted on by the second person, and so on.

During the early stages of a relationship, the individuals involved operate in terms of the personal theories, representations, and communication habits they bring with them from previous experiences. As interpersonal communication progresses, each begins to acquire some knowledge of the other's ways of sensing, making sense of, acting, and reacting. Gradually, through combination, recombination, blend, mutation, compromise, and unspoken negotiation, the joint rules by which their particular relationship will operate begin to emerge.

As we encounter another person and initiate a relationship, we have two concerns—being perceived positively by the other person and evaluating the other person. Most people want to be perceived by others as worthy human beings, and therefore, we try to act in a manner we believe will be seen favorably by the other person. Most job applicants, for example, will not put their feet on the interviewer's desk or chew gum during a job interview. In general, we believe that a person who puts feet up on a desk and chews gum does not understand the rules of the workplace, is not showing respect to the interviewer, and, therefore, won't be a good employee. The gum-chewer might be a brilliant accountant, but probably will not get past the first interview.

We make evaluations in a similar manner in other types of relationships, too. For example, we have often heard people refer to others as "my type" or "not my type." This means that some individuals have an idea of the characteristics (often physical) of a person who will make a good relationship partner, and they look for that type of person to date. Good friends sometimes know that this particular pairing will eventually lead to relationship disaster, but are powerless to stop someone from getting into yet another bad relationship.

Stage Two: Exploration

The second stage of relational development, *exploration,* picks up shortly after the initial encounter, as the participants begin exploring potentials of the other person and the possibility of further pursuing the relationship. In this phase we gather information about the other person's style, motives, interests, and values. This knowledge serves as the basis for assessing the merits of continuing the relationship.

This stage may be characterized by small talk—but the importance of this talk is anything but small. All relationships begin with the participants trying to find out information about each other. Beyond observing what a person looks like from the outside, we need to know what the person is like "on the inside" in order to feel comfortable talking about topics of more depth than the weather or the score of the last football game. Sometimes this conversation is difficult because we really don't know what the other person likes to talk about. Sometimes this conversation is formalized, as in a job interview

FIGURE 11.6 Relationship stages are reflected in nonverbal as well as verbal behavior patterns.

in which the interviewer has a set list of questions to ask of each applicant, or in an examination at the doctor's office that involves a specific list of questions in order to make a diagnosis.

Although exploration may be hard work, it is often enjoyable to get to know another person and to hear what he or she has to say about particular topics. Future conversations get easier as we learn more about people and get to know their likes and dislikes better.

Stage Three: Intensification

If the relationship progresses, it moves into a third phase, which Mark Knapp and Anita Vangelisti have labeled the *intensifying* stage.[21] In reaching this level, the participants have arrived at a decision—which they may or may not verbalize—that they wish the relationship to continue. As the relationship progresses, they acquire a good deal of knowledge about each other and, at the same time, create a number of joint rules, a shared language, and characteristic relational rituals. A relationship at this stage may stall, deteriorate, or continue to develop.

At this stage of a relationship, people often consider themselves "close friends." People at this stage are more likely to share deeper secrets (such as their fear of failure or past drug use), to use more personal terms or nicknames for each other, and to develop symbols that have a private meaning. For example, items that were bought together (like a favorite lamp or chair) or events that were shared (like getting soaked in a rainstorm while waiting for a taxi) are used as the basis for intimate conversations.[22] We also intensify our relationships nonverbally by touching each other more frequently and in more intimate ways.

Stage Four: Formalization

Should the relationship progress further, some formal, symbolic acknowledgement binding the individuals to one another is common. In the case of a love relationship, the formal bonding may take the form of engagement or wedding rings. With an individual being hired for a job, the employee and employer may sign a contract. Where two persons are entering a business partnership, the relationship may be formalized by ratifying legal agreements.

During this stage, the individuals advance in their joint creation of relational rules, including the development of shared symbols and preferred and characteristic patterns of conversing. The meanings of these verbal and nonverbal behaviors become standardized. Over time, the relationship develops a distinctiveness that distinguishes it in subtle and not-so-subtle ways from the many other relationships in which the individuals have been involved.

Formalization is a very important stage in any relationship. This is the stage in which people announce to the world that they are committed to each other. This commitment may be indicated nonverbally (for example, with an engagement ring) or by referring to a person in a different way (for example, "this is my fiancé").

Although the beginning of this process may be very exciting (such as planning a wedding or getting a first job), the relationship can develop repetitive communication patterns. These patterns may be positive or negative. For example, some couples may enjoy greeting each other in the same way every day when they return from work ("So how was your day?") while others find that they have the same fight ("Why are you always late?") over and over again.

Stage Five: Redefinition

With the passage of time, people inevitably grow and develop, creating pressure for change on the other person in the relationship, as well as on the relationship itself. As a consequence, a need for redefining some of the joint rules of the relationship often arises. There are many classic illustrations of these types of situations: perhaps a teenager no longer wants to be so closely supervised by his or her parents, or an employee wants more latitude on the job than when first hired. In each instance, changes in the individuals place strains on their relationships and on the accepted and often difficult-to-change rules and patterns that have developed.

Sometimes the needed redefinition is a very gradual, natural, and easily manageable part of the evolution of a relationship. In other instances, when change is too rapid or extreme, or resistance too great, a deterioration process begins. The couple who fights about

FIGURE 11.7   *Symbols and Rituals of Bonding*

one partner's chronic lateness may resolve their difficulties by agreeing to meet in a location in which the prompt partner can do something while waiting for the other person. An employer with an employee who is chronically late may file a formal reprimand and warn the person that his or her job is in jeopardy if the behavior does not change.

Stage Six: Deterioration

Initially, the deterioration may go unnoticed, as people in a relationship begin more and more to "go their own ways" physically and symbolically. Things that once were shared no longer are. Words or gestures that once mattered no longer do. Once-glowing prospects for the future at a particular job become blurred and faded. Rules that grew naturally in a love relationship during its development now seem confining and are followed with resignation.

Once the deterioration process has reached this point, it is quite likely that the relationship is headed for dissolution, as the behaviors of each person come to make less and less difference to the actions and reactions of the other. Physical separation and the dissolution of any remaining legal or contractual obligations are the final steps in the often painful process of terminating a relationship.

Communication researcher Steve Duck has identified four phases in the dissolution process, which can be summarized as follows:[23]

"Self-Talk" Phase
- Focusing on the other partner's behavior
- Evaluating our own contribution and adequacy in the relationship
- Emphasizing negatives of the relationship
- Considering withdrawal
- Identifying positive aspects of alternative relationships

Interpersonal Communication Phase
- Deciding to confront the problem openly
- Confronting
- Negotiating and discussing
- Exploring possibilities for repair and reconciliation
- Assessing costs of withdrawal or reduced intimacy
- Separating

Group and Social Communication Phase
- Agreeing with the partner as to how to relate to one another following dissolution of the relationship
- Initiating gossip/discussion in social groups
- Constructing and telling face-saving and blame-placing stories and accounts of what happened
- Considering and dealing with the effects on our other social groups

"Grave Dressing" and Public Communication Phase
- "Rebounding"
- Replaying, analyzing, and moralizing—postmortem replay of events
- Distributing our own version of the break-up story publicly

Relationships do not necessarily move through these stages in an orderly way. They may stall in any one stage, back up and go forward again, or stop at one point for an extended period of time.

Relational Patterns

As relationships evolve, characteristic communication patterns develop. These relational patterns are the result of joint rules that have developed between the people involved. In this section, we will briefly consider four of the most common of these communication patterns: (1) supportive and defensive climates; (2) dependencies and counter-dependencies; (3) progressive and regressive spirals; and (4) self-fulfilling and self-defeating prophecies.[24]

Supportive and Defensive Climates

"I appreciate how supportive you were last night when I was upset."
"Do you have to criticize and judge everything I do?"
"I wish you would appreciate me more."
"It seems as though you find fault with me no matter what I say or do."
"You're being so defensive!"

The orientations of individuals within relationships and their patterns of communicating with one another create the climate of communication. Climates and individual behaviors can be characterized along a continuum from highly *supportive* to highly *defensive*. Each statement above is a comment on how supportive or defensive the speaker perceives another person—and the relationship overall—to be at a particular point in time.

There are a number of communication behaviors that tend to create and maintain defensive climates within relationships:[25]

- *Evaluating.* Judging other's behavior
- *Controlling.* Striving to control or manage other's behavior
- *Developing strategy.* Planning techniques, hidden agendas, and moves to use in relationships, as you might in a chess game
- *Remaining neutral.* Remaining aloof and remote from others' feelings and concerns
- *Asserting superiority.* Seeing and expressing yourself as more worthy than others
- *Conveying certainty.* Assuming and acting as though you are absolutely certain in your knowledge and perceptions

In contrast, the following behaviors are seen as contributing to a supportive climate:

- *Describing.* Describing rather than judging or evaluating the other person's behavior
- *Maintaining a problem orientation.* Focusing on specific problems to be solved
- *Being spontaneous.* Dealing with situations as they develop, without a hidden agenda or "master plan"
- *Empathizing.* Looking at things from the other person's viewpoint
- *Asserting equality.* Seeing and presenting ourselves as equal to others
- *Conveying provisionalism.* Maintaining a degree of uncertainty and tentativeness in our thoughts and beliefs

Dependencies and Counterdependencies

The dynamics of dependency and counterdependency are prevalent in many relationships at various points in time. A *dependency relationship* exists when one individual in a relationship who is highly dependent on another for support, money, work, leadership, or guidance generalizes this dependency to other facets of the relationship.

The classic example of this kind of relational dynamic develops between children and their parents or, in some cases, between therapists and their patients.[26] In both instances, one individual has particular needs or goals that are being met by the other individual or individuals in the relationship. The dependent pattern may become more generalized, so that one person comes to rely on the other in a broad range of circumstances that are unrelated to the original basis for dependency. When this occurs, a dynamic is set in motion that can have farreaching impact and consequences for the individuals as well as the relationship. Whether people are discussing politics, sex, or religion, whether they are trying to decide where to eat or where to live, the dependent person comes to take cues from the other, on whom he or she has learned to rely, as the following conversation might suggest:

Alice: I think we should go to The Tavern for lunch. How does that sound?

Jenny: Fine.

Alice: Come to think of it, The Tavern is likely to be crowded at this hour. How about the Corner Grill?

Jenny: Sure, that sounds great, too.

In other relationships, or in the same relationship at other points in time, the dependency is in the opposite direction. In these circumstances, one individual relates to the other not as a dependent but, instead, as a *counterdependent*. While the dependent individual complies with the other person in the relationship across a broad range of topics, the counterdependent person characteristically disagrees, as the following scenario illustrates:

Alice: I think we should go to The Tavern for lunch. How does that sound?

Jenny: I'm tired of The Tavern.

Alice: How about the Corner Grill?

Jenny: That's no better. I was thinking of a place with nice salads.

Alice: What about The Attic?

Jenny: It's really not worth all this time deciding. Let's just go to The Tavern and be done with it.

In the first circumstance, we can assume that whatever Alice suggests, Jenny would follow. In the second, it seems likely that whatever Alice suggests, Jenny would disagree.

As dependencies and counterdependencies become a habitual way of relating, they guide, shape, and often overshadow the specific content of conversation. Eventually, at the extreme, the content of what the individuals say comes to have little impact on the dynamics. When person A says "yes," person B agrees. Or, when A says "no," B consistently disagrees.

Progressive and Regressive Spirals

When the actions and reactions of individuals in a relationship are consistent with their goals and needs, the relationship progresses with continual increases in the level of harmony and satisfaction. This circumstance can be described as a *progressive spiral*. In progressive spirals, the reciprocal message processing of the interactants leads to a sense of "positiveness" in their experiences. The satisfaction each person derives builds on itself, and the result is a relationship that is a source of growing pleasure and value for the participants.

The opposite kind of pattern can also develop, in which each exchange contributes to a progressive decrease in satisfaction and harmony. In these circumstances—*regressive spirals*—there is increasing discomfort, distance, frustration, and dissatisfaction for everyone involved. Perhaps the simplest example of a regressive spiral is provided by an argument:

> ***Ann:***   Will you try to remember to do the dishes tomorrow morning before you go to work?
>
> ***Mike:***   You know I get really sick of your nagging all the damn time!
>
> ***Ann:***   If you were a little more reliable and a little less defensive, we might not need to have these same discussions over and over again.
>
> ***Mike:***   You're hardly the one to lecture me about memory or defensiveness. If you remembered half the things you've promised to do, we would have a lot fewer arguments. It's your defensiveness, not mine, that causes all of our problems. . . .

Like dependencies, spirals often take on a life of their own, fueled by the momentum they themselves create. What begins as a request to do the dishes can easily become still another in a string of provocations in a relationship where regressive spirals are common. And, by contrast, "Hi, how are you?" can initiate a very positive chain of events in a relationship characterized by frequent progressive spirals.

Over time, the spirals that characterize any relationship alternate between progressive and regressive. However, in order for a relationship to maintain strength, momentum, and continuity, the progressive phases must outweigh and/or outlast the regressive periods.

Factors That Influence Patterns

We have looked at the role communication plays in the evolution of relationships and the patterns that develop within them. In this section, we will focus on the factors that influence these patterns. A number of elements have an impact on interpersonal communication. Particularly important are stage and context of interaction, interpersonal needs, and style, power, and conflict.

Stage of Relationship and Context

Communication patterns in a relationship vary greatly from one stage to another. Naturally, people meeting each other for the first time interact in a different manner than people who have lived together for several years. The nature of interpersonal patterns also varies depending on the context in which conversation is taking place. People meeting in a grocery store are quite likely to act and react differently to one another than if they are talking in a bar or at a business meeting. Together, these two factors account for much of the variation in the patterns of communication within relationships.

Interpersonal Needs and Styles

Beyond the rather direct and obvious impact of stage and context, the interpersonal needs and styles of the individuals involved represent other influences on communication within relationships.

Often noted as especially important in this way are the interpersonal needs for *affection, inclusion,* and *control.* William Schutz has suggested that our desires relative to giving and receiving affection, being included in the activities of others and including them in ours, and controlling other people and being controlled by them are very basic to our orientations to social relations of all kinds.[27]

We each develop our own specific needs relative to control, affection, and inclusion, as we do in other areas. The particular profile of needs we have, and how these match with those of other people, can be a major determinant of the relational patterns that result. For instance, we could expect that one person with high needs for control and another with similarly strong needs to be controlled would function well together. The former would fall comfortably into a dominant leadership role, while the latter would be very willing to follow. If, on the other hand, two people who work or live together have similarly high (or low) needs for control, one might predict a good deal of conflict (or a lack of decisiveness) within the relationship.

Interpersonal *style* also plays a key role in shaping the communication patterns that emerge in relationships. As discussed earlier, some people are more comfortable operating in an outgoing, highly verbal manner in their dealings with others, while others characteristically adopt a more passive and restrained interpersonal style, due either to preference or apprehension about speaking in social situations. Those who use a more outgoing style deal with their thoughts and feelings in a forthright, assertive manner.[28] If they want something, they ask for it. If they feel angry, they let others know. If they feel taken advantage of, they say so. If they don't want to comply with a request, they have little trouble saying "no!" In contrast to an externalizing style of interpersonal communication, the internalizing style involves "absorbing" the verbal and nonverbal messages of others, giving the outward appearance of acceptance, congeniality, and even encouragement, regardless of one's thoughts or feelings.[29] For any of several reasons, people who are prone to use the internalizing style often "bottle up" thoughts, opinions, and feelings. If they are angry, it is seldom apparent from what is said. If they disagree, they seldom say so. If they feel taken advantage of, they may allow the situation to continue rather than confront it openly.

Though few of us use either style exclusively, we often favor one approach over the other in the majority of our dealings with people; and, depending on the style of the people with whom we are in relationships, this factor alone can become a primary influence in shaping our interactions and our relationships, as is suggested in the following conversation:

> ***Tom:*** Georgia, you wouldn't mind taking me home tonight after work, would you? I know I impose on you a lot, but Mary needed the car again today, and I know you're the kind of person who doesn't mind helping out now and then.
>
> ***Georgia:*** Well, I was going to stay late tonight, but if you have no other way, I . . .

> ***Tom:*** Hey thanks, Georgia. I was sure I could count on you. How are things any-
> way? Really busy, I'll bet. Well, listen, I'd better get back to work. I'll meet you
> by your car at 5:00. Thanks again.

Tom's externalizing style, in combination with Georgia's internalizing style, will no doubt be critical factors in defining many of the interactions that take place between them.

Power

Interpersonal communication within relationships is also shaped by the distribution of power. Where one individual is employed by the other, for instance, the relationship is *asymmetrical,* or uneven, in terms of the actual power each has in the job situation.[30] The employer can exercise more control over that facet of their relationship—so long as the other person does not quit—simply as a consequence of the uneven control over resources and decision making.

There are many similar situations where asymmetries affect interpersonal communication. The relationship between a therapist and a patient, a teacher and a student, a parent and a child, or a supervisor and supervisee are among the most common examples. In each, one member of the relationship has control over certain facets of the other's life, a circumstance that generally has a substantial impact on the interpersonal communication patterns that develop.

In peer–peer, colleague–colleague, or other relationships of this type, there is the potential for symmetry. Where this possibility exists, interpersonal communication creates rather than perpetuates any dependencies that result.

Conflict

The presence of *conflict*—"an incompatibility of interest between two or more people giving rise to struggles between them"—can have a major impact on communication dynamics.[31] Communication researcher Alan Sillars suggests that when people are involved in conflict situations they develop their own personal theories to explain the situation. These theories, in turn, have a great influence on how interactants deal with one another.

Sillers finds that there are three general communication strategies used in conflict resolution:[32]

- *Passive-indirect methods.* Avoiding the conflict-producing situation and people
- *Distributive methods.* Maximizing one's own gain and the other's losses
- *Integrative methods.* Achieving mutually positive outcomes for both individuals and the relationship

Implications and Applications

- Being competent in interpersonal communication involves applying our understanding of communication and interpersonal relationships to everyday life. The goal is to use our knowledge to increase our interpersonal satisfaction and effectiveness from our own perspective, as well as from the perspective of those with whom we interact.[33]

• Self-awareness in relationships can contribute to interpersonal communication competence. Psychologist Carl Rogers offers the following personal observations on therapeutic relationships, which can be applied in many other types of relationships as well:[34]

In my relationships with persons I have found that it does not help, in the long run, to act as though I were something that I am not.

I find I am more effective when I can listen acceptingly to myself and can be myself.

I have found it of enormous value when I can permit myself to understand another person.

I have found it enriching to open channels whereby others can communicate their feelings, their private perceptual worlds, to me.

I have found it highly rewarding when I can accept another person.

The more I am open to the realities in me and in the other person, the less do I find myself wishing to rush in to "fix things."

Life, at its best, is a flowing, changing process in which nothing is fixed.

• Empathy and respect for others' opinions, knowledge, and perspective generally enhances communication.

• Listening, observing, and interpreting are vital to communication competence in relationships. Every person reacts to a situation in his or her own way; some people are more interpersonally sensitive than others. The following guidelines can be helpful:[35]

Practice your listening, observation, and interpretation skills.

Try not to be distracted by an emotion-arousing word, phrase, or action.

Adapt to the situation.

Listen to and observe the total person. Attend to both the verbal and nonverbal channels.

Strive to interpret messages according to the other person's codes and meanings, not your own.

Be aware of potential gender-based differences in communication.

• One of the benefits of studying communication is its value for analyzing our relationships and the communication behaviors of our acquaintances, friends, family, colleagues, and intimates. This knowledge can sometimes be productively shared with others to help them better understand their own communication in relationships. Sharing interpersonal perspectives effectively requires sensitivity:

Describe rather than criticize.

Be specific and avoid generalizations.

Focus comments on communication behaviors that the other person can change.

Select a time and place for discussions of relationships that is appropriate and meets the needs of all parties.

Strive to make the discussion and suggestions you may have for others constructive, not destructive.[36]

Summary

In this chapter, we have examined the relationship between communication and relationships. We have also discussed a number of ways of thinking about and characterizing relationships, and explored common communication patterns that can occur. Communication plays a central role in the development and evolution of all human relationships. Relationships also provide perhaps the most important context in which we attempt to use our communication abilities to achieve particular goals and meet particular needs.

In the most general sense, a relationship exists whenever there is reciprocal message processing—when two or more individuals are reacting to one another's verbal and nonverbal behavior. It is by means of interpersonal communication that relationships are initiated, develop, grow, or deteriorate.

Intentionally-established relationships can be considered from several perspectives: whether they are dyadic or triadic; whether they are task-oriented or social in purpose; whether they are short- or long-term; whether they are casual or intimate. We also have discussed dating, love, and marital relationships.

Relationships progress through a series of relatively predictable stages, beginning from an initial social encounter, progressing to stages of increasing interaction and joint rule creation. Many relationships involve some formalized acknowledgement of their status, such as marriage or a legal business contract. A relationship may stall in one of these stages, back up and go forward again, or stop and remain in one stage for an extended period of time.

Over time, communication patterns develop in relationships. Often these dynamics take the form of defensiveness or supportiveness, dependencies or counterdependencies, progressive or regressive spirals, or self-fulfilling or self-defeating prophecies. These dynamics can have a far more significant impact on the form and development patterns of relationships than does the content of interaction.

A number of factors, such as stage and context, interpersonal needs and style, distribution of power, and the presence of conflict play a role in facilitating the development of particular patterns.

Notes

1. The discussion of dyads and triads draws on the excellent summary of work on this topic provided by William Wilmot in *Dyadic Communication,* 3rd ed. (New York: Random House, 1987).

2. Wilmot, 1987, pp. 121–129.

3. William M. Kephart, "A Quantitative Analysis of Intra-Group Relationships," *American Journal of Sociology,* Vol. 55, 1950, pp. 544–549.

4. Julia T. Wood and Christopher C. Inman, "In a Different Mode: Masculine Styles of Communicating Closeness," *Journal of Applied Communication Research,* Vol. 21, 1993, pp. 279–296.

5. Wilmot, 1987, pp. 121–129.

6. Fred Davis, "The Cabdriver and His Fare: Facets of a Fleeting Relationship," in *Interpersonal Dynamics.* Ed. by Warren G. Bennis, David E. Berlew, Edgar H. Schein, and Fred I. Steele (Homewood, IL: Dorsey, 1973), pp. 417–426.

7. See Michael D. Scott and William G. Powers, *Interpersonal Communication: A Question of Needs* (Boston: Houghton Mifflin, 1978), for a useful discussion of the role of needs in interpersonal communication and relational development.

8. See Joseph Luft, *Of Human Interaction* (Palo Alto, CA: National Press Books, 1969); Sidney M. Jourard, *The Transparent Self* (Princeton, NJ: Van Nostrand, 1964); and Stella Ting-Toomey, "Gossip as a Communication Construct." Paper presented at the Annual Conference of the Western Speech Communication Association. Los Angeles, February, 1979.

9. Based on summary provided by Stephen W. Littlejohn, *Theories of Human Communication,* Third ed. (Belmont, CA: Wadsworth, 1989), p. 161, adapted from Shirley J. Gilbert, "Empirical and Theoretical Extensions of Self-Disclosure," in *Explorations in Interpersonal Communication.* Ed. by Gerald R. Miller (Beverly Hills: Sage, 1976), pp. 197–216.

10. James J. Lynch, *The Broken Heart: The Medical Consequences of Loneliness* (New York: Basic Books, 1979).

11. See discussion in E. Friedman, A. H. Kathcher, J. J. Lynch, and A. A. Thomas, "Animal Companions and One-Year Survival of Patients after Discharge from a Coronary Care Unit," *Public Health Reports,* 95, 1980, pp. 307–312; T. F. Garrity, L. Stallones, M. B. Marx, and T. P. Johnson, "Pet Ownership and Attachment as Supportive Factors in the Health of the Elderly," *Anthrozoos,* 3, 1989, pp. 35–44; and J. M. Siegel, "Stressful Live Events and the Use of Physician Services among the Elderly: The Moderating Role of Pet Ownership," *Journal of Personality and Social Psychology,* 58(6), 1990, pp. 1081–1086.

12. Edwin J. Thomas, *Marital Communication and Decision-Making* (New York: Free Press, 1977), p. 1.

13. See extensive discussion of dating and marriage, summarized in this section, in Michael J. Beatty, *Romantic Dialogue: Communication in Dating and Marriage* (Englewood, CO: Morton, 1986).

14. Anita L. Vangelisti, *Handbook of Family Communication* (London: Lawrence Erlbaum, 2004).

15. Ascan F. Koerner and Mary Ann Fitzpatrick, "Communication in Intact Families," in *Handbook of Family Communication.* Ed. by Anita L. Vangelisti (London: Lawrence Erlbaum, 2004), pp. 177–196.

16. Koerner and Fitzpatrick, 2004, pp. 177–196.

17. Koerner and Fitzpatrick, 2004, pp. 177–196.

18. Barbara J. Wilson, "The Mass Media and Family Communication," in *Handbook of Family Communication.* Ed. by Anita L. Vangelisti (London: Erlbaum, 2004), pp. 563–593.

19. William B. Gudykunst and C. M. Lee, "An Agenda for Study Ethnicity and Family Communication," *Journal of Family Communication,* Vol. 1, 2001, pp. 75–85.

20. The discussion of stages of development of relationships draws on the work of Mark L. Knapp and Anita L. Vangelisti in *Interpersonal Communication and Human Relationships* (Boston: Allyn & Bacon, 1992), and Murray S. Davis, *Intimate Relations* (New York: Free Press, 1973).

21. Knapp and Vangelisti, 1992, pp. 37–38.

22. Leslie A. Baxter, "Symbols of Relationship Identity in Relationship Cultures," *Journal of Social and Personal Relationships,* Vol. 4, 1987, pp. 261–280.

23. Based on Steve Duck, "A Topography of Relationship Disagreement and Dissolution," in *Personal Relationships 4: Dissolving Personal Relationships* (New York: Academic Press, 1982).

24. See discussion of spirals and prophecies in Wilmot, 1987, pp. 121–129, and in Paul Watzlawick, Janet H. Beavin, and Don D. Jackson, *Pragmatics of Human Communication* (New York: Norton, 1967), pp. 51–54.

25. Jack R. Gibb, "Defensive Communication," *Journal of Communication,* Vol. 11, Sept. 1961, p. 41. Also see discussion of supportiveness–defensiveness in Steven A. Beebe and John T. Masterson, *Family Talk: Interpersonal Communication in the Family* (New York: Random House), 1986, pp. 145–150.

26. See Robert R. Carkhuff and Bernard G. Berenson, *Beyond Counseling and Therapy* (New York: Holt, 1967).

27. William Schultz, *The Interpersonal Underworld* (Palo Alto, CA: Science and Behavior Books, 1968).

28. See Colleen Kelley, "Assertion Theory," in *The 1976 Annual Handbook for Group Facilitators.* Ed. by J. William Pfeiffer and John E. Jones (La Jolla, CA: University Associates, 1976); Sharon and Gordon Bowers, *Asserting Yourself* (Reading, MA: Addison-Wesley, 1976); and Colleen Kelley, *Assertion Training* (La Jolla, CA: University Associates, 1979).

29. Brent D. Ruben, "The Machine Gun and the Marshmallow: Some Thoughts on the Concept of Communication Effectiveness." Paper presented at the annual conference of the Western Speech Association (Honolulu: November, 1972), and Brent D. Ruben, "Communication,

Stress, and Assertiveness: An Interpersonal Problem-Solving Model," in *The 1982 Annual Handbook for Group Facilitators*. Ed. by J. William Pfeiffer and John E. Jones (La Jolla, CA: University Associates, 1982).

30. Watzlawick, et al., 1967, pp. 67–71.

31. Herbert W. Simons, "The Carrot and Stick as Handmaidens of Persuasion in Conflict Situations," in *Perspectives on Communication in Social Conflict*. Ed. by Gerald R. Miller and Herbert W. Simons (Englewood Cliffs, NJ: Prentice Hall, 1974), pp. 177–178. See also review of definitions and approaches to conflict in Brent D. Ruben, "Communication and Conflict: A System-Theoretic Perspective," *The Quarterly Journal of Speech,* Vol. 64, 1978, pp. 202–210.

32. Alan L. Sillars, "Attributions and Communication in Roommate Conflicts," *Communication Monographs,* Vol. 47, 1980, pp. 180–200.

33. See discussion of communication competence in Brian H. Spitzberg and William R. Cupach, *Interpersonal Communication Competence* (Beverly Hills: Sage, 1984). Also see discussion in Littlejohn, p. 182.

34. Carl Rogers, *On Becoming a Person: A Therapist's View of Psychotherapy* (Boston: Houghton Mifflin, 1970), pp. 15–27.

35. Adapted from Beebee and Masterson, 1986, pp. 182–183.

36. Based on Beebee and Masterson, 1986, pp. 217–219; Gibb, 1961.

12 Groups

In this chapter

Why . . .

- Groups often don't measure up to our expectations.

- Group size is important to group effectiveness.

- The "wheel" communication pattern leads to efficiency but low satisfaction.

- Common roles emerge in groups of all kinds.

- It's good to bring a laptop to a meeting.

- Too much cohesiveness can be detrimental to groups.

Each of us spends a great deal of time in groups of various kinds. As members of families, peer groups, clubs, work groups or teams, religious groups, and other social groups, we are selectively exposed to the world around us. As we grow from infancy to adulthood, the groups in which we participate generate a wide range of demands and opportunities for us; and, in the process of adjusting to them, we develop, change, and grow.

As with relationships, groups are created and maintained by people engaged in reciprocal message processing. As we shall see, the communication process makes groups possible and is essential to every facet of group functioning.

Groups differ from relationships in terms of the number of people involved, the resources available for decision making, and the complexity of the communication dynamics that result. The presence of additional individuals and more complex communication dynamics is, on the one hand, a very positive characteristic of groups. With increased size comes additional people to address issues, undertake projects, and solve problems. On the other hand, the larger size also leads to problems associated with agreeing on goals, ensuring that information is available to all group members, defining roles and responsibilities, providing appropriate leadership, creating cohesiveness, and avoiding undue pressure on individuals toward conformity. See Table 12.1.

Groups: Fiction and Fact

A decision about this year's group project has to be made. The board—of which you are a newly-elected member—has proposed a service project to help homeless people in the community. A meeting of the group is scheduled to approve the recommendation and begin the planning process.

This group has a fairly simple and straightforward agenda. A decision has to be made, and a recommendation is on the table. You envision a brief meeting of the group at which members will share information and opinions and begin planning together to achieve the common goal.

The meeting is scheduled at what is supposed to be a good time for everyone. Eleven members of the group are present at the designated starting time. One member arrives fifteen minutes later. Six people are absent, and no one is sure why.

As discussion proceeds, it becomes clear that five of the members present disagree with the proposed project.

TABLE 12.1 *Characteristics of Groups: Consequences of Size*

Benefits	Costs
Additional Members to Assist with Activities	Effort Needed to Develop Consensus on Goals
	Effort Needed to Keep Members Informed
Additional Members to Participate in Decision Making	Effort Needed to Include Members
	Effort Needed to Counteract Pressures Toward Conformity
Additional Resources for Problem Solving	Effort Needed for Leadership

Three members in attendance are vocally opposed to the idea. (Two don't like the idea, and the third—an unsuccessful candidate for board membership during the last election—doesn't feel the board sought enough input from members in arriving at its recommendation). Of those not present, two people are reportedly opposed to the idea, but no one seems to know the reasons for their disapproval.

The other three members in attendance haven't spoken; one looks angry, one bored, and a third seems to be working on an unrelated writing assignment of some kind while others are engaged in discussion.

Unfortunately, the realities of group life often do not match our expectations.[1] In the abstract we tend to think of groups as collections of active, supportive, and enthusiastic people, working together rationally and unemotionally to pursue shared goals. In fact, groups are composed of individuals with varying motivations, emotions, attachments, perspectives, and needs who come together to negotiate a framework for communication that permits collective action. While this goal seems to be relatively straightforward, the process by which individuals pursue it may not be.

Why People Join Groups

People join groups to pursue individual needs in a social context. Groups assist individuals in meeting a number of goals, including: socializing and companionship, support for personal development or change, spiritual growth, and economic gain. A number of factors go into individual decisions as to which groups to join, among them:[2]

- Attractiveness of the group's members—including physical, social, and task attractiveness
- Attractiveness of the group's activities and goals
- Attractiveness of being a member of a particular group—personal, social, symbolic, occupational, or economic benefits

Types of Groups

Task and Social Dimensions: Productivity and Morale

Groups are created to serve a number of goals. Often, the primary objective is *productivity*—the completion of a task or job. Examples are organizing a party, building a house, or carrying out community service projects. We can distinguish several types of task-oriented groups:[3]

- *Duplicated activity group.* Each member does the same job. Examples: All members plant trees or prepare letters for mailing.
- *Assembly line group.* Each member works on a different part of the task. Examples: Some members dig holes, others plant trees, and others water and clean up; or some members fold letters, others add the stamps, and others stuff and mail.

- *Judgmental, problem-solving and decision-making group.* Members of the group identify and choose among possible answers, strategies, or options. Examples: A group decides how many and what kind of trees to plant, where to plant them, and plans the planting process.

There are also groups in which the primary goal is to create positive *morale*—and to facilitate members achieving personally- or socially-oriented goals, such as interpersonal support, encouragement, and diversion. Social clubs and discussion groups are examples. See Figure 12.1.

To a greater or lesser extent, most groups serve a combination of task-, personally-, and socially-oriented goals. Even in what might seem to be a rigidly task-oriented group, such as a work group or team on an industrial assembly line where productivity is the primary measure of success, good morale is also important. This is especially the case if members of a task group will need to work together for some period of time. In such cases, good morale may enhance productivity; and, conversely, poor morale can undermine it. Within groups whose goals are primarily social, task orientation can also be essential, even in deciding where to meet, what projects to undertake, where to eat, or what movies to attend. Most groups—such as families, service clubs, or religious or professional groups—require a fairly even balance between concern for productivity and morale. Task orientation is necessary to carry out group activities; personal and social orientation are necessary to encourage full participation and to encourage positive feelings by members toward the group and one another.

FIGURE 12.1 Membership in various groups can be an important part of our lives.

Contrived and Emergent Groups

Some groups are *emergent*. Such groups form naturally out of the spontaneous activities of individuals. Acquaintances who become friends and begin to go places and do things with one another provide an example of an emergent group.

More often, groups are *contrived*—intentionally formed for specific purposes.[4] Contrived groups typically have specific, stated goals or objectives, such as to serve the community, to share professional interests, to complete a work project, to help members quit smoking, or to support a political candidate. Sometimes, groups that are initially emergent shift to contrived, such as when acquaintances decide to form a club or work group.

Group Development

Group Communication Networks

In a two-person relationship, there is the possibility of only one reciprocal communication linkage. With three interactants, there are six possible message-processing pairs: person 1 with person 2, person 1 with person 3, person 2 with person 3, persons 1 and 2 with person 3, persons 1 and 3 with person 2, and persons 2 and 3 with person 1. When we consider the possible interpersonal linkages in a group of four members, there are twenty-five potential communication relationships! The addition of just one more person creates the potential for nineteen additional communication linkages.[5]

In groups that are emergent, reciprocal message-processing linkages—*networks*—develop naturally, often spontaneously. Networks begin to form as individuals meet and get to know one another. With the passage of time, the network becomes well-developed as all members of the group participate in interaction. Theoretically, as shown in Figure 12.2, the network will evolve to include all group members, at least minimally.[6]

In actual practice, a number of patterns of linkage are possible, as shown in Figure 12.3. In the *circle* network, each group member interacts with two other people. Person A interacts with Person B and Person E, Person B with Person A and Person C, and so on. The *wheel* configuration describes a situation in which all messages flow through one individual—Person A. Person A interacts directly with all members of the group, but none of the others interact directly with one another. In a *chain,* members interact in a serial, straight-line manner. The *all-channel* pattern denotes a network in which each member of a group sends messages to, and receives messages from, every other member. In any group, some linkages in networks are utilized more and others less; some people become central to the network, others peripheral; still others may become isolated from others in the network. And, clearly, patterns change over time.

Stages of Development

Groups that are formed to accomplish a specific task (such as writing a report) may follow a predictable pattern. Studies of the development of task-oriented groups suggest that they move through the following phases:[7]

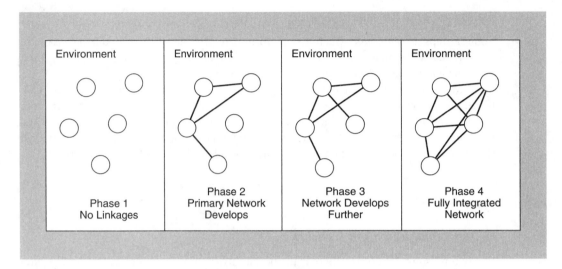

FIGURE 12.2   The development of linkages in a group is marked by the emergence of networks that connect individuals to one another and define the unit. A group need not progress through all phases but may move from a stage of high integration to stages of lower integration and back again periodically.

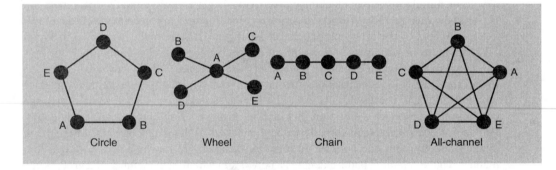

FIGURE 12.3   In studies of common group communication networks, such as those shown here, centralized networks (like the "wheel") contributed to rapid performance, but the error rate was high. Low centralization (such as provided in the "circle") was found to be associated with a high degree of individual satisfaction. Researchers also noted that being in a key position in a network, one requiring that information be channeled through one individual, led to information "overload."

Source: Harold J. Leavitt, "Some Effects of Certain Communication Patterns on Group Performance," *Journal of Abnormal and Social Psychology, 46,* (1951), pp. 38–50; M. E. Shaw, "Some Effects of Unequal Distribution of Information Upon Group Performance in Various Communication Nets," *Journal of Abnormal and Social Psychology, 49,* (1954), pp. 547–553.

1. Orientation phase
2. Conflict phase
3. Emergence phase
4. Reinforcement phase

The first stage, *orientation,* consists of getting acquainted, expressing initial points of view, and forming linkages relative to the task at hand. In the early stages of a group's work, the discussion tends to focus on "small talk," such as the weather, the setting, circumstances that brought the individuals together, goals of the group, and so on.

As the group proceeds to work on its task, roles and responsibilities are considered. During the *conflict* phase, the expression of differing points of view leads to polarization. Gradually, accommodations are made among members and subgroups with differing view points, as the group begins to take on an identity of its own in the *emergence* phase. As the group's project nears completion, cooperation among individuals in the network increases, as does support for—and *reinforcement* of—the group's solution.[8]

These stages are general descriptions of the development of a group. Not all groups follow these stages in precisely this order. Some research indicates that many groups may not proceed in this orderly fashion at all.[9] Sometimes groups move from one stage to another and then back again. Nevertheless, whether or not a particular group follows this model, this sort of typology helps us to understand the nature of group process.

A number of factors influence the dynamics of groups as they evolve. Among these are: the amount of structure within the group; the time available to the group for completion of the task; the group size; the group members' attitudes and feelings about the task, topic, and one another; and the nature of the task.[10] The following task characteristics are particularly important to a group's progress:[11]

- *Task difficulty.* The amount of effort required to complete the job
- *Solution multiplicity.* The number of reasonable alternatives available to solve the problem
- *Interest and motivation.* Interest generated by the task
- *Cooperation requirements.* The degree to which cooperation by group members is necessary to complete the task
- *Familiarity.* The extent to which the group has had experience with a particular task

Group Culture: Symbols, Rules, and Codes

As networks develop, symbols, rules, and codes of various types emerge and become standardized through communication, as shown in Figure 12.4. The process creates the group's *culture.* Some aspects of group culture develop naturally, as with slang phrases among members of a club or social group, or informal "dress codes" in a peer group. In other instances, symbols, rules, and codes result from systematic efforts by members of a group. In such cases, symbols and rules are created to give the group an identity, to differentiate it from others, or to identify or differentiate a particular group from a larger unit of which it is a

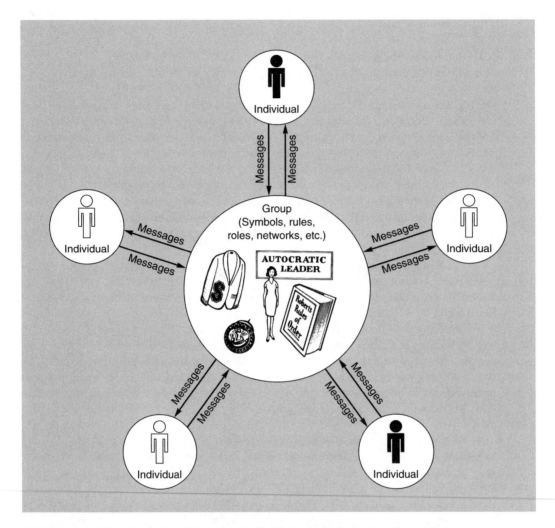

FIGURE 12.4   Through their verbal and nonverbal behavior individuals collectively create the groups to which they belong and the cultures, symbols, rules, jargon, and other conventions characteristic of each. Once created, the culture of the group "acts back upon" its members. Over time, individuals are greatly influenced by the group, and in turn individuals collectively create the group.

part. The decorated jackets of street gangs serve this function, as do handshakes, team names and logos, or the "secret words" of fraternities and sororities.

Culture plays a pervasive role in the dynamics of groups. It provides members of a group with a sense of individual and collective identity and contributes to the development of order, structure, and cohesiveness in the overall operation of the system.

Terrence Deal and Allen Kennedy observed major corporations and developed a description of elements of culture that can be applied to small groups as well as to large organizations.[12] They discuss the values, heroes, and rites and rituals characteristic of every culture.

Values are the basic concepts and beliefs of a group. They form the heart of a group's culture and establish the standards of achievement. Core values (such as customer service or "people come first") indicate what is important to a group. Group members who support the group's values are more likely to succeed. For example, members of a research and development team in a high technology company may be expected to quickly invent products that are innovative and ahead of the competition. People in this type of group are rewarded for being risk-taking. A person who continually says, "I don't think we can do this," would be unlikely to succeed in this type of group.

Cultures and groups often have *heroes* who personify the group's values. These people (whether real or fictitious) provide role models for group members to follow. Heroes may be people who began a highly successful organization (like Walt Disney) or people who became memorable by overcoming a difficult time in the group's life. For example, a group of students working on a class project may valorize the person who brought a laptop to the group meeting, thereby saving the group from endless hours taking notes and typing the final paper.

Rites and rituals are the routines of everyday life in a group. These activities may consist of nothing more significant than everyone in a group shaking hands and introducing themselves at the beginning of an exercise, or they may be elaborate, formal ceremonies like initiation rituals. These activities communicate and reinforce the values of the group. Although some rites and rituals are traditional and maintained over time, groups must be careful to adapt their rites and rituals as the membership of the group changes and society's attitudes toward various beliefs progresses. For example, hazing is no longer an appropriate way to initiate a person into a campus organization.

Decision Making

One of the major activities of most task-oriented groups is decision making. Decisions range from simple and straightforward questions such as when to hold a meeting, to more complex and entangled questions about group policy and activities. Rules that guide decision making in small informal groups emerge naturally as members spend time with one another. In larger, more structured groups, decision-making sessions are generally convened and given a specific name—*meetings*. During meetings, the behaviors of individuals follow a number of reasonably well-defined rules, some emerging spontaneously, with others following group traditions, formalized bylaws, or parliamentary procedure.

There are a number of methods by which groups can make decisions, among them: consensus, compromise, majority vote, decision by leader, and arbitration.[13]

Consensus

Consensus refers to a process which requires that a group arrive at a collective decision with which all members genuinely agree. For example, through discussion, it becomes apparent that every member of a club likes the idea of doing a service project for senior citizens, and the group decides to undertake this kind of project.

The following rules have been developed to help a group reach consensus:[14]

1. Members should avoid arguing for their "pet" proposals.
2. Groups should avoid "us against them" stalemates in which each side in a dispute must either "win" or "lose."
3. Members should not comply with a group majority if they do so only to avoid conflict.
4. Groups should not use rules for decision-making that allow them to avoid conflict, such as a "majority wins" rule.
5. Groups should view differences of opinion among members as natural and helpful.
6. Members should consider that their early, initial agreements are suspect and premature.

Compromise

Compromise is a process of negotiation and give-and-take to arrive at a position that takes account of—but may not be completely consistent with—the preferences of individual members. For example, some members of a club want to do a service project for senior citizens, while others favor a project for the homeless. Through discussion, the group decides to undertake a project for homeless seniors.

Majority Vote

Majority voting is a method for arriving at group decisions mathematically. A decision is made when it is supported by a majority of members. In very formal groups, there may be a specific definition for majority (for example, 50 percent plus 1 or two-thirds). For example, four members want to do a project for senior citizens; six want to do something for the homeless. The decision is six-to-four in favor of a homeless project.

Decision by Leader

Leader decision making involves the imposition of a resolution by a group's leader. In this instance, it is a decision by proclamation. For example, the group is unable to meet because of bad weather, and a decision is made by the club president that this year the group will do a service project for senior citizens.

Arbitration

Agreement through a process of formal negotiation between parties unable to reach a decision by other means is called *arbitration.* For example, two subgroups exist within the club. One is determined to do a project for seniors, while the other insists that something should be done for homeless people in the community. Members of each group have very strong personal convictions about the matter. Discussion and a trial vote reveals that there is a five to five split, with no one willing to change his or her position. An imposed decision risks permanently alienating members. The head of the local community agency coordinating the organization is invited to the next meeting to help the group reach a decision.

More often than not, arbitration is used in conflicts between, rather than within, groups—for instance, a deadlock between labor and management over terms of a contract. These groups may also have very specific rules for arbitration.

Roles and Responsibilities

In small informal groups, member roles and responsibilities develop primarily as the result of informal, often unverbalized, agreements, as illustrated in Figure 12.5. In larger and more formal groups, individual roles and responsibilities may be made explicit. In clubs, for instance, the responsibilities and duties of officers, committee members, and other positions are generally detailed in written bylaws or a constitution. And in workgroups or teams, the mission, goals, time constraints, and resources available may be specified.

In a now classic article on group roles, Benne and Sheats outlined three types of roles that develop in groups over the course of time:[15] (1) roles related to the completion of the task, (2) roles related to building and supporting the group, and (3) individualistic roles. Within each of these broad categories, a number of specific roles are identified.

Task-Oriented Roles

- *Initiator-contributor.* Suggests or proposes new ideas or changed ways of regarding the group problem or goal

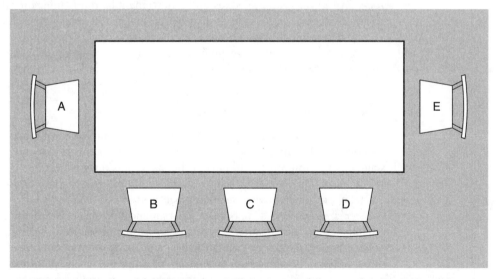

FIGURE 12.5 Studies of seating patterns in groups suggest that people who sit in positions A, C, and E are more vocal contributors to discussions than people in positions B or D. Often, people with more dominant personalities tend to choose the high participation positions while others, who prefer to avoid high levels of participation, avoid them.

Source: Mark L. Knapp and Judith A. Hall, *Nonverbal Communication in Human Interaction,* 5th ed. (Belmont, CA: Wadsworth, 2002), p. 163.

- *Information-seeker*. Asks for clarification of suggestions made in terms of their factual adequacy and for authoritative information and facts pertinent to the problem being discussed
- *Opinion-seeker*. Asks for clarification of the values pertinent to what the group is undertaking, of values involved in a suggestion made, or of values in alternative suggestions
- *Information-giver*. Offers facts or generalizations which are "authoritative" or relates his or her own pertinent experience to the group problem
- *Opinion-giver*. States his or her belief or opinion pertinent to a suggestion made or to alternative suggestions
- *Elaborator*. Spells outs suggestions in terms of examples, offers a rationale for suggestions previously made, and tries to understand how an idea or suggestion would work out if adopted by the group
- *Coordinator*. Shows or clarifies the relationships among various ideas and suggestions, tries to pull ideas and suggestions together, or tries to coordinate the activities of various members of subgroups
- *Orienter*. Defines the position of the group with respect to its goals by summarizing what has occurred, points to departures from agreed-on directions or goals, or raises questions about the direction the group discussion is taking
- *Evaluator-critic*. Subjects the accomplishment of the group to some standard or set of standards of group functioning in the context of the group task
- *Energizer*. Prods the group to action or decision, attempts to stimulate or arouse the group to "greater" or "higher quality" activity
- *Procedural-technician*. Expedites group movement by doing things for the group—performing routine tasks such as distributing materials or managing objects for the group (e.g., rearranging the seating)
- *Recorder*. Writes down suggestions, makes a record of group decisions, or writes down the results of the discussion

Group-Building and Support Roles

- *Encourager*. Praises, agrees with, and accepts the contribution of others
- *Harmonizer*. Mediates the differences between other members, attempts to reconcile disagreements, relieves tension in conflict situations through jesting
- *Compromiser*. Operates from within a conflict by offering a compromise, admitting a mistake, or moving toward another position
- *Gatekeeper/expediter*. Attempts to keep communication channels open by encouraging or facilitating the participation of others or by regulating the flow of communication
- *Standard setter*. Expresses standards for the group to attempt to achieve in its functioning or applies standards in evaluating the quality of group processes
- *Group observer*. Keeps records of various aspects of group process and feeds such data with proposed interpretations into the group's evaluation of its own procedures
- *Follower*. Goes along with the movement of the group, more or less passively accepting the ideas of others, serving as an audience in group discussion and decision making

Individualistic Roles

- *Aggressor.* May work in many negative ways, including deflating the status of others, expressing disapproval of the values, acts or feelings of others, attacking the group or the problem it is working on, joking aggressively, or showing envy toward another's contribution by trying to take credit for it
- *Blocker.* Tends to be negative and stubbornly resistant, disagreeing and opposing without or beyond reason, and attempting to maintain or bring back an issue after the group has rejected it
- *Recognition seeker.* Works in various ways to call attention to himself or herself, including boasting, reporting on personal achievements, acting in unusual ways, or struggling to prevent being placed in an "inferior" position
- *Self-confessor.* Uses the audience opportunity the group setting provides to express personal, nongroup-oriented "feeling," "insight," or "ideology."
- *Dominator.* Tries to assert authority or superiority by manipulating the group or certain members of the group
- *Help seeker.* Attempts to call forth "sympathy" responses from other group members or from the whole group
- *Special interest pleader.* Speaks for the "small business owner," "the grass roots" community, the "soccer mom," "labor," and so on, usually cloaking his or her own prejudices or biases in the stereotype which best fits his or her individual need

Leadership

No doubt the role that receives the most attention in any discussion of groups is that of the leader. The basic role of a leader is to coordinate the activities of individuals so that they contribute to the overall goals and general adaptability of the group.

In groups of two, three, or four individuals, patterns of leadership are almost totally the result of the needs, preferences, and communication styles of the individuals involved. Leadership may well be a subtle, even unnoticeable, aspect of the group's operation. In larger groups, leadership is an essential, formalized, and often highly visible element in the day-to-day and long-term functioning of the group. In either case, the role involves the design, implementation, and/or supervision of procedures, policies, or mechanisms necessary to bring about the desired coordination of the individuals and activities of the group.

Functions of Leadership

Leadership is conducted through communication. But leaders are responsible for accomplishing certain goals. The basic functions of leadership fall into two categories: (1) group maintenance functions, and (2) group achievement functions. A synthesis of these functions is provided by Baird and Weinberg.[16] They list:

Group Maintenance Functions
- Promoting participation
- Regulating interaction

- Promoting need satisfaction
- Promoting cooperation
- Arbitrating conflict
- Protecting individual rights
- Providing exemplary behavior
- Assuming responsibility for group failure
- Promoting group development

Group Achievement Functions

- Informing
- Planning
- Orienting
- Integrating
- Representing
- Coordinating
- Clarifying
- Evaluating
- Stimulating

Approaches to Leadership

Leadership is an interactional process that helps people in organizations manage their environment. Effective leaders plan and select actions that help organizations or groups accomplish their goals. In addition, they may assist individuals to understand the obstacles they face in accomplishing their tasks so that they can be overcome. There are a variety of points of view as to what constitutes good leadership.[17]

Good-Leaders-Are-Born Approach.   The traditional view held that leadership is a *trait*—an ability one inherits. In this perspective, "good leaders are born not made." The assumption is that leadership qualities are inherent within one's personality. Either we possess or do not possess these qualities. According to this approach, the challenge of leadership involves finding people who have "the right stuff." This theory was often used to keep certain groups of people out of leadership positions, and it is not widely followed today.

One-Best-Style Approach.   Another approach views leadership as a matter of style. Decision making can be wholly centralized or can be totally diffused among members of a group. If the decision making is centralized (controlled by the leader), the leadership style may be characterized as *autocratic*. The autocratic leader uses authority to direct group activities. Typically, this type of leader tightly controls information, assigns members to roles and responsibilities, and has formal systems of accountability. When authority is shared, the leadership style is described as *democratic* or *participatory*. This type of leader gets members of the group involved in decision making and has a more open sharing of information. Moreover, roles and responsibilities are determined, at least in part, by the group. A third approach to leadership—*laissez-faire*—is a "hands-off" style, in which no authority is exercised by the leader. From the perspective of the "one-best style" approach, the challenge of leadership is determining whether the autocratic, democratic, or laissez-faire style of leadership is most effective in a given situation.

Based on studies comparing leadership styles and their effects, it was first thought that the democratic style was superior in terms of group productivity and morale. However, further research confirmed that some groups functioned very well with more authoritarian leadership. Examples are military groups, surgical units, and athletic teams. A reasonable conclusion is that there is no ideal leadership style for all groups and circumstances; rather, the appropriateness of a particular style depends on the nature and purpose of the group.[18]

Contextual Approach.   The contextual approach views leadership as the result of individual abilities (inherited plus learned), the purposes of the group, pressures put on the group from outside, and the way members in the group talk, work, or relate to one another.[19]

Bormann and Bormann offer the following description of this approach to leadership:

> The contextual view recognized that some people learn to play the game of being leader and that they tend to have certain opening moves they use in starting the game whenever they join a new work group. To some extent, the way they try to be leader depends upon what they think about the group. They do not approach the squad at basic training in the army with the same expectations they display toward a peer discussion group. . . . Such an explanation provides a more complete view of leadership than does either the trait approach or the one-best-style approach. It includes the idea that leaders are to some extent born, but it also suggests that potential leaders can acquire skills and improve talents.[20]

No matter which leadership style is chosen, it is important to remember that, as communication scholar J. Kevin Barge reminds us:[21]

- Leadership is enacted through communication.
- Leaders refine, develop, and modify the organizing systems of their organizations or groups to maintain viability in a complex, changing environment.
- The key to successful leadership in the future is the ability to coordinate diverse groups of people working on differing tasks in a changing and unstable environment.

Follower and Member Issues

For the individual, leadership is an important element that differentiates the involvement in a group from participation in relationships. In relationships, each individual has a direct hand in creating and controlling the system, its culture, communication patterns, rules, and roles. This is not often the case with groups, since we are usually initiated into—rather than initiating—them.

Becoming a participant in any group involves an initiation into the culture and communication patterns of the unit. Our training for membership in groups begins during our earliest years. As a child in a family, for instance, a good deal of compromise, accommodation, and fitting in is required. The child must learn the family's rules as to what to do, when to do it, what to say, and where to say it.

RESEARCH PROFILE

Leading from Afar • *Stacey L. Connaughton*

In our increasingly globalized world, organizational employees may be located at great distances from each other. Professor Connaughton's research demonstrates that maintaining communication through mediated channels contributes to employees' satisfaction with their jobs.

• • •

In recent years, innovative technologies have enabled a number of nontraditional ways of leading. One of the more interesting new challenges in leadership occurs when leaders are physically distant from their subordinates. The leader may be located in New Jersey but her employees may work in China and Peru. In this case, the distance between leader and subordinate is one of both physical geography and time.

But, if you've ever been in a long distance romantic relationship, you know that distance can sometimes pose challenges to a relationship. Similarly, physical distance can affect manager–employee relationships in various ways. Trust might be challenged; cross-cultural communication issues may surface; and distanced employees may feel "cut off" from those at corporate headquarters.

In spite of physical distance, however, managers still need to effectively lead. But, although distanced leadership is becoming more common, we know little about how leaders effectively lead across time and space. How does leading people from afar differ from leading people who are co-located? Must distanced leaders always incorporate some face-to-face communication with their far-flung employees in order to lead them effectively? What communicative behaviors on the part of the leader are related to distanced employees' job satisfaction and satisfaction with their manager? What communicative behaviors from the distanced leader are associated with distanced employees' productivity and performance?

To answer these questions, I have interviewed distanced leaders in large, global organizations and distributed surveys to their distanced employees. One interesting finding from this research is that as long as distanced employees believe they have access to their leader (through mediated channels or face-to-face), physical distance does not appear to affect their job satisfaction or satisfaction with their distanced leader.

As organizations continue to expand around the globe and as technology enables us to communicate with people who are not physically present with us, distanced work relationships are likely to remain commonplace in many organizations. Through research we can begin to capture what communicative variables are critical to achieving key organizational outcomes such as distanced employees' satisfaction and productivity.

Later, as the child seeks to attain membership in various other groups, a similar process operates. Entry into certain clubs, fraternal orders, and religious groups makes this process of fitting in a very explicit part of the initiation of a new member into the unit. Even in those social and work groups where there is no formal apprenticeship, internship, or trial period, the individual must come to terms with the group's rules and realities in order to be accepted and to function effectively as a member.

Thus, in those instances in which one's role requires *adjustment* to the situation rather than the *creation* of that situation, the initial function of communication is identifying and fitting oneself to the ongoing rules and structures made by others. This generally means that becoming a member of a group is a less active, less creative, more accommodating—and for some a more frustrating—process than becoming part of a relationship.

Cohesiveness

Cohesiveness refers to group loyalty.[22] A cohesive group is one in which members have a "team spirit" and are committed to the group's well being. As Ernest and Nancy Bormann note in *Effective Small Group Communication,* the essence of the concept of cohesiveness is aptly reflected in the motto of Alexandre Dumas's *Three Musketeers:* "All for one and one for all."

The relationship between communication, cohesiveness, and performance is important in any group. It is through communication that cohesiveness—or the lack of it—is fostered. Moreover, the presence or absence of cohesiveness influences the patterns and quality of communication within a group. When present, cohesiveness also encourages task and social dimensions of productivity and good morale:[23]

- Cohesive task groups are more productive. They do more work because members work cooperatively, distribute the work load well, and use time efficiently.
- Cohesive groups have higher morale because their members value and feel like they are a part of the group. Members pay attention to, appreciate, spend time and effort with one another, and share success as well as failure.
- Cohesive groups have efficient and effective communication because channels are open. Members are present, receptive, and committed to ensuring the communication necessary to promote productivity and high morale.

Symptoms of Too Little Cohesiveness: Boredom and Indifference

There are a number of symptoms and consequences of low cohesiveness.[24] These include a lack of member involvement, the absence of enthusiasm, and minimal question asking. Meetings are quiet, even boring, with members behaving in a polite but apathetic manner. Even important decisions are handled routinely, and the prevailing sentiment is best expressed as, "Let's get this over with."

Symptoms of Too Much Cohesiveness: The Groupthink Syndrome

Cohesiveness and loyalty to the group can have a down side. In *Groupthink,* Irving L. Janis explains that decision-making groups can actually be *too* cohesive.[25] Within highly cohesive groups, pressure to agree with the group can become very powerful. A *norm,* or accepted standard, of avoiding disagreement may develop. The group can be so cohesive and team-oriented that opinions that contradict the majority view may go unverbalized and/or be inadvertently overlooked. The *groupthink syndrome* occurs because members place great value on loyalty and being a team player. One of the characteristics of groupthink that makes it particularly troublesome is that the process often occurs without the awareness of the participants.

Groupthink Warning Signs. The presence of certain factors signals the potential for groupthink. These include:[26]

- *Overestimation of the group's power and morality.* Assuming the group is not accountable to others and that it is pursuing the morally correct course of action
- *Closed-mindedness.* Ignoring or distorting alternative viewpoints
- *Pressures toward conformity.* Subtle and not-so-subtle influence toward agreement among group members and lack of willingness to acknowledge or discuss differences of opinion

Consequences of groupthink may include: an incomplete survey of alternatives and options, failure to examine risks of preferred choices, failure to reappraise initially-rejected alternatives, poor information search, selective bias in processing information at hand, and failure to work out contingency plans.[27]

Conflict in Groups

At various stages in the development of any group, conflict is inevitable. The conflict may have to do with disagreements over a group's goals, member roles or responsibilities, decision making, resource allocation, group dynamics, relationships among particular individuals, or any of a number of other factors.

Conflict is not inherently a problem. In fact, while the experiencing of conflict is generally unpleasant, we know that without conflict, quality, diversity, growth, and excellence may be diminished for individuals, relationships, or groups. Thus, the goal is not necessarily to eliminate conflict. Rather, the objective in any situation should be to better understand conflict, to be able to identify its origins, to be able to determine its potential for making a positive contribution, and to be able to resolve or manage it productively.

A number of approaches have been developed to analyze and resolve conflict within groups. One interesting approach classifies conflict based on two dimensions:[28]

- *Assertiveness.* Behaviors intended to satisfy our own concerns
- *Cooperativeness.* Behaviors intended to satisfy the concerns of others

Considered in combination, these two dimensions describe five different styles of conflict.[29] See Figure 12.6.

1. *Competitive style.* High in assertiveness and low in cooperativeness. Example: the tough competitor who desires to defeat others—a "fight orientation."
2. *Accommodative style.* Low in assertiveness and high in cooperativeness. Example: the easygoing, undemanding, and supportive follower.
3. *Avoiding style.* Low in assertiveness, low in cooperativeness. Example: the low-profile, indifferent, group isolate—a "flight orientation."
4. *Collaborative style.* High in assertiveness, high in cooperativeness. Example: the active, integrative problem solver.
5. *Compromising style.* Moderate in assertiveness, moderate in cooperativeness. Example: the "meet-you-half-way," "give-up-something-to-keep-something" approach.

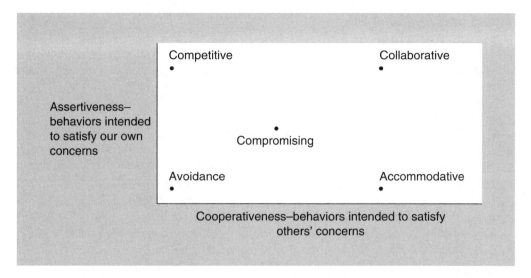

FIGURE 12.6   *Five Conflict-Management Styles and Their Relationships*

Source: Thomas L. Ruble and Kenneth W. Thomas, "Support for a Two-Dimensional Model of Conflict Behavior," *Organizational Behavior and Human Performance,* 16 (1976): 143–155. (Current edition is titled *Organizational Behavior and Human Decision Processes.*) Copyright © 1976 by Academic Press, Inc. Reprinted with the permission of the publishers.

This framework is useful for understanding origins of conflict within groups. Moreover, it suggests how certain styles and strategies can be helpful in resolving and managing conflict.

Mediated Groups

As new communication technologies continue to be developed, more and more group interaction is taking place through mediated channels. For example, a group of engineers may "meet" in a video-conference in which each engineer sits alone in a conference room watching a monitor that projects images of the other group members who are sitting in various other locations around the world. Another group may use a computer program to help them analyze a large body of information and come to a decision. Still another group of citizens may log on to their local computer network and exchange messages about a topic of concern to them, such as the new school budget. Some college instructors have set up discussion rooms, listservs, or message boards so that their students can continue class discussion online.

These mediated modes of discussion have the potential to link together people who live and work in very remote locations. The potential for creating a global sense of community is enormous. As this technology becomes available to more people throughout the world, the possibilities for new types of group interaction will continue to expand.

Implications and Applications

- Groups are complex social systems made up of individuals who bring their own unique orientations—perspectives, goals, needs, values, experiences, styles, and motivations—to group membership.

- Groups are successful to the extent that the diverse orientations of members can be coordinated, channeled, and/or focused.

- Success has two dimensions: productivity and morale. From the perspective of productivity, a group is successful when the job is done. In terms of morale, a group is successful when people feel satisfied. Sometimes these two outcomes go together in groups; sometimes they do not. For instance, taking time to focus on members' personal and social needs, which may contribute to good morale, is time taken away from work on completing a task. However, if a group is to work together on more than a single task, effort spent to foster positive morale in the short-run often is rewarded by contributing to increased productivity in the longer term. And, even in the short-run, poor morale can have major consequences in terms of the quality of decision making and on productivity.

- The communication dynamics and networks that emerge within a group often by accident frequently take on a life of their own. Once particular cliques or subgroups form, for instance, they are often self-perpetuating.

- The way in which new members are initiated into groups is a critical aspect of group development. The kind of orientation new members receive, and the place they initially occupy in group communication networks, may have long-term consequences for the new members' thoughts about, and actions toward, the group.

- Every group has its own culture and its unique symbols, rules, and codes. These serve to contribute to the group's identity and provide a basis for commonness among members.

- Often without the intention of group members, cultures support and encourage some kinds of behavior—for instance, cooperativeness, aggressiveness, service, or racial or gender bias—while discouraging others. By analyzing communication patterns and practices, one can become aware of the implicit values and behaviors that are endorsed and encouraged by particular group cultures. This knowledge can be put to good use by individual members and the group as a whole to evaluate and refine goals and operations.

- Decision making is the central activity of many groups. When we think about quality decision making, we think in terms of *what* decision is made. *How* decisions are made, however, is often as important. Issues related to the "how" of decision making have to do with the *process* a group goes through in deciding. Issues related to the "what" have to do with the *product* of group decision making. Various decision-making methods are available; and each has pluses and minuses in terms of the quality of the process and product. A decision made by a knowledgeable leader for the group may be a better decision than one less informed members would reach through discussion and compromise. However, discussion and compromise are likely to result in better feelings and greater commitment to the decision by members, because they play a more active part in the process. Ideally, decision making should be undertaken in a way that provides the best of both a process- and product-orientation.

- Communication researcher Randy Hirokawa notes that groups need to fulfill a set of critical functions to make successful decisions.[30] His list includes:

  1. The group must come to understand the nature of the dilemma it faces.
  2. Group members must agree on the requirements for an acceptable solution.
  3. The group must identify a range of realistic alternative proposals for solutions.
  4. The group needs to thoroughly and accurately assess the positive consequences of each alternate proposal.
  5. The group must thoroughly and accurately assess the negative consequences of each alternative proposal.[31]

- Cohesiveness is an important element of successful groups in terms of performance, morale, and effective communication. Techniques that foster group cohesiveness include:[32]

  Increasing the amount of communication among members

  Giving a group an identity and emphasizing it: talking about the group as a group

  Building a group tradition by recognizing special dates or occasions

  Emphasizing teamwork and striving to increase the attractiveness of participation in the group

  Encouraging the group to recognize good work

  Setting clear, attainable group goals

  Providing rewards for the group

  Treating members like people worthy of respect and dignity, not like parts in a machine

- Extreme pressure toward group loyalty and being "team players," can stifle dissent and critique—both of which can play essential parts in creativity and quality decision making. Some techniques that can be used to lessen the likelihood of the groupthink syndrome include:[33]

  Leaders can encourage members to be critical.

  Leaders can avoid stating their own preferences and expectations at the outset.

  Members of the group can discuss the group's deliberations with trusted associates outside the group and report back to the group on their reactions.

  Experts can be periodically invited to meetings and should be encouraged to challenge the views of group members.

  A member who is articulate and knowledgeable can be appointed to the role of devil's advocate, with the task of looking for alternatives, questioning the group's direction, and assuring that possible objections are considered.

  Leaders can allocate time during each meeting to review minority, opposing, or alternative points of view.

- Conflict is an inevitable, and not necessarily a negative, aspect of group life. It is important to learn to recognize the potentially positive functions of conflict for the individual and for the group as a whole. Learning to understand and manage conflict, rather than always striving to eliminate or suppress it, can be productive.

Summary

We spend a great deal of time in groups of various kinds—working at our jobs, participating in clubs and associations, attending community or religious functions, and taking part in social activities. The groups in which we participate over the course of our lifetime create a wide range of demands and opportunities for us; and, in the process of adjusting to these, we develop, change, and grow.

As with relationships, groups are created and maintained by people engaged in reciprocal message processing. Groups differ from relationships in terms of the number of people involved, available resources, and complexity. Groups are created to serve a number of goals and purposes. Some groups serve primarily task-oriented functions and emphasize performance. Others stress personally- or socially-oriented functions and morale. Most groups are concerned with both types of goals. Groups may be contrived or emergent. In small social units, group communication networks evolve naturally. In larger and more formalized groups, networks are often purposefully established to regulate the flow of information.

Groups move through a series of stages as they evolve. The dynamics involved depend on a number of factors, including the difficulty of their tasks, the number of alternative solutions, and the interest created by the tasks. Groups develop a culture—their own symbols, rules, and codes.

The major activity of some groups is decision making, and a number of methods are available for doing this. Roles and responsibilities also are central to the functioning of groups. In smaller groups, roles and definitions of responsibility evolve naturally. Some roles are related to task completion. Others have to do with team building and support; still others are individualistic. In larger, more structured groups, roles and responsibilities are often formal rather than informal, created rather than natural, explicit rather than implicit. Leadership accomplished through communication is basic to groups of all kinds.

Cohesiveness is an important factor in group functioning. It is important for productivity, morale, quality decision making, and effective communication. The groupthink syndrome occurs when members—often unknowingly—become preoccupied with maintaining cohesiveness within a group. Conflict is an inevitable, and often productive, aspect of group functioning.

Mediated communication allows us to participate in groups even if the members are not in the same location. Technology such as the Internet allows group members to overcome barriers of time and space.

Notes

1. See discussion of "realistic" and "unrealistic" views of groups in Ernest G. Bormann and Nancy C. Bormann, *Effective Small Group Communication,* 4th ed. (Edina, MN: Burgess, 1988), pp. 2–4.

2. Gerald L. Wilson and Michael S. Hanna, *Groups in Context: Leadership and Participation in Small Groups* (New York: Random House, 1986), pp. 110–114; and Bormann and Bormann, 1988, pp. 64–72.

3. Based on distinctions suggested in Charles Pavitt and Ellen Curtis, *Small Group Discussion: A Theoretical Approach,* 2nd ed. (Scottsdale, AZ: Gorsuch Scarisbrick, 1994), pp. 26–29.

4. See Lee Thayer, *Communication and Communication Systems* (Homewood, IL: Irwin, 1968), pp. 188–190.

5. A formula for computing the number of such linkages has been provided by William M. Kephart in "A Quantitative Analysis of Intra-Group Relationships," *American Journal of Sociology,* Vol. 55, 1950, pp. 544–549.

$$PR = \frac{3^N + -2^{N+1} + +1}{2}$$

Note: PR is the number of potential relationships, and N is the number of persons involved.

6. See Richard W. Budd, "Encounter Groups: An Approach to Human Communication," in *Approaches to Human Communication.* Ed. by Richard W. Budd and Brent D. Ruben (Rochelle Park, NJ: Hayden-Spartan, 1972), especially pp. 83–88; and Gerald Egan, *Encounter: Group Processes for Interpersonal Growth* (Belmont, CA: Brooks/Cole, 1970), pp. 69–71.

7. B. Aubrey Fisher, "Decision Emergence: Phases in Group Decision-Making," *Speech Monographs,* Vol. 37, 1970, pp. 53–66, and *Small Group Decision Making* (New York: McGraw-Hill, 1974); see also B. Aubrey Fisher and Donald G. Ellis, *Small Group Decision Making* (New York: McGraw-Hill, 1990), pp. 153–157.

8. Marshall Scott Poole and Jonelle Roth, "Decision Development in Small Groups (IV): A Typology of Group Decision Paths," *Human Communication Research,* Vol. 15, 1989, pp. 323–356.

9. See Fisher, 1970, and discussion in Stephen W. Littlejohn, *Theories of Human Communication,* 5th ed. (Belmont, CA: Wadsworth, 1996), pp. 292–293.

10. Wilson and Hanna, 1986, pp. 27–30.

11. Marvin E. Shaw, "Scaling Group Tasks: A Method for Dimensional Analysis," *JSAS Catalog of Selected Documents in Psychology,* Vol. 8, 1973, M. S. 294. See discussion in Wilson and Hanna, 1986, pp. 28–29.

12. Terrence E. Deal and Allen A. Kennedy, *Corporate Cultures: The Rites and Rituals of Corporate Life* (Reading, MA: Addison-Wesley, 1982), pp. 21–84.

13. Based on Wilson and Hanna, 1986, pp. 68–71.

14. These rules were developed by J. Hall and W. H. Watson, "The Effects of a Normative Intervention of Group Decision-Making Performance," *Human Relations,* Vol. 23, 1970, pp. 299–317. For a more comprehensive discussion of consensus rules, see Pavitt and Curtis, 1994, pp. 433–436.

15. Kenneth Benne and Paul Sheats, "Functional Roles of Group Members," *Journal of Social Issues,* Vol. 4, 1948, pp. 41–49.

16. John E. Baird, Jr., and Sanford B. Weinberg, *Group Communication,* 2d ed. (Dubuque, IA: Brown, 1981), p. 215.

17. Based on discussion by Bormann and Bormann, 1988, pp. 127–130 and J. Kevin Barge, *Leadership: Communication Skills for Organizations and Groups* (New York: St. Martin's Press, 1994), chap. 1.

18. Bormann and Bormann, 1988, p. 129.

19. Bormann and Bormann, 1988, p. 129.

20. Bormann and Bormann, 1988, p. 129.

21. Barge, 1994, chap. 1.

22. Bormann and Bormann, 1988, p. 55.

23. Based on Bormann and Bormann, 1988, p. 55.

24. Bormann and Bormann, 1988, pp. 56–57.

25. Irving L. Janis, *Groupthink: Psychological Studies of Policy Decisions and Fiascos,* 2nd ed. (Boston: Houghton Mifflin, 1982). See discussion in Littlejohn, 1996, pp. 286–287.

26. Wilson and Hanna, 1986, pp. 197–198; based on Janis, 1967.

27. Wilson and Hanna, 1986, p. 198; based on Janis, 1967.

28. T. L. Ruble and K. W. Thomas, "Support for a Two-Dimensional Model of Conflict Behavior," *Organizational Behavior and Human Performance,* Vol. 16, 1976, pp. 143–155. See discussion in J. P. Folger and M. S. Poole, *Working Through Conflict* (Glenview, IL: Scott, Foresman, 1984), pp. 40–41.

29. Ruble and Thomas, 1976; Folger and Pool, 1984, p. 41.

30. See, for example, Randy Y. Hirokawa, "Group Communication and Decision-Making Performance: A Continued Test of the Functional Perspective," *Human Communication Research,* Vol. 14, 1988, pp. 487–515.

31. Pavitt and Curtis, 1994, p. 283.

32. Bormann and Bormann, 1988, pp. 74–76; see also Pavitt and Curtis, pp. 96–97.

33. Janis, 1982; see discussion in Littlejohn, 1996, pp. 286–287.

13 Organizations

In this chapter

Why . . .

- There are several schools of thought about organizations, work, and management.

- Communication is essential to contemporary theories of organizational quality.

- Organizational cultures are created and maintained through communication.

- Diversity presents important opportunities for organizations.

Communication and Organizations

We spend a significant amount of time in organizations during our lifetimes—attending school, working, and participating in professional, religious, political, health, civic, and other organizations. We look to these organizations for fulfillment of our physical, psychological, social, spiritual, political, and economic needs.

While organizations come in many different shapes and sizes, all have a good deal in common in terms of communication. Communication makes possible the coordination of activity by several individuals, without which any form of social organization would be impossible.

295

Communication is also essential to the day-to-day functioning of organizations. It is through communication that members of organizations: (1) define goals, (2) delineate the roles and responsibilities of members, (3) coordinate operations, (4) establish information networks, and (5) develop the culture and climate, all of which guide the behavior of members. In the sections that follow, we will examine each of these organizational activities and their relationship to communication.

Organizational Goals

A *goal* is the objective that guides the activity of an organization. It is the benchmark against which the effectiveness, success, viability, and adaptability of the organization can be assessed. Communication plays an important role in setting goals, in monitoring progress toward them, and, where appropriate, in periodic goal redefinition.

Some organizations are formed with the primary goal of manufacturing and marketing consumer goods—producing automobiles, computers, or bread, for instance. For other organizations, the "product" is a service. Hospitals, schools, or libraries are examples of this type of organization.

As with any system, the survival and growth of an organization depend on the availability of adequate resources. Organizations provide goods and services, while in exchange they typically receive financial compensation.

The presence of productivity goals is not a unique characteristic of organizations. As we have seen, relationships and groups also may be task-oriented. The distinguishing characteristic of organizational goals is to be found in the *origin* and *clarity* of the goals. In relationships and small, informal groups, the goals for the enterprise may emerge as the system evolves. With organizations, goals are usually more formally established or consciously set. This is not to say that initial organizational goals may not evolve. They can and often do. Through major reorganizations, goal reformulation, or more subtle evolutionary processes, goals may change over time.

Roles and Responsibilities

In any organization, the completion of the product- or service-oriented task requires a *division of labor*—the partitioning of the larger tasks into small parts and the delineation of roles. A *role* is a set of behaviors—a job to be done, a position to be filled, or a function to be carried out.

In relationships and groups, the roles individuals play—and their responsibilities to others in the social unit—generally evolve out of the interaction among members as the unit develops. In these instances, the process of role delineation is informal, as in gangs or high school cliques. In organizations, the division of labor and role definition is highly formalized.

The formalization of roles has several aspects:

1. Specification of roles themselves
2. Establishment of a process of selecting people to fill these roles

3. Determination of responsibilities associated with the roles
4. Development of procedures for moving from one role to another

Each of these aspects is clearly and formally delineated in the form of "job titles," "hiring policies," "job descriptions," and "promotion and termination procedures."

Fundamental aspects of role relationships—the ways in which roles are related to one another—are also formalized in most organizations. Formal organization charts, such as those shown in Figure 13.1, portray these relationships. They indicate a *chain of command* and *reporting lines*—who reports to whom.

Many organizations today are in a state of transition. Formal organizational charts may be eliminated or changed frequently as organizations rapidly evolve to meet the dynamics of the marketplace. Structures change. Many organizations have "flattened" their hierarchy or eliminated layers of management that impede the flow of communication and

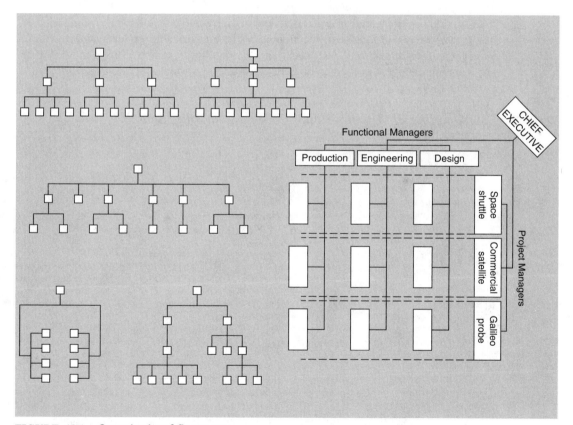

FIGURE 13.1   *Organizational Structures*

Source: Everett M. Rogers and Rehka Agarwala-Rogers, *Communication in Organizations* (New York: Free Press, 1976); Henry Mintzberg, *Structures in Fives: Designing Effective Organizations* (Englewood Cliffs, NJ: Prentice Hall, 1983); and Henry L. Tosi, John R. Rizzo, and Stephen J. Carroll, *Managing Organizational Behavior* (Cambridge, MA: Blackwell, 1994).

slow down decision making. More and more decisions are made at the lowest possible level of the hierarchy. Individual employees have been given more responsibilities in their day-to-day dealings with clients or customers to improve service and facilitate communication with individuals both inside and outside the organization. Various available organizational communication channels are listed in Box 13.1.

Management Functions

Another basic consideration in the design and day-to-day functioning of an organization that directly involves communication has to do with management. Organizations need processes for planning, decision making, financial oversight, monitoring the activities of the organization, coordinating activities of its component parts, evaluating the organization's functioning in comparison with other organizations and the environment, and so on. These are typically considered *management functions.*

In organizations, management is an essential, formalized, and highly visible element in the day-to-day and long-term functioning of the unit. Like group leadership functions, management functions may be very centralized, or authority can be diffused in varying degrees among members of the organization, resulting in *participatory management.*

BOX 13.1 • *A Sampling of Organizational Communication Channels*

Memo	The Grapevine
Telephones	Satellite Video
Newsletters	Lectures
Electronic Mail	Manuals
Business Luncheons	Bulletins
Videotape Presentations	Live Internet Streaming Video
Training Sessions	Directory of Employees
Conferences	Guest Speakers
Speeches	Annual Reports
Paging Systems	Announcement Flyers
Meetings	Paycheck Stub Messages
Grievance Interviews	DVDs
Family Picnics/Events	Charts and Graphs
Workshops	Posters
Ad Reprints	Suggestion Box
Exhibits and Displays	Teleconferences
Slide Presentations	Committees
Daily Interpersonal Contact	Social Get-Togethers
Fax	Counseling Interviews

Source: Adapted in part from R. Wayne Pace, *Organizational Communication,* Englewood Cliffs, NJ: Prentice Hall, 1983, pp. 45–56.

Organizational Theories

To a large extent, the orientation that is taken relative to management depends on the prevailing views of human nature within an organization. Traditionally scholars have identified three main schools of thought regarding human nature.[1] Each of the three suggests a set of principles and assumptions about how individuals behave in organizations, and each has its own implications regarding the functions management and communication should serve. A fourth perspective has become popular in recent years.

Scientific Management

The *scientific management* approach to organizational behavior is a collection of theories developed by business practitioners and academics. The most visible figure in the field was Frederick W. Taylor, whose 1911 book, *Scientific Management* embodied the philosophy and theory of the approach.[2] In this view, humans in organizations are seen as being motivated primarily by material rewards. By implication, maximum productivity is presumed to be achievable by employees who are clear on what they are to do and to whom they are responsible, and who are rewarded appropriately.

Essentially, then, the scientific school views the organization as a *machine*. Like a machine, an organization is seen as being effective to the extent that it runs efficiently. Workers are the vital cogs in the organizational machine and are understood to be motivated primarily by financial considerations. The task of a manager is to engineer work and the workplace environment in order to achieve maximum productivity and profitability through the use of formal authority and formal, downward channels of communication.

A clear and specific organizational structure, job specialization, fair rewards, defined rules, and distinct lines of responsibility and authority are regarded as basic. The purpose of communication is to provide information to employees that will clarify the tasks they are to perform and to reward them monetarily, according to their accomplishments.

Human Relations

What has come to be referred to as the *human relations school* of organizational behavior set forth a more social view of work life. Chester Barnard's 1938 book, *The Functions of the Executive,* was a major impetus for this perspective, as were the well-known Western Electric, Hawthorne Plant studies, which focused on working conditions, morale, and productivity.[3] Researchers F. J. Roethlisberger and William J. Dickson (1939) set up experimental work rooms and groups to study the impact of such factors as the length of the work day, the length of the work week, and the introduction of breaks during the day.[4] Much to their surprise, they found that regardless of what specific changes they introduced into the experimental environment—whether they shortened or lengthened working hours, days and weeks, for instance—worker productivity improved. Every change they made in the environment seemed to increase productivity. By the end of the two-year study, efforts to explain the increased productivity led to an examination of every imaginable explanation including environmental factors, worker fatigue and monotony, wage incentives, method of supervision, even temperature, humidity, and seasonal variation.

Ultimately, the researchers concluded that differences in productivity were not due to specific changes. Rather, greater productivity resulted from the positive interpersonal relationships and unusual level of supervisor attention present in the experimental group at every phase of the research. The experiment had fostered closer working relations and had established greater confidence and trust in the supervisors than were present in the normal work situation.

If the *machine* is the image that best captures the thinking of scientific management, the *family* serves a comparable function for the human relations approach. Organizations are seen as effective when they address worker needs, build trust, and encourage collaboration. In this perspective, workers are thought to be motivated primarily by the desire for job satisfaction, recognition, attention, and participation in decision making. Managers, accordingly, strive to create a supportive, open and trusting workplace climate where employees collaborate, are appreciated, and feel valued.[5]

This view provides a less mechanistic approach to human behavior in organizations. People are seen as being motivated by social, as well as economic, goals. Therefore, workers are thought to be most highly motivated when they are socially involved with colleagues and when they have been involved in making decisions that affect them.

In this school of thought, communication is seen as a means of facilitating social interaction and participation in organizational decision making. Achieving this objective is regarded as the primary function of management.

Systems

General systems theory seeks to provide an integrating approach to knowledge developed in fields as seemingly diverse as biology, sociology, communication, and engineering. Central to this framework is an emphasis on living systems and the way in which they maintain themselves through ongoing interactions between their parts and their environments.[6]

The systems perspective views individuals, relationships, groups, and organizations as interacting with and dependent on one another and their environment. Human behavior in organizations is seen as being shaped by the organization—its goals, roles, rules, culture, climate, networks, and so on. Simultaneously, organizations are seen as being influenced by the individuals, relationships, and groups that compose them.

Communication is viewed as the process through which organizations emerge and evolve and the basis upon which individuals, relationships, groups, and organizations relate to their surroundings and to one another. Communication also serves in decision making and control of the system as a whole in its efforts to adapt to its environment. In this perspective, management functions emphasize the need for effective communication and information systems to facilitate interaction, coordination, and adaptability.

Organizations are viewed as *complex systems*. Management's task is to create and guide organizations so that they are open and responsive to the needs and opportunities of the environment. Workers and the units of which they are a part are viewed as components of the organizational system, and information flow and feedback within and among these subsystems is understood to be necessary to the adaptability of the individuals, their units, and the organizations as a whole in their marketplace environment.

RESEARCH PROFILE

Critical Cultural Studies in Organizations • *Stan Deetz*

Contemporary scholars view organizations through a more critical lens than more traditional theorists of the past. Professor Deetz's work encourages more democratic processes in organizations which foster more productive cooperation among organizational stakeholders.

• • •

My teaching, research, and organizational interventions have usually been described as a form of critical cultural studies. Critical cultural studies (CCS) examine our communicative practices and processes of knowledge construction in light of both moral and practical commitments to inclusion and shared decision making. CCS provides a theory of communication but also a way of living. CCS asks for personal courage to identify and challenge assumptions behind ordinary ways of perceiving, conceiving, and acting and to recognize the influence of history, culture, and social positioning on perceptions, meanings, and actions. For example, the theory of communication embedded in CCS enables us to see how thoughts, feelings, and the very ways we perceive the world are outcomes of social processes. Understanding the social/historical/political processes through which our experiences are constructed can cast in doubt some of the most secure and personal understandings of our

world and ask us to make choices usually made for us by others.

To study communication, then, is to study the constitution of human experiences—how we get our meanings—rather than how they are expressed. This is important since, unfortunately, while opportunities for expression are protected in our society and usually in our organizations, the communication processes of producing our experiences are often very unbalanced, favoring specific dominant interests. Communication systems thus display much systematic distortion, and our freedom of speech is of limited value if we simply express meanings that dominant interests prefer. I study how these distortions occur and how we can form systems that give a greater opportunity for diverse interests to influence the formation of our personal identities, knowledge, values, and decisions. I aim to bring important conflicts into decision making that have been suppressed or overlooked. Most of my work does this in regard to corporate organizations looking both at internal practices and their external consequences for society. In my work, organizations are largely described as political sites dominated by some values at the expense of others. This work encourages the exploration of alternative communication practices that allow greater democracy and more productive cooperation among stakeholders through reconsidering organizational governance and decision-making processes.

Reviewing the scientific management, human relations, and systems schools of thought is a useful way to highlight differences between concepts of human behavior in organizations and implications for management and communication functions. The three perspectives provide broad frameworks for thinking about management and communication and serve as a backdrop for more specific approaches to management practice.

Quality

The word *quality* has become one of the most familiar terms in organizations today. From Ford's early use of the slogan "Quality is Job 1," to language on inspection tags in pockets of new garments, the preoccupation with "quality" is pervasive in contemporary organizational thought and practice.

The *quality school* of organizational behavior and management practice builds on previous schools of thought. Following the traditions of scientific management, the control of quality of products and services, and the idea of continually striving to improve work processes are basic concepts of contemporary quality thinking. Reflecting the perspectives of the systems school, the quality approach regards organizations as effective when they are responsive to the demands and opportunities of the environment—specifically to customers and other key groups that influence and are influenced by the organization. And, consistent with the views of the human relations approach, the quality approach sees workers as seeking involvement, collaboration, and the opportunity to do high quality work.

Rather than viewing the organization as a *machine,* a *family,* or a *system,* the dominant metaphor for theorists concerned with quality in organizations is *team,* as shown in Figure 13.2. Managers are viewed as *coaches* who coordinate worker expertise and marketplace information to assess, meet, and exceed the product and/or service expectations of customers.

Among the most noted contributors to the development and popularization of the quality approach are Walter Shewhart, W. Edwards Deming, Joseph Juran, and Phillip Crosby.[7] Walter Shewhart, often referred to as the father of the quality approach, developed theories and techniques for preventing variability in manufacturing processes through statistical process control techniques. W. Edwards Deming is best known for his contributions to Japanese industry, in which he served as an advisor as a part of the post–World War II reconstruction effort. His impact was substantial, and the Japanese named their most prestigious quality award, the Deming Prize, in his honor. Another name associated with the quality school is Joseph Juran, who emphasized the importance of continuous improvement and attention to consumers, describing quality as "fitness for use as perceived by the customer."[8] Phillip Crosby has also played an important role in popularizing the quality approach. He developed the Quality College in 1980, where an estimated five million people have attended courses.[9]

School of Thought	Organizational Image
Scientific Management	*Machine*
Human Relations Management	*Family*
Systems Management	*System*
Quality Management	*Team*

FIGURE 13.2 *Images of Organizations*

Among the corporations to pioneer the quality approach were organizations like Motorola, AT&T, Xerox, Proctor & Gamble, IBM, Ford, Disney, Federal Express, General Motors, and Johnson & Johnson. Studies indicate that more than three-fourths of the corporations in the United States have active quality programs aimed at enhancing competitiveness, operational efficiency, productivity, cost-effectiveness, customer responsiveness, employee involvement, and ultimately market and financial position.[10]

In education, quality programs have been implemented within a number of school systems, colleges, and universities, using the labels TQ (total quality), CI (continuous improvement), OD (organizational development), and TQM.[11] Generally, these programs apply the concepts of corporate quality programs, but adapt the framework and concepts to the specific needs, values, and goals of educational institutions. These programs emphasize quality in academics, work processes, teamwork, service encounters, management, and interpersonal relationships. Studies indicate that 92 percent of colleges and universities are integrating quality concepts, practices, and tools into the curriculum, 75 percent are applying quality to the administration of the institution, 92 percent have implemented plans to survey the various publics they serve, and 83 percent will institute faculty development efforts relative to quality.[12]

Quality: Core Concepts. "Quality" is certainly a familiar term, but what exactly does it mean in an organizational context, and what are the core concepts associated with the quality approach? Though the terminology varies somewhat from setting to setting, author to author, and program to program, six values are common to the various approaches:[13]

1. Service orientation
2. Leadership
3. Information
4. Process improvement and collaboration
5. Communication
6. Continuous improvement

Service Orientation. The quality school of thought places great emphasis on understanding and addressing the needs and expectations of *stakeholders*—individuals and groups for whom an organization provides products or services and/or on whose assessment of the quality of these activities the support and reputation of the organization depends.[14] Within the quality framework, these stakeholders are variously called *customer, constituencies, consumers, publics, clients, audiences, beneficiaries,* or *users.* See Figure 13.3.

The focus on service to consumers is based on a recognition that it is ultimately their judgments of the quality of a product, service, or institution—translated into marketplace behaviors—that are necessary to the continuing health of the organization. Traditionally, the word *quality* was associated with inherent features, characteristics, or attributes of a product, service, or process. The contemporary quality approach adds the stipulation that in order to possess quality, the needs and expectations of consumers must be satisfied. Conventionally, then, the quality of a product such as an automobile would be determined by a technical evaluation of the inherent attributes of the product. The new approach focuses

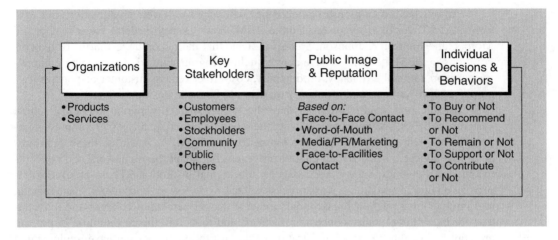

FIGURE 13.3 *Organizational Quality Framework*

on the consumer: What does the customer want, expect, and value in a car? Reliability? Speed? Economy? Size? Service? A courteous dealer? How do these factors rank relative to one another? Does a particular product meet these requirements and expectations? If so, it has quality; if not, it doesn't. After-the-fact judgments of quality focus on consumer satisfaction and loyalty: How satisfied is a customer with a particular automobile? Would he or she buy another? How likely is he or she to recommend the car to a friend?

The quality perspective suggests that, practically—as well as theoretically—speaking, the definition of quality is dictated by the behaviors of consumers in a competitive marketplace for goods and services. No matter how organizational "insiders" assess the value of a particular product or service as producers/creators, these judgments are made in a vacuum, limited, and inevitably incomplete, if they don't take account of the perceptions of consumers for whom the products and/or services are intended.

Most basically, the concept of service orientation suggests that it is essential to:

1. Identify constituencies for which the organization provides products or services
2. Determine and anticipate their needs and expectations
3. Satisfy—or, ideally, exceed—those needs and expectations

Leadership. A fundamental tenet of the quality approach is that leaders are most effective when they are personally involved in creating, communicating, explaining, reinforcing, and exemplifying the organization's mission, vision, values, and service orientation. Ideally, senior leaders' involvement will include a visible commitment to employees' growth, development, and satisfaction, and should encourage participation and collaboration among all personnel. Through ongoing personal involvement in activities such as planning, communication, reviews of performance, and recognition of individual and unit achievements, senior leaders serve as role models, reinforcing the organization's mission, vision, and values, and encouraging improved leadership at all levels.

Information.   A third value of the quality approach is information. The basic concept underlying this value is that organizational well-being, and a service orientation, are possible only with effective systems for information acquisition, analysis, and use. This includes identifying, studying, and comparing one's own activities to those of *benchmark* organizations—organizations which represent a standard of excellence and are a focal point for performance comparison and improvement.

Process Improvement and Collaboration.   The fourth value emphasized by the quality approach is process improvement and collaboration. Organizations are viewed as complex systems with numerous internal and external components which interact with and depend on one another. These interactions may take the form of exchanges of goods, services, capital, and information. The viability of organizations as systems and their ability to meet expectations of external stakeholders depend largely on whether and how effectively and efficiently these internal interactions take place. A simple example of a *process* that is common in nearly all organizations is recruiting. Whether one thinks of a business, a club, or a university, recruiting new members is a basic process. One can dissect the recruiting process in any organization to identify the specific steps in the process, the order in which they are performed, who performs them, and the procedures used. Through careful and systematic study it is also possible to determine whether there may be steps that could be shortened or eliminated, procedures that could be streamlined, additional training that could be provided to assist the people to function more efficiently, technology that could be introduced to expedite the process, and so on, and the result would be an improved recruiting process, one which might be more efficient, more effective, more responsive, and thereby better meet the needs of the organization and the potential recruits.

Traditionally, organizations have been structured around essential functions. Thus, a typical manufacturing company has divisions or departments of production, sales, operations, marketing, finance, research and development, and so on. Each division is organized hierarchically, with the staff in that area reporting to supervisors who report to managers, who in turn report to directors, who report to vice presidents, who ultimately report to a president and/or chief executive officer. The result: elaborate vertical structures and reporting relationships within each functional area of the organization.

Vertical structures, sometimes called *silos,* facilitate interaction *within* functional divisions. At the same time, they set up obstacles to interaction and collaboration *between* units. Individuals and departments often become detached from the overall mission of the organization. As a result, work process fragmentation, compartmentalization, and an "it's not my job" mentality tend to evolve. Thus, for example, the research and development division may design a product without the benefit of full collaboration with manufacturing, operations, and marketing, leading ultimately to any of a number of unfortunate outcomes, such as a wonderful design for a product which the company can not easily manufacture and for which there is no longer a viable market.

Simpler, "flatter," better-integrated organizations and work processes, which facilitate cross-functional and cross-divisional collaboration and teamwork, are better able to address consumer expectations, aligning individuals and functional units with the organization's mission, and improving organizational quality overall. In the case of manufacturing, the

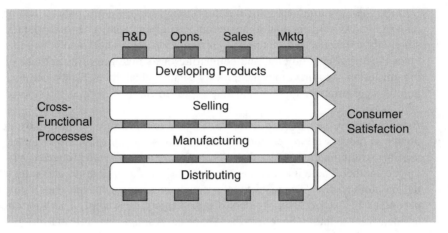

FIGURE 13.4   *Cross-Functional Approach to Key Organizational Processes*

quality approach promotes structures and work process patterns that integrate functions—for instance, research and development, purchasing, marketing, sales, and perhaps even suppliers and customers, as shown in Figure 13.4.

Communication.   Communication is the process through which organizational directions are set, leadership and collaboration take place, information is gathered and disseminated to and from internal and external stakeholders, and work process coordination and collaboration occurs. It is also the mechanism through which relationships are formed and developed—relationships which are essential to the creation of a culture and spirit of teamwork that is necessary to support and maintain a service orientation, collaboration, and an overall organizational commitment to excellence.

Continuous Improvement.   The sixth quality value is continuous improvement. Organizational excellence is not seen as occurring naturally. Rather, it requires a substantial commitment to time and resources to a process of continuous improvement and ongoing change—what many writing in the quality area have called a "journey."

Continuous improvement implies a commitment by everyone within the organization to a repetitive process, consisting of planning and testing improvements, evaluating outcomes, learning from failures as well as successes, implementing and sustaining successes, planning and testing improvements, and so on.

Quality Strategies and Processes.   What is the process by which the core quality concepts, values, and practices are implemented within an organization? Broadly speaking, the quality process has two phases.

1. Assessment
2. Improvement

Quality Assessment.   Fundamentally, *assessment* is a strategy for evaluating the performance of an organization in relation to the expectations of its constituencies, and the organization's mission and vision.

One of the most widely used assessment tools is the Malcolm Baldrige National Quality Award. The Baldrige Award, signed into law on August 2, 1987, was initiated with the intent of improving quality and workmanship in the United States. The National Institute of Standards and Technology (NIST) directs the award program.[15]

Companies interested in being considered for the award must complete a comprehensive self-study and application process. Awards are given in three categories: manufacturing, service, and small business, with no more than two awards per category per year.

The development of the criteria for 1988 resulted in seven categories, which have changed slightly over the years. The criteria include the following categories:

1. Leadership
2. Strategic planning
3. Customer and market focus
4. Measurement and knowledge management
5. Human resource development and management
6. Process management
7. Business results

Over the years a number of organizations have developed their own Baldrige-based assessment systems, tailored especially to their organization's needs. Among these are the Johnson & Johnson's "Signature of Quality Award," New York State's "Governor Excelsior Awards," and Rutgers "Excellence in Higher Education."[16]

Quality Improvement.   Quality improvement involves developing plans and strategies, working to enhance organizational excellence in any of the aspects mentioned in the foregoing discussion. Basic to the improvement process are groups or teams—often referred to as *quality* or *process improvement teams.* A *team* simply is a group composed of individuals representing various facets and levels of a unit or process earmarked for study and improvement. The team includes individuals with a broad base of knowledge and experience with the processes being addressed, and typically includes representatives from various stakeholder groups—managers and workers; often consumers and suppliers also participate. The team works together, with the guidance of a group facilitator, to clarify and eliminate gaps, and to develop an approach for ongoing monitoring and improvement. Team activities typically consist of the following:

- Planning improvements
- Studying the process to be improved
- Understanding the problem
- Collecting information
- Using tools and techniques to analyze and interpret the information
- Identifying solutions
- Implementing and managing changes
- Evaluating results

Other improvement tools include strategic planning, advisory groups, work process design or redesign groups, quality and service skills instruction/training, partnerships with other organizations, and external consultation.

As should be apparent from the brief review of the four approaches to organization thought, each approach has strengths and limitations. No one approach solves all problems or satisfies all critics.

This is certainly true for the organizational quality approach, which was seen by some early enthusiasts as a prescription to cure all the ills of contemporary organizations. What has become clear from the accumulating experience of organizations where the approach has been utilized over a period of time is that the quality approach can provide a useful way of thinking about the components of an organization, the necessary interactions between these components, and the processes and outcomes that are critical to excellence.[17] The approach also suggests some practical strategies that can be useful in assessing and improving an organization.

But there is no guarantee nor any particular magic in the process. In fact, some have described the quality approach as "organized and systematic common sense." When the approach is most effective, these outcomes occur because there is a genuine commitment to assessment and improvement within the organization and the core concepts discussed in this chapter are thoughtfully applied in a manner that makes sense for the particular organization.

Communication Networks

Network Functions

As with relationships and groups, organizations have their origins in *communication networks*—reciprocal message processing linkages. From the perspective of an organization, the functions of communication networks include:

1. Providing the means for coordinating the activities of individuals, relationships, groups, and other subunits within the organization
2. Providing mechanisms for directing the activities of the organization as a whole
3. Facilitating the exchange of information within the organization
4. Ensuring the flow of information between the organization and the external environment in which it exists

Network Size

One important differentiating characteristic of organizations is size. We have seen from previous discussions that an increase in the number of individuals in a social unit dramatically increases the number of reciprocal communication linkages that are possible and necessary to connect the people involved. This is a problem of major proportions within large organizations.

In small groups, little needs to be done to formalize communication networking. People can generally talk to whom they wish, about what they wish. When the group gets together, whatever happens, happens. In organizations, given the incredibly large number of potential two-person linkages, formalization of face-to-face and mediated communication networks is essential. See Figure 13.5.

Internal Networks: Message Flows within Organizations

Downward Message Flows.   Generally speaking, formalized lines of information that flow within organizations correspond closely with the lines of authority. The most familiar pattern of formalized information flow is from management to employees—from a supervisor to a supervisee.

In such circumstances, messages flow "downward" from people in positions of relatively greater authority to others in the organization who report to them—directly or through intermediaries. Messages transmitted downward generally serve one or more of the following functions:[18]

1. Specifying a task to be performed
2. Providing instructions about how to perform a task
3. Providing information about the reason for a particular task that needs to be performed
4. Providing information about organizational policies or practices
5. Providing information about an employee's performance
6. Providing information about the organization and its mission

Upward Message Flows.   Messages channeled from supervisees to supervisors—from individuals in organizational groups, departments, or divisions to people occupying managerial roles—represent what is called an *upward message flow.* Upward communication has several functions, including:[19]

1. Providing input for decision making
2. Advising about supervisees' information needs
3. Providing information regarding supervisees' level of receptivity to information, satisfaction, and morale
4. Providing a potentially constructive outlet for grievances and complaints
5. Allowing superiors to assess the effects of previous downward communication
6. Helping supervisees cope with problems and facilitating their involvement

Horizontal Message Flows.   What are often called *horizontal communication networks* refer to linkages that connect individuals at the same level of authority within an organizational group, department, or division. Functions of horizontal information sharing include:[20]

1. Coordinating planning and execution of tasks
2. Providing for collective problem solving
3. Facilitating common understanding
4. Resolving differences
5. Developing supportive and productive work relationships

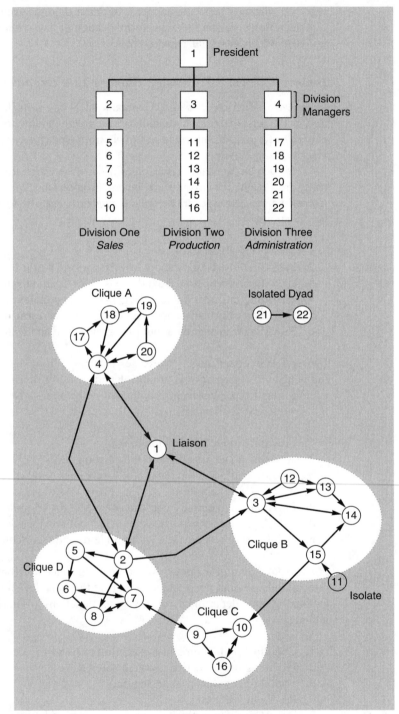

FIGURE 13.5 The chart at the top depicts the *formal organization* and *chain of command* within a typical hierarchic company. The drawing underneath illustrates the *communication network* among members of the company. Within the company, there are four *cliques*—subsystems of individuals who interact with one another relatively more than with others. There is also an *isolate* (11), an *isolated dyad* (21 and 22), and a *liaison* (1)—an individual interlinking various cliques.

Adapted with the permission of The Free Press, a Division of Simon & Schuster Adult Publishing Group, from *Communication in Organizations* by Everett M. Rogers and Rekka Agarwala-Rogers. Copyright © 1976 by the The Free Press. All rights reserved.

Informal Message Flows.   Aside from the formalized, intentionally designed linkages, other *informal,* or *emergent, networks* inevitably develop among individuals and subunits in any group or organization. These informal networks—which include the *grapevine*—serve to link individuals to one another in much the same way as do formal networks. Unlike their formalized counterparts, however, informal linkages come into being primarily because of the personal and social needs of the members.

Sometimes informal communication networks correspond closely in structure to the formal systems. For instance, a supervisor and his or her subordinates may regularly have lunch together and discuss personal and professional matters. Often, formal and informal networks are very different. A shipping clerk may ride to work with a secretary to the Vice President for Operations, for instance. In any case, informal networks established between workers in different departments, through e-mail, at after-hours get-togethers, at the tennis court, or on the way to and from work, are important channels within any group or organization. These networks have a substantial impact on both the content and flow of messages in the more formalized networks.

Informal networks:[21]

1. Are generally face-to-face
2. Are less constrained by organizational and political restraints
3. Move messages rapidly
4. Tend to be more the result of the situation than the people or their roles
5. Tend to develop more often within organizational workgroups, departments, or divisions than between them
6. Generally transmit information that is accurate, though often somewhat incomplete, leading to misinterpretation

External Networks: Relating to Other Organizations and Publics

Inflow: Research and Surveillance.   All groups and organizations depend on various constituencies, stakeholders, or *publics,* in the larger environment for their survival. Volunteer groups rely on contributors, business organizations on consumers and the government, hospitals on patients and physicians, advertising agencies on their clients and the public, newspapers on their subscribers and advertisers, and so on. *External networks* connect the organization with these publics and to the larger environment.

External networks also enable the system to gather information from the environment. Through market research, monitoring and analysis of various information sources, and direct surveillance of competitors and other environmental factors, organizations receive information necessary to identify and respond appropriately to environmental change, threat, opportunity, or challenge.

Outflow: Advertising, Marketing, and Public Relations.   External networks are also used to provide external publics with information that members of the group or organization think desirable, proper, or necessary. The terms *advertising, marketing,* and *public relations* refer to activities that involve the transmission of messages into the environment with the goal of informing and systematically influencing these publics and possibly engaging them in dialogue.

Mediated Communication Networks

In many organizations, face-to-face interaction between members on a regular basis may be impossible due to the large number of people involved or to physical separation. Therefore, in most enterprises, mediated communication is essential. The traditions of the mail and telephone are now supplemented or in some cases replaced by fax, teleconferences, online computer systems, e-mail, voice-messaging systems, and many other new communication media.

Organizational Communication Networks in Action

In the ongoing dynamics of organizational communication, networks seldom operate in the straightforward, rational, predictable manner one might infer from a description of possible types of networks and directions of message flow. In actuality, the functioning of communication networks is exceptionally complex, often unpredictable, sometimes uncontrollable, and frequently chaotic. See Figure 13.6.

In any organization, messages are being sent simultaneously in a variety of directions. In such circumstances, "breaks" in the network, distortion, contradiction, and confusion inevitably occur—they are more the rule than the exception. And, as in other communication situations, the message a manager or a subordinate thinks he or she is sending in an e-mail or through face-to-face conversation is often quite different than the message others receive. Furthermore, the sheer size of an organizational network and the

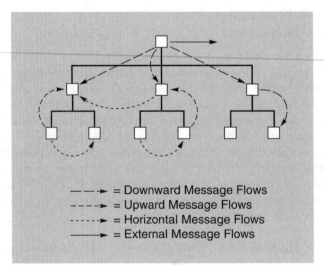

FIGURE 13.6

RESEARCH PROFILE

Communication Network Analysis • Ronald E. Rice

We are linked together through our communication networks. Professor Rice's research explores the relationships between these networks and resources, power, ideas, diversity, and job satisfaction, among other important aspects of our lives.

• • •

I have conducted research in the areas of communication science, public communication campaigns, computer-mediated communication systems, methodology, organizational and management theory, information systems, information science and bibliometrics, and social networks. One of my primary theoretical and methodological approaches is *communication network analysis*. Network analysis is the study and interpretation of influences on, forms of, and outcomes from, patterns of relations among entities. The entities may be people, organizations, words, events, and so forth. The relations may be communication, trade, co-occurrences, hierarchies, and so forth. The strength of such relations can be measured by frequency, attraction, length, financial value of transactions, dependency, and so forth. The overall structure of a network, the relationships among the network members (the entities), and the location of a member within the network are critical factors in understanding social behavior. These networks influence, among other things, access to resources, the distribution of social and organizational power, the spread of new ideas as well as diseases, career success and mobility, workplace diversity, job satisfaction, and even personal health and longevity.

My research has applied these concepts and methods to studying

- How new information systems change interactions among organizational departments and transform organizational structures
- How communication among organizational members influences those members' attitudes toward such new information systems
- How organizational relationships affect who seeks help from whom in understanding how to use a new information system, or what personal traits and problem characteristics affect who is influential in an organization
- How users of computer-mediated communication systems interact within and across their groups over time
- How different industries combine resources when technologies, such as television and computers, converge
- How researchers, articles, conferences, and journals represent different scientific interest areas
- How adolescents' friendship networks influence who uses drugs

distance between the top and bottom levels of the hierarchy intensify problems. Distance generally increases the likelihood of information loss, distortion, and the likelihood of distrust and suspicion.

The difficulties associated with information flow in organizations are described—in the extreme case—by Osmo Wiio:[22]

- If communication can fail, it will.
- If a message can be understood in different ways, it will be understood in just the way that does the most harm.
- There is always somebody who knows better than you do what you meant by your message.
- The more communication there is, the more difficult it is for communication to succeed.

Clearly, the complexity of organizational networks and that of the communication process combine to make organizations one of the most challenging contexts for those interested in studying or applying an understanding of the nature of communication and its impact on human behavior.

Organizational Culture

As interaction takes place through the networks of any organization, verbal and nonverbal behavior patterns develop and become routinized. Over time, they become important social realities for the organization—what can be called the organization's "culture." An *organizational culture,* is the sum of its symbols, events, traditions, standardized verbal and nonverbal behavior patterns, folk tales, rules, and rituals that give the organization its character or "personality." See Figure 13.7.

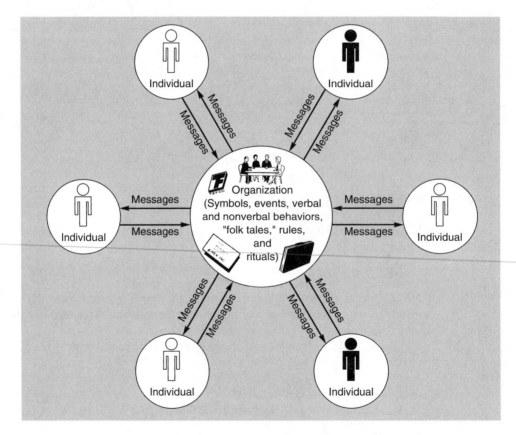

FIGURE 13.7 *Organizational Culture* Through their verbal and nonverbal behavior individuals collectively create the organizations to which they belong and the symbols, events, standardized verbal and nonverbal behavior patterns, "folk tales," rules, rituals, and other conventions characteristic of each.

Origins of Organizational Cultures

Organizational cultures grow out of the communication activities of individual members. Though organizational cultures are the products of human communication, they can take on an objective quality and "act back on" individuals within an organization, as depicted in Figure 13.7.

Symbols are one important element of the culture of many organizations. Trademarks, buildings, office furnishings, and uniforms are examples of symbols that are often a visible facet of an organization's culture. See Figure 13.8. Sometimes organizational symbols develop naturally, as with informal dress codes among employees of a company. In other instances, symbols—trademarks or slogans, for instance—are purposefully developed and actively promoted.

Space is another important organizational symbol. In many organizations, rules are developed for use in allocating space to employees, such that the location, size, and decor of an employee's office or workspace reflect his or her position. Larger, more elaborately furnished and decorated offices go to individuals of a higher rank within the organization. Lesser officials may have smaller, modestly decorated offices; people at still lower levels may have no private workspace, separated from one another by portable partitions or bookcases and file cabinets. For reasons that may make little sense to an outsider, carpeting in a vacated office might be ripped up and thrown away, rather than being left for a new occupant whose rank within the organization would not merit carpeted floors. These actions are regarded as necessary to preserve the culture. Variations are substantial from one organization to the next, as suggested.

As more employees telecommute (work at home or take their offices with them on the road), organizations are adapting their spaces. Some organizations have eliminated

FIGURE 13.8 Business cards are personal, portable symbols of organizational affiliation.

most individual offices and have replaced them with large areas that contain desks, telephones, data ports, and other office equipment that are shared by people who only occasionally are physically present at the office. For these organizations, electronic communication (e-mail, PDAs, pagers, etc.) has replaced the need to have all organizational employees present in one physical location. Other organizations have opened up their office spaces and created larger rooms in which people work together irrespective of job title or status. These spaces are designed to bring together people working on various facets of a task and to increase communication among people with different types of expertise.

Events like the annual picnic, the annual holiday party, or the management retreat also contribute to and reflect an organization's culture. They serve much the same functions for the culture of an organization as do birthdays, anniversaries, and reunions for individuals, relationships, and families.

The language used to talk about an organization is also a reflection of and, at the same time, an influence on its culture. An organization in which people talk about promotions in terms of military language like "fighting one's way to the top" is likely to have quite a different culture than one where promotions are described in terms of "members of a family working together to help one another succeed." We can distinguish between corporations based on whether their cultures are like academies, clubs, fortresses, or baseball teams, depending on the language used by the employees.[23]

Organizational "folk tales" or stories are another important facet of an organization's culture. Most organizations have a collection of favorite stories about notorious past and present personnel, organization achievements or failures, and memorable moments in the life of the organization. For example, one employee might say: "Did anyone tell you about the guy a few years back who tried to bargain his way to a higher salary by boasting to management of an offer from another company? They wished him luck in his new position, and asked him how soon he would be leaving." Or: "Let me tell you about the security guard who asked the president for her ID." Implicit in these stories are statements about organizational values, ethics, management practices, and other facets of life in the organization. Through stories and storytelling, organizational cultures are transmitted from one generation of employees to another.

Functions of Organizational Cultures

Organizational cultures play a central and pervasive role in the dynamics of organizations of all kinds, and they serve many important communication functions for those who create and participate in them, including:

1. Providing people within these units with a sense of individual and collective identity
2. Contributing to the establishment of structure and control
3. Aiding with the introduction of members to the customs and traditions of the organization
4. Fostering cohesiveness among members of the organization

Assimilation, Socialization, and Innovation in Organizations

Becoming a member of an organization requires an initiation into the culture through processes referred to as *socialization* and *assimilation*. Even in organizations with no formal apprenticeship or internship, the individual must come to terms with the organization's culture to be accepted and function effectively as a member. The formal communication networks play a role in this process, but informal networks are even more essential to learning the ropes.

Within any unit—an individual, relationship, group, organization, or society—there is a tension between influences that contribute to cultural stability and continuity and those that contribute to cultural innovation and change. Stability within organizations is fostered when members of the unit carry cultural traditions forward with them in time. Innovation and change call for departures from tradition. Sometimes innovations are introduced intentionally. At other times, change happens by accident because of the way individuals cope with and internalize the culture of the organization. Cultural continuity and cultural innovation are equally necessary to the survival and prosperity of organizations over time.

Organizational Climate

Climate is another aspect of organizations in which communication plays a direct role and one which is closely related to culture. An organization's *climate* is the atmosphere or tone members of the organization experience as they go about their daily routines. Climates are created through communication. In turn, climates influence organizational members and are perpetuated through organizational communication processes. Even as consumers, we may have a sense that not all organizations—department stores, hospitals, or schools, for instance—feel the same although their product or service may be similar. Often, differences in the feeling we get are a reflection of differences in the organizational climates, which were created and maintained through communication.

In very general terms, we can talk about climates being positive or negative. Positive—supportive—climates have been described as having the following characteristics:[24]

1. Supportiveness of supervisor–supervisee communication
2. Perceived quality and accuracy of downward communication
3. Perceived openness of the supervisor–supervisee relationship
4. Opportunities for and degree of influence of upward communication
5. Perceived reliability of information from subordinates and coworkers

Studies show that where supportive climates exist, job satisfaction is high and productivity may improve as well.[25] Generally speaking, a positive climate and high levels of satisfaction will be reflected in the positive treatment of clients and consumers, as well as colleagues.

Organizational climates, whether positive or negative, are self-perpetuating. Individuals tend to be attracted to—and selected to participate in—organizations in which members share their values, needs, attitudes, and expectations. Individuals with incompatible orientations are less likely to stay or be retained, if they do initially affiliate themselves.

Organizational Diversity

According to the U.S. Bureau of Labor Statistics and other sources, by the year 2008 70 percent of new entrants into the work force will be women and minorities. By 2010, the U.S. workforce will be 34 percent nonwhite.[26] These changes reflect dramatic changes in the U.S. population. A diverse group of customers is demanding products and services that meet their particular needs. Thus, issues of diversity have a particular importance for today's organizations as they attempt to meet the needs of the future.[27]

Many organizations have introduced training programs to help their employees deal with and manage the increasing diversity of the work force.[28] For example, in many organizations, innovations to improve quality include listening to the employees who have direct contact with the product and encouraging more employee input into decision-making processes. Training programs designed to address these issues include helping employees to develop the communication skills necessary to effectively present their ideas to a diverse audience and to understand the viewpoints and ideas of others.

Diversity expert Barbara Walker contends that: (1) people work best when they feel valued; (2) people feel most valued when they believe that their individual and group differences have been taken into account; (3) the ability to learn from people regarded as different is the key to becoming fully empowered; and (4) when people feel valued and empowered, they are able to build relationships in which they work together interdependently and synergistically.[29]

Thus, dealing with diversity in organizations consists of fully utilizing an employee's abilities based on an acknowledgement of the employee's uniqueness.[30] This concept means that organizations should not only allow but should encourage employees to use their own individual styles rather than expecting all employees to fit a particular corporate mold. This management philosophy emphasizes work output (how well a job is done), not necessarily the means used to obtain that work (how the employee went about accomplishing the task). For example, some employees may be more comfortable learning how to use a new computer program by reading the manual, others may do a better job by asking their coworkers for advice, and still others may just begin to hit keys and see what happens. The important thing for the organization should be how well the employee learned the new program, not what method he or she used to accomplish the task.

A survey of 4,191 employees from three organizations identified seven themes for diversity effectiveness:

1. *Climate.* General perceptions about the organization's ability to manage diversity
2. *Hiring practices.* What types of people are asked to join an organization

3. *Promotion practices.* Diverse people being promoted and welcomed into managerial jobs
4. *Training and development.* Amount and type of training and help offered to employees
5. *Equity and fairness.* General sense of fairness and respect
6. *Visible commitment.* Reflected by gender and minority–nonminority ratios, recognition for achievements, and other visible and tangible signs
7. *Politics in the workplace.* Perceptions that favoritism exists[31]

Organizations that score highly in each of these areas are more likely to be places that welcome and benefit from a more diverse work force.

There are five major problem areas that have been associated with diversity:

1. Stereotypes and their associated assumptions
2. Actual cultural differences
3. Exclusivity of the "white male club" and its associated access to important information
4. Unwritten rules and double standards for success which may be unknown to women and minorities
5. Lack of communication about differences[32]

Organizations that ignore these problem areas are not dealing effectively with diversity in their work force.

Diversity presents challenges for today's organizations. Nevertheless, the benefits of acknowledging work force diversity are great. Many companies have been very successful, especially in meeting the needs of a diverse market, by valuing the diversity within their own work forces and making use of the talents of a multicultural work force.

Implications and Applications

- Organizations have multiple constituents, or publics; and communication is the means through which the needs and expectations of these individuals and groups are identified and addressed.
- In many respects, an organization's most important constituents are internal. Each staff member, work group, or division has a contribution to make to the organization as a whole. Moreover, these constituents have needs and expectations—financial, informational, and social needs, for instance—which must be accommodated and coordinated if the unit is to perform efficiently and effectively.
- Organizations also have a number of external publics—customers and suppliers, for example—upon whom the viability of the organization depends.
- Organizational quality can be evaluated based on:[33]

  Technical quality. The adequacy of the products and services, and technical skills of staff. For example: clinical skills of hospital staff, or clerical skills of college secretarial personnel.

Administrative quality. The adequacy of management policies, procedures, practices, and staff. For example: billing systems in hospitals or course registration systems in colleges.

Relationship quality. The adequacy of the interpersonal communication and relationship building skills of staff. For example: a physician's interpersonal skills for relating to patients or a college receptionist's relationship skills in dealing with students or visitors.

- When internal publics evaluate an organization, they typically base their judgments on technical or administrative factors. "Insider" assessments of the quality of a college, for example, are generally based on an evaluation of administration, research, teaching, and service, using academic and technical criteria. External publics often take technical quality for granted or are unable to assess it. In the case of a college, for instance, students, parents, and members of the public at large are typically unable to make or understand assessments based on administrative practices or faculty research. Instead, their images are often based on what they can more easily see and comprehend, such as the quality of faculty and staff interpersonal communication and relationships.[34]
- The image of an organization with its external publics is influenced by mediated communication (news coverage, Web sites, advertising, public relations initiatives, and so on) and especially by face-to-face contact with representatives of the organization. Thus, the preoccupied college official who seems indifferent to a student's problem or the faculty member who is unavailable to meet with a student, unknowingly and unintentionally provide the basis for stories that may be told and retold to friends, parents, and acquaintances. From this perspective, every contact between an organizational employee and a "constituent" is an encounter that either contributes to or detracts from the perception—and the reality—of organizational quality.[35] Interactions between representatives of an organization and its external publics are critical communication links that are vital to the continued viability of any organization.

Summary

Communication, as we have seen, is as essential to the emergence of organizations as it is for the development of individuals, relationships, and groups. Without message processing even the simplest coordination between individuals would be impossible. In small organizations with a dozen people and large enterprises of several thousand employees, communication is critical to defining goals, delineating individual roles and responsibilities, controlling the organization's operations, establishing networks, and creating the organization's culture and climate.

A goal is the objective a system is designed to achieve. It is the benchmark against which the effectiveness, success, viability, and adaptability of the system can be assessed.

Organizations are formed with product- or service-oriented goals. A division of labor and a delineation of roles are needed to achieve these goals. A role is a set of defined behaviors— a job to be done, a position to be filled, or a function to be carried out. Relationships between roles may be indicated by reporting lines and formal organizational structure.

Organizational systems need a control mechanism for planning, decision making, financial oversight, monitoring operations, coordinating activities, and evaluating organizational functioning. These are management functions. The way in which they are carried out in an organization depends on the prevailing view of the nature of human behavior in organizations. The scientific management, human relations, systems, and quality views provide four ways of thinking about organizational behavior, management, and communication functions.

Communication networks serve important functions within organizations. Formal message flow through networks in an organization may be downward, upward, or horizontal. Informal networks are also basic to organizations. External networks link an organization to its environment. Face-to-face networks in organizations are increasingly supplemented by mediated communication. In the ongoing dynamics of organizational communication, networks seldom operate in the straightforward, rational, and predictable manner suggested by descriptions of the types of networks and the direction of message flow.

Organizational cultures emerge over time as a result of interactions among organization members. An organization's culture is the sum of its symbols, events, standardized verbal and nonverbal behavior patterns, "folk tales," rules, and rituals that give the organization a character or personality.

Communication also results in the creation of organizational climates. A climate is the atmosphere or tone experienced by members of an organization as they go about their daily routines.

Diversity is one of the major opportunities facing contemporary organizations.

Notes

1. See discussion in Everett M. Rogers and Rekha Agarwala-Rogers, *Communication in Organizations* (New York: Free Press, 1976); Gerald M. Goldhaber, *Organization Communication*, 4th ed. (Dubuque IA: Wm. C. Brown, 1993); and R. Wayne Pace, *Organizational Communication* (Englewood Cliffs, NJ: Prentice Hall, 1983).

2. Frederick W. Taylor, *Scientific Management* (New York: Harper & Row, 1911).

3. Chester I. Barnard, *The Functions of the Executive* (Cambridge, MA: Harvard University Press, 1938).

4. F. Roethlisberger and W. Dickson, *Management and the Worker* (Cambridge, MA: Harvard University Press, 1939).

5. See Everett M. Rogers and Rekha Agarwala Rogers, 1976.

6. James G. Miller, "Living Systems," *Behavioral Science, 10,* 1965, pp. 193–237; Brent D. Ruben and John Y. Kim, *General System Theory and Human Communication* (Rochelle Park, NJ: Hayden Books, 1975); L. Thayer, *Communication and Communication Systems* (Homewood, IL: Richard Irwin, 1968); Brent D. Ruben, *Communication and Human Behavior* (Englewood Cliffs, NJ: Prentice-Hall, 1992); and Ludwig von Bertalanffy, *General System Theory* (New York: Braziller, 1968).

7. See discussion in R. G. Lewis and D. H. Smith, *Total Quality in Higher Education* (Delray Beach, FL: St. Lucie Press, 1994).

8. Lewis & Smith, 1994, p. 54.

9. Lewis & Smith, 1994, pp. 57–58.

10. A. Hiam, *Does Quality Work? A Review of Relevant Studies* (New York: The Conference Board, 1993).

11. See discussion in Brent D. Ruben, *Pursuing Excellence in Higher Education.* (San Francisco: Jossey-Bass, 2004); Brent D. Ruben, *Quality in Higher Education* (New Brunswick, NJ: Transaction Books, 1995); Lewis & Smith, 1994; and Daniel T. Seymour, *The IBM-TQM Partnership with Colleges and Universities: A Report* (Washington, D.C.: American Association of Higher Education, 1993).

12. Total Quality Forum V, *A Report of Proceedings of the Total Quality Forum V: Rise to the Challenge: Best Practices and Leadership* (Schaumberg, IL: Motorola University, 1993).

13. See Ruben, *Quality in Higher Education,* 1995.

14. Brent D. Ruben, *Excellence in Higher Education: A Baldridge-based Guide to Assessment, Improvement and Leadership* (Washington, D.C.: National Association of College and University Business Officers, 2003); and Brent D. Ruben and Jennifer Lehr, *Excellence in Higher Education: Organizational Quality Self-Assessment Framework for Colleges and Universities* (Dubuque, IA: Kendall-Hunt, 1997).

15. National Institute of Standards and Technology, *The 1994 Malcolm Baldrige National Quality Award Criteria* (Washington D.C.: U.S. Department of Commerce, 1994).

16. Brent D. Ruben, *Excellence in Higher Education: A Baldridge-based Guide to Assessment, Improvement and Leadership* (Washington, D.C.: National Association of College and University Business Officers, 2003).

17. M. A. Hiam, 1993.

18. An excellent research summary and discussion of information flow is provided in Pace, 1983, Chapter 5. Values of downward information flow based on the work of Daniel Katz and Robert Kahn, *The Social Psychology of Organization* (New York: Wiley, 1966), are discussed on pp. 39–41.

19. Pace, 1983, p. 47.

20. See Pace, 1983, p. 53.

21. See discussion and summary of research by William L. Davis and J. Regis O'Connor, "Serial Transmission of Information: A Study of the Grapevine," *Journal of Applied Communication,* Vol. 5, 1977, pp. 61–72, and discussion in Pace, 1983, pp. 57–58.

22. Osmo Wiio, *Wiio's Laws—and Some Others* (Espoo, Finland: Weling-Goos, 1978), laws 1.2, 2, 3, and 4.

23. Carol Hymowitz, "Which Corporate Culture Fits You?" *The Wall Street Journal,* July 17, 1989, p. B1.

24. An excellent discussion of the organizational climate concept and current research is provided by Raymond L. Falcione and Elyse A. Kaplan, "Organizational Climate, Communication and Culture," in *Communication Yearbook 8.* Ed. by Robert N. Bostrom (Beverly Hills: Sage, 1984), pp. 285–300. See also discussions of climate and its impact on customer relations and on perceptions of organization quality in Karl Albrecht and Ron Zemke, *Service America! Doing Business in the New Economy* (Homewood, IL: Dow Jones/Irwin, 1985); and Wendy Leebov, *Service Excellence: The Customer Relations Strategy for Health Care* (Chicago: American Hospital Association, 1988).

25. Falcione and Kaplan, 1984, pp. 295–296.

26. Hewitt Associates, *Timely Topics* (February 2004). For extensive discussions of the changing nature of the workforce and the implications for organizations see: Taylor Cox, Jr., *Creating the Multicultural Organization: A Strategy for Capturing the Power of Diversity* (San Francisco: Jossey-Bass, 2001); Lee Gardenswartz, Anita Rowe, Patricia Digh, and Martin Bennett, *The Global Diversity Desk Reference: Managing an International Workforce* (San Francisco: Pfeiffer, 2003); R. Roosevelt Thomas, Jr., et al., *Harvard Business Review on Managing Diversity* (Boston: Harvard Business School Publishing, 2001).

27. Several authors in the field of communication have dealt with the issues of organizational diversity; for example, Lea P. Stewart, "Facilitating Connections: Issues of Gender, Culture, and Diversity," in *Communication Ethics in an Age of Diversity.* Ed. by Josina M. Makau and Ronald C. Arnett (Urbana: University of Illinois Press, 1997), pp. 110–125; Lea P. Stewart, "Gender Issues in Corporate Communication," *Women and Men Communicating: Challenges and Changes,* 2nd ed. Ed. by Deborah J. Borisoff and Laurie P. Arliss (Prospect Heights, IL: Waveland, 2001), pp. 171–184.

28. L. Duke, "Cultural Shifts Bring Anxiety for White Men," *Washington Post,* January 1, 1991, pp. A1, A14.

29. Barbara A. Walker, "Valuing Differences: The Concept and a Model," in *Valuing Differences in the Workplace.* Ed. by M. A. Smith and S. J. Johnson (Alexandria, VA: ASTD, 1991), pp. 7–16.

30. C. L. Brown and B. Sykes, "Implementing Diversity: The Quiet Conflict," presented at the Conflict and Diversity Conference, Temple University, Philadelphia, PA, 1992.

31. Heidi Brinkman, "Key Issue of the 1990s: Workforce Diversity," *TeamWorks,* April 1992, pp. 1–2.

32. L. Copeland, "Valuing Diversity, Part 2: Pioneers and Champions of Change," *Personnel,* Vol. 65, No. 7, 1996, pp. 44–49.

33. Brent D. Ruben, "Quality of Care: Insights from Patients, the Social Literature, and the Pet Shop," 1990.

Unpublished paper presented at the Mid-Atlantic College Health Association, Silver Springs, PA, Oct. 1990.

34. Brent D. Ruben, "The Health Caregiver–Patient Relationship: Pathology, Etiology, Treatment," in *Communication and Health: Systems and Applications.* Ed. by E. B. Ray & L. Donohew (NJ: Lawrence Erlbaum, 1990), pp. 51–68; Ruben, 1991; Brent D. Ruben and June C. Bowman, "Patient Satisfaction: Critical Issues in the The-

ory and Design of Patient Relations Training," *Journal of Healthcare Education and Training,* Vol. 1, No. 1, 1986, pp. 1–5; and B. D. Ruben, D. Christensen and N. Guttman, *College Health Service: A Qualitative Analysis of the Patient Perspective.* Unpublished Report, 1990.

35. Albrecht and Zemke, 1985; Wendy Leebov, *Service Excellence: The Customer Relations Strategy for Health Care.* Chicago: American Hospital Association, 1988.

14 Cultures and Societies

In this chapter

Why . . .

- First impressions are often based on cultural assumptions.

- Cultural symbols are different but yet all the same.

- Cultural rules guide behaviors such as handshaking.

- Culture is largely invisible.

- Adjusting to a new culture or situation has a number of predictable stages.

- The global village may be a nice place to live—or not.

Following the 9-11 World Trade Center disaster, cultural issues took on a new importance for many Americans. Differences in language, religion, dress, and names, which may have drawn little attention previously, suddenly became vitally important symbols in communication and information processing. In the wake of the tragedy, being identified as Muslim, an Arabic speaker, or of Middle Eastern descent suddenly became differences that made a difference—in the way one was viewed and treated. Even in the absence of specific knowledge about one's background or nationality, assumptions, misperceptions, misunderstandings, and cultural stereotyping were rampant. Here is one example.

A restaurant owner escorted a visitor through the kitchen to the back door of one of Baltimore's oldest Indian restaurants. His purpose was to show the visitor a crime scene. The owner, a sixty-year-old American citizen, pointed to the back steps and exterior of the building and explained that that's where four pint bottles filled with flammable liquid were thrown and exploded. A teenage prank? Possibly, the more likely conclusion was that the homemade bombs were thrown because the restaurant owner had a beard and wore a turban—symbols for some that he might be associated with those to blame for the WTC disaster.

The owner explained that he wore a colored turban, not a white one with a tail like Osama bin Laden. A month after the WTC tragedy, the owner reported that his business was down 30–40 percent, and he was nervous to go out in public, fearing he'd be treated as a terrorist. He commented to the reporter that he wondered how long Americans like him would be viewed with suspicion.

Numerous newspaper articles during the months following 9-11 reported similar events. In one of these, false rumors that a Hindu doctor was involved in an FBI terrorism investigation became so widespread that the physician took out an ad in the local paper in an effort to combat the rumors. (*Washington Post,* October 3, 2001, p. C01.)

The aftermath of the events of 9-11 dramatized, perhaps to a greater extent than in recent history, the critical role of culture and cultural symbols, and their pervasive impact on human communication.

All of these examples, and many more that can be seen in the passage above, reflect the influence of culture on our perceptions, attitudes, and behaviors. In this chapter, we will examine the nature of culture and how it influences and is influenced by our communication. In addition, we will look at the nature of intercultural communication and its pervasiveness in today's society.

The Nature of Culture

"Culture," like "communication," is a familiar term to most people. Partly because of this familiarity, the term is used in a number of different ways. The most common usage of "culture" is as a synonym for country or nation. If we come across several people conversing in a language other than English, or notice a woman wearing a veil over her face, we may say they are from another culture, meaning, in this case, that they seem to be from another country.

At other times, the term is used to refer to desired qualities or attributes. For instance, someone who uses "street language," is sloppy in his or her eating habits, or lacks a knowledge of the arts, might be described as "uncultured"—meaning unrefined, uneducated, or unsophisticated.

To those who study human behavior, "culture" has a more precise definition. It is not regarded as something one has or does not have, nor is it something which is thought of as being positive or negative. In fact, culture is not some thing at all, in the sense that an object can be touched, physically examined, or located on a map. Rather, it is an idea or a concept, which E. B. Tylor in 1871 described as having to do with "that complex whole which includes knowledge, belief, art, morals, law, custom, and any other capabilities and habits acquired by . . . member[s] of [a] society."[1]

From the point of view of communication, *culture* can be defined as the complex combination of common symbols, knowledge, folklore, customs, language, information-processing patterns, rituals, habits, and other behavioral patterns that link and give a common identity to a particular group of people at a particular point in time.

The Relationship between Communication and Culture

Let's examine the concept of culture and its relationship to communication in more detail: First, it is helpful to remind ourselves that all social systems—relationships, families, groups, organizations, and societies—develop and maintain cultures.[2] And they do so through communication.

In each relationship, for instance, a *relational culture* emerges naturally over time. As we discussed in earlier chapters, couples may have "our songs," dates of special significance, unique terms of endearment, and shorthand verbal and nonverbal codes—such as special phrases or gestures that have a unique meaning to the individuals involved. Each of these has a particular meaning and significance because of their shared communication history.

The same process occurs in groups and organizations, though a larger number of people are involved. As communication networks emerge and evolve, shared patterns and realities develop. In each, as we have seen, particular words or phrases, approaches to leadership, norms of behavior, or conventions of dress emerge as a result of communication and mutual adaptation of the members.

Societies, about which we have more to say later, are larger and more complex social systems, yet the same communication dynamics are at work. The symbols of a society are perhaps the most visible signs of culture.

Symbols are basic to the culture of each society. Spoken and written language are the most basic cultural elements, but other symbols serve this same role. Particular objects, places, people, ideas, documents, songs, historic events, monuments, heroic figures, architectural styles, and even folk tales may be important to a culture. See Figure 14.1.

As illustrated in Figure 14.2, flags of any one country are distinctive. Yet, if we analyze them in terms of physical characteristics such as their form, overall size, composition, and weight, most are really quite similar. Composed of pieces of cloth that vary from one another in little more than color, flags play important symbolic roles in human affairs. They mark territories, represent particular geographic locations, symbolize political or religious ideologies, and provide a symbol of commonality and unity for the residents of the territories they symbolize.

For Americans, the Statue of Liberty, the World Trade Center, Abraham Lincoln, the concept of freedom of speech, the Constitution, and *The Star Spangled Banner* have particular meanings, and their shared appreciation unites members of a culture in a common identity. While the specific elements of culture vary from one society to another, the linking and collective identity functions they serve are comparable within all societies.

Within societies, as in other social systems, communication is the means through which individuals create, share, and perpetuate culture, as illustrated in Figure 14.3. Shared verbal and nonverbal communication patterns, orientations toward religion, politics, gender, courtship, child rearing, race, and other facets of social life also become a part of the culture of any society.

FIGURE 14.1   A variety of verbal and nonverbal message sources provide visible traces of culture that confront individuals within societies.

Cultures—whether of relationships, groups, organizations, or societies—serve several common functions related to communication:

- Linking individuals to one another
- Creating a context for interaction and negotiation among members
- Providing the basis for a common identity[3]

FIGURE 14.2 Flags are societal symbols.

As is apparent by this point, the relationship between culture and communication is complex. Cultures are the by-product of the communication activities that take place in relationships, groups, organizations, and societies. Indeed, were it not for our human capacity for symbolic language, we would be unable to develop a common culture. And, without communication and communication technology it would be impossible to pass along the elements of our culture from one place to another and from one generation to the next. At the same time, our individual communication preferences, patterns, and behaviors are developed as we adapt to the cultural demands and opportunities we encounter over the course of our lifetimes.

As much as it is accurate to say that culture is defined, shaped, transmitted, and learned through communication, the reverse is equally correct.[4] In effect, then, there is a reciprocally-influencing, or reciprocally-defining, relationship between human communication and culture. Through communication we shape our cultures; and, in turn, our cultures shape our communication patterns.[5]

Characteristics of Culture

The idea of culture and its relationship to communication can be made clearer by discussing the following common characteristics of cultures: (1) Cultures are complex and multifaceted; (2) cultures are invisible; (3) cultures are subjective; and (4) cultures change over time.

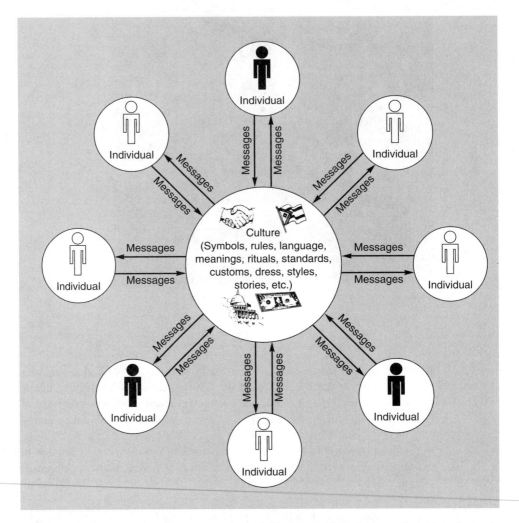

FIGURE 14.3 The relationship between the individual and culture is mutually influencing and reciprocally defining. Culture is created and perpetuated through the communication activities of individuals. Collectively, their behaviors provide the realities—symbols, rules, language, standards, customs, etc.—to which each individual must adapt in order to be part of the unit.

Cultures Are Complex and Multifaceted

The complexities of culture are most apparent, and potentially most problematic in terms of communication, at the level of societies. Here, language differences are often involved, along with fundamental issues such as social customs, family life, dress, eating habits, class structure, political orientations, religion, customs, economic philosophies, beliefs, and value systems.[6] See Figure 14.4.

Particular cultural elements such as these do not exist in isolation but, instead, influence one another in a number of subtle ways. For example, values of a societal culture

FIGURE 14.4 *Comparing Culture: Culturegrams* People in different countries have differing attitudes toward housework, favored sports, other aspects of social life, and even greeting rituals.

Japan
- Nearly 80 percent of all Japanese live in cities, even though there is room for growth in rural areas.
- Because body language is important, Japanese often expect others to sense their feelings without verbal communication.
- Most Japanese marriage ceremonies take place in hotels.
- Baseball is Japan's national sport.

Kenya
- Kenyans take pride in their efforts to preserve African wildlife.
- Kenyans are more willing to trust a person who will look them in the eye.
- Kenyan men do not do household chores and rarely cook.
- Kenya's economy is based on agriculture, which employs 75 percent of the workforce.

Lebanon
- It is extremely impolite to leave someone's home just after eating.
- The Lebanese do not ask about a person's religion; that would be considered an attempt to categorize someone.
- The main meal of the day is eaten between noon and 3 p.m.
- The parliament has an equal number of seats reserved for Christians and Muslims.

Puerto Rico
- Puerto Rico became a commonwealth of the United States with its own constitution in July 1952.
- One beckons by waving all fingers with the palm down.
- Women do not change their surnames when they marry.
- Every town honors its patron saint annually with several days of festivities.

Russia
- New Year's Day is the most popular holiday in Russia.
- When entertaining, Russians put more food on the table than they can eat to indicate abundance.
- Soccer is the favorite sport in Russia.
- Victory Day (May 9th) commemorates the end of World War II and is deeply important to most Russians.

Spain
- During the 16th century, Spain was one of the most powerful empires in the world.
- Spaniards stand close and frequently touch one another on the arm while conversing.
- Team sports are not part of school programs, so people join private clubs.
- Accepting a second serving is one of the best ways to show appreciation to the cook.

Source: CultureGrams, World Edition, www.culturegrams.com.

have an impact on economics and vice versa; and both influence and are influenced by social customs, religion, and family life. Consider this illustration: The tendency toward large families in some cultures is explained not only by custom but also by economics, religion, health, and the level of technology. In an agrarian society where infant mortality is high due to disease and poor health conditions, a couple may have many babies in order to be certain to have enough healthy children to farm and help with other duties necessary to the survival of the family unit. In North America and Europe, the decreasing size of families is also influenced by many of these same cultural factors, including economics, customs, available technology, social conditions, and evolving gender attitudes.

If we examine the verbal and nonverbal communication patterns in any culture, the same pattern of complexity and association is apparent. Greeting forms, gestures, conversational topics and formats, dress, language habits, courtship practices, eye-contact preferences, uses of space, orientations toward time, gender roles, orientations toward elders, and attitudes toward work all influence and are, in turn, influenced by a variety of cultural dimensions.

In Saudi Arabia, for example, gender differences are very pronounced. Traditional women wear dark robes (abayah) and veils (hijab) in public. Men do not approach women to initiate interaction in a social setting, nor do they look directly at a woman or do anything else that might be interpreted as a sign of interest. These gender role differences extend to other social settings as well. For instance, a Saudi male may invite a married man to dinner at his home with the expectation that the guest will not bring his wife. Even in those situations in which a couple is invited, the wife may be met at the door by the host's wife and entertained in a separate area of the home, leaving the men to dine alone. Many restaurants have separate entrances and special areas where women and children are expected to dine.

These traditional Saudi gender orientations are puzzling and objectionable to a North American. However, they can be understood in relation to the entire Arabic culture. They are the tip of what can be thought of as the "cultural iceberg."[7] In the case of the Arabic culture, the Islamic religion and tradition prescribe a very different role for women than for men. Saudi women are treated as they are because of a long-standing concern for protecting them from what are seen as the harsh realities of public life. For this same historical reason, the traditional dress of the Saudi women is designed to conceal and protect her from invasions of privacy that are regarded as rude and inappropriate.

Yet another example of the way in which facets of culture and communication are influential is apparent in business situations in Saudi Arabia. Saudis place great value on family, friends, and relationships. As a result, in Saudi business dealings, a substantial amount of time is spent discussing family, friends, and "how things are going." In fact, two businessmen meeting one another for the first time might devote their initial meeting to discussing only these topics, engaged totally in what North Americans often think of as "small talk." Only after the Saudi feels he knows and trusts the other person does he feel disposed to talk business—what *he* is more apt to regard as "small talk." From the perspective of North American culture, where a great premium is placed on efficiency and problem solving in business affairs, the Saudi business communication behavior may well be frustrating and difficult to comprehend. In a culture like Saudi Arabia, where a high premium is placed on supportive and socially-oriented communication, the highly task-oriented, "time-is-money" style of North Americans is equally annoying and often quite ineffective.

While every culture is unique in many respects, it is also possible to identify general patterns of similarity and difference, as illustrated in Figure 14.4. These and other themes are helpful analytically. In terms of orientation toward communication practices, cultures can be described in terms of three general themes: high and low context, individual and collective orientation, and monochronic and polychronic perspective toward time.[8]

High and Low Context Cultures. Communication and culture scholar Edward Hall defines *context* as "information that surrounds an event; it is inextricably bound up with the meaning of that event."[9] He indicates that cultures of the world—and the communication practices of individuals within those cultures—range from *high* to *low context.*

> A high context (HC) . . . message is one in which *most* of the information is already in the person, while very little is in the coded, explicit, transmitted part of the message. A low context (LC) communication is just the opposite; i.e., the mass of the information is vested in the explicit code.[10]

In Japanese, Arab, and Mediterranean cultures, for example, there is an extensive overlapping of personal, social, and work relationships. Because of these overlapping communication networks, these are high-context cultures; and, therefore, many everyday communication activities do not require much background information. The people who work together spend so much time together socially and in family activities that they are very well-informed about many aspects of one another's lives. Thus, when they converse, much can be taken for granted because of the rich communicative history of their relationships. Hall contrasts such cultures with low-context peoples, such as North Americans, Germans, Swiss, Scandinavians, and other northern Europeans, who tend to compartmentalize their personal relations, work relationships, and other aspects of their lives.[11]

Interactants within high- or low-context cultures have few problems interacting with one another. People from high-context cultures rely more on nonverbal cues and on what they know about a person's background to guide them through a conversation, while people from low-context cultures are more likely to ask the other person direct questions about their experiences, attitudes, and beliefs.[12] However, conversations across context types can become quite problematic, as when a North American and a Middle Easterner meet for the first time to engage in negotiations or to conduct business affairs.

Individual and Collective Orientation.[13] Feelings of responsibility toward the group is a feature of cultures that may vary from intense concern about the group's welfare and perceptions to a primary emphasis on the importance of individuals and their desires. Simply put, in individualistic cultures, the individual's goals are of prime importance while in collective cultures, the group's goals are supreme.

The United States is an example of a relatively individualistic culture. In the U.S., competition is encouraged, and each person is expected to be responsible for his or her own actions. Success is typically defined in terms of individual accomplishment—"working one's way up the ladder." When an American is asked what he or she does for a living, the response usually begins with a job title, followed by a description of his or her work responsibilities.

In Japan, traditionally a more collectively-oriented culture, things are quite different. Individuals are responsible to and for the entire group and are expected to adhere to group values and rules. A Japanese person responding to the question, "What do you do for a living?" is more likely to begin by explaining where he or she works, and only then to describe what he or she does, reflecting the greater importance attached to the work of the group than to one's own personal accomplishments.

Monochronic and Polychronic Time.   Time—a dimension of importance in many communication situations—is particularly vital to understanding cultures and differences between them. Hall distinguishes between two orientations to time: monochronic and polychronic. *Monochronic time* describes the orientation of people who pay attention to, and do, only one thing at a time. *Polychronic* refers to people who attend to and do many things at once.

In monochronic cultures, time is thought of as a commodity, as something to be counted, managed, allocated, and spent. Monochronic time is divided quite naturally into segments to be scheduled. In a monochronic system, a schedule or agenda becomes extremely important, as does completing tasks in a timely manner. In these cultures, people talk about time as though it were money, as something that can be "spent," "saved," "wasted," and "lost."[14]

Whereas scheduling, attention to time management, and the compartmentalization of personal and work-related activities are important in monochronic cultures, people in polychronic cultures have a much more fluid approach to such matters. Life in the United States—especially business life—clearly exemplifies the monochronic orientation, which is also a part of the cultures of Switzerland, Germany, and Scandinavia. In contrast are time-flexible Mediterranean cultures.[15] Individuals from monochronic cultures may get frustrated dealing with people from polychronic cultures and vice versa. For example, a North American business person attending a conference in Spain may expect the meetings and meals to begin and end at the times printed on the schedule. When the lunch that was scheduled to begin at noon doesn't start until 1:00 or 1:30, the attendees from polychronic cultures may seem unconcerned. Those from monochronic cultures experience the "delay" as a problem and are likely to become agitated.

Differences between high- and low-context and monochronic and polychronic cultures are useful for characterizing cultures and also help to explain some of the problems that occur in intercultural communication, a topic we will discuss in more detail later. Box 14.1 provides an interesting perspective on this issue.

Cultures Are Invisible

Most of what characterizes the culture of a relationship, group, organization, or society is as invisible to the individuals it envelops as the air that surrounds them. For each of us, our culture—and its many influences—is so subtle and pervasive that it often goes unnoticed. It's there now, it's been there as long as anyone can remember, and few of us have reason to think much about it.

BOX 14.1

Cultural variations in orientation to time, pace of life, or as it is sometimes referred to, tempo, are topics of both practical and theoretical interest. How does one study these differences systematically? Robert Levine uses three interesting, naturalistic methods that involve comparing measures of three types across cultures. First, he measures the amount of time it takes for a random sample of men and women pedestrians to walk sixty feet. Second, he observes a sample of postal workers and measures the amount of time it takes for them to transact a request for stamps. Third, he measures the accuracy of fifteen randomly selected bank clocks in the downtown area of a city as a way of assessing the concern with accuracy of timekeeping within the culture. Beyond the description provided here, there are a number of details and controls employed in all three measurement techniques to assure their validity and reliability, and the three measures are then combined to provide an overall pace-of-life score. Based on these scores, Switzerland, Ireland, Germany, Japan, and Italy, in that order, were the fastest paced cultures of the thirty-one cultures he studied, and Mexico, Indonesia, Brazil, El Sal-

vador, and Syria, the slowest. The U.S. and Canada ranked in the middle at fifteenth and sixteenth, respectively

Levine found that five factors accounted for the overall pattern of differences between faster- and slower-paced cultures, health of a culture's economy, degree of industrialization, size of population, climate, and cultural orientation toward individualism–collectivism. In general, wealthier, more industrialized, more densely populated, cooler, and more individualistic cultures were more fast-paced.

Levine used a similar research method to study thirty-six cities within the U.S. and not surprising, found a number of differences. In addition to measuring walking speed, he also measured bank teller transaction speed, talking speed, and the percentage of people wearing wrist watches. Seven of the top ten most fast-paced cultures were in the Northeast—Boston, Buffalo, and New York City ranking at the top of the list. Six of the ten slowest-paced cities were in California, and two were in Tennessee. The three slowest were Los Angeles, Sacramento, and Shreveport, LA.

Source: Robert Levine, *A Geography of Time* (New York: Basic Books, 1997).

In many parts of North America, we take the English language for granted, as we do a number of nonverbal conventions. For instance, business associates in our culture think little about the familiar two- or three-pump handshake greeting, intermittent eye glances, and two-and-a-half to four feet of space separating interactants when they first meet. In a similar way, we take for granted the many relational, group, and organizational cultures that guide and shape our lives. The romantic glances and expressive touch between intimates and the conventions of dress and jargon in our various groups and organizations become natural behaviors to the people involved.

Sometimes we do become aware of the existence and nature of our cultures. When this occurs, it generally happens in one of three ways: (1) violation of a cultural convention, (2) cross-cultural contact, or (3) scholarly analysis.

1. *Violation of a cultural convention.* When someone within our culture violates taken-for-granted cultural practices or standards, it tends to attract our attention. In the case

of the customary handshake ritual, for instance, we think little about it unless our expectations are violated. If, when meeting an individual for the first time, he or she takes hold of our hand with a very weak or exceptionally overpowering grip, we are likely to take note. Our reaction would be even more pronounced if a person we were meeting were to pump our hand four, five, six, or seven times, and only then reluctantly let go. And imagine our response if someone reached out to shake hands in the middle of a long conversation! We have a similar reaction when a new acquaintance stares incessantly, or stands five or more feet from us during casual conversation. As with so many other facets of our lives, we have been learning the cultural conventions for greeting and conversing with one another since we were children; and we generally think nothing about these conventions unless or until they are violated.

The same process occurs in relational cultures. Perhaps the most striking example happens when one individual in an intimate relationship "senses that something is wrong" because the other person doesn't look at his or her partner "the way he or she is used to," or no longer seems to "joke around" in the accustomed way. When our expectations are violated, we realize at some level of awareness that we have acquired a number of patterns, customs, habits, and meanings which we simply take for granted.

2. *Cross-cultural contact.* The second way in which we can be alerted to the presence and impact of our culture is when we encounter people from another culture and observe major differences between their behavior and our own. To many Europeans, men kissing one another on the cheek as a greeting goes unnoticed, while this same behavior startles North Americans. The Japanese habit of closing the eyes when concentrating on a question may be quite traumatic to the Canadian business person who has no idea how to interpret the action. Similarly, the "street language" and dress of an urban youth may be striking to someone raised in a wealthy suburb, whose verbal and nonverbal behavior, in turn, may also seem strange to urban residents. Travel—domestic and especially international—is certainly the most powerful way to increase our awareness of cultural differences.

Without necessarily being aware of it, these circumstances afford us some of our only opportunities to observe the subtle and pervasive influence our own cultures and subcultures have upon us. In either of these two kinds of circumstances, we know intuitively that "something is wrong" and that we feel somewhat uncomfortable, though we may not know exactly what is troubling us.

3. *Scholarly analysis.* The third way we can become aware of our culture is through studying our own or others' descriptions of it. Figure 14.4, providing overview descriptions of several cultures, stimulates this kind of cultural awareness.

Cultures Are Subjective

Because we have grown up with and take our cultures so much for granted, we are largely unaware of their subjective nature. To the people involved, aspects of culture are rational and make perfect sense, though they may not to "outsiders." We may easily come to assume that things are the way they "should be"—intermittent glances during casual conversation, shaking hands in a business setting, waving to an acquaintance, and so on.

An excellent example of this kind of assumption making is provided by colors. Obviously, red is red, and orange is orange. And, we all know that red is *not* orange, right? Not necessarily, as illustrated in Figure 14.5. The taken-for-granted language people use to describe color and the ways they categorize and perceive color around them may vary considerably from one culture to another. In Western cultures and language communities, we divide the color spectrum into six more or less distinct categories—red, orange, yellow, green, blue, and purple. We seldom think about the fact that these divisions are arbitrary, as are their labels. They are the result of the historical influence of European culture in the western world. People in certain other language communities divide the color spectrum differently. Historically the Shona people of Zimbabwe and the Bassa of Liberia, for instance, had fewer categories. The Shona divided the spectrum into four parts, which are pronounced *cipsuka, cicena, citema,* and *cipsuka. Cipsuka* appears two times, because it refers to colors at both the red and purple ends of the spectrum. The Bassa used two major categories—*ziza* and *hui.*[16]

Examples such as these help to remind us that the cultural patterns, codes, and realities we take for granted are not necessarily "true" or "right." A more theoretically appropriate view is that our cultures are the way they are because we and our ancestors created them in particular ways. We have come to accept their correctness in the same way that other people (see Box 14.2) have come to accept the rightness of their cultures—through communication.

Ethicist Thomas Donaldson[17] has identified the core values which he believes reflect cultural traditions around the world.

1. *Respect for human dignity.* Individuals must not treat others simply as tools; in other words, they must recognize a person's value as a human being.
2. *Respect for basic rights.* Individuals and communities must treat people in ways that respect people's basic rights.
3. *Good citizenship.* Members of a community must work together to support and improve the institutions on which the community depends.

English:

red	orange	yellow	green	blue	purple

Shona:

cipsuka	cicena	citema	cipsuka

Bassa:

ziza	hui

FIGURE 14.5

From *Word Play* by Peter Farb, Copyright © 1973 by Peter Farb. Used by permission of Alfred A. Knopf, a division of Random House, Inc. and Brandt and Hochman Literary Agents, Inc.

BOX 14.2

Differing perceptions about symbols and their meanings are commonplace when individuals from distinct cultures interact. Conflicts in the Middle East have provided any number of dramatic illustrations. The meaning of gunfire provides one particularly vivid example. In both Iraq and Afghanistan, there have been a number of instances where wedding ceremonies, which include the firing of guns into the air as a part of the traditional celebration, have been interpreted as the sites of organized military action and responded to based on this interpretation. In one such case in which forty Iraqis were killed, debates swirled as to meaning of the gun fire that emanated from the group. Were the victims simply participating in a wedding ritual or were they part of an overt military action, which would justify the air strike they triggered? Offering a personal interpretation of the event, one soldier said simply: "We took ground fire and we returned it. . . . we operated within our rules of engagement." The debate continues as to whether those killed were wedding guests or willful military combatants.

Source: "Iraqis Blame U.S. for Wedding Attack, Despite Denial," Alastair Macdonald, Reuters News Service/Yahoo News, May 20, 2004.

Although we may want to believe that these precepts are valued in all cultures, many of the events of contemporary world affairs seem to call this belief into question. If values such as "respect for dignity and basic rights" and "good citizenship" are, indeed, universal cultural values, it seems clear that the meaning of these words and phrases varies considerably among cultures or at least among some individuals in various cultures.

Cultures Change over Time

Cultures and subcultures do not exist in a vacuum. We carry the influence of these cultures with us as we participate in any number of relationships, groups, or organizations. As we as individuals change, we provide an impetus for the change of cultures of which we are a part. In this sense we are each agents of cultural change.

In addition to natural, evolutionary cultural developments that inevitably occur, other cultural changes occur in a more intentional revolutionary way. In recent years, for example, concerned African Americans, Latinos, women, gay males and lesbians, and handicapped individuals have focused attention on the discriminatory conventions and practices that have become a part of our society's culture. Efforts by members of these groups have not only accelerated and directed cultural developments within the society as a whole but have undoubtedly had an impact on the cultures of relationships, groups, and organizations, as well.

A Word of Caution

Efforts to identify and classify cultures based on an analysis of the identification of similarities and differences among them has a long and respected academic tradition. The results of these efforts are helpful for understanding the nature of culture and the processes through which cultures develop and evolve.[18] At the same time, this kind of analysis has very practical value for those seeking to understand and function effectively in particular cultures or in cross-cultural settings in general.

In undertaking this kind of analysis, and in using the information which results, there is the very real danger of cultural stereotyping—of adopting overly gross generalizations about individuals representing particular national, regional, religious, or ethnic groups. It is important to remember that what can be said about a group never fully applies to the individuals who compose it. In our efforts to classify and understand the commonalities within another culture, we would do well to remind ourselves of the incredible diversity that we find within our own culture, and to recognize that a similar degree of diversity exists in other cultures, as well.

The Role of Mediated Communication

Many institutions within society contribute to the creation, perpetuation, and evolution of culture. Families play a very basic part in this process, as do churches, schools, corporations, the government, and the business community. Mediated communication also plays an indispensable role.

Mediated communication extends our creating, duplicating, and storing capabilities. Our technology broadens the pool of messages available in common to individuals. Some of these mediated messages relate to our relational, group, and organizational cultures. Cell calls, e-mail, and photographs serve this purpose for relationships, in much the same way that printed constitutions, badges, and emblems serve this function for groups. Brochures, newsletters, and video products, similarly, contribute to the culture of organizations. At the societal level, the cultural contribution of mediated communication is immense. Mass media institutions such as newspapers, radio, television, books, and film have long played a fundamental role in packaging and transmitting cultural information, as do libraries and museums.[19]

Advertising also contributes to our cultural information base. Ads promote our market-based economic system and urge us to become consumers. Sporting events provide another interesting illustration of the ways in which mediated, especially mass, communication can serve as a carrier of cultural messages as discussed by Dan Nimmo and James Combs in *Mediated Political Realities.* Sporting events present a story of "heroic deeds and untimely errors, dramatic climaxes, and the euphoria of the victors along with the gloom of the vanquished."[20]

Even video and computer games provide implicit cultural messages. Video games come equipped with a "reset" button that allows the player to have a fresh start at any time without any consequence with each new game.

> Many video games offer the consumers a pause control. When a player desires to take a break from a particular game and to return later, the touch of a button makes this possible. When the individual returns, hours or days later, he or she will find the game patiently waiting at

the same place it was when stopped, another luxury unfortunately absent in everyday encounters.[21]

Mass communication also plays a role in commercializing cultural symbols. Not only people, but also fictional characters, are commercialized through mass communication, as with Big Bird, Spiderman, or Mickey Mouse. So, too, mass communication is essential in the commercialization of places, among them Disney World, Central Park, Cancún, Las Vegas, New York, and Paris.

Mediated messages are a kind of cultural mirror, combining with the messages of face-to-face communication to provide a menu and an agenda of concerns, issues, values, personalities, images, and themes that occupy a central role in the symbolic environment to which individuals must adapt. In this way, mediated communication plays a fundamental role in the socialization process of the individual and in so doing contributes at the same time to the stability and order of social systems.[22]

Cultural Adaptation

Adapting to a culture is a matter of socialization and persuasion. It involves learning appropriate personal representations, maps, rules, and images of the relationships, groups, organizations, and society of which we are members.

Most of the learning is natural and inevitable. We would learn to speak our native language, for example, whether we were ever formally taught it or not. We absorb cultures—become Americans, Kenyans, Italians, Macedonians—with virtually no effort or awareness on our part that it is happening. Even less obviously, we adapt to and absorb the cultures of relationships, groups, and organizations in which we become involved. We become "a corporate person," "a stockbroker," "a Protestant," or "masculine" or "feminine" with very little effort on our part, as we take on the cultural conventions of our gender, friends, family, ethnic groups, profession, and society.

Cultural adaptation also involves persuasion, as with the education provided by family, church, and school aimed at providing the knowledge, values, and rules that others deem necessary.

Because we tend so easily and so thoroughly to adapt to our own cultures, it is often a difficult and stressful matter to readjust to others. Newly retired, divorced, or widowed people, for instance, often find the adjustment to their new situation extremely difficult. Adjusting to the subculture of a prison often presents the same problems; and, once this adjustment has taken place, readjustment to the culture of the "outside world" upon release can be even more difficult.

These kinds of adjustments represent what has been called *culture shock,* feelings of helplessness, withdrawal, paranoia, irritability, and a desire for a home.[23] Initially, culture shock was thought to be a *disease*—a malady contracted by persons who were suddenly transplanted from one geographic locale to another. Symptoms associated with the illness were noted to include frustration, anger, anxiety, feelings of helplessness, overwhelming

RESEARCH PROFILE

Adaptation and Intercultural Communication • *Young Yun Kim*

In today's world, people are continually crossing cultural boundaries. Professor Kim's work helps people understand and adapt to their roles as sojourners.

● ● ●

Millions of people change homes each year crossing cultural boundaries. Immigrants and refugees resettle in search of a new life, side by side with temporary sojourners finding employment overseas as artists, musicians, writers, accountants, teachers, and construction workers. As well, diplomats and other governmental agency employees, business managers, Peace Corps volunteers, researchers, professors, military personnel, and missionaries carry out their work overseas for varying lengths of time. Individuals such as these are the contemporary pioneers venturing into an unfamiliar terrain where many of the "business-as-usual" ways of doing things lose their relevance. Even relatively short-term sojourners, such as exchange students, must be at least minimally concerned with building a healthy functional relationship to the host environment in ways similar to the native population.

As they confront their predicaments and actively engage in new learning, they are embarking on a gradual, long-term process of growth beyond their original cultural perimeters.

This description, in a nutshell, points to the reality of cross-cultural adaptation that I have tried to understand and explain through my research and theorizing. I began to study this phenomenon about two-and-a-half decades ago as a graduate student from South Korea. Since that time, the main aim in my work has been a search for a general theory, a comprehensive and systematic intellectual guide as we examine what happens when we cross cultural boundaries and what factors facilitate or impede adaptation. I am convinced that our ability to communicate in accordance with the norms and practices of the local culture is at the heart of successful adaptation. As we undertake this project of cross-cultural adaptation, we are also embarking on a path of personal development—one in which we stretch ourselves out of the familiar and reach for a deepened and more inclusive understanding of human conditions, including our own.

loneliness, and excessive fears of being robbed, cheated, or eating dangerous food.[24] As the following story indicates, the turbulence that goes with the experience of physical relocation can apparently be traumatic for animals as well as humans:

> In the spring of 1972, the United States and China exchanged gifts of animals as gestures of goodwill between countries. The Chinese pandas, Hsing-Hsing and Ling-Ling, quickly adjusted to the National Zoo in Washington, D.C. After a few days, they were in excellent health, standing on their heads and wiggling their rumps. Milton and Matilda, the two musk oxen sent to Peking, did not make a healthy adjustment to the [Beijing] Zoo—they suffered from postnasal drip and a skin condition that caused them to shed their hair. . . .[25]

The explanation provided by Dr. Theodore Reed, director of the National Zoo, who accompanied the oxen to China, was that their runny noses and other symptoms were the result of culture shock and the rigors of travel—"hearing Chinese spoken instead of English, seeing new faces, new uniforms, new surroundings, and eating Chinese hay and grain."[26] Within several months, Milton and Matilda recovered, as a result of antibiotics and what Reed described as "tender loving care."

As one might predict even from this brief story, the medical view of cultural adjustment has broadened in recent years to include an emphasis on psychology, sociology, and especially, communication. In fact, in his classic book *Silent Language,* Edward Hall described culture shock as "simply the removal or distortion of the familiar cues one encounters at home and the substitution of them by other cues which are strange."[27]

Stages of Cultural Adaptation

There have been numerous attempts to describe and delineate the stages of cultural adaptation.[28] These writings suggest that there are generally four phases, as shown in Figure 14.6.

1. Phase 1 is a "honeymoon" period during which individuals adjusting to a new culture are excited by the novelty of the people and new surroundings or situations.

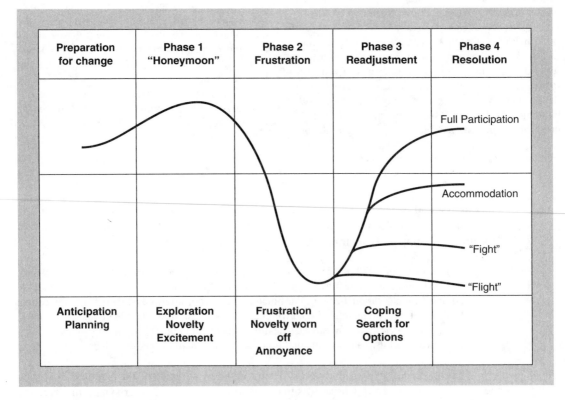

FIGURE 14.6 *Stages of Adaptation in a New Environment*

Source: Based on review of literature on stages of adaptation presented in *Adaptation to a New Environment,* by Daniel J. Kealey (Ottawa, Canada: Canadian International Agency, Briefing Centre, 1978).

2. Phase 2 is a period in which fascination and novelty often turn into frustration, anxiety, and even hostility, as the realities of life in an unfamiliar environment or circumstance become more apparent.
3. Phase 3 marks the beginning of the readjustment process, as individuals begin to develop ways of coping with their frustrations and the challenge of the new situation.
4. In Phase 4, the readjustment continues. During this period, several outcomes are possible. Many individuals regain their balance and comfort level, developing meaningful relationships and an appreciation of the new culture. Other individuals are unable fully to accept the new culture but find a way to cope with it adequately for their purposes. A third response is simply to find a way to "make the best of it," though with substantial personal discomfort and strain. Some are unable to reach even this level of adjustment and find their only alternative is to retreat from the situation.

When an individual is adjusting to the culture of a new society thousands of miles from home, where the geography, climate, rituals, customs, lifestyles, and languages are unfamiliar, with no companions and no prospect of returning to their home country for several years, cultural adaptation may be a very intense and stressful experience.

The same dynamics of adaptation occur in more common circumstances. Any time we move from one area to another, enter a new relationship, start a new job, move in with new roommates, or find ourselves in a novel situation, we are likely to go through these same stages of adaptation as the adjustment to new people, new expectations, new symbols, and new cultural realities takes place.

Often, the initial enthusiasm in a new country, community, job, organization, relationship, or situation gives way to frustration, disappointment, and even some degree of depression, as it becomes apparent that the new situation is not all we had imagined it would be. Gradually, we begin to adapt, as we revise our expectations downward, develop new understanding, and apply the skills necessary to cope with the new relationship, group, organization, or circumstance. In some instances, we adjust fully. In others, we give the appearance of fitting in but never really become comfortable.

Sometimes our resistance to the situation is substantial. In some cases individuals may be unable to continue and may decide to withdraw. See Figure 14.6.

Intercultural Communication

The topic of intercultural communication—or, as it's sometimes termed, cross-cultural communication—has become increasingly popular as a theme in recent years, and a growing number of writings in the field are dedicated to providing an overview of theory and research in the area.[30]

What, exactly, is intercultural communication?

Whenever we interact with someone from another culture, we are engaged in *intercultural communication*. Given our definition of culture, this means that every communication situation is intercultural *to some degree*. In any communication situation, each person brings unique symbols, meanings, preferences, and patterns that reflect the many cultures of which they have been a part over the course of their lifetime.

As we meet new people, we are in the process of negotiating the beginnings of a new relationship and relational culture. From the first moments of contact between two individuals, we begin a process of intercultural communication, mutual exploration, negotiation, and accommodation. At the instant we take notice of a person, we don't know whether we have similar knowledge levels, backgrounds, orientations toward time, political philosophies, gestural patterns, greeting forms, religious orientations, or even a common language capability. And we don't know whether or not we have had similar experiences in previous relationships, groups, or organizations.

As we interact, we use communication to reduce our uncertainty about the situation and the people involved.[31] We talk and listen to one another. We study appearance, dress, adornments, posture, and walk. Gradually, we begin to acquire information that helps us to determine what we have in common and where we differ. As the process continues, the pool of common information available to us grows steadily and with it the possibilities of which we are becoming a part.

While the process may sound quite simple, the complexities and potential problems are substantial. Communication scholar Joseph DeVito offers the following guidelines for avoiding barriers in intercultural communication:[32]

1. Recognize the differences between yourself and the culturally different person. When in doubt, ask questions; avoid assuming similarities. At the same time, however, do recognize the value of seeking out similarities and emphasizing these points of contact.
2. Recognize that differences exist within any group. Do not stereotype, overgeneralize, or assume that differences within a group are not important.
3. Remember that meaning is in the person and not in the words or in the gestures used. Check your meanings with those of the other person. Make sure that any assumed similarity (or difference) in meaning really exists.
4. Be aware of the cultural rules operating in any intercultural communication context. . . . Become sensitive to the rules that the other person is following. Be careful not to assume that your rules are the only valid or logical ones. When in doubt, ask.
5. Avoid negative evaluation of cultural differences, both verbally and nonverbally. See cultural customs and rules (your own as well as those of others) as arbitrary and convenient rather than as natural and logical.
6. Guard against cultural shock by learning as much as possible about the culture you will enter. Read, talk with people from that culture and those who have had experience in the culture, and view films, for example.

Societies—Complex Cultural and Communication Systems

A *society* is a complex social system composed of a large number of diverse, geographically dispersed, and mutually dependent individuals, groups, and organizations in pursuit of interrelated goals. Societies—like other social systems—are created, defined, and maintained through communication.

National and International Networks

Two types of communication networks are basic to the functioning of a society: (1) national networks, and (2) international networks. *National networks* are the pathways *within* a society that connect individuals, groups, and organizations to one another. See Figure 14.7. The functions served by these networks include

1. Providing the means through which information is conveyed among members of a society
2. Facilitating the coordination of often diverse activities of individuals, groups, and organizations within a society
3. Supplying the channel through which collective decisions are made and implemented

In a democratic society, many of the critical linkages in the national network will be provided by individuals elected or chosen to represent a particular group or organization.

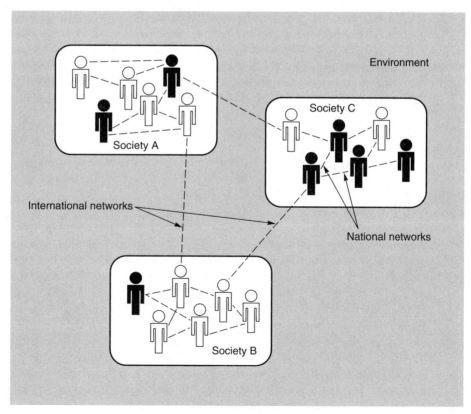

FIGURE 14.7   *National and International Networks*

Members of a community select individuals to represent their concerns and point of view to other groups at a regional or state level. At a still higher level, representatives from regions, states, and other groups and organizations join to pool information, discuss common concerns, set priorities, and make decisions for the society as a whole.

This process of collaboration and collective decision making results in the creation of recommendations, policies, and laws. Information about these deliberations and their outcomes is then distributed to members of the society using a variety of pathways. News and public affairs media programming, political campaigning, government publications, Web sites, and other mass communication channels operate in combination with interpersonal communication. Collectively, these national networks create what Karl Deutsch termed the "nerves of government."[33]

Besides the national networks, so essential to the functioning of a society, *international networks* are also extremely important. These transnational networks are linkages *between* societies.

Interpersonal contact by tourists, foreign service personnel, and representatives to the United Nations and other international agencies plays an important role in linking societies to one another. Other pathways are those created through international news and entertainment programming, international banking transactions, governmental propaganda, and intelligence operations. Functions served by international networks include

1. Providing societies access to information necessary to identify and adapt to the needs and challenges of the environment and the world community
2. Supplying the means through which information is conveyed among societies
3. Facilitating the identification and coordination of often diverse needs, activities, and perspectives of various societies
4. Providing the pathways through which international collaboration is possible

International Communication: The Global Village—Fact or Fiction

A number of popular and scholarly writers, including Marshall McCluhan, have pointed optimistically to a future in which citizens of the world would be linked together in what we might think of as a "world community" or "global village." The image is of a massive network in which individuals in all societies would be united throughout communication. Scholars envision "an information world," an extension of today's growing number of advanced information societies.

To some extent, this envisioned future has already become reality. Live television broadcasts from throughout the planet have become commonplace; Cable News Network (CNN) is available in more than ninety countries; newspapers are printed and distributed throughout the world via satellite; and the international distribution systems for books, videotapes, CDs, and software are all realities of life.

Formal and informal international relations, and tourism, are other significant contributors to global communication. There is little question that increased face-to-face interaction along with mediated communication have facilitated dramatic increases in the flow of information around the world, increasing exposure to one another's cultures, perspectives, and leaders.

Complexities Abound

With the recognition that global information sharing is indeed a growing reality come new questions from some quarters as to whether a global village is really a desirable goal. Indeed, some are suggesting now that the barriers that could be diminished through information and communication technology may be quite important to maintain.

Although most of us would probably regard cultural change as desirable, not all share this view. As we have seen, for some, the intrusion of messages from other cultures is negatively valued. Detractors contend that communication across cultural boundaries can contribute to a "melting pot" effect, and fear that valued distinctions between cultures or societies often become blurred in the process. To those who see this melting down of differences as threatening to the distinctiveness of a particular relationship, group, organization, culture, or society, intercultural communication and change may be actively resisted.

It is also argued that economic dependency on countries that produce communication hardware has implications for dependency on these same providers for content and programming—CDs, computer programs, and the content of television shows, for instance. Many are concerned because they see North American culture linked to our communication products and services. For a less industrialized country or those with different ideologies, the prospect of enabling its citizens to be linked to the world community in order to have access to U.S. prime time television—HBO, MTV, or the Playboy Channel—raises some obvious questions. Can a culture hope to preserve its identity, political or ideological integrity, or its traditional values when its citizenry receives a steady diet of music videos and programs such as *Die Hard, The Sopranos,* and *Total Recall*? Concerned about precisely these issues, several European countries limit "American cultural imperialism" by placing quotas on the invasion of U.S. programs.[39]

This potential for economic and cultural control raises fundamental questions. Is it possible for an individual, organization, or society to be dependent on others economically and technologically but be uninfluenced by their cultural messages? Or does control of communication media, products, and services imply cultural influence and dependency? Clearly, the challenge is to reap the benefits of global communication without unnecessarily sacrificing individual and cultural integrity and independence in the process.

Another important issue has to do with the nature of communication as it relates to increasingly optimistic predictions about improvements in international cooperation and understanding. While we can certainly think of many situations where increased communication has contributed to improved intercultural and international relations, we can also identify any number of circumstance where more communication seems to lead to a deterioration in relations. Many examples could be drawn from areas of international conflict, and perhaps most vividly for North Americans, those associated with the events leading to the 9-11 tragedy and the actions which have followed. While one could question the quality and effectiveness of the message sending and receiving associated with these circumstances, it is clear that communication was not absent.

Examples such as this remind us that more communication media, networks, messages, and services, alone provide no guarantee of improved international understanding or cooperation. The capability of communication and the sharing of a common symbolic environment do not automatically lead to shared or converging ways of thinking or behaving, common value orientations or similar information processing patterns for the individuals involved. In all fundamental respects, a war, an argument, or a divorce, are as much a product of communication as are peaceful coexistence, a reconciliation, or a marriage. Occasionally, "negative" outcomes develop because of a lack of a common base of information or reciprocal message processing. More often, however, these results occur because of the *presence* rather than *absence* of communication. As we know, even when two individuals are confronted by the same messages, their ways of selecting, attaching meaning and significance, and retaining information may inhibit—or even preclude—the chance for mutual understanding, agreement, or convergence. The problem of human rights in many countries of the world does not seem to be the result of a "breakdown" in reciprocal message processing. Virtually all of us have access to messages relative to the problems of human rights and some "awareness" of the problem. But access to and awareness of messages are not necessarily good predictors of whether and how the messages will be used— "message sent" does not equal "message received."

The area of international communication and relations provides a vivid example of a fundamental communication insight—more communication doesn't necessarily make things better. This is an important idea with profound implications for understanding the complexity of communication in relationships in general, and in international affairs more specifically.

In the short run, at least the presence of communication and commonly available messages are not necessarily more likely to produce convergence than divergence, love than hate, understanding than misunderstanding, peace than war. In the long run, we can speculate that the ever-increasing pool of shared "fast" and "slow" messages (see Figure 14.8)—along with common needs and goals—will lead to an increasingly predictable and shared world culture. And, while simply increasing the number of communication situations provides no guarantee of improved world relationships, efforts to improve our individual communication skills, such as listening, empathy, and respect, can certainly help to bridge the gap.

Implications and Applications

- Each relationship, group, organization, and society has a culture that is to some extent unique.
- As we engage in communication, we are at the same time contributing to the creation or maintenance of the cultures of our relationships, groups, organizations, and/or so-

In the United States

Fast Messages	Slow Messages
Prose	Poetry
Headlines	Books
A Communiqué	An Ambassador
Propaganda	Art
Cartoons	Etchings
TV Commercials	TV Documentary
Easy Familiarity	Print
Manners	Deep Relationships
	Culture

FIGURE 14.8 *Examples of Fast and Slow Messages*

From *Understanding Cultural Differences: German, French and Americans* by Edward T. Hall and Mildred R. Hall. Copyright © Edward T. Hall and Mildred R. Hall. Originally published by Intercultural Press 1989. Reproduced with the permission of Edward T. Hall.

cieties. Each time we behave in a culturally-consistent manner—adhere to the usual practices of a group, follow conventional patterns of dress or speech at work, or use a traditional greeting or gesture—we help to reinforce and perpetuate that culture.

- Cultures are so basic to our lives that we usually take them for granted.
- We tend to assume our own cultural practices are correct; and contrasting cultures are often regarded as *wrong* rather than simply *different.*
- Mediated communication contributes to the processes of creating, maintaining, and changing cultures. News and entertainment programs portray particular cultural images—about male and female roles, for example—and these images become a part of the culture to which we must adapt. Even sporting events and video games reflect and promote certain cultural themes.
- When we move from one locale, relationship, or job to another, we go through a process of adaptation as we learn to fit ourselves with the new culture. Depending on the degree of difference between the previous and new circumstances—and our own expectations and adaptability—we may experience "culture shock."
- Every communication situation is somewhat intercultural in the sense that no two people have precisely the same cultural backgrounds. The greater the difference in cultural backgrounds, the greater the communication challenge and the less likely that "message sent" will equal "message received." However, some situations in which we assume there are no major cultural differences—for instance, all parties were raised in the United States and speak English as their first language—can still present major intercultural challenges as a result of differing family, religious, ethnic, occupational, or geographic influences.

- Potentially important components of intercultural communication competence are:[34]

  Respect for people whose behaviors and cultures differ from our own

  Knowledge of the cultures involved

  Willingness to acquire knowledge of others' cultures

  Empathy for others' situations

  Sensitivity to cultural differences in language, conversational rules, and nonverbal behavior

  A nonjudgmental approach to different cultural patterns

  Tolerance for new and ambiguous situations

  The capacity to balance task- and support-role orientation

  Self-awareness

Summary

From the point of view of communication, culture can be defined as the complex combination of common symbols, knowledge, folklore conventions, language, information-processing patterns, rules, rituals, habits, lifestyles, and attitudes that link and give a common identity to a particular group of people at a particular time.

All social systems—relationships, groups, organizations, and societies—develop and maintain cultures through communication. The symbols of a society are among the most visible signs of culture. Cultures link individuals to one another, provide the basis for a common identity, and create a context for interaction and negotiation among members. The relationship between culture and communication is reciprocally-defining: Through communication we shape our cultures; and in turn, our cultures shape our communication patterns.

Cultures are complex and multifaceted, invisible, and subjective; and cultures change over time. We become aware of cultures through violations of cultural conventions, cross-cultural contact, and scholarly analysis.

Mediated communication plays an important role in the creation and maintenance of cultures. By extending our capacity to create, duplicate, and store messages, our technology broadens the pool of information available in common to individuals in relationships, groups, organizations, and societies. The cultural information base of a society consists of news, information, and entertainment programming. Mediated messages are a kind of cultural mirror, combining with the messages of face-to-face communication to provide an agenda of concerns, issues, values, personalities, and themes that occupy a central role in the symbolic environment to which individuals must adapt.

Adapting to a culture is a natural process of developing appropriate personal theories, representations, maps, and images of the cultures of which we are members. Because we adapt to our own cultures so easily and thoroughly, it is frequently a difficult and stressful matter to adjust to others, often resulting in what has been called "culture shock."

We are engaged in intercultural communication when we interact with people from other cultures. Every communication situation involving someone we don't know well is intercultural to some degree. As we meet new people, we negotiate the beginnings of new relationships and new relational cultures.

A society is a complex social system composed of a large number of diverse, geographically dispersed, and mutually-dependent individuals, groups, and organizations in pursuit of common goals. Societies are created, defined, and maintained through communication among the individuals who compose them. Societies operate by means of national and international networks. These networks provide the means through which information is conveyed among members of a society, facilitate the coordination of diverse activities within a society, and supply the channel through which collective decisions are made and implemented. An information society is one in which communication and information play a central role economically and socially, as in, for example, the United States, Japan, Brazil, and England.

Many writers have pointed optimistically to a future in which citizens of the world would be linked together in a global village. As this seems to be an increasingly likely possibility, concerns are being expressed that the intrusion of messages from other cultures can be destructive economically and socially. Moreover, the availability of common messages among members of different societies does not assure common understanding, acceptance, or peace. However, the ever-increasing pool of shared environmental information—along with new common needs and goals—seems likely to lead to a more predictable and shared world culture than the one guiding relations between countries of the world today. The increasing number of communication situations alone provides no guarantee of improved world relationships, but efforts to improve our individual communication skills can help to bridge the gap.

Notes

1. E. B. Tylor, quoted in Marvin E. Wolfgang and Franco Ferracuti, *The Subculture of Violence* (New York: Tavistock, 1967), p. 95.

2. See Lee Thayer, *Communication and Communication Systems* (Homewood, IL: Irwin, 1968), p. 47.

3. The establishment of a personal and group identity has long been a critical function of culture. One of the most significant recent changes is a rise of scholarship that focuses more directly on culture and identity politics. The following two books exemplify this trend: M. P. Orbe, *Constructing Co-cultural Theory: An Explication of Culture, Power, and Communication* (Thousand Oaks, CA: Sage, 1997); and Dolores V. Tanno and Alberto Gonzalez (Eds.), *Communication and Identity Across Cultures.* (Thousand Oaks, CA: Sage, 1998). The following article explores the way in which ideology affects the manner in which people (including scholars) talk about intercultural–

interethnic relations in the context of the United States: Young Y. Kim, "Unum and Pluribus: Ideological Underpinnings of Interethnic Communication in the United States," *International Journal of Intercultural Relations,* Vol. 23, 1999, pp. 591–611.

4. See Edward Hall, *The Silent Language* (New York: Doubleday, 1959), pp. 50–52.

5. An acknowledgment for this phraseology is due to Marshall McLuhan and the well-known adage of his time: "We shape our tools and thereafter our tools shape us."

6. The publication *How to Map a People* (Provo, UT: Brigham Young University, David M. Kennedy Center for International Studies, 1976) was among the early efforts to provide a broad overview of the multiple dimensions of culture. The Center also developed a number of country- and culture-specific overviews based on this framework, several of which are summarized in Figure 14.4. More

recently, any number of similar cultural profiles have been published. The *Culture Shock Guides to Customs and Etiquette* series (published by Arts Center Publishing Company, a division of Barnes & Noble, New York, NY) includes more than 20 such publications.

7. For the phrase "cultural iceberg" we are indebted to the writings of Donald Timkulu, "The Cultural Iceberg" (Ottawa, Canada: Canadian International Development Agency, Briefing Center), 1980.

8. Edward T. Hall, *Beyond Culture* (Garden City, NY: Anchor Press/Doubleday, 1979); and Edward T. Hall and Mildred Reed Hall, *Understanding Cultural Differences: Germans, French, and Americans* (Yarmouth, ME: Intercultural Press, 1989).

9. Hall and Hall, 1989, p. 6.

10. Hall, 1976, p. 91.

11. Hall and Hall, 1989, pp. 6–7.

12. William B. Gudykunst, "Culture and Development of Interpersonal Relationships," in *Communication Yearbook 12.* Ed. by James A. Anderson (Newbury Park, CA: Sage, 1989), pp. 315–354. See also Stephen W. Littlejohn, *Theories of Human Communication,* 5th ed. (Belmont, CA: Wadsworth, 1996), p. 259.

13. This discussion is adapted from Joseph A. DeVito, *Human Communication: The Basic Course,* 6th ed. (New York: HarperCollins, 1994), pp. 422–424, and William B. Gudykunst, *Bridging Differences: Effective Intergroup Communication* (Newbury Park, CA: Sage, 1991), based on the work of Hall, 1979 and Hall and Hall, 1989.

14. Hall and Hall, 1989, p. 13.

15. Hall and Hall, 1989, p. 14.

16. Peter Farb, *Word Play: What Happens When People Talk* (New York: Vintage, 1993).

17. Thomas Donaldson, "Values in Tension: Ethics Away from Home," *Harvard Business Review,* September–October 1996, pp. 53–54.

18. An excellent example of this kind of study is provided by Kim, 1999.

19. See Todd Hunt and Brent D. Ruben, *Mass Communication: Producers and Consumers* (New York: HarperCollins, 1992); Richard W. Budd and Brent D. Ruben, eds. *Beyond Media: New Approaches to Mass Communication,* 2nd ed. (New Brunswick, NJ: Transaction, 1988); and Herbert Schiller, *Culture, Inc.: The Corporate Takeover of Public Expression* (New York: Oxford University Press, 1989), especially Chapter 2, "The Corporation and the Production of Culture," for a more detailed discussion of mass communication and mass production and distribution of culture.

20. A summary of a more lengthy discussion provided by Dan Nimmo and James E. Combs, *Mediated Political Realities* (New York: Longman, 1983). See Chapter 6 "Fantasies of the Arena: Popular Sports and Politics."

21. Robbi L. Ruben, "Lessons of Videogaming," unpublished paper, Rutgers University, November, 1989.

22. Hugh D. Duncan, *Communication and Social Order* (London: Oxford University Press, 1962); and Hugh D. Duncan, *Symbols in Society* (New York: Oxford University Press, 1968), especially Parts II and III.

23. Jolene Koester, "Communication and the Intercultural Reentry: A Course Proposal," *Communication Education,* Vol. 33, 1984, p. 251.

24. *Guidelines for United States Navy Overseas Diplomacy* (Washington, DC: Department of Navy), p. 33.

25. *Guidelines for United States Navy,* p. 33.

26. *Guidelines for United States Navy,* p. 33.

27. Hall, 1959, p. 199.

28. See Young Y. Kim, *Communication and Cross-Cultural Adaptation* (Clevedon, England: Multilingual Matters, 1988). Excellent summaries of writing and research in the area of cultural adaptation are also provided by Marjorie H. Klein, "Adaptation to New Cultural Environments," in *Overview of Intercultural Education, Training and Research. Volume I: Theory.* Ed. by David S. Hoopes, Paul B. Pedersen, and George W. Renwick (Washington, DC: Society for Intercultural Education, Training and Research, 1977), pp. 50–56; David Reed Barker, in "Culture Shock and Anthropological Fieldwork," paper presented at the conference for the Society for Intercultural Education, Training and Research, Mount Pocono, PA., 1980; and by Daniel J. Kealey in *Adaptation to a New Environment* (Ottawa, Canada: Canadian International Development Agency, Briefing Centre, 1978). See also, Colleen Ward, Stephen Bochner, and Adrian Furaham, *Psychology of Culture Shock, 2nd ed.* (London, England: Taylor & Francis, 2001).

29. William B. Gudykunst and Young Yun Kim, *Communicating with Strangers: An Approach to Intercultural Communication,* 4th ed. (New York: McGraw-Hill, 2003).

30. Among the most comprehensive surveys of the field are: William B. Gudykunst and Young Y. Kim, *Communicating with Strangers: An Approach to Intercultural Communication,* 4th ed. (New York: McGraw-Hill, 2003); Stella Ting-Toomey, *Communicating Across Cultures* (New York: Guilford, 1999); Myron W. Lustig and Jolene Koester, *Intercultural Competence: Interpersonal Communication Across Cultures,* 4th ed. (Boston: Allyn & Bacon, 2002); Larry A. Samovar and Richard E. Porter, *Intercultural Communication: A Reader, 9th ed.* (Belmont, CA: Wadsworth, 1999).

31. DeVito, 1994, pp. 442–443.

32. Karl Deutsch, *The Nerves of Government* (New York: Free Press, 1966).

33. Philip Revzin, "La Boob Tube: Europe Complains about U.S. Shows," *The Wall Street Journal,* October 16, 1989, pp. 1–10.

34. Based on summary of research and discussions in Gudykunst and Kim, 2003; Young Y. Kim, *Communication and Cross-Cultural Adaptation* (Clevedon, England: Multilingual Matters, 1988); Brent D. Ruben and Daniel J. Kealey, "Behavioral Assessment of Communication Competency and the Prediction of Cross-Cultural Adaptation," *International Journal of Intercultural Relations,* Vol. 3, No. 1 (Spring, 1979), pp. 15–48; Brent D. Ruben, "Human Communication and Cross-Cultural Effectiveness," *International and Intercultural Communication Annual,* Vol. 4, 1978, pp. 95–105; and others.

15 Public and Mass Communication

In this chapter

Why . . .

- The difference between interpersonal and mass communication is a matter of degree.

- Understanding public speaking is basic to understanding public and mass communication.

- Communication apprehension is a major problem for many.

- Sporting events, video games, and ads for credit cards can teach powerful lessons.

- Public and mass communication are both causes and effects of behavior.

Communication occurs in a number of contexts and forms. In this chapter, we focus on communication that takes place in a public or mass media context. Public and mass communication play a critical role in creating and disseminating the messages that are central to our activities as individuals, and in relationships, groups, communities, organizations, and societies.

What Is Public and Mass Communication?

The terms *public* and *mass* communication can be contrasted with intra- or interpersonal communication. Unlike these more private and personal forms of communication, public and mass communication refer to situations in which messages are created and disseminated to a *relatively* large number of receivers, in a setting that is *relatively* impersonal. Public speaking, concerts, theatre, and public debates are examples of public communication. Communication involving mass media such as newspaper and magazine articles, television and radio programs, movies, and advertising are examples of mass communication.

The term *relatively* is italicized in this definition in the previous paragraph because what is "public" or "mass," and what is not, is often a matter of degree. When, for example, does communication between individuals in a group or organization qualify as public communication? Most of us would agree that when three or four people who know each other well speak to each other it is certainly interpersonal or perhaps group communication, but not public or mass communication. On the other hand, we would get little disagreement that if the message were presented to 250 employees at an annual meeting of a division of the organization, it would be "public communication," and if the presentation were a professionally produced videotape, most communication scholars would also agree that it qualifies as mass communication. But, what if the communication event consisted of prepared and rehearsed remarks (perhaps via fax or e-mail) to 5, 10, 25, or 50 people, who didn't know each other all that well? At what point does the situation become "public" and/or "mass" communication? It is our view that there is no magical threshold test for when a communication situation is and when it is not public or mass communication. However, there are some general guidelines which are helpful in differentiating these situations from others. Public and mass communication situations tend to be characterized by:

- *An audience.* Generally, a large number of people are involved in the event, so much so that a communicator tends to think of intended receivers in aggregate terms—as an audience rather than as individuals. Giving a speech to a class would fit the definition, while rehearsing in front of roommates would not.
- *Impersonality.* The source often does not know all participants personally, and this lack of knowledge, the situation, and the number of people involved make it difficult for a communicator to send "personalized" messages. Even though a speaker may know some receivers very well, he or she may not be able to acknowledge or make use of this knowledge, and must instead use a "to whom it may concern" approach.
- *Planned, predictable, and formal.* The communication process is planned, predictable, and/or formalized. The physical setting in which the event (a public speech or network news program) takes place may be arranged in a particular way (e.g., seating or layout of a setting) and may follow a predetermined agenda.
- *Source control.* The source has disproportionate control over determining what messages are created and disseminated. For example, the communicator sets and manages the agenda, and determines the content.

- *Limited interactivity (feedback).* Audience members have limited means of reacting to the source or his or her message, and have little ability to shape the course of the communication event. "Negotiation" of the content does not occur in the sense we're used to experiencing it in interpersonal or most group settings. In most mass communication situations, the message sender and the act of message sending is separated from the message receiver and the act of receiving in time, space, or both, often making interaction and feedback difficult. Often the feedback a speaker receives is too delayed to alter the source's current content. If during a speech the speaker notices that half the audience is yawning, the speaker could adapt and liven up the material. If, however, an audience member does not appreciate the sexist nature of a television's reporter's language, the best one could hope to do would be to write a letter or e-mail and trust that the reporter will receive the message and care enough to try and prevent future occurrences of such language. In an interpersonal context, this delay would not occur, and one could almost instantly amend one's language to best suit the audience.
- *Source centrality.* The source has easy and direct access to all receivers, but receivers may not have the same access to one another. For example, the television public speaker addresses all members of the viewing audience; however, members of the audience cannot address one another.

Traditionally, when characterizing "mass" communication situations, one additional condition is present:

- *Mass media are involved.* Traditional mass media are radio, television, film, newspapers, magazines, and books. Newer media, such as the Internet, broadcast e-mail, electronic bulletin boards, chat rooms, listservs, and "mass fax" also fit the definition of mass media.

The Role of Public and Mass Communication

Although the differences between public and mass communication and other forms of communication are sometimes a matter of degree, these forms and contexts of communication are important to understand in their own right precisely because of the characteristics listed above: A large number of people are typically involved in the audience; the communication event is planned, relatively predictable, formal, and impersonal; the source exercises great control over message content, with little opportunity for interaction with or among recipients, and in the case of mass communication, media are involved that tend to further extend the reach of human communication and their role in shaping our cultures. In addition to the familiar public and mass communication channels, many institutions within society contribute to the creation, perpetuation, and evolution of culture. Schools play a very basic part in the creation, distribution, and sharing of culture, as do churches, governments, and the business community.

Effects of Health Communication Campaigns • *Itzhak Yanovitzky*

"Friends don't let friends drive drunk," "Just say no," and "Your brain on drugs" are famous examples of health communication campaign messages. Professor Yanovitzky's research examines the effectiveness of mediated messages such as these and also the interpersonal choices we make when seeking and receiving health-related information.

• • •

I conduct innovative research in the area of indirect (or mediated) effects of health communication campaigns on health behavior and processes of social influence. Specifically, my work demonstrates that many public health communication campaigns are able to influence the behavior of target audiences indirectly by promoting change in public health policy (e.g., laws mandating stiffer sanctions against drunk drivers, increasing taxation on tobacco products, and offering free mammograms to women with low or no income) or otherwise stimulating social change related to a particular

health behavior (e.g., the decline in the social acceptability of smoking). In this context, I also investigate the strategic use of communication by advocacy groups to promote changes in health policy (often referred to as media advocacy).

My research in the area of social influence and strategic communication seeks to advance a more complete understanding of social influence processes as well as explore norms-based message strategies that are particularly conducive to attitudinal and behavioral change across a wide range of health behaviors. It focuses on the relative contribution of multiple sources of social information (e.g., family members, close friends, peers, and local and national media) and different processes of social influence (conformity, social comparison, and compliance) to the formation, modification, and maintenance of human behavior. This line of research is currently used to inform the development of effective communication-based interventions in dangerous drinking and substance use among adolescents, college students, and young adults.

Understanding Public Communication[1]

One of the most common public communication events is the public speech.

It is important to remember in a public communication context that both the speech and its presentation can and should be considered separately. Obviously, the speech does not exist apart from its presentation. From a practical point of view, however, preparing a speech and preparing a presentation are separate phases of a public communication situation.

The Speech

Preparation for a speech falls into four general categories:[2]

1. *Preparing to create the speech.* This step involves:
   - Discovering ideas and evidence
   - Gathering and organizing information
   - Assessing the audience
   - Analyzing and focusing the topic
   - Developing a thesis
   - Reaching conclusions

2. *Drafting the speech.* Public communicators at this stage try to give a structure and form to their presentation. This step involves creating introductions and conclusions, using evidence to support major conclusions, developing and placing specific examples, and developing visual aids.

3. *Revising.* This step may involve major changes to the presentation. In this step, the communicator pays particular attention to structure, logic, evidence, examples, and further development. The speaker must make sure that he or she has given the audience what they need to be informed, persuaded, or for other intended communication goals to be realized.

4. *Editing.* This step consists of fine tuning. During this stage the speaker pays particular attention to mechanics such as transitions between major points, delivery and appearance, citing sources, and presentation style.

The Presentation

Preparing the presentation consists of the following four stages:

1. The first and most important activity is *preparing the speech,* as described. Once this is done, preparation for the presentation can begin.

2. *Rehearsal.* The public communication event (for example, a speech, a concert, a play) should be rehearsed. Depending on the formality of the situation, a dress rehearsal may

FIGURE 15.1 Great orators use a variety of rhetorical strategies to motivate and inspire their audiences.

be held that includes simulating the situation as closely as possible. Anyone who has ever participated in a wedding rehearsal knows how important it is to completely prepare for the event so that everyone knows his or her role. Less formal events call for rehearsals that help plan the timing of the event or speech, and familiarize speakers with the setting and any technology to be used in the presentation.

3. Advanced preparation includes *developing flexible presentation strategies* (such as changes in the length of the presentation or additional gestures) that can be used as necessary to react to feedback from the audience. For example, if an audience seems confused by a presentation, the effective public communicator is ready to explain major points in more detail or to provide additional examples. If the audience appears bored or already familiar with some ideas being presented, a good speaker will condense parts of the presentation or vary his or her vocal tone, speak directly about issues of concern to this audience, or use more interesting graphics to win back the attention of the audience.

4. *Other presentation elements* such as clothing need to be attended to before a public communication event. Dress is an important unifying force for audiences and speakers. Politicians often wear caps with particular insignias to indicate that they identify with their audience. This type of nonverbal cue signifies the message, "I'm one of you." On other occasions, the public communicator may want to distance himself or herself from the audience. Religious leaders often wear different clothing while conducting services in order to reinforce their roles as spiritual advisors.

Although we have discussed these steps as if they were sequential, in reality the sequence may be adjusted based upon the circumstances.[3]

Audience Analysis and Adaptation.   Effective public communication always involves consideration of the audience. The most basic information that is necessary to find out about an audience is demographic. For example, people of any age may be interested in learning about a new technique for fly fishing provided that they are fishing enthusiasts. On the other hand, it would be unwise to speak about casino gambling to a group of people who do not gamble because of their religious beliefs. The importance of any given demographic factor varies depending on the speaker and the topic of the speech.

Some demographic features that may be important in planning a public presentation include age, gender, race, ethnicity, religion, socioeconomic status, educational level, sexual orientation, and geographical location.

A good speech is adapted to a particular audience to the degree that the speaker would have to change it (by modifying examples or word choice, for example) for another audience. If a speaker can deliver a speech to another audience without making any changes, the speech is not specific enough for the intended audience.

Developing a Purpose and a Thesis.   As we discussed earlier, one of the major differences between public communication and interpersonal communication is that public communication usually has a predetermined purpose established by the communicator. In arriving at the purpose, a communicator needs to answer three general questions with respect to the potential audience for the message:[4]

- Who are they?
- What do we want them to know, believe, or do as a result of this speech?
- What is the most effective way of composing and presenting the speech to accomplish that aim?

In interpersonal communication, ideas may be presented spontaneously without much advanced preparation. In a public communication event, a great deal of time is typically devoted to advance thinking about who the audience is, what we want them to gain from listening to us, and what strategies will best accomplish these goals.

One of the ways in which public communicators clarify the purpose for their speeches is through the development of a thesis. The *thesis* of a speech is the one main definite idea to which all others are subordinated. If we think of the topic of the speech as a question, then the thesis is the answer to that question. It is a specific statement of purpose. Effective theses are:[5]

1. *Restricted.* A good thesis limits the scope of what can be discussed in detail in the time allotted to a speech. For example, trying to describe the changing roles of women on television from 1980 to 2005 in five minutes would be extremely ambitious. A twenty-minute speech on the changing role of the main characters in a specific program would be a more restricted and reasonable topic.

2. *Unified.* A thesis should present one dominant idea. There may be more than one idea a communicator wants to convey, but they should all be unified by some other idea. For example, an effect may have more than one cause so that a speaker may need to discuss three causes, but these causes are united under a single common theme.

3. *Precise.* In a good thesis, a restricted, unified idea is presented with clarity. There should only be one possible interpretation. There is no place for ambiguous or vague language ("voting for this candidate will make all the difference") or cliches in an effective thesis.

Without an effective thesis we often end up treating the entire subject area as a thesis and rambling around purposelessly. We may be providing accurate information to the audience, but it has no clear point. In addition, we have no criteria for selecting and ordering material so we leave ourselves open to the audience asking, "What is the point of this?" Effective public communicators always ask themselves, "What exactly about my subject is the point?"[6] When listening to public presentations, we can judge their effectiveness using these criteria to examine the thesis presented.

Making an Argument.   Making an argument, or *persuasion,* is an attempt to win over or convince an audience to agree with a particular position or to pursue some course of action.[7] There are two general approaches to making an argument: emotional appeals which produce belief or reasoned appeals which produce conviction. For example, a speaker who graphically describes an accident that resulted from drunken driving is using emotional appeals to persuade an audience not to drink and drive. A speaker who presents numerous facts demonstrating the negative consequences of credit card debt is using reasoned appeals to persuade an audience not to abuse their credit cards.

There are many techniques that are used in efforts to persuade audiences, for example:[8]

- Using repetition
- Associating one's claim with something already thought of positively by the audience or associating opposing claims with something already thought of negatively by the audience
- Purposely omitting relevant information
- Using emotional, connotative language
- Using emotional appeals such as guilt, fear, love, and so on
- Appealing to human needs such as the need for ego gratification, reassurance of worth, emotional and physical security, love, creative outlets, power, roots, immortality
- Creating cognitive dissonance by presenting inconsistent ideas
- Arguing from ethos or the source's credibility
- Appealing to cultural values
- Using content appeals based on reasoning and evidence

While persuasive public communicators may make use of some or all of these approaches, effective and ethical persuasion should be based heavily on content appeals using reasoning and evidence. Except with hostile audiences in cases in which the goal is to change the direction of already held attitudes, content appeals should be balanced with controlled emotional and other appeals as long as those appeals work within the structure of the argument. With hostile audiences, speakers need to be as unemotional as possible, because any emotion aroused in the audience will intensify already held attitudes. Unless the goal is to reinforce these pre-existent attitudes, all content appeals should use two-sided arguments in which the speaker both provides positive arguments for his or her claims and raises and refutes strong arguments for opposing claims.

Public communicators can develop effective arguments by following these suggestions:[9]

- Make limited claims.
- Avoid overstatement; especially words like "never," or "nobody," or "everybody."
- Be open about uncertainties.
- Control tone; especially avoid over-emotionalism.
- Avoid frequent or heavy use of sarcasm.
- In addition to using solid reasoning and credible evidence, use devices to keep the audience's attention and sympathy. For example, intelligent use of understatement, overstatement, metaphor, allusion, humor, and controlled emotions is effective.
- Be sure to produce a clear, logical structure for the presentation with a clear purpose at all points.

Use of Evidence.   Evidence to support an argument consists of a series of reasons or facts, details, examples, references, and quotations. Facts do not speak for themselves; they only speak for those who know how to use them, to put them in a strategic place, and to explain their significance. It is important for a speaker to choose a thesis based on an examination of evidence rather than choosing the evidence to support the thesis. Evidence should be used wisely. There is no need to use evidence to support statements that one can reasonably expect an audience to accept without support. Statements that are needed to make a persuasive point, however, should be supported.

An easy way to check the necessity for evidence is by using a pyramid structure of three levels with the thesis at the peak as the first level.[10] At level two, supply those statements which, if accepted, would persuade an audience to accept the thesis. At level three, provide evidence for all level two statements that members of the audience might hesitate to accept. Little time has to be spent giving evidence to support level three statements, which ought to be non-controversial facts.

Visual Aids. There are four types of visual aids that help public communicators convey their messages to large audiences:[11]

1. The *actual object* being talked about. For example, a person giving a presentation on dog grooming might demonstrate on a real dog.
2. A *model* of the object. If the real object is too large (for example, an airplane) or too difficult to bring to the event (for example, a rare butterfly), a model may be constructed.
3. *Mediated objects* such as pictures, movies, or computer programs.
4. *Mediated models* such as slides, charts, graphs, or diagrams.

Visual aids function to add interest to a presentation by giving the audience something to examine. They may also clarify what the speaker is saying by providing a visual illustration of the points being made. In addition, visual aids like PowerPoint can jog a speaker's memory and be used as visual "notes."

There are several guidelines for preparing effective visual aids:

- *Make them visible.* It is frustrating for an audience to be shown a visual aid that is not easily visible. Good public communicators make sure their visual aids are large enough to be seen. Remember that a slide that looks nice on a computer screen may not show up effectively when projected to a large auditorium.
- *Make them simple.* Avoid too much detail to keep the visual aid from being confusing. Omit information that is not directly relevant to your thesis.
- *Make them complete.* Although it is important to make visual aids simple, it is also important to present all the needed visual information. Don't leave out important information or the audience may be confused.
- *Make them appropriate.* Good visual aids fit the purpose, tone, and content of the presentation. If the speech is a serious one designed to persuade an audience not to drink and drive, demonstrating the latest drinking game would not be appropriate.
- *Make them communicative.* Good visual aids add something to the speech. Speakers use them because they have a purpose, not just for appearances.
- *Make them relevant.* It is important to display a visual aid only when you are talking about the subject and remove it as soon as you have moved on to another point. If you have finished speaking about dog grooming and are now talking about cats, for example, it will distract the audience if you still have a dog on display.

Communication Apprehension.   Communication apprehension, anxiety before and during a public communication event, is a natural part of the public communication experience. Everyone feels anxiety when speaking or performing in front of a large audience. In fact, some communication scholars have argued that a slight degree of anxiety leads to better performances because people who do not feel any anxiety may fail to adequately prepare for a public communication event and, therefore, not perform to the best of their abilities. Thus, controlled anxiety may be desirable for effective performance.

The normal range of communication apprehension can be controlled by several techniques:[12]

- *Attitude.* Face each public communication opportunity as a challenge to get a message to a large audience and not as an insurmountable obstacle.

- *Experience.* The more experience a person has in public communication situations, the easier it is to face the next situation.

- *Preparation.* Never attempt to "just wing it" during a public communication event. Even speeches that seem totally spontaneous may have been thought out far in advance. Obviously, it is impossible to have a comment memorized for every public situation we might ever face, but some type of advanced preparation will improve our performance in almost any type of public or mediated event.

- *Gestures.* Often gestures that are appropriate for interpersonal communication situations "get lost" in a public communication context. Effective public communicators learn to modify or enlarge their natural repertoire of gestures to reach a larger audience. Gestures can often be an effective way to manage our anxiety by using extra energy that otherwise might get transformed into nervous habits like excessive blinking or gripping the podium too tightly.

- *Remembering that most physiological reactions are not perceived by the audience.* It is important to remember that the audience rarely perceives the anxiety a public communicator might feel. Even when they do, signs of slight anxiety such as a wavering voice or shaking hands will usually be perceived with empathy and not criticism.

- *Talking to the audience as individuals, not just as a group.* Mild anxiety can often be managed by addressing remarks to individual members of the audience. Talking directly to several people makes a public communication situation seem more interpersonal in nature. It is often easier to think about the individual people in an audience and their opinions rather than try to address the group as a collective.

Making eye contact with individuals in an audience can often help to allay anxiety. Many people become anxious when talking to a group, but their anxiety is lessened when they begin to "talk to" particular individuals in the audience. Receiving individual feedback instead of just seeing a sea of faces is often enough to turn an anxiety-provoking public communication event into a more pleasant, rewarding experience.

- *Recognizing that audience members are friendly and want the speaker to succeed.* Most audiences are composed of individuals who desire the speaker to do a good job. Audiences are rarely openly hostile to a speaker. Knowing that the audience is on the speaker's side can help an individual to be a more effective speaker. Sometimes, however, we know that the audience disagrees with us. This often occurs in a persuasive speaking situation when we are trying to convince an audience to change their attitudes. Nevertheless, even if the audience is antagonistic toward a speaker's opinion or point of view, audience members still want the speaker to give a good presentation.

Understanding Mass Communication

In many respects, mass communication is an extension of public communication. Particularly where traditional mass media are involved, the informative, persuasive, or entertaining messages of public communication efforts can be amplified, multiplied, duplicated, and distributed far beyond the context of a lecture hall or concert with the aid of communication technology.

As with public communication, mass communication is generally a more formalized, planned, and purposeful process than face-to-face communication. To a greater extent than in many other contexts of communication, economic considerations also are important. The production of news or television programming, advertisements, and political campaigns are extremely expensive undertakings. Even production of a campus newsletter, or the purchasing of space for a classified advertisement in a community newspaper involves an expense. And, as we shall see, questions of social impact are also important when one considers mass communication, because of the potential for the rapid and widespread distribution of messages made possible by traditional and newer mass media.

Production, Distribution, and Consumption

The industrial revolution brought an age in which the mass production, distribution, and consumption of *manufactured goods* was central to the economic and social fabric of our society. In a similar way, the communication revolution has brought us to an age in which the basic commodity is *information*. Mass communication organizations produce, distribute, and market information products and services.[13]

- *Production* refers to the creation, gathering, packaging, or repackaging of information.
- *Distribution* relates to the movement of mass communication products from the point of production to the point of consumption. The movement may occur immediately, as with a live television broadcast, or it may involve substantial time delays, as with magazines, books, films, or taped programs.
- *Consumption* refers to the uses, impacts, and effects that mass communication can have for a single individual, a relationship, group, organization, or society. Examples include: being informed, entertained, persuaded, educated, humored, motivated, or deceived. For a society, the influences of mass communication may be social, political, cultural, economic, or technological.

This process is illustrated in Figure 15.2.

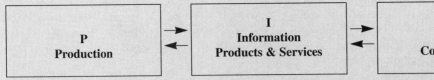

P
Production

I
Information
Products & Services

C
Consumption

Description:
Mass communication
organizations create and
distribute information products
and/or services

Description:
Information products and/or
services are distributed
to an audience

Description:
Information products and
services compete for attention,
acceptance, and use among
audiences

ORGANIZATIONS:
- Television Network
- Newspaper Publishers
- Movie Producers
- Magazine Publishers
- Book Publishers
- Record Companies
- Advertising Agencies
- Public Relations Firms
- Libraries
- Museums
- Information Services
- Etc.

PRODUCTS/SERVICES:
- Television Programs
- Newspapers
- Movies
- Magazines
- Books
- Records/Tapes/CDs/MP3s
- Ads
- Public Relations Campaigns
- Documents
- Exhibits
- Research Reports/Databases
- Digital Media
- Etc.

AUDIENCES:
- Individuals
- Couples, Families,
  Co-Workers, Etc.
- Groups
- Organizations
- Societies

USES/IMPACT:
- Information
- Entertainment
- Persuasion
- Education
- Diversion
- Motivation
- Deception
- Socialization
- Etc.

FIGURE 15.2   *P ↔ I ↔ C Model of Mass Communication*

The economic relationship between the consumers and producers may be direct, in-direct, or a blend of the two. In the case of movies, CDs, or DVDs, consumers directly underwrite production costs through their purchases. Television and radio producers and distributors are supported by advertisers who want to gain access to consumers of those mass communication products. In such instances, consumers provide indirect financial support of production and distribution each time they purchase advertisers' products. With newspapers and magazines, cable and satellite radio and television, and Internet services, the economic link between consumers and producers is partially direct—through payment of subscription charges or provider connection fees. It is also partially indirect—through the purchase of advertisers' products. In the case of software products—computer programs, video games, CDs, DVDs, or MP3s—audience members pay directly.

Information Products and Services

Information products are collections of messages—textual, visual, or vocal—organized in a particular way for a particular purpose or use by a particular audience. Information products include not only news but also entertainment, public relations and advertising, computerized databases, even museum exhibits or theatrical performances.

Information services are activities associated with the preparation, distribution, organization, storage, or retrieval of information. Information services include news or editorial research, public relations consulting, and electronic information delivery.

The Audience

The term *audience* refers to the group of individuals who have the potential for being exposed to and using an information product or service. In the terminology of Information or Computing Science, the audience is the *user group*.

Traditionally, when talking about mass communication, "audience" evokes an image of a very large, diverse group of viewers or readers all being exposed to the same information at more or less the same time and all unknown to the information producers. However, fax machines, CD-ROMs and MP3 players, PDAs (like Palm Pilots), and computers suggests the value of a broadened concept of audience. New media make it easier to direct messages to specific segments of a mass audience. This view of "audience" does not presume that the user group must be of a specific size, nor be particularly diverse, nor that all of its members be exposed to the same information at the same time, nor that members of the group be unknown to the information producers. More basic is the requirement that the information product involved must have been purposefully produced and distributed by an organization for a particular constituency.[14] A network television program fits this definition, as does a DVD produced for a corporation, a church electronic newsletter, or a museum exhibit.

This approach to mass communication takes account of:

- Traditional mass media and newer technologies
- Convergence among once distinct mass communication media, products, and services
- Interactive capabilities of many mass communication media
- Active decision-making roles played by mass communication producers *and* consumers
- Complex individual, social, economic, and cultural dynamics that contribute to the interplay between mass communication producers and consumer groups
- General and specialized mass communication producers, products, services, and consumer groups

Four Basic Functions of Mass Communication

Mass media and mass-mediated communication serve a number of functions. Sociologist and mass communication scholar, Charles Wright, describes four: surveillance, correlation, socialization, and entertainment.[15]

Surveillance.   Media provide a constant stream of news-related messages which enable audience members to be aware of developments in the environment that may affect them. *Surveillance* may consist of a warning function, alerting members of the audience to danger—a hurricane or pollution of the water or air or a terrorist alert, for example.

Mass-mediated communication also serves a *status conferral function;* individuals, organizations, and issues that are reported on by mass media tend to be seen as significant by members of the audience. Additionally, mass-mediated communication serves an *agenda-setting function* in that it helps to set the public agenda as to issues, individuals, and topics of concern to mass media audience members.

Correlation.   Mass media serve to interrelate and interpret information about the events of the day. The *correlation function* serves to help audience members determine the relevance that surveillance messages have for them.

Socialization.   Partly as an extension of the surveillance and correlation functions, mass-mediated communication socializes individuals for participation in society. Mass media provide common experiences, foster shared expectations as to appropriate and inappropriate behaviors. Mass-mediated communication also plays a central role in the transmission of cultural heritage from generation to generation.

Entertainment.   Mass media are a pervasive source of mass entertainment and provide the basis for diversion and release for audience members. See Figure 15.3.

Broader Functions of Mass Communication

Packaging and Distribution of Culture.[16]   In any society, mass communication institutions package and distribute the cultural knowledge base. This knowledge base consists of the news and entertainment programs, public relations, and advertising, along with other information products and services provided by libraries, museums, theme and amusement parks, cable and satellite services, software producers, computer services, art galleries, sports, and even shopping malls.[17]

Mass media such as newspapers, television, and film have long played a fundamental role in packaging and transmitting cultural information. However, when we think more broadly, we realize that many other organizations whose primary function is not mass communication in the usual sense of the term also serve these same functions.

Popularizing and Validating Function.   While the concept of a cultural information base may seem abstract, its consequences are not. Through mass communication, concepts of what is real and make-believe, or right and wrong, are distributed from place to place and from generation to generation, and in the process, are popularized and sanctioned. News, entertainment, sports, and advertising programming tell us stories about people and how they live, provide insights into how people think, and portray the consequences of particular behaviors. In subtle ways, they provide lessons about relationships, family life, war, crime, music, religion, and politics. Whether the topic is sex, violence, fitness, drugs, or racial issues, they contribute to the visibility, currency, and validity of the topics they address.

FIGURE 15.3 This picture from Spain demonstrates the influence of American media products in our global world.

News and Information.   Sometimes intentionally, but more often unintentionally, news and informational programming have the effect of popularizing and validating particular concerns and ideologies (ways of thinking) by focusing on some while ignoring others. Even interviews and public opinion polls contribute to the popularity and legitimacy of certain issues through the choices that information producers make. Interviews and polls, for example, deal with particular topics and questions. Many topics are available, but only some are included. To ask respondents their opinions on environmental pollution, the actions of a local political figure, or a governmental policy is to state by implication that these are important topics of the day. Their importance is further underscored when the results of the poll are published. These selected topics are given a visibility and legitimacy that is not afforded to other topics of perhaps equal significance but which were not selected for examination.

Mass communication news and informational programming contributes to the popularization and legitimation of culture through the selection of what is and what is not "news." For example, the selection and repeated rebroadcasting of particular images, events, or excerpts from a political speech elevate the visibility, permanence, and significance that are associated with these sights or "sound bites." Mass communication also contributes to the cultural agenda by the interpretation (or lack of interpretation) of news events, and through the way "causes" and "effects" are implied.

Entertainment and Advertising.   Entertainment programs contribute importantly to the web of culture, often in subtle ways. They provide commentary on how people should live, look, think, talk and relate to others. Advertisements also provide strong cultural messages regarding economics and consumption: They urge us to become consumers. Encouraging consumption is a universal theme in advertising and many kinds of promotion. However, rarely is the message "We want you all to get out there and buy goods and services whether you need or can afford them" made explicit. One area where this theme *is* apparent is in

FIGURE 15.4   People who choose to get their information through newspapers have a wide variety of choices in contemporary society.

advertising for credit cards. College students are a prime target of these campaigns. Direct mailings and "take an application" posters urge their audience "to establish your credit now" and assure that "you have been pre-approved" or that the bank will "say yes" when you apply. The implicit economics lesson is a simple one: It is important to be a consumer, it is necessary to establish credit—the sooner the better—and it is good to buy on credit.

Sports: Heroes and Villains.   Sporting events provide another interesting illustration of the ways in which mass communication serves as a carrier of cultural messages. Dan Nimmo and James Combs, in *Mediated Political Realities,* discuss how sports programming prepares viewers for political participation in society. Sporting events, particularly when distributed by mass media, are presented as suspense-filled contests with heroes and villains. They present a story of the "triumph of justice or the intervention of fortune, . . . heroic deeds and untimely errors, dramatic climaxes, and the euphoria of the victors along with the gloom of the vanquished."[18] Sports commentators contribute further to the melodramatic nature of sports by introducing rivalries and quarrels among players, salary and contract disputes, fights and fines, winning and losing, romance and death. Sporting events teach about playing by the rules, losing gracefully, sportsmanship, competition, and persistence.[19]

The influences of these themes can be seen as influencing the way other facets of life are viewed. Media coverage of politics or criminal trials, for example, often places more emphasis on rules, tactics, and "spin" strategies than on issues of right or wrong, guilt or innocence.

Video and Computer Games: Control and Consequences.   Video games—another somewhat less obvious form of mass communication—also provide implicit cultural messages. Trees, people, houses, animals, and other cars buzz back and forth across the road in front of your metallic red Lamborgini as you screech around the turns. Suddenly a bike pulls out in front of you and you are forced to swerve off the road into a ditch, where your car crashes into a brick wall and blows up.[20] Is this a problem? Not if the press of a button brings you back to the start of the track in the same shiny car—and this is exactly how things work in the world of video-gaming. One of the strongest messages that video games send is immortality, and the possibility to redo what went wrong without consequence.[21]

Not only is violence in these types of entertainment media prominent and consequential, it has increased dramatically and continues to do so.[22] When video games first appeared in the 1970s, they contained simple and apparently harmless content. In the 1980s, games like Pacman, which featured a yellow orb chasing and being chased by ghosts, became dominant. In the 1990s, more violent video games became popular, including Mortal Kombat, in which realistic human fighters battle to the death. Today, the level of violence has increased substantially. A study of popular video games found that nearly 80 percent of the games were violent in nature. And 21 percent of these games portrayed violence toward women.[23]

Commercializing Function. Mass communication often plays a role in giving commercial value to and helping to sell particular cultural symbols. In this sense, mass communication institutions are part of the cultural industry, which the United Nations Educational, Scientific, and Cultural Organization (UNESCO) describes as an industry involved in the large-scale production, reproduction, storage, or distribution of cultural goods and services.[24]

Herbert Schiller, a communication and culture scholar, writes that increasingly, "cultural creation has been transformed into discrete, specialized forms, commercially produced and marketed. Speech, dance, drama (ritual), music, and the visual and plastic arts have been vital, indeed necessary, features of human experience from earliest times. What distinguishes their situation in the [present] . . . era are the relentless and successful efforts to separate these elemental expressions of human creativity from their group and community origins for the purpose of *selling them* to those who can pay."[25]

Mass communication plays a major role in the commercialization of celebrities, brand names, art objects, music, and other elements of culture. This is especially obvious in areas where the popularization of particular individuals through public and mass communication has given great value to them, their names, and anything associated with them. One example is the endorsement of clothes or other products by music or sports figures. Another is the selling of autographs. Commercialization also takes place when a celebrity's name is added to other products, services, or ideas as a way of enhancing value or marketability. Ironically, public and mass communication play a role in giving celebrities commercial value, and are then used to enhance and market the value of products or services they endorse.

Social Contact and Sense of Community. Mass communication consumption can serve as a substitute for human contact, helping individuals avoid isolation and loneliness. As noted by mass communication researchers Robert Kubey and Mihaly Csikszentmihalyi:

> Those who lack structured interactions with other people due to unemployment, divorce, widowhood, personality factors, or declining health are more likely than others to turn to

television for companionship, information, and escape. Older people who are widowed and/or retired, for example, are among the heaviest television viewers.[26]

Interactive media—chat rooms, listener call-in radio, 900 numbers, and computer bulletin boards—may be seen as serving mass communication and interpersonal communication functions at the same time.

Mass communication gives people a sense of community and connection to others. It can also provide a stimulant to interaction to the extent that we share the same interests as other information consumers. Reading the morning newspaper, attending a particular concert, participating in an online message board discussion, or viewing the weekend football or basketball game may facilitate interaction by providing topics for conversation.

In general then, mass communication plays a major role in the production and distribution of social realities. In our society, and in most others, the mass media are the major providers of standardized messages regarding people, products, situations, and events—

RESEARCH PROFILE

Media Industries • Joseph Turow

What we see on television, hear on the radio, watch at the movies, or listen to on our CD players is the product of media industries. Professor Turow's research examines media companies and how they shape the images that are presented to us and their influence on our perceptions of the world.

• • •

I believe that what fundamentally separates mass communication from interpersonal, small group, or organizational communication is not the size of the audience (it may be large or small) or even the use of media technology (televised communication can, for example, be mass or interpersonal). Rather, what distinguishes mass communication is that industries are involved in creating and distributing messages for audiences.

An industry is a grouping of companies that use technology to work together in a regularized way to produce and distribute goods and services. The huge resources gathered by many media firms create the potential for using technologies such as radio, movies, and television to reach millions or even billions of people. In the twenty-first century, industrial processes are also making it possible to target millions of people at the same time with messages that are modified to match what the companies know about each individual. It already happens on the Internet. Soon it will happen on your TV.

Media companies are usually in business to make money from the materials they produce and distribute, which is another characteristic that sets them apart from such communication activities as gossip among friends and construction of an Internet site by a class. But by surrounding huge populations with words, sounds, and images, media firms go beyond mere money making. They contribute to the notions people carry in their heads about what society is like, how they fit in, and what power they have to change things for the better.

Why do major media in society present certain images and not others? How do those images relate to issues of power and control in society by producers, advertisers, lobbyists, and government agencies? What government and business policies might be implemented to guide society's entertainment and news media toward messages that encourage active citizenship and social involvement? These are difficult but fascinating and important questions that I have tackled through my mass media research.

messages that often have a major influence on the understandings, knowledge, and images members of the audience develop.

The Effects of Public and Mass Communication

In general terms, there are two ways of thinking about public and mass communication effects. One focuses on the communicator, the message, and the technology. The second emphasizes the audience members.[27]

The Communicator/Producer Perspective

The communicator/producer-centered approach sees the source, message, technology, information products and services as controlling influences on audience members.[28] This way of thinking is suggested by statements such as "His speeches and media campaign made him a winner," or "Decaying morals within society are a consequence of increasing sexuality in public communication, television, records, and music videos." Each statement implies a *causal relationship* between public and mass communication on the one hand and individual, group, or societal behavior on the other.

The Audience/Consumer Perspective

Consumer approaches emphasize the role audience members play in public and mass communication outcomes.[29] While most communicator/producer theories may portray audience members as *passive* and *controlled,* the audience/consumer perspective emphasizes their *active* and *controlling* role. This way of thinking is implied in the statement "When I hear a political speech filled with over-simplification and generalization, I just tune it out," or "Today's audience members are sophisticated enough to enjoy all forms of television, CDs, and music videos without being adversely influenced."

The tension between views of mass communication as highly influential (those emphasizing source/producer influences) and those which view audience members as more powerful (emphasizing the consumer perspective) is ongoing. Do violent movies cause people to develop violent tendencies, or do individuals' needs for violence lead them to watch (and producers, therefore, to continue to create) violent programs? As we have seen earlier, attempting to explain communication outcomes in a one-way, cause-and-effect manner—as is characteristic of the $S \rightarrow M \rightarrow C \rightarrow R = E$ paradigm—may underestimate the fundamentally interactive, mutual influence that systems theories believe are fundamental to communication. The systems framework implies that outcomes (or effects) are the result of interactions that take place over time between the individual and physical and social environment.

Uses and Gratifications

The foundation of the consumer approach to mass communication theory comes from a tradition called "uses and gratifications," originally advanced by Elihu Katz, Jay Blumler, and Michael Gurevitch.[30]

[The uses and gratifications approach] . . . views members of the audience as actively utilizing media contents, rather than being passively acted upon by the media. Thus, it does not assume a direct relationship between messages and effects, but postulates instead that members of the audience put messages to use, and that such usages act as intervening variables in the process of effect.[31]

This perspective views audience behavior as being guided by the pursuit of particular goals and needs.[32] One of the particular benefits of the uses and gratifications approach is that it provides a generalized way of thinking about mass communication "effects." That is, rather than viewing mass communication and its effects as a unique and specialized form of human communication, mass communication outcomes were seen as arising from interactions between individuals and the environment, in the same manner as in interpersonal, group, organizational, and other settings. As Littlejohn puts it: "Media are considered to be only one way of meeting personal needs, and the individuals may meet their needs through the media or in some other way."[33]

Dependency Theory[34] extended the core concepts of the uses and gratifications approach and helped to reconcile this view with earlier theories that envisioned mass media as extremely powerful in bringing about effects in the audience members. Dependency theories suggest that audience members do rely on media to meet their needs, but they come to depend on some media more than others and, moreover, their dependence on media both influences, and is influenced by, their needs and uses. Thus, some individuals may depend largely on particular mass media for their information on current events (such as cable TV), while others may meet their needs for diversion and entertainment using other media (such as the Internet). Depending on the choices made by members of the audience, particular media will become more important and influential, while others become less so. The Dependency model also suggests that in times of societal change and conflict, audiences members are more likely to question social institutions and their own beliefs and, in such circumstances, the importance of mass media increases for audience members.[35]

Integrating Perspectives

Both the communicator/producer and audience/consumer perspectives are valuable to understanding the dynamics of public and mass communication. Communicator-oriented approaches remind us that public and mass communication sources play an important and influential role in our lives through the creation, packaging, commercialization, validation, and distribution of the information that fills our environment—information with which we must organize ourselves in order to function.

Consumer-oriented theories stress the role individual audience members play in explaining the impact of mass communication. They emphasize the significant role of individual needs and uses, attitudes, and beliefs in the dynamics of message reception. In so doing, they remind us that as consumers we play an active role in the communication process and in determining its effects.

How can these two perspectives be integrated? Consider the following analogy: "High-powered sports cars cause accidents." It is true that high-powered sports cars are involved in a number of accidents—more accidents than cars lacking such power. Are the cars themselves to blame? Would we eliminate all these accidents if we stopped producing fast cars? To what extent are the drivers to blame?

One can certainly speed and drive recklessly in a Corvette. The car *is* designed for high performance. But these same behaviors are also possible in a Honda Civic, if a driver chooses to *use* it in these ways. However, we can't take this argument too far; without a car, after all, there can be no speeding or reckless driving. We might, therefore, want to conclude that in any given instant a high-powered sports car *contributes to,* but does not itself *cause,* accidents. Thus, accidents are the result of particular *patterns of consumption in relation to product characteristics and availability.*

If we think of public—and particularly mass—communication, the case of high-powered cars provides a helpful analogy because it involves a relationship between technology and human behavior. As with cars and drivers, it seems reasonable to assume that communication technologies and products facilitate but are seldom the sole cause of audience behavior. Generally, the effects that occur between public and mass communicators and consumers are *mutually causal,* or *mutually controlling.*

As with the Corvette, the influences of public and mass communication result from *both:*

1. The availability of particular messages and technologies with particular characteristics and capabilities
2. The uses to which audience members attend to, interpret, remember, and use those messages

Thus, the "effects" of public and mass communication are the result of particular *patterns of message reception in relation to characteristics and availability of messages and technology.* Communicators, messages, and technologies play an important role in defining, influencing, and shaping the available options, direction, and limits of those uses. As audience members we influence the impact of public and mass communicators, individual and institutional, through the choices we make—to attend or not, buy or not, read or not, listen or not, watch or not, and so on. Over the long term, these choices influence what is made available to us through public and mass communication, which in turn influences the range of choices we have available, and so on, and so on.

Implications and Applications

As producers of public communication and consumers of mass media, we have a number of responsibilities.

Perhaps the most important of these is to behave ethically. It is easy to see why ethical behavior is so important for public speakers. As speakers, we must always try to present the most accurate information that is available to us. Outright lies and even stretching the truth are not acceptable in a public context. In fact, speaking ethically enhances one's credibility. It is well known that speakers who present information that is contradictory to their point of view and who then effectively refute this information are more persuasive than speakers who ignore opposing arguments.

Today's information-rich society is providing more opportunities for unethical behavior using technology. For example, it is very easy to send a potentially harmful message to thousands of people via e-mail. Some people pass along obscene or offensive messages. While we have the right to view all of the information that is available to us on the World Wide Web, we do not have the right to consciously inflict harm on others. It is every individual's responsibility, ultimately, to make sure that his or her messages are not inappropriate or harmful to others.

To become more effective consumers and producers of public or mediated messages, we should expose ourselves to a variety of media and to a variety of products in these media. There is a wealth of information available today in mediated formats, but much of it is repetitious and designed to appeal to a mass audience. Unfortunately, the plot of the latest "reality" show or action/adventure movie is much like the plot of last year's big hit of the same genre. It is important to seek out alternative mediated messages to expand our knowledge about the role of communication in the contemporary world. For example, look for films directed by African-American or women directors. Listen to college radio stations or National Public Radio. Read magazines designed for audiences interested in particular topics such as politics, hobbies, or self-development. Go to museums that contain collections focused on unfamiliar topics. All of these experiences improve our own abilities to communicate by enhancing our personal experiences of the world and helping us to understand others' experiences of it.

Summary

Public and mass communication play a critical role in creating and disseminating messages. Public and mass communication refer to situations where messages are created and disseminated to a *relatively* large number of receivers, in a setting that is *relatively* impersonal. Public speaking, theatre, and public debates are examples of public communication. Communication involving mass media such as newspaper and magazine articles, television and radio programs, and advertising are examples of mass communication. The term *relatively* is italicized, because what is "public" or "mass" and what is not is often a matter of degree.

The public speech is one common example of public communication. The speech and its presentation should be considered separately. Preparation for a speech falls into four general categories: preparation, creating the speech, revising, and editing. The presentation consists of preparing the speech, rehearsal, developing presentation strategies, and other presentational elements. Audience analysis and adaptation, developing a purpose and thesis, making an argument, the use of evidence, visual aids, and communication apprehension are all important considerations in understanding the dynamics of public communication.

Mass communication is an extension of public communication involving technology. Key considerations in the process include production, distribution, and consumption; information products and services, and the audience. Four basic functions of mass communication are: surveillance, correlation, socialization, and entertainment. Broader functions of mass communication include: the packaging and distribution of culture, the popularizing and validating function, the commercializing function, and social contact and sense of community.

Broadly speaking, there are two ways of thinking about public and mass communication effects. One emphasizes the role played by the communicator/producer; the other the role played by the audience/consumers. Both perspectives are valuable for understanding mass communication, and can and should be integrated for a comprehensive view of the process.

Notes

1. We would like to thank Alan Stewart for his contributions to this section.

2. Adapted from Bert E. Bradley, *Fundamentals of Speech Communication,* 5th ed. (Dubuque, IA: Wm. C. Brown, 1988), pp. 21–28; Stephen E. Lucas, *The Art of Public Speaking,* 5th ed., (New York: McGraw-Hill, 1995); and Alan D. Stewart, unpublished class notes.

3. Alan D. Stewart, unpublished class notes.

4. Lucas, 1995, p. 91.

5. James M. McCrimmon, *Writing with a Purpose* (Boston, MA: Houghton Mifflin, 1974), pp. 16–18.

6. Alan D. Stewart, unpublished class notes.

7. Alan D. Stewart, unpublished class notes.

8. See Bradley, 1988, pp. 326–336; and Patricia Kearney and Timothy G. Plax, *Public Speaking in a Diverse Society* (Mountain View, CA: Mayfield, 1996), pp. 328–334.

9. Alan D. Stewart, unpublished class notes.

10. For a more detailed discussion see J. Vernon Jensen, *Argumentation: Reasoning in Communication* (New York: D. Van Nostrand, 1981), pp. 128–134; and Charles U. Larson, *Persuasion: Reception and Responsibility,* 6th ed. (Belmont, CA: Wadsworth, 1992), pp. 178–185, 190–192.

11. Alan D. Stewart, unpublished class notes.

12. Adapted from Bert E. Bradley, *Fundamentals of Speech Communication,* 5th ed., (Dubuque, IA: Wm. C. Brown, 1988), pp. 39–44; and Alan D. Stewart, unpublished class notes.

13. A detailed discussion of the P-I-C framework is provided in Todd Hunt and Brent D. Ruben, *Mass Communication Producers and Consumers* (New York: HarperCollins, 1993), from which the summary provided in this section is drawn.

14. John V. Pavlik and Shawn McIntosh, *Converging Media* (Boston: Allyn and Bacon, 2004).

15. Charles R. Wright, *Mass Communication: A Sociological Perspective,* 3rd ed. (New York: Random House, 1986), pp. 3–28.

16. For a more detailed discussion of mass communication and culture, see Hunt and Ruben, 1993.

17. Hunt and Ruben, 1993.

18. Dan Nimmo and James E. Combs, *Mediated Political Realties* (New York: Longman, 1983), p. 126.

19. Nimmo and Combs, 1983.

20. Robbi L. Ruben, "Lessons of Videogaming," unpublished paper, Rutgers University, November 1989.

21. R. Ruben, 1989.

22. Craig A. Anderson and Karen E. Dill, "Video Games and Aggressive Thoughts, Feelings, and Behavior in the Laboratory and in Life," *Journal of Personality and Social Psychology,* Vol. 78, 2000, pp. 772–790.

23. T. L. Dietz, "An Examination of Violence and Gender Role Portrayal in Video Games: Implications for Gender Socialization and Aggressive Behavior," *Sex Roles,* Vol. 38, 1998, pp. 425–442.

24. UNESCO, *Cultural Industries: A Challenge for the Future of Culture* (Paris: UNESCO, 1982), p. 21.

25. Herbert Schiller, *Culture, Inc.: The Corporate Takeover of Public Expression* (New York: Oxford University Press, 1989), pp. 30–31.

26. Robert Kubey and Mihaly Csikszentmihalyi, *Television and the Quality of Life: How Viewing Shapes Everyday Experience* (Hillsdale, NJ: Lawrence Erlbaum, 1990), p. 168.

27. For a more detailed discussion of mass communication effects see Hunt and Ruben, 1993, Chapter 3.

28. See Carl I. Hovland, Irving L. Janis, and Harold H. Kelley, *Communication and Persuasion* (New Haven: Yale University Press, 1953); Charles R. Wright, *Mass Communication: A Sociological Perspective,* 3rd ed. (New York: Random House, 1986), pp. 3–28; Walter Lippman, *Public Opinion* (New York: Macmillan, 1921); Donald L. Shaw and Maxwell E. McCombs, *The Emergence of American Political Issues* (St. Paul, MN: West, 1977), p. 5; Maxwell E. McCombs and Donald L. Shaw, "The Agenda Setting Function of the Mass Media," *Public Opinion Quarterly,* 36:2 (1972), pp. 176–187; Maxwell E. McCombs and Donald L. Shaw, "Structuring the Unseen Environment," *Journal of Communication,* 26:2 (Spring 1976), p. 18; Wright, pp. 154–155; George Gerbner et al., "The Mainstreaming of America: Violence Profile No. 11," *Journal of Communication,* 30 (Summer 1980), pp. 10–29; George Gerbner and Larry Gross, "Living with Television: The Violence Profile," *Journal of Communication* 26 (Spring 1976), pp. 173–199; Elizabeth Noelle-Neumann, "Return to the

Concept of the Powerful Mass Media," in H. Eguhi and K. Sata, eds., *Studies of Broadcasting* (Tokyo: Nippon Kyokii, 1973), pp. 67–112; Joshua Meyrowitz, *No Sense of Place* (New York: Oxford University Press, 1985), pp. 16–23; Marshall McLuhan, *Understanding Media* (New York: McGraw-Hill, 1964), p. 7; Harold A. Innis, *The Bias of Communication* (Toronto: University of Toronto Press, 1951); and Harold A. Innis, *Empire and Communication,* rev. ed. (Toronto: University of Toronto Press, 1972).

29. See Hadley Cantril, *The Invasion from Mars: A Study in the Psychology of Panic* (Princeton: Princeton University Press, 1940); Paul Lazarsfeld, Bernard Berelson, and Hazel Gaudet, *The People's Choice* (New York: Columbia University Press, 1948); Everett M. Rogers, *Diffusion of Innovations* (New York: Free Press, 1962); Everett M. Rogers and Floyd Shoemaker, *Communication of Innovations: A Cross-Cultural Approach* (New York: Free Press, 1971); Everett M. Rogers and Ronny Adhikarya, "Diffusions of Innovations: An Up-to-Date Review and Commentary," in Dan Nimmo, ed., *Communication Yearbook 3* (New Brunswick, NJ: Transaction Books, 1979), pp. 67–82; Elihu Katz, Jay Blunder, and Michael Gurevitch, "Uses of Mass Communication by the Individual," in W. Phillips Davison and Frederick Yu, eds., *Mass Communication Research: Major Issues and Future Directions* (New York: Praeger, 1974); Jay Blumler and Elihu Katz,

eds., *The Uses of Mass Communication* (Beverly Hills, CA: Sage, 1974); and Lee Thayer, "On the Mass Media and Mass Communication: Notes Toward a Theory," in Richard W. Budd and Brent D. Ruben, eds., *Beyond Media: New Approaches to Mass Communication* (New Brunswick, NJ: Transaction Books, 1988), pp. 64–70.

30. The "uses and gratifications" concept was originally advanced by Elihu Katz, Jay Blumler, and Michael Gurevitch in "Uses of Mass Communication by the Individual," in *Mass Communication Research: Major Issues and Future Direction.* Ed. by W. P. Davidson and F. Yu (New York: Praeger, 1974), pp. 11–35, and discussed in Jay Blumer and Elihu Katz, Eds., *The Uses of Mass Communication* (Beverly Hills, CA: Sage, 1974).

31. Katz, Blumler, and Gurevitch, 1974, p. 1.

32. For an excellent discussion of uses, gratifications, and dependency theories, see Stephen W. Littlejohn, *Theories of Human Communication,* 6th ed. (Belmont, CA: Wadsworth, 1999).

33. Littlejohn, 1999, p. 350.

34. Littlejohn, 1999.

35. Sandra J. Ball-Rokeach and Melvin L. De Fleur, "A Dependency Model of Mass-Media Effectives," *Communication Research,* Vol. 3, 1976, pp. 3–21; and Melvin L. DeFleur and Sandra J. Ball-Rockeach, *Theories of Mass Communication* (New York: Longman, 1982), pp. 240–241.

Index